VIBGYOR.

久保帯人

The new workspace I moved into last year is a bit small, but at dawn, when I open the front door after work, I can see the sunrise. The sky lights up like a fiery rainbow. Lately I've been working until sunrise just to catch the sky. It's not that I have to work all night because I sleep till noon every day. I mean, just look at that sunrise.
-Tite Kubo

BLEACH is author Tite Kubo's second title. Kubo made his debut with *ZOMBIE POWDER*, a four-volume series for *WEEKLY SHONEN JUMP*. To date, *BLEACH* has been translated into numerous languages and has also inspired an animated TV series that began airing in Japan in 2004. Beginning its serialization in 2001, *BLEACH* is still a mainstay in the pages of *WEEKLY SHONEN JUMP*. In 2005, *BLEACH* was awarded the prestigious Shogakukan Manga Award in the *shonen* (boys) category.

BLEACH
Vol. 16: NIGHT OF WIJNRUIT
The SHONEN JUMP Manga Edition

STORY AND ART BY
TITE KUBO

English Adaptation/Lance Caselman
Translation/Joe Yamazaki
Touch-Up Art & Lettering/Mark McMurray
Design/Sean Lee
Editor/Yuki Takagaki

Managing Editor/Frances E. Wall
Editorial Director/Elizabeth Kawasaki
VP & Editor in Chief/Yumi Hoashi
Sr. Director of Acquisitions/Rika Inouye
Sr. VP of Marketing/Liza Coppola
Exec. VP of Sales & Marketing/John Easum
Publisher/Hyoe Narita

Printed in the U.S.A.

Published by VIZ Media, LLC
P.O. Box 77010
San Francisco, CA 94107

SHONEN JUMP Manga Edition
10 9 8 7 6 5 4 3 2 1
First printing, December 2006

PARENTAL ADVISORY
BLEACH is rated T for Teen and is recommended
for ages 13 and up. This volume contains
fantasy violence.

THE WORLD'S
MOST POPULAR MANGA

www.viz.com

www.shonenjump.com

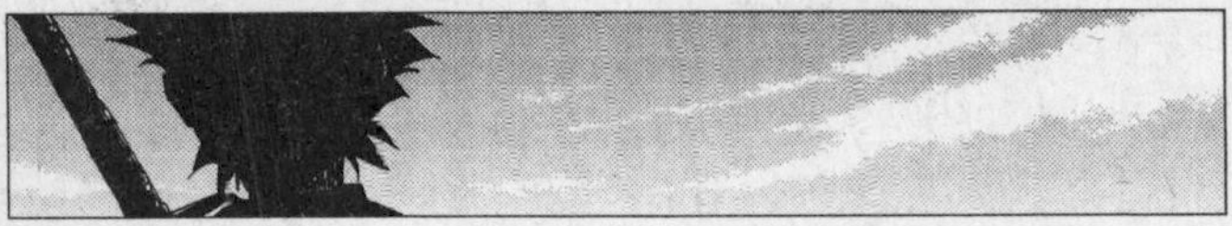

The mane of the sun pouring down
Erases the footprints on thin ice
Do not fear deception
The world already lies atop deception

BLEACH 16 NIGHT OF WIJNRUIT

Shonen Jump Manga

STARS AND

Rukia Kuchiki

Tôshirô Hitsugaya

Ichigo Kurosaki

plot

Ichigo and the others struggle to rescue Rukia, who awaits death in a tower of the Seireitei. But Ichigo's decisive battle with Byakuya Kuchiki is delayed while Yoruichi puts him through a crash course on achieving Bankai. Meanwhile, the murder of Captain Aizen casts a pall over the entire Seireitei. Suspecting Gin Ichimaru of the deed, Tôshirô challenges him to a duel. But when Momo suddenly appears between them, Tôshirô finds himself switching from avenger to the accused!

BLEACH ALL

浮竹十四郎

Jûshirô Ukitake

雛森桃

Momo Hinamori

Gin Ichimaru

市丸ギン

STORIES

BLEACH16

NIGHT OF WIJNRUIT

Contents

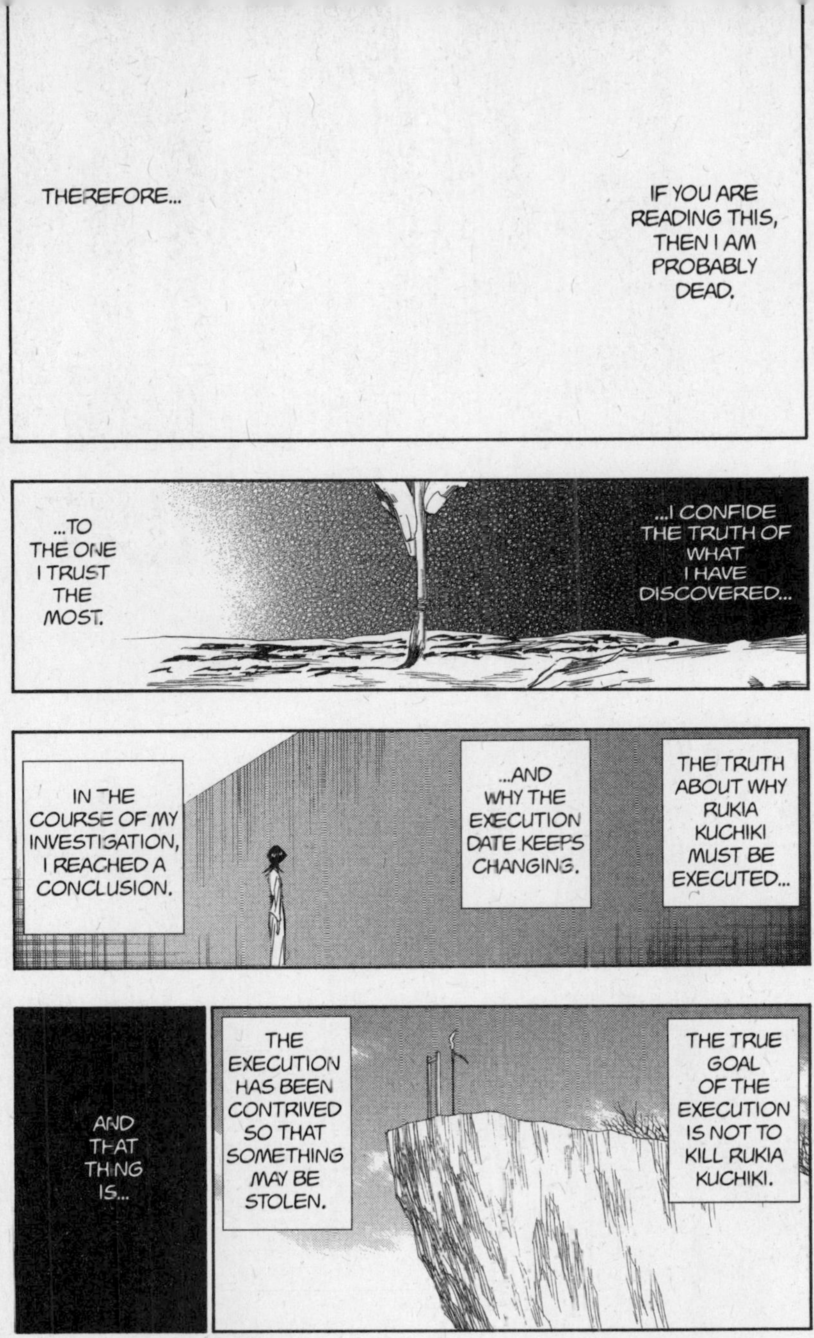
IF YOU ARE READING THIS, THEN I AM PROBABLY DEAD.
THEREFORE...
...I CONFIDE THE TRUTH OF WHAT I HAVE DISCOVERED...
...TO THE ONE I TRUST THE MOST.
THE TRUTH ABOUT WHY RUKIA KUCHIKI MUST BE EXECUTED...
...AND WHY THE EXECUTION DATE KEEPS CHANGING.
IN THE COURSE OF MY INVESTIGATION, I REACHED A CONCLUSION.
THE TRUE GOAL OF THE EXECUTION IS NOT TO KILL RUKIA KUCHIKI.
THE EXECUTION HAS BEEN CONTRIVED SO THAT SOMETHING MAY BE STOLEN.
AND THAT THING IS...

131. The True Will

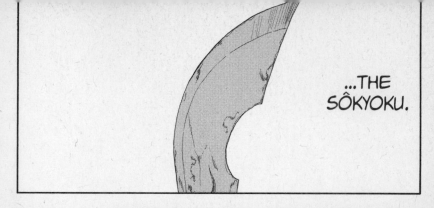

...THE SÔKYOKU.
THE SÔKYOKU, WHOSE SEAL IS ONLY REMOVED FOR EXECUTIONS...
...HAS THE DESTRUCTIVE POWER OF ONE MILLION ZANPAKU-TÔ IN ITS BLADE. THE TAKKA* HAS THE DEFENSIVE POWER TO BLOCK AN EQUAL NUMBER OF ZANPAKU-TÔ.
FURTHERMORE, WHEN USED TO EXECUTE A SOUL REAPER, ITS POWER CAN BE MOMENTARILY INCREASED BY SEVERAL DOZEN TIMES.
*EXECUTION STAND
THE ONE WHO PLOTTED RUKIA'S EXECUTION ...
...INTENDS TO USE THE SÔKYOKU TO DESTROY NOT ONLY THE SEIREITEI, BUT THE ENTIRE SOUL SOCIETY AS WELL.
THE NAME OF THAT DESPICABLE PERSON IS...

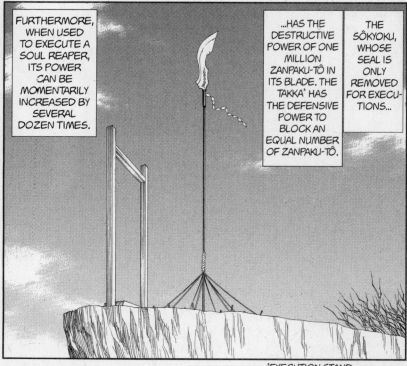

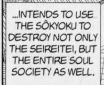

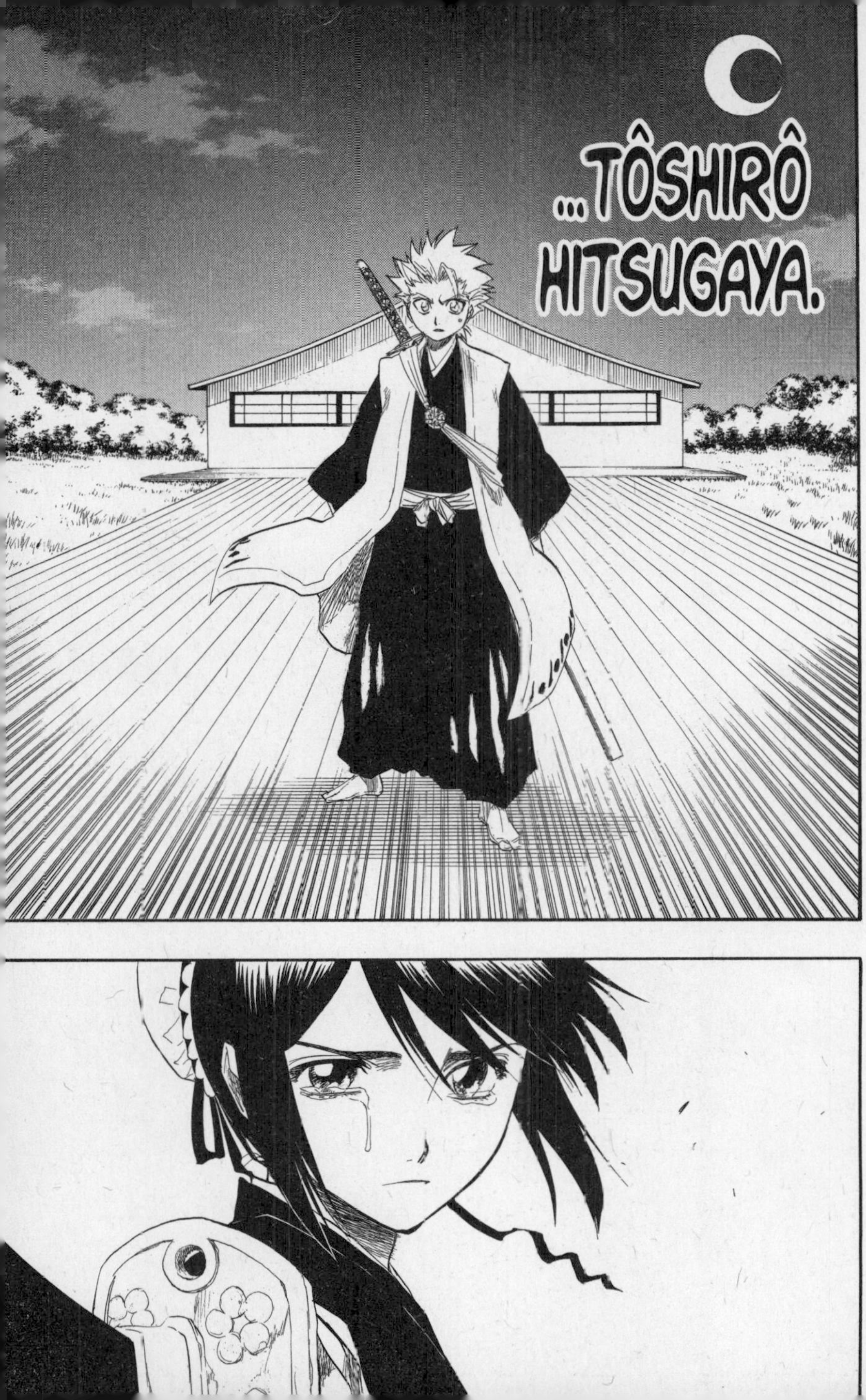
...TÔSHIRÔ HITSUGAYA.

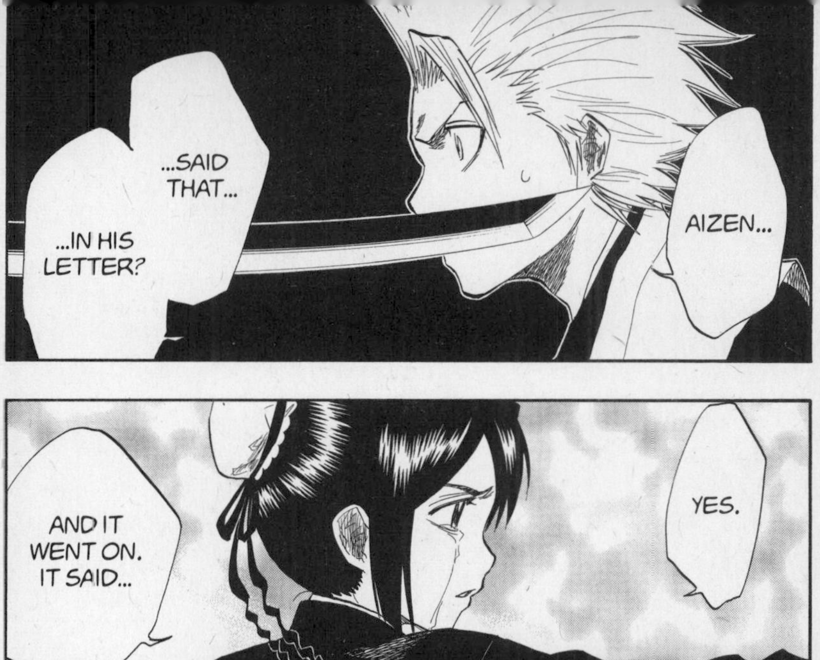
AIZEN...
...SAID THAT...
...IN HIS LETTER?
YES.
AND IT WENT ON. IT SAID...
..."TONIGHT I HAVE CALLED HIM OUT TO THE HIGASHI DAISHÔHEKI.*
"I MUST FOIL HIS PLAN AT ALL COSTS.

*THE SACRED EASTERN WALL

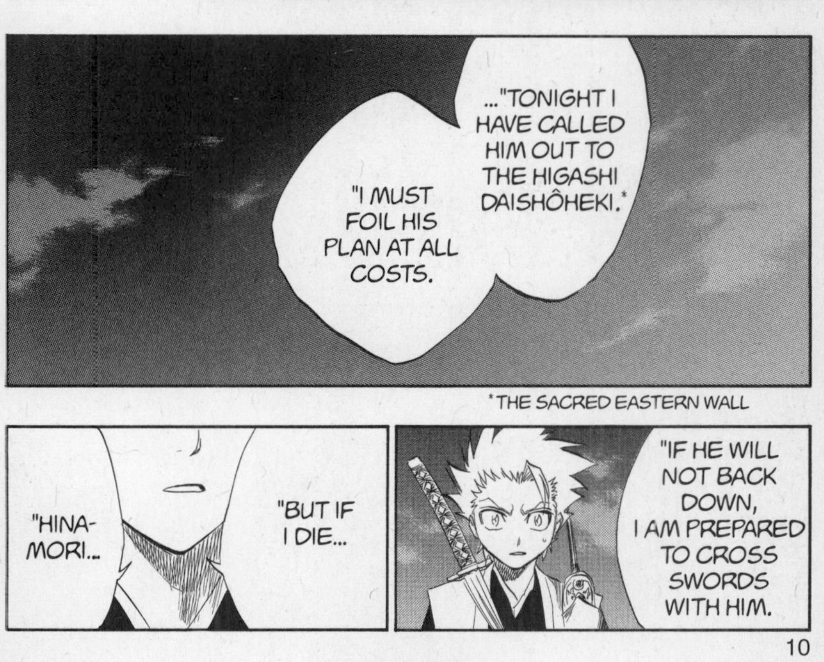
"IF HE WILL NOT BACK DOWN, I AM PREPARED TO CROSS SWORDS WITH HIM.
"BUT IF I DIE...
"HINA-MORI...

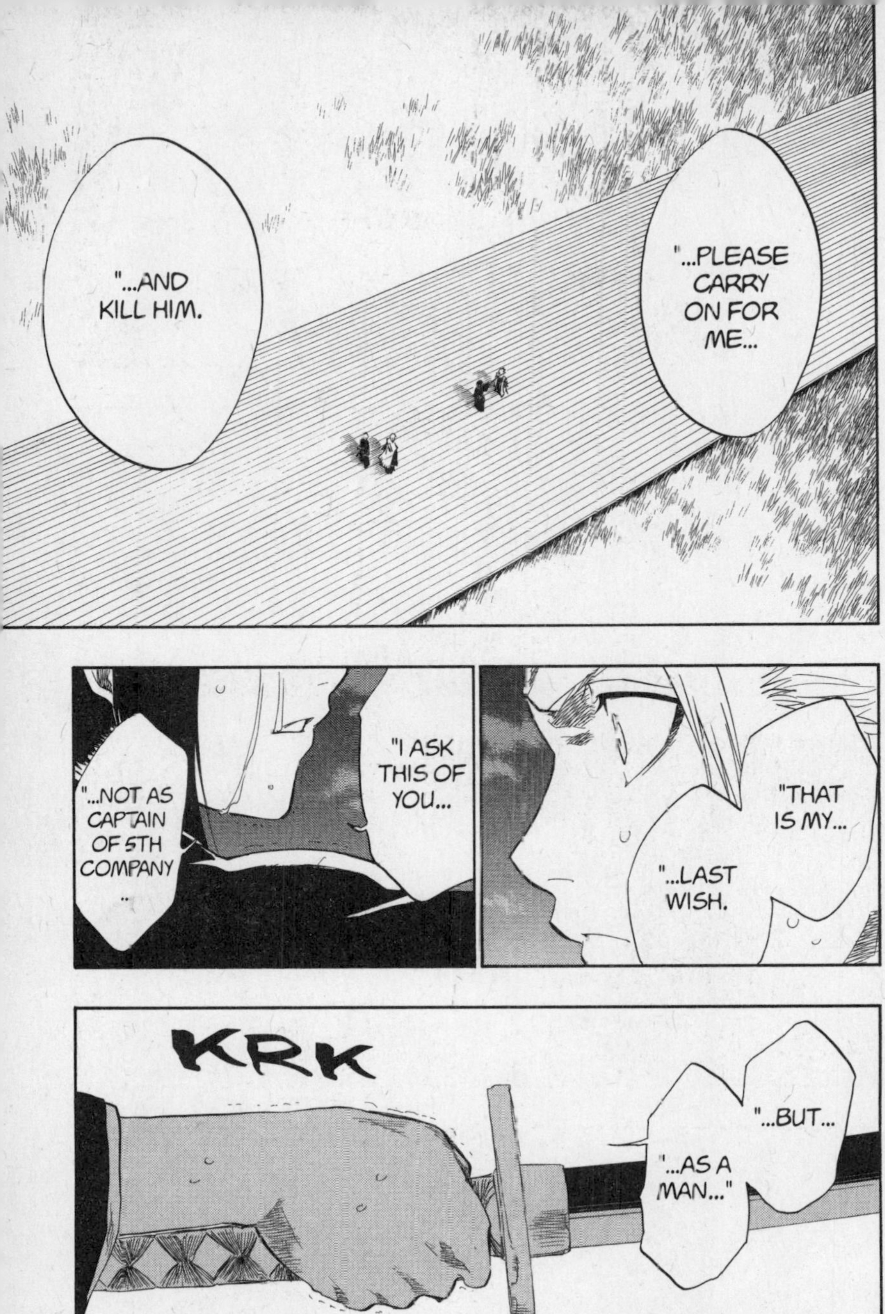
"...PLEASE CARRY ON FOR ME...
"...AND KILL HIM.
"THAT IS MY...
"...LAST WISH.
"I ASK THIS OF YOU...
"...NOT AS CAPTAIN OF 5TH COMPANY ..
KRK
"...BUT...
"...AS A MAN..."

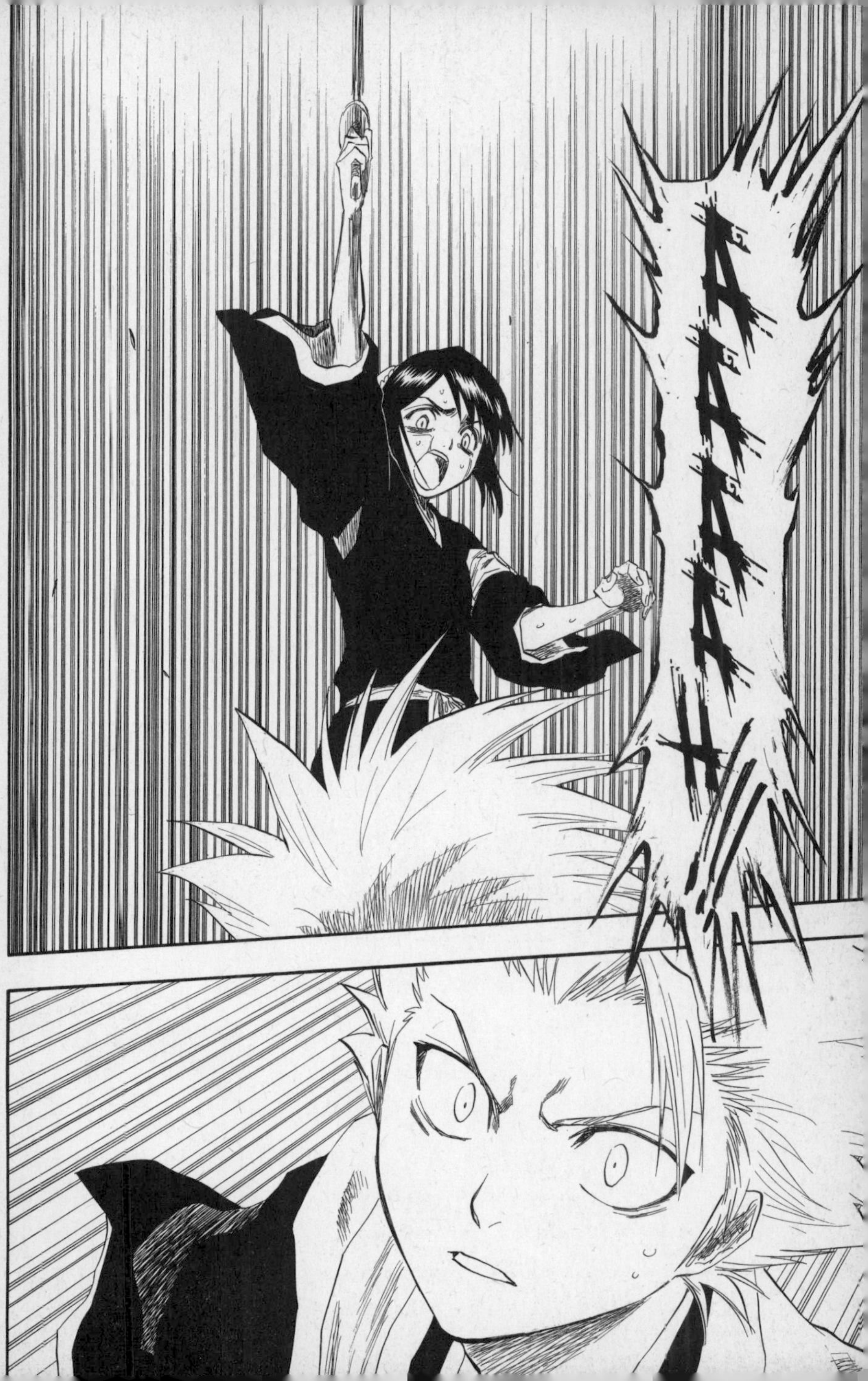
AAAAAH

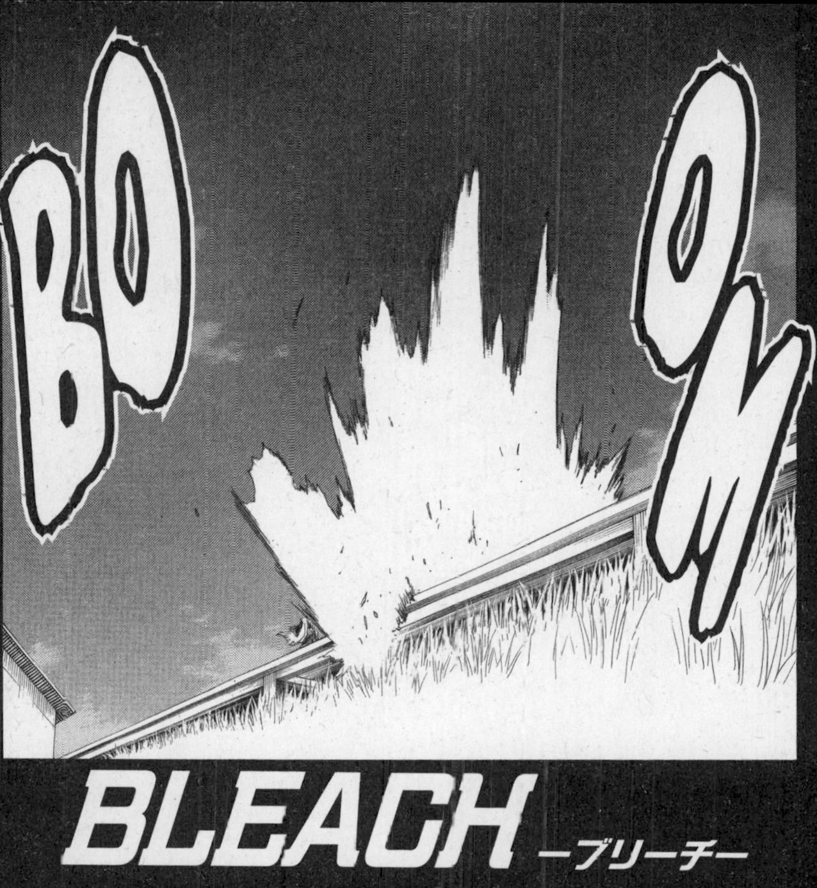
BOOM

BLEACH —ブリーチ—

131. The True Will

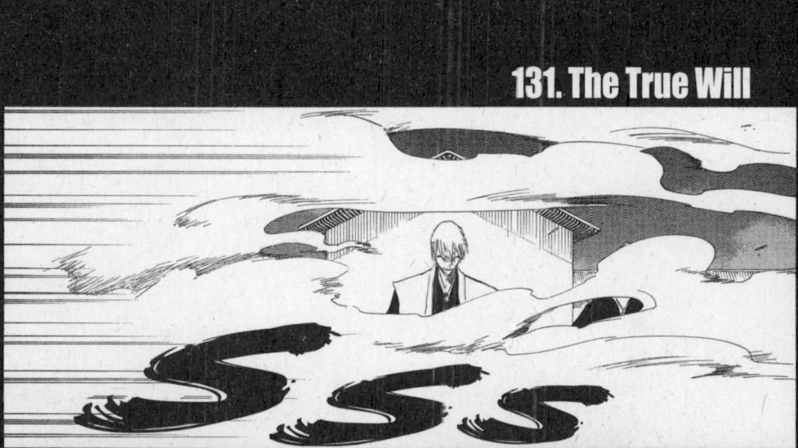
SSS

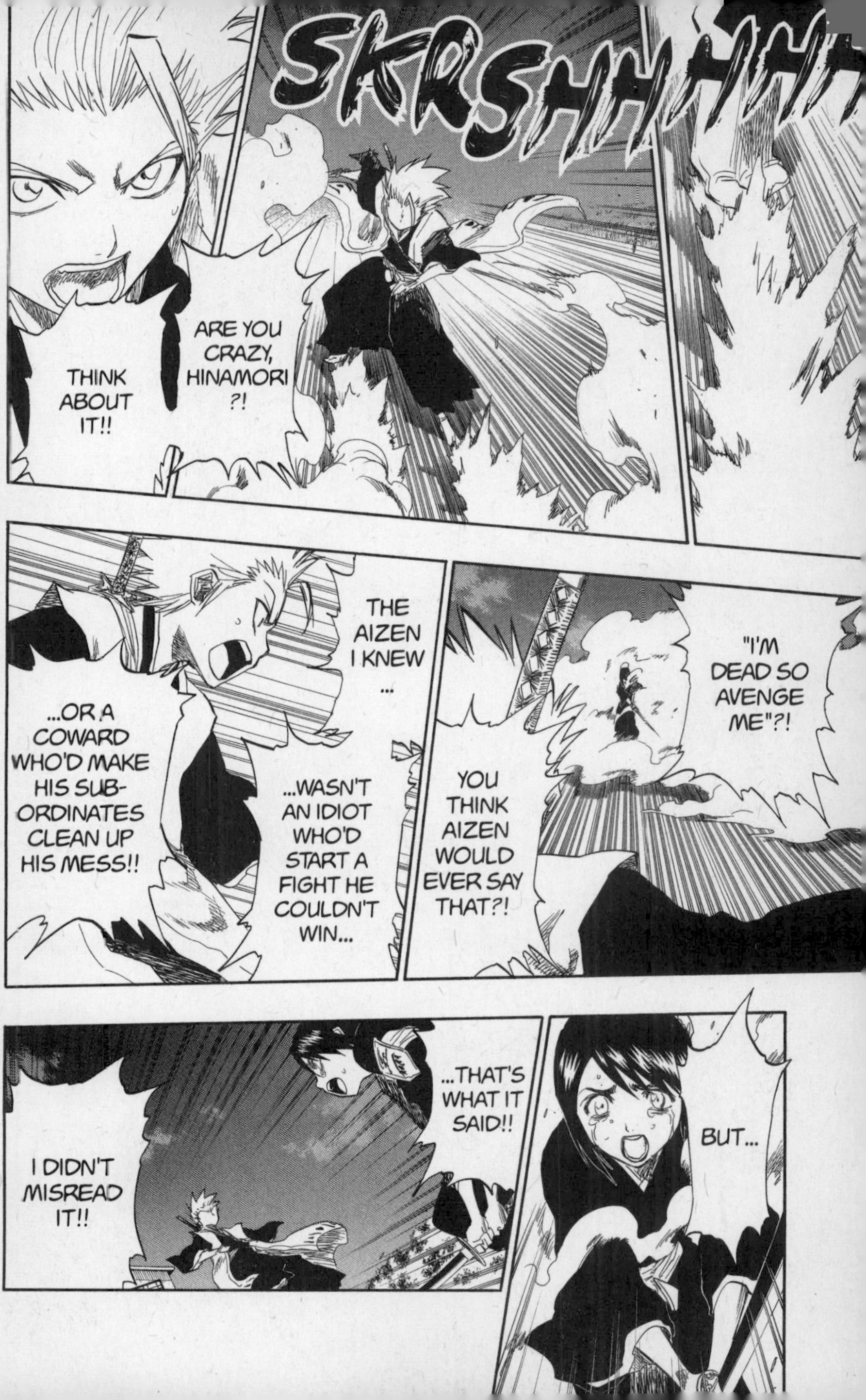
SKRSHHHH
ARE YOU CRAZY, HINAMORI?!
THINK ABOUT IT!!
"I'M DEAD SO AVENGE ME"?!
YOU THINK AIZEN WOULD EVER SAY THAT?!
THE AIZEN I KNEW ...
...WASN'T AN IDIOT WHO'D START A FIGHT HE COULDN'T WIN...
...OR A COWARD WHO'D MAKE HIS SUB-ORDINATES CLEAN UP HIS MESS!!
BUT...
...THAT'S WHAT IT SAID!!
I DIDN'T MISREAD IT!!

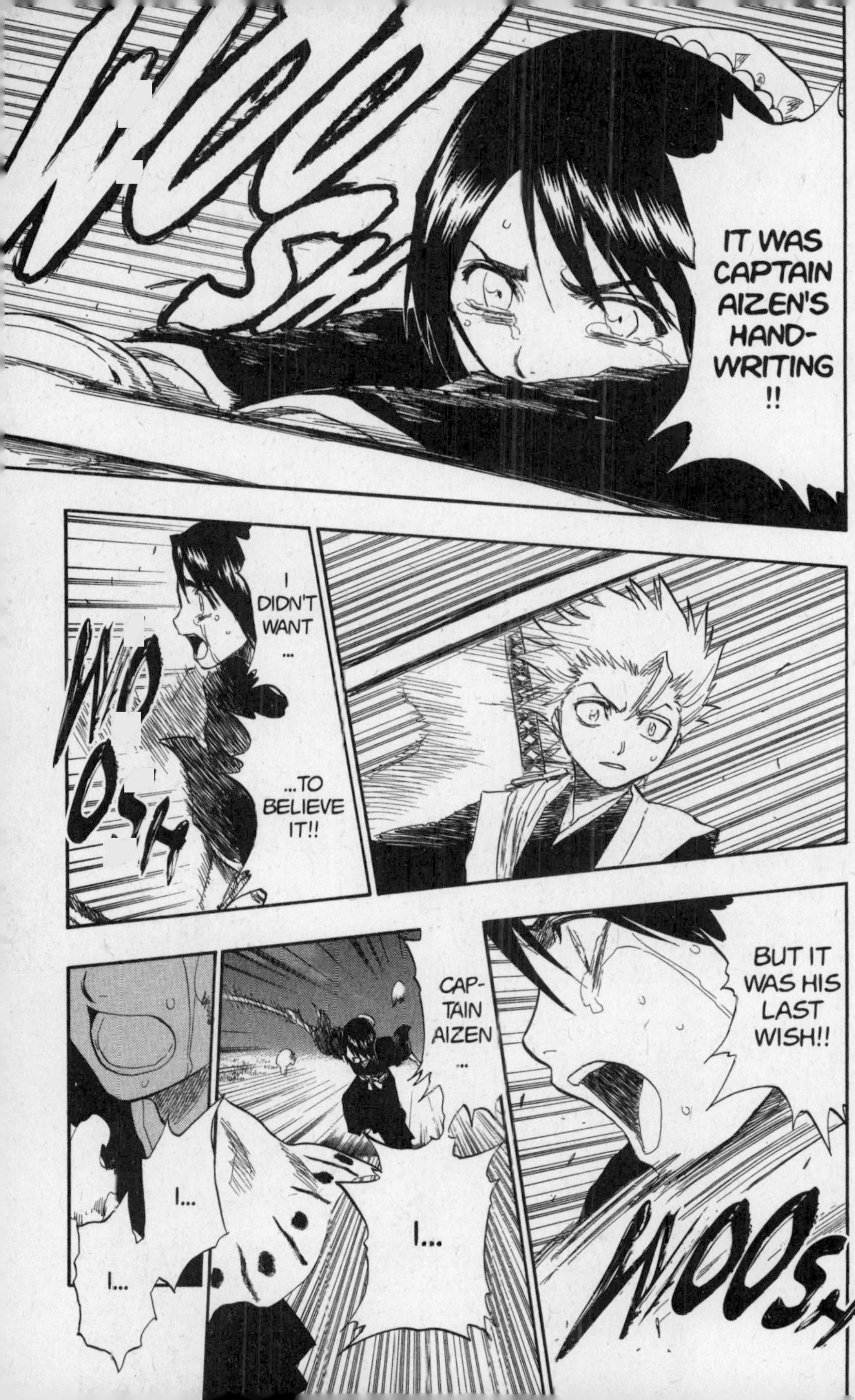
IT WAS CAPTAIN AIZEN'S HAND-WRITING !!
I DIDN'T WANT ...
...TO BELIEVE IT!!
BUT IT WAS HIS LAST WISH!!
WOOSH
CAP-TAIN AIZEN ...
I...
I...
I...

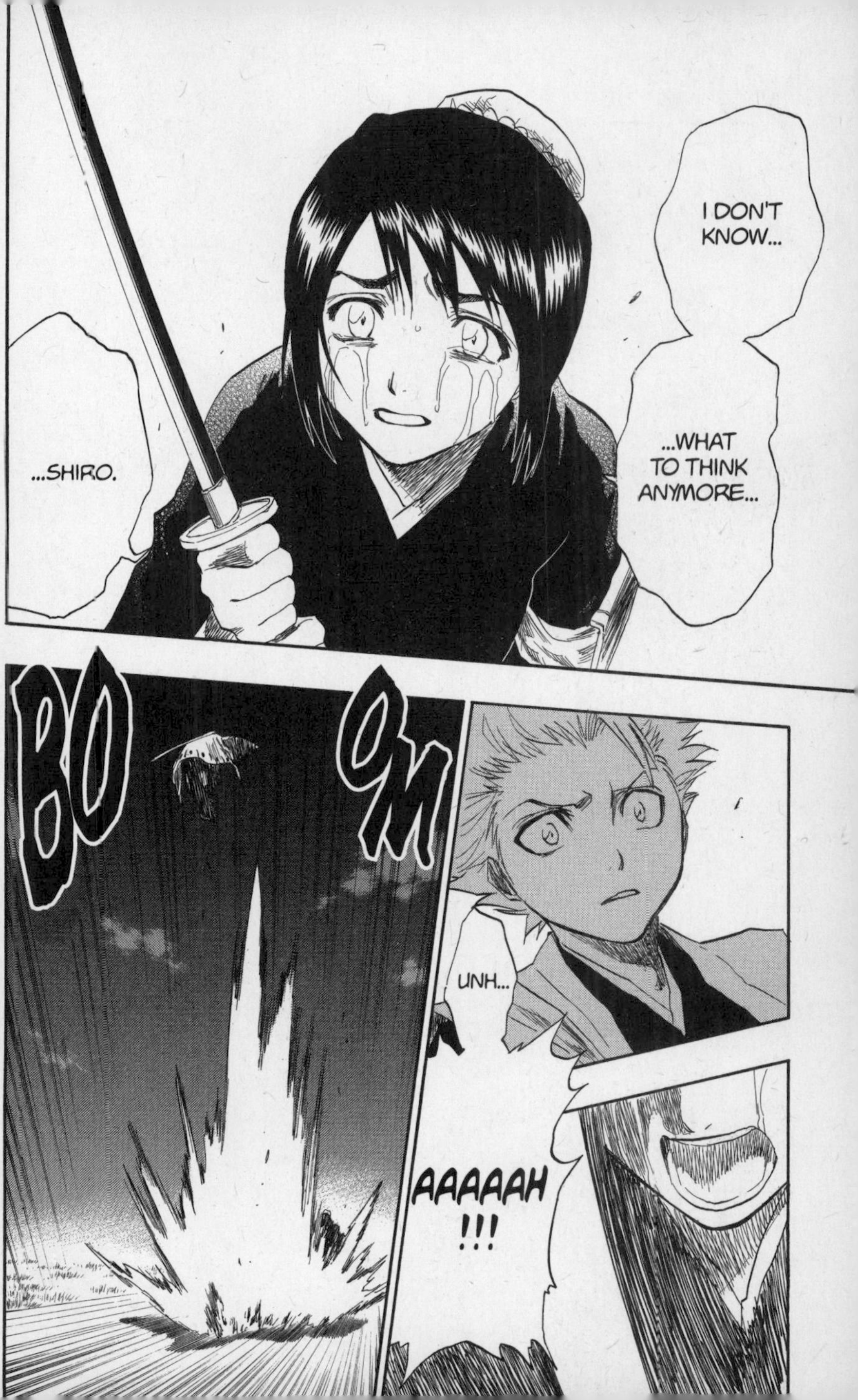
I DON'T KNOW...
...WHAT TO THINK ANYMORE...
...SHIRO.
UNH...
AAAAAH!!!
BOOM

READ THIS WAY

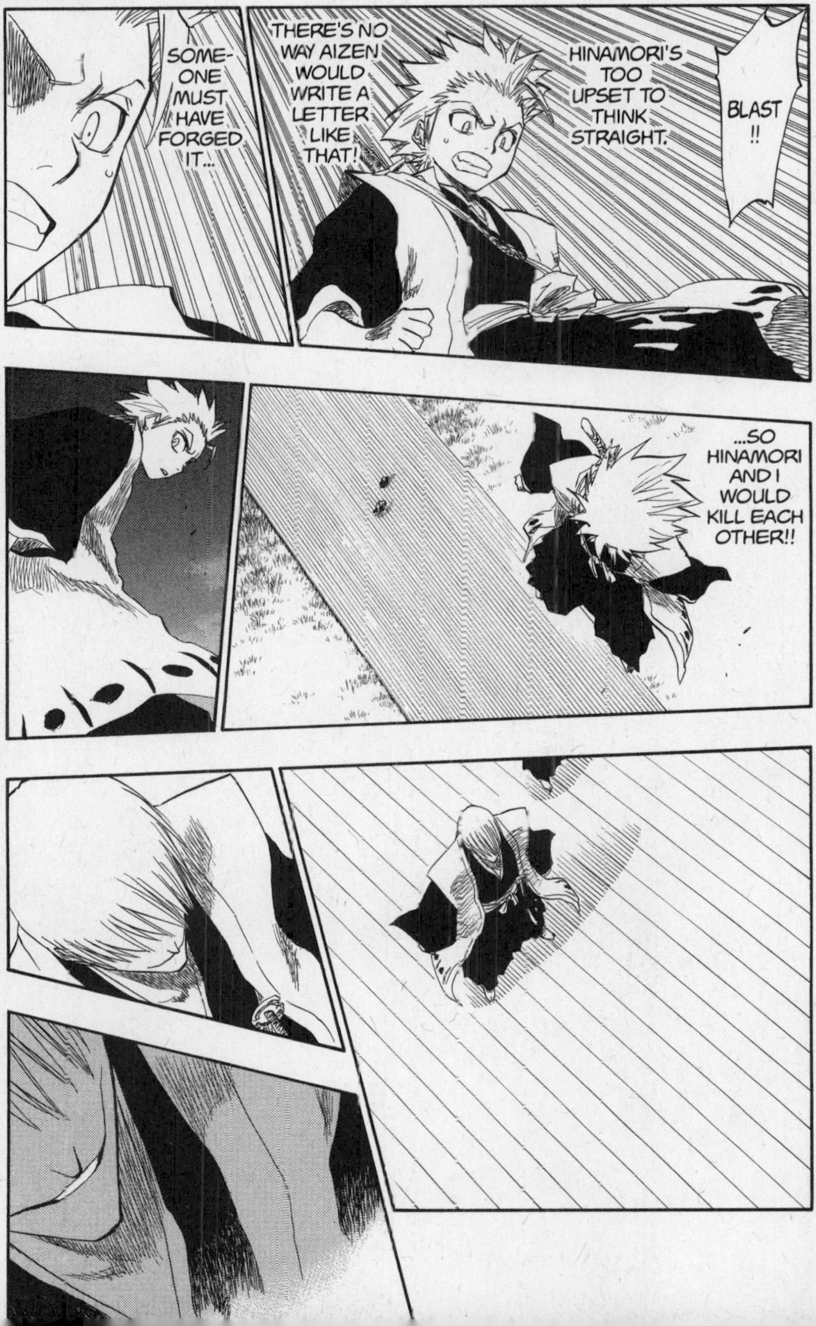
BLAST !!
HINAMORI'S TOO UPSET TO THINK STRAIGHT.
THERE'S NO WAY AIZEN WOULD WRITE A LETTER LIKE THAT!
SOME-ONE MUST HAVE FORGED IT...
...SO HINAMORI AND I WOULD KILL EACH OTHER!!

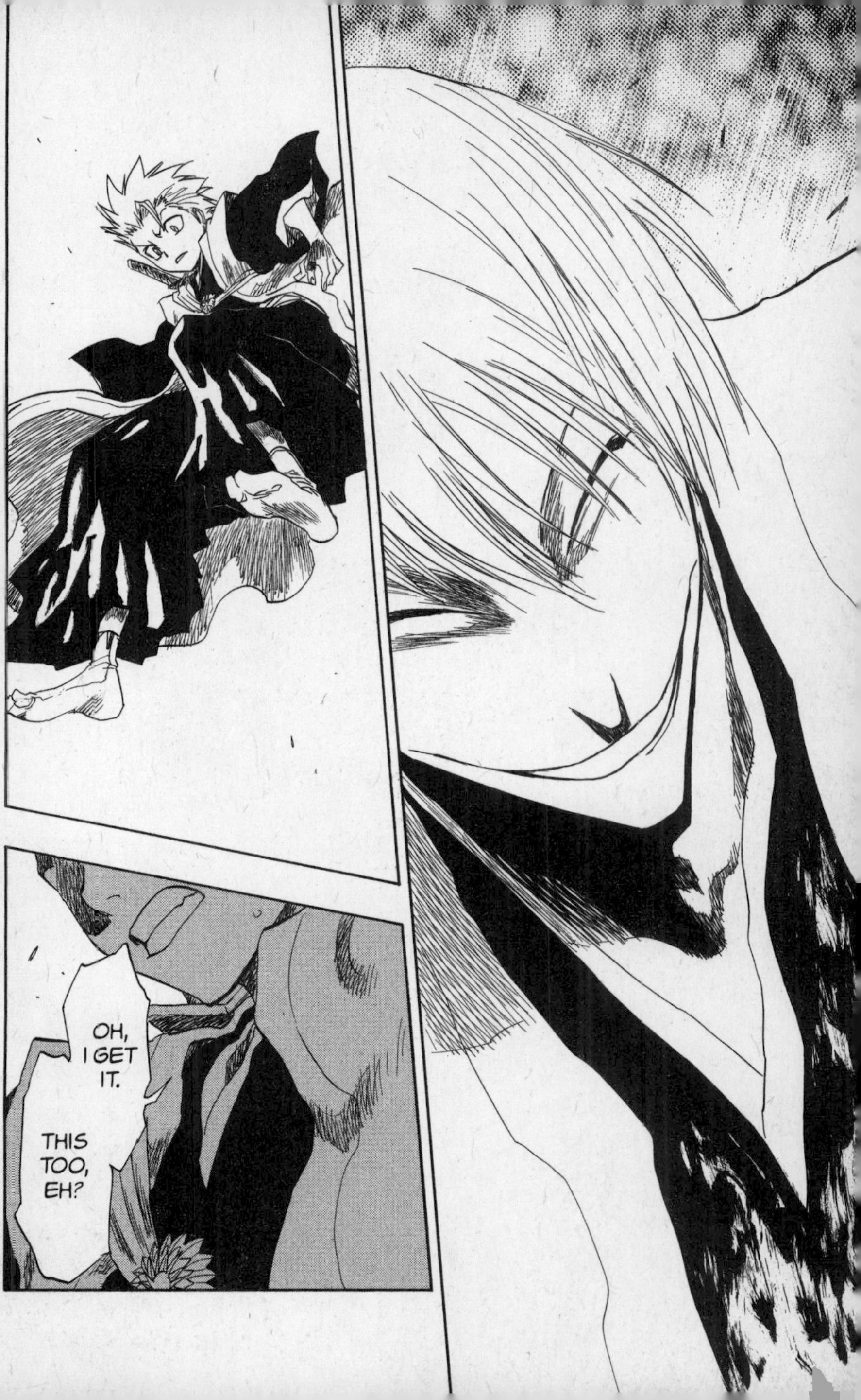
OH, I GET IT.
THIS TOO, EH?

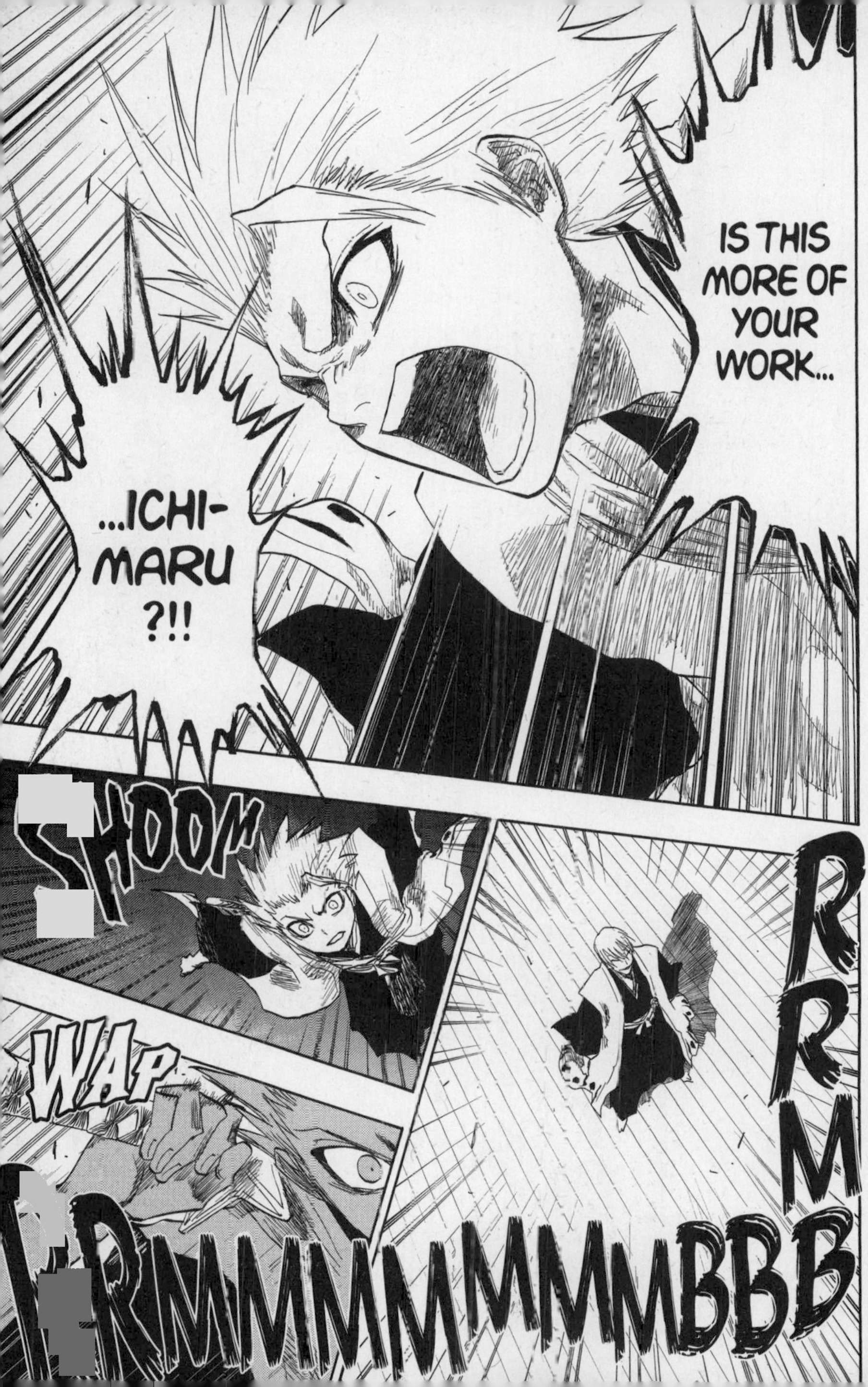
IS THIS MORE OF YOUR WORK...
...ICHIMARU ?!!
RRRM
SHOOM
WAP
RMMMMMMMBBB

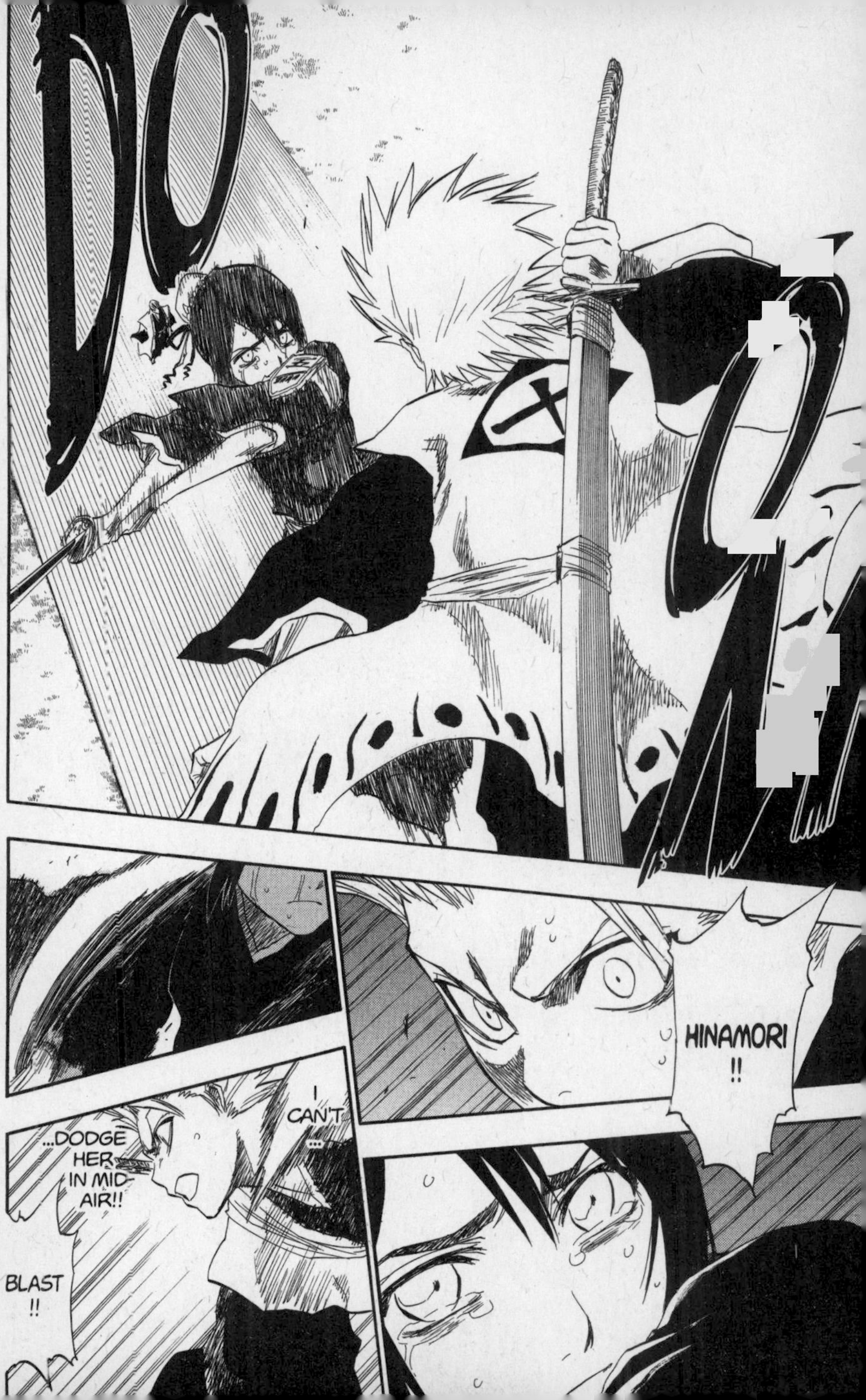
DO
HINAMORI !!
I CAN'T ...
...DODGE HER IN MID-AIR!!
BLAST !!

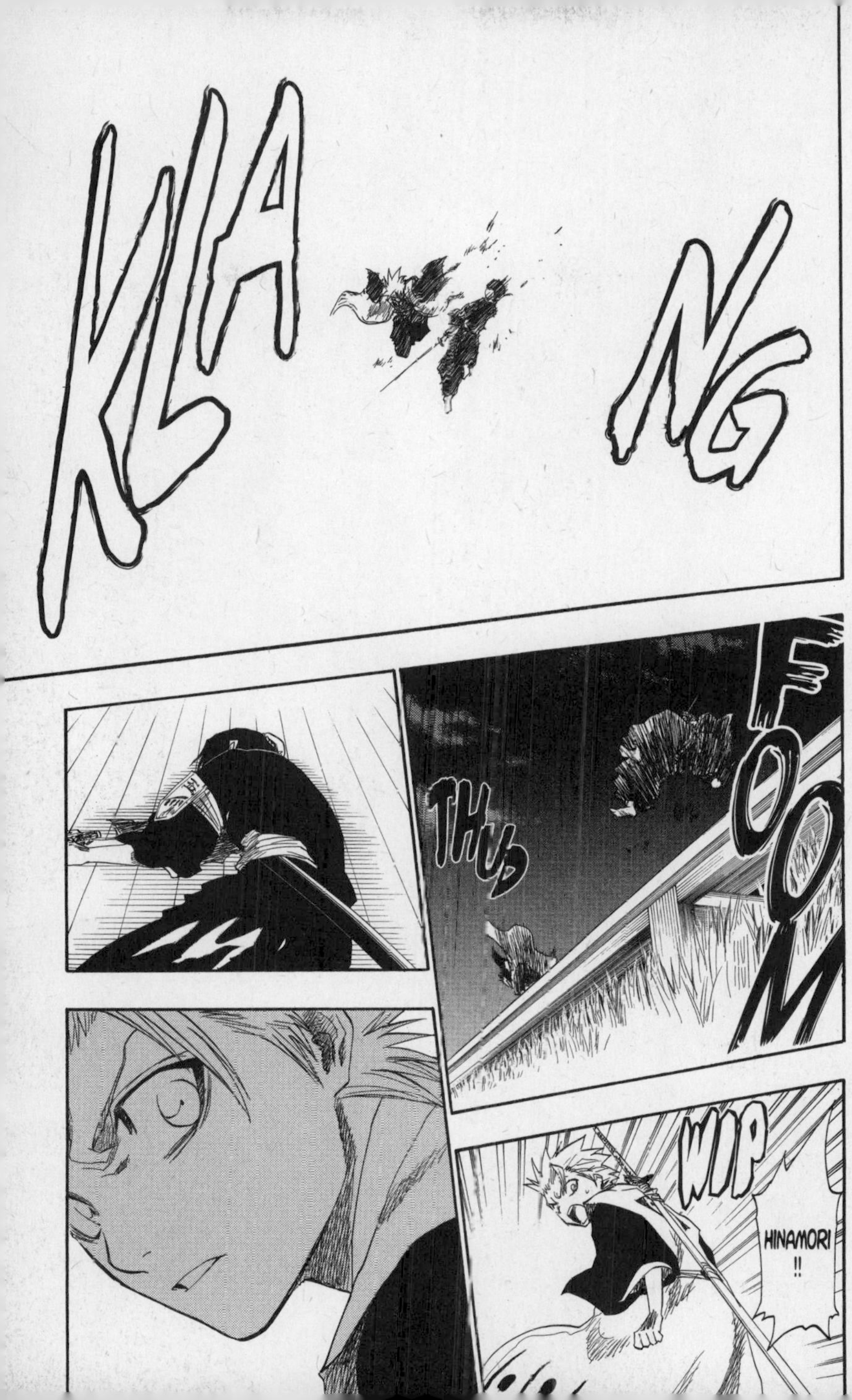
KLANG
FOOOM
THUD
WIP
HINAMORI!!

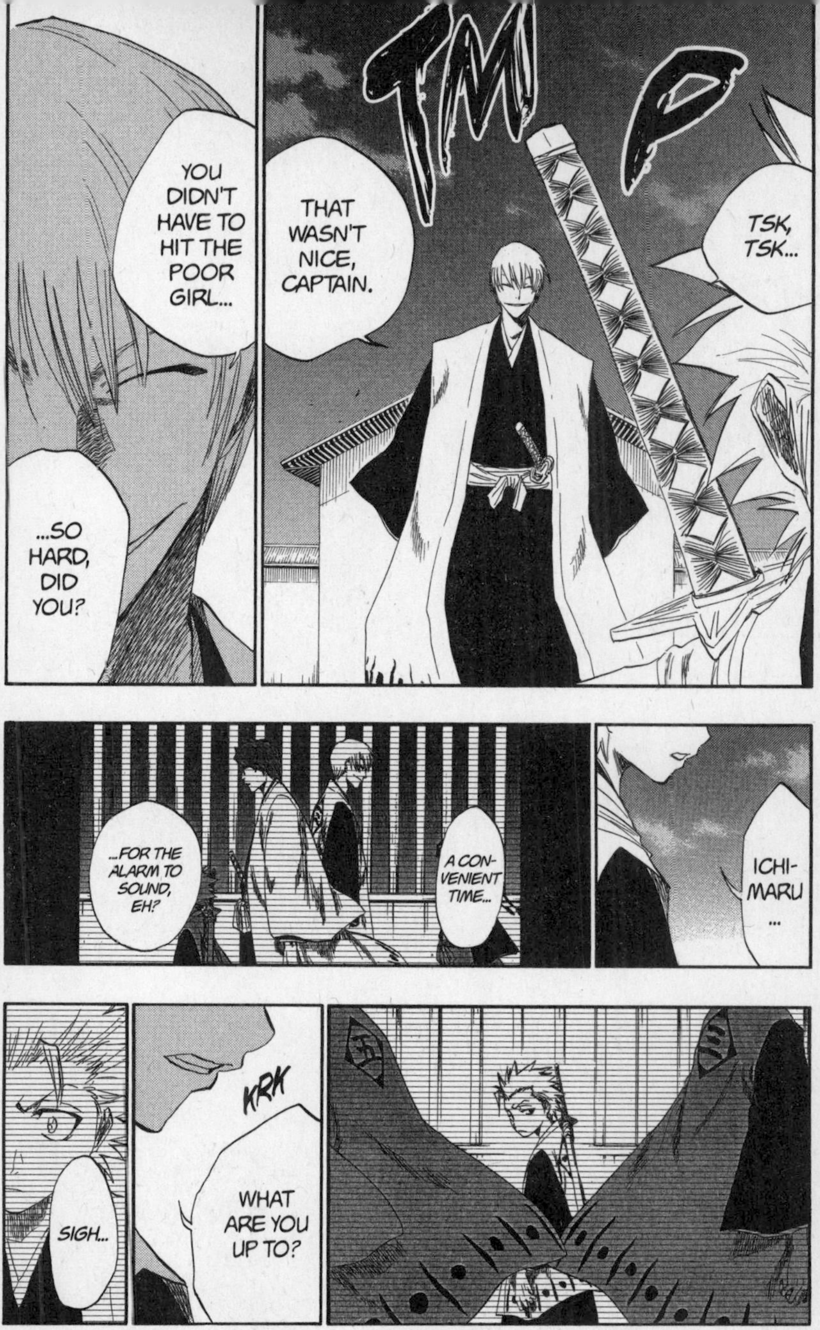
TMP
TSK, TSK...
THAT WASN'T NICE, CAPTAIN.
YOU DIDN'T HAVE TO HIT THE POOR GIRL...
...SO HARD, DID YOU?
ICHI-MARU ...
A CON-VENIENT TIME...
...FOR THE ALARM TO SOUND, EH?
KRK
WHAT ARE YOU UP TO?
SIGH...

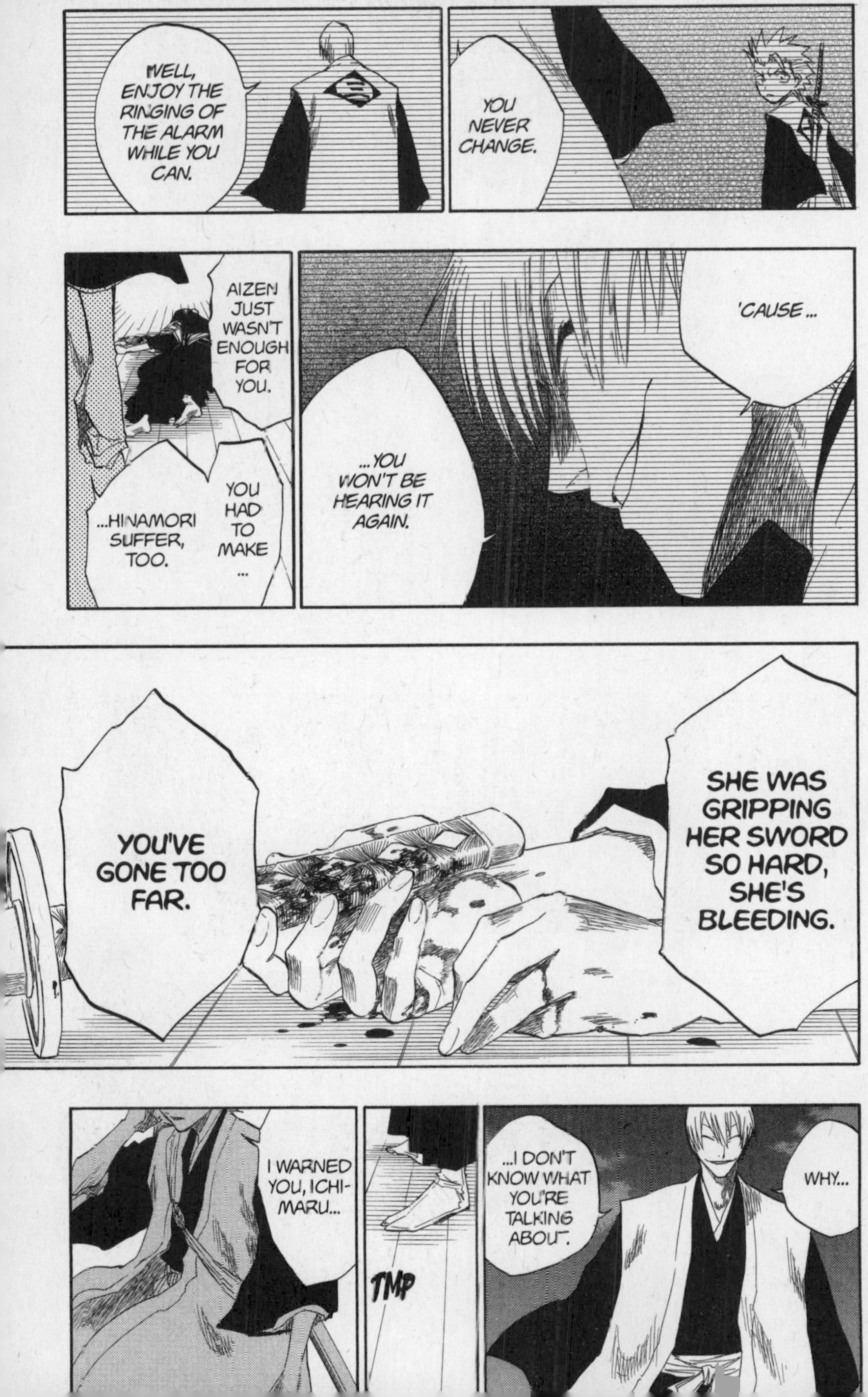
YOU NEVER CHANGE.
WELL, ENJOY THE RINGING OF THE ALARM WHILE YOU CAN.
'CAUSE ...
...YOU WON'T BE HEARING IT AGAIN.
AIZEN JUST WASN'T ENOUGH FOR YOU.
YOU HAD TO MAKE ...
...HINAMORI SUFFER, TOO.
SHE WAS GRIPPING HER SWORD SO HARD, SHE'S BLEEDING.
YOU'VE GONE TOO FAR.
WHY...
...I DON'T KNOW WHAT YOU'RE TALKING ABOUT.
TMP
I WARNED YOU, ICHI-MARU...

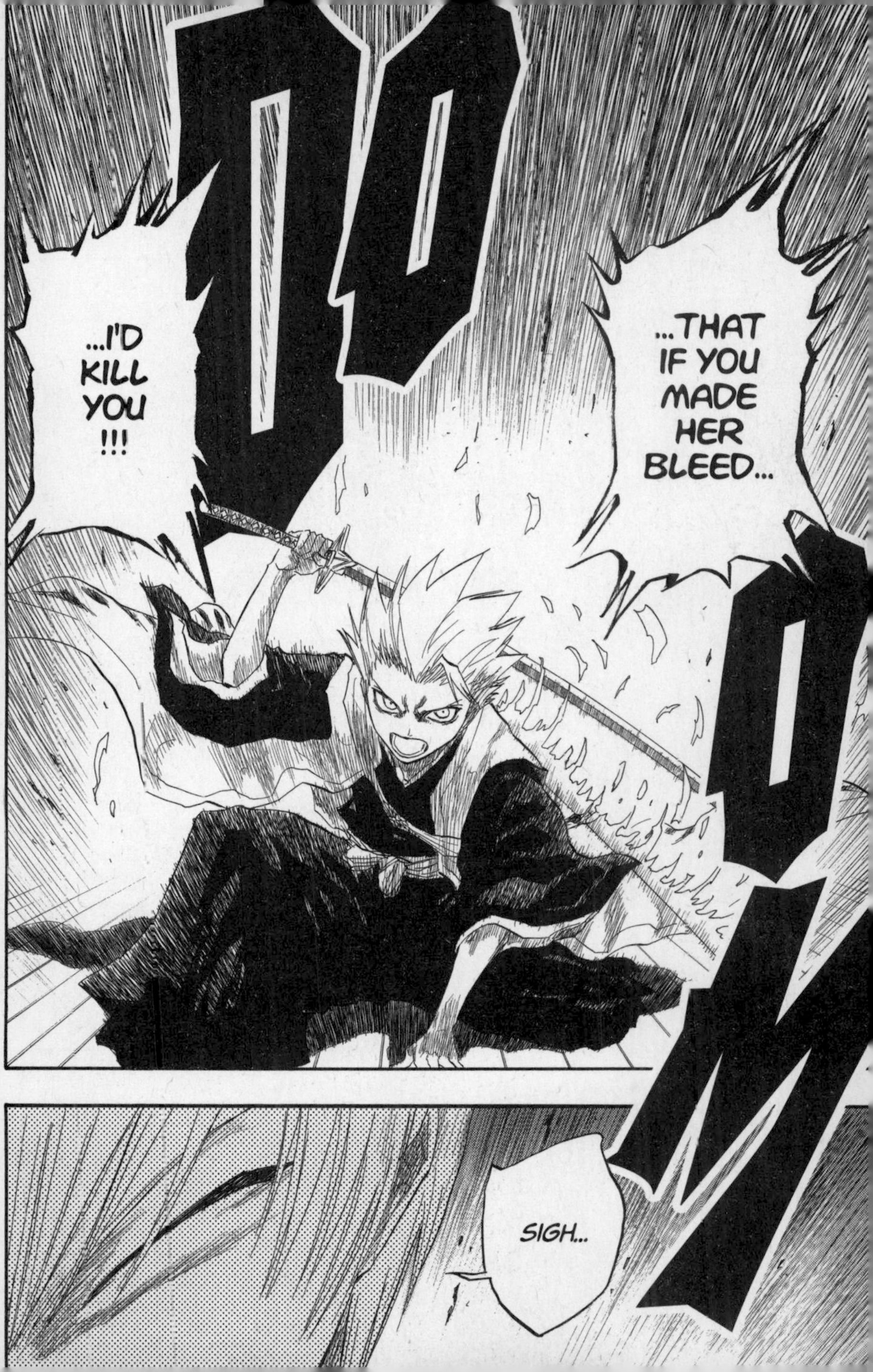
...THAT IF YOU MADE HER BLEED...
...I'D KILL YOU !!!
SIGH..

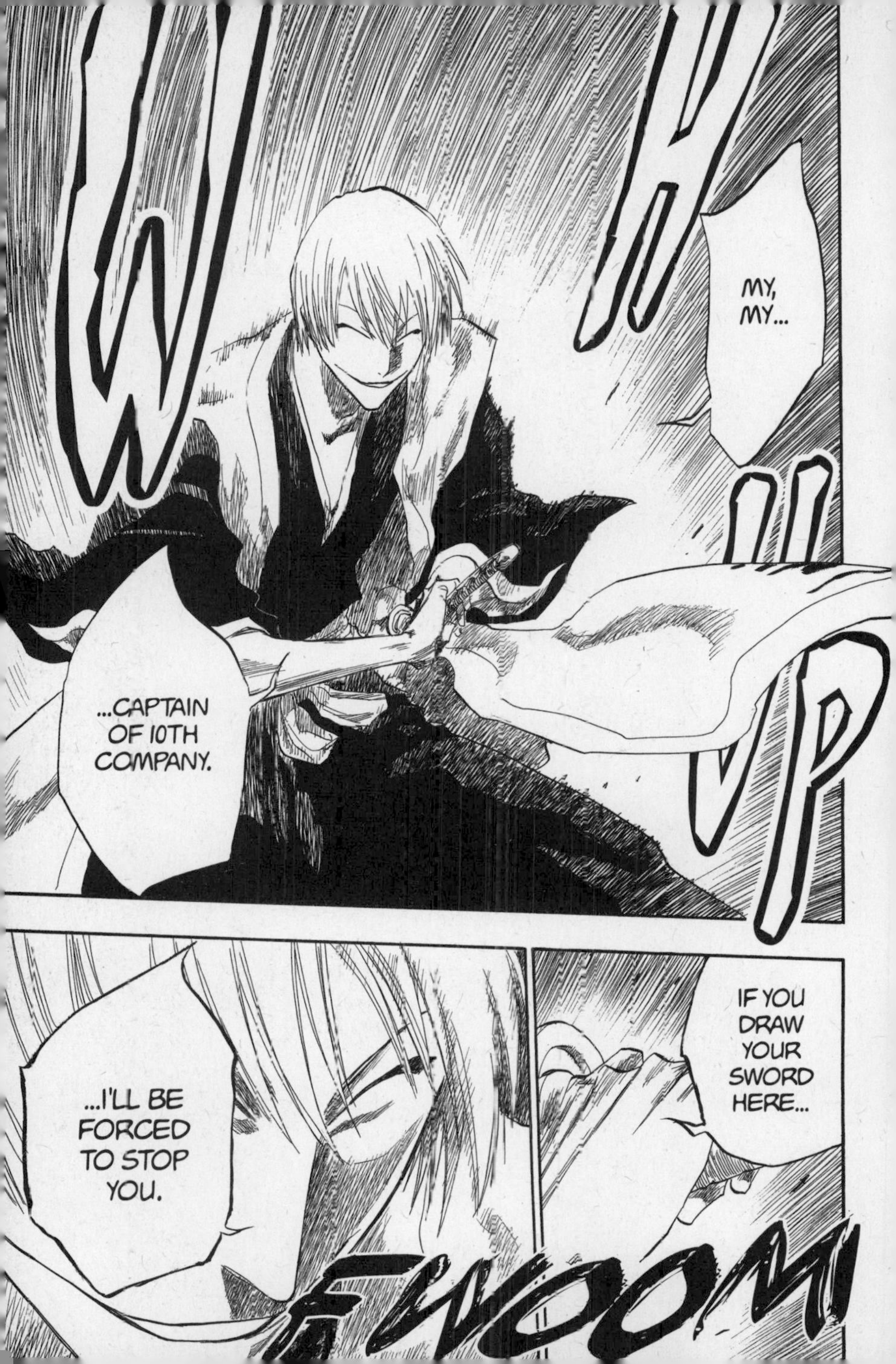
WHUP
MY, MY...
...CAPTAIN OF 10TH COMPANY.
IF YOU DRAW YOUR SWORD HERE...
...I'LL BE FORCED TO STOP YOU.
FWOOM

MEANWHILE IN THE WORLD OF THE LIVING, SERIES 4
SHE'S ONLY IN 5TH GRADE, BUT SHE CAN WRITE IN CURSIVE!
YUZU'S Super HEARTFELT DIARY
AUGUST 8, CLOUDY.
ICHIGO CAME HOME THIS MORNING OUT OF THE BLUE. I WAS KIND OF SURPRISED SINCE DAD HAD SAID THAT ICHIGO WOULD BE GONE ALL SUMMER. I WAS REALLY HAPPY TO SEE HIM! HE SAID HE'D LOST HIS TICKET FOR THE BULLET TRAIN AND COME HOME. HOW CUTE! ♡
WHAT SHALL WE DO TOGETHER TOMORROW? ♡

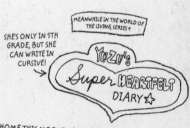

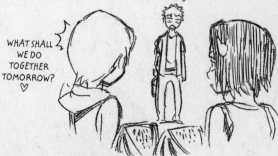

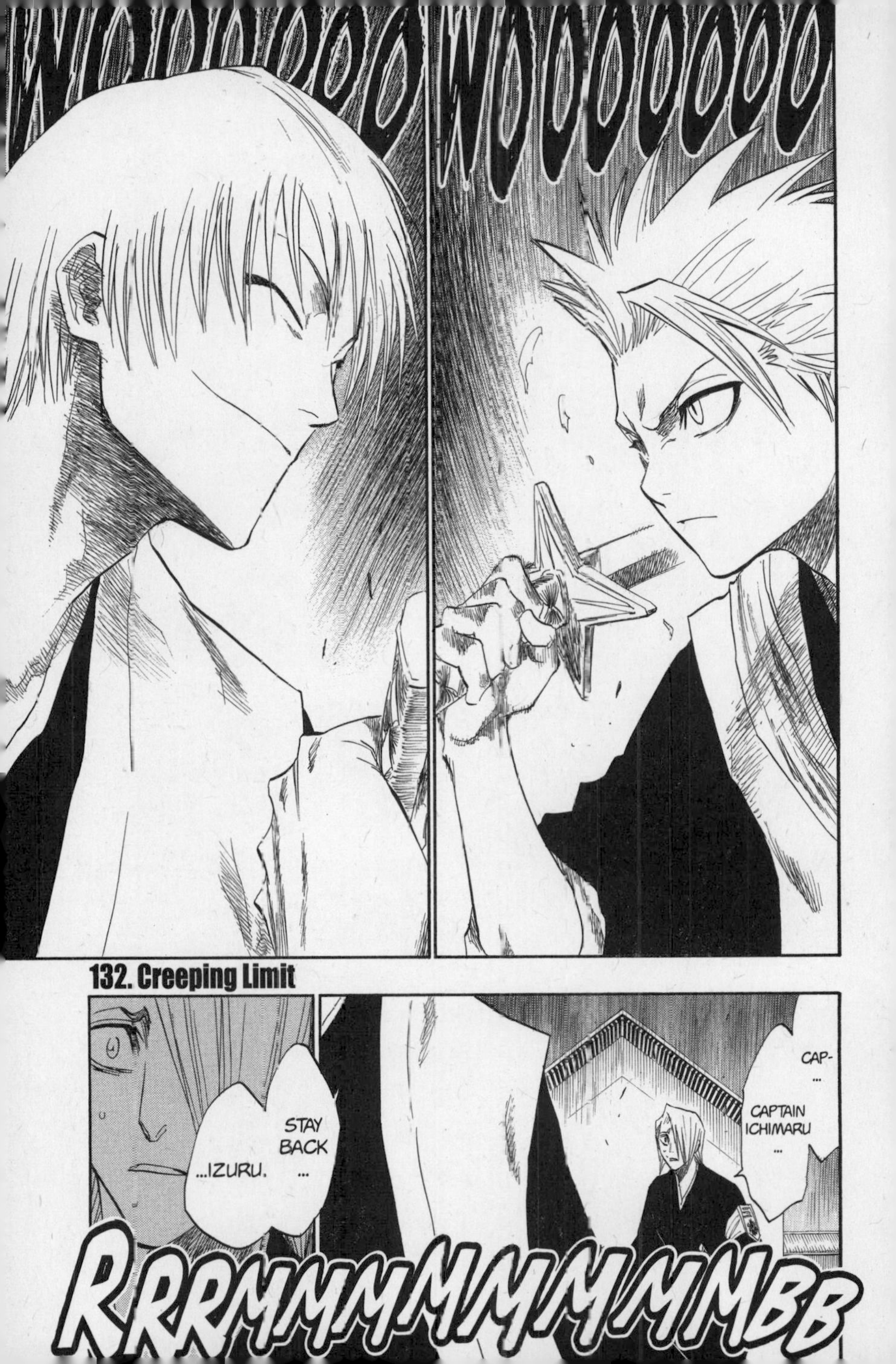
WOOOOOOOO
WOOOOOOO
132. Creeping Limit
CAP- ...
CAPTAIN ICHIMARU ...
STAY BACK ...
...IZURU.
RRRMMMMMMMMMBB

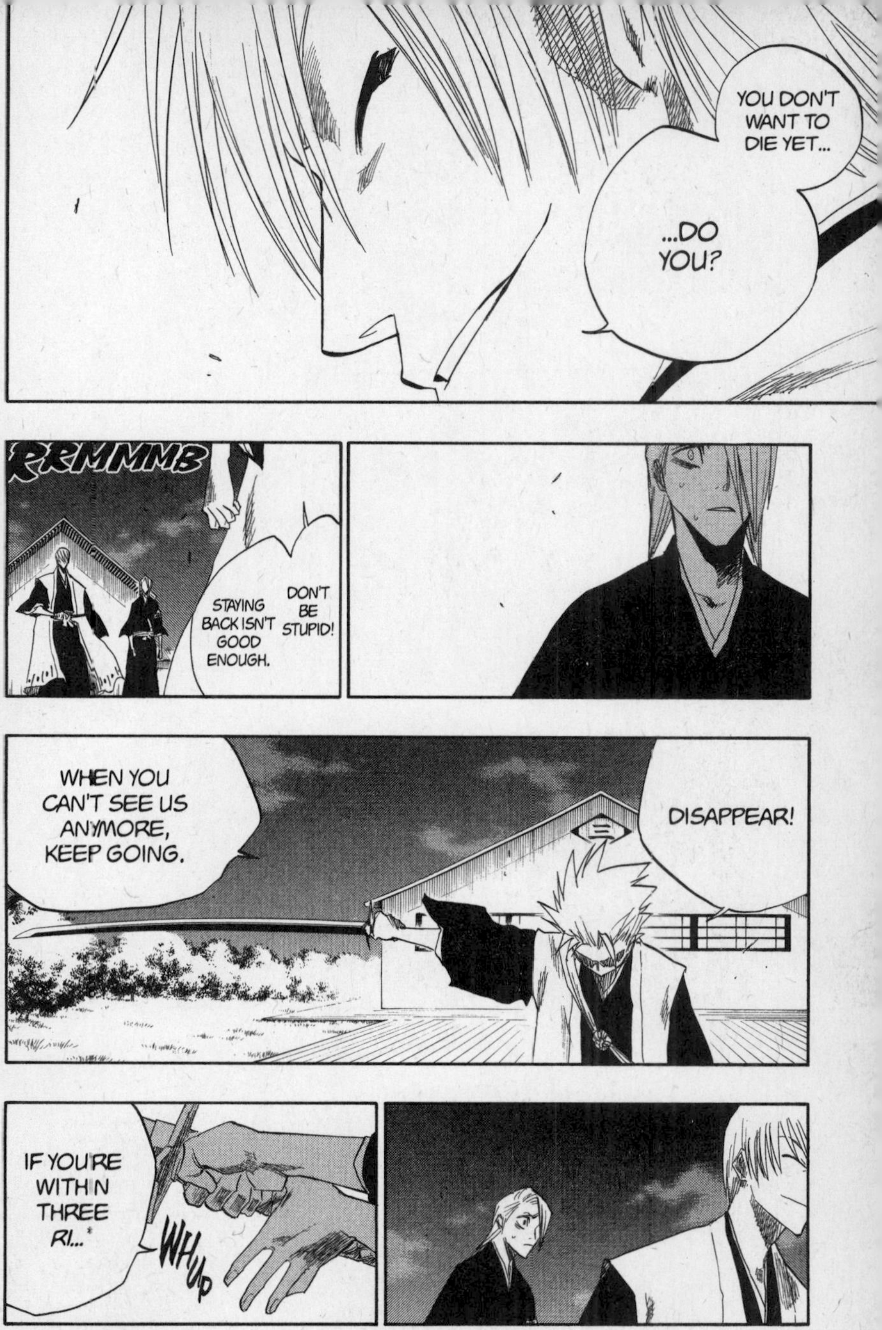
YOU DON'T WANT TO DIE YET...
...DO YOU?
RRMMMB
DON'T BE STUPID!
STAYING BACK ISN'T GOOD ENOUGH.
DISAPPEAR!
WHEN YOU CAN'T SEE US ANYMORE, KEEP GOING.
IF YOU'RE WITHIN THREE RI...*
WHUP

*About 7.3 miles

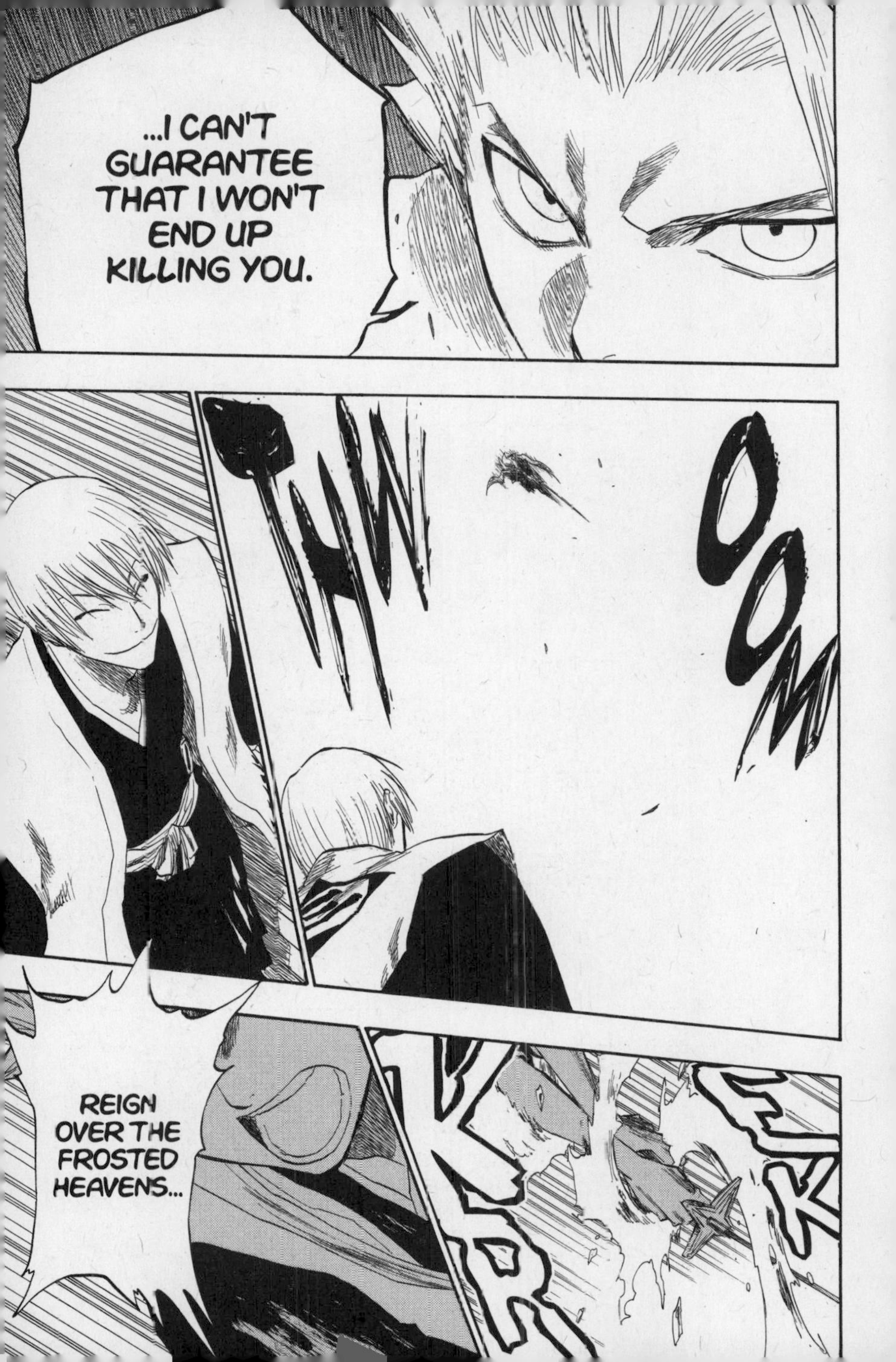
...I CAN'T GUARANTEE THAT I WON'T END UP KILLING YOU.
THWOOM
REIGN OVER THE FROSTED HEAVENS...

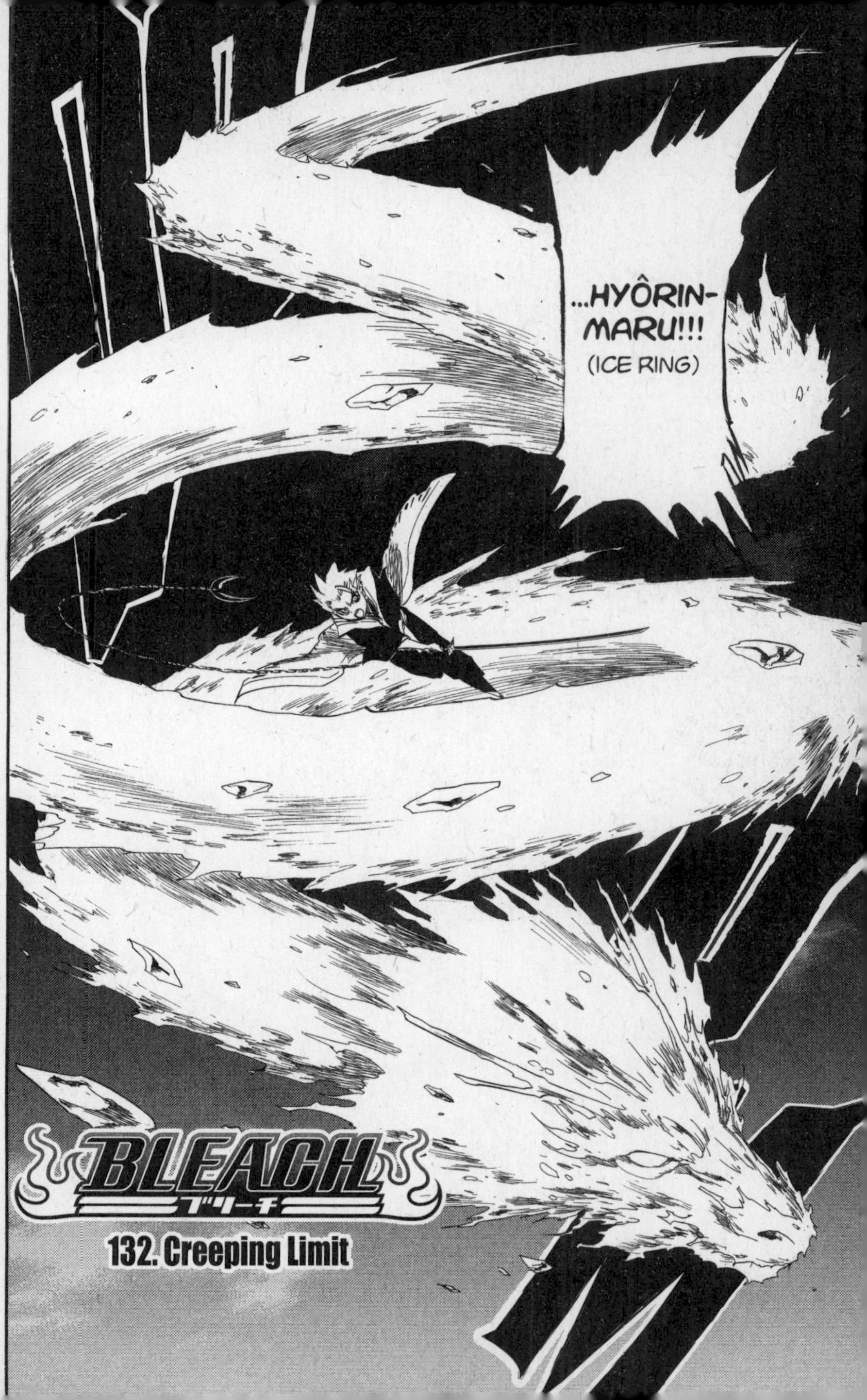
...HYÔRIN-
MARU!!!
(ICE RING)
BLEACH
ブリーチ
132. Creeping Limit

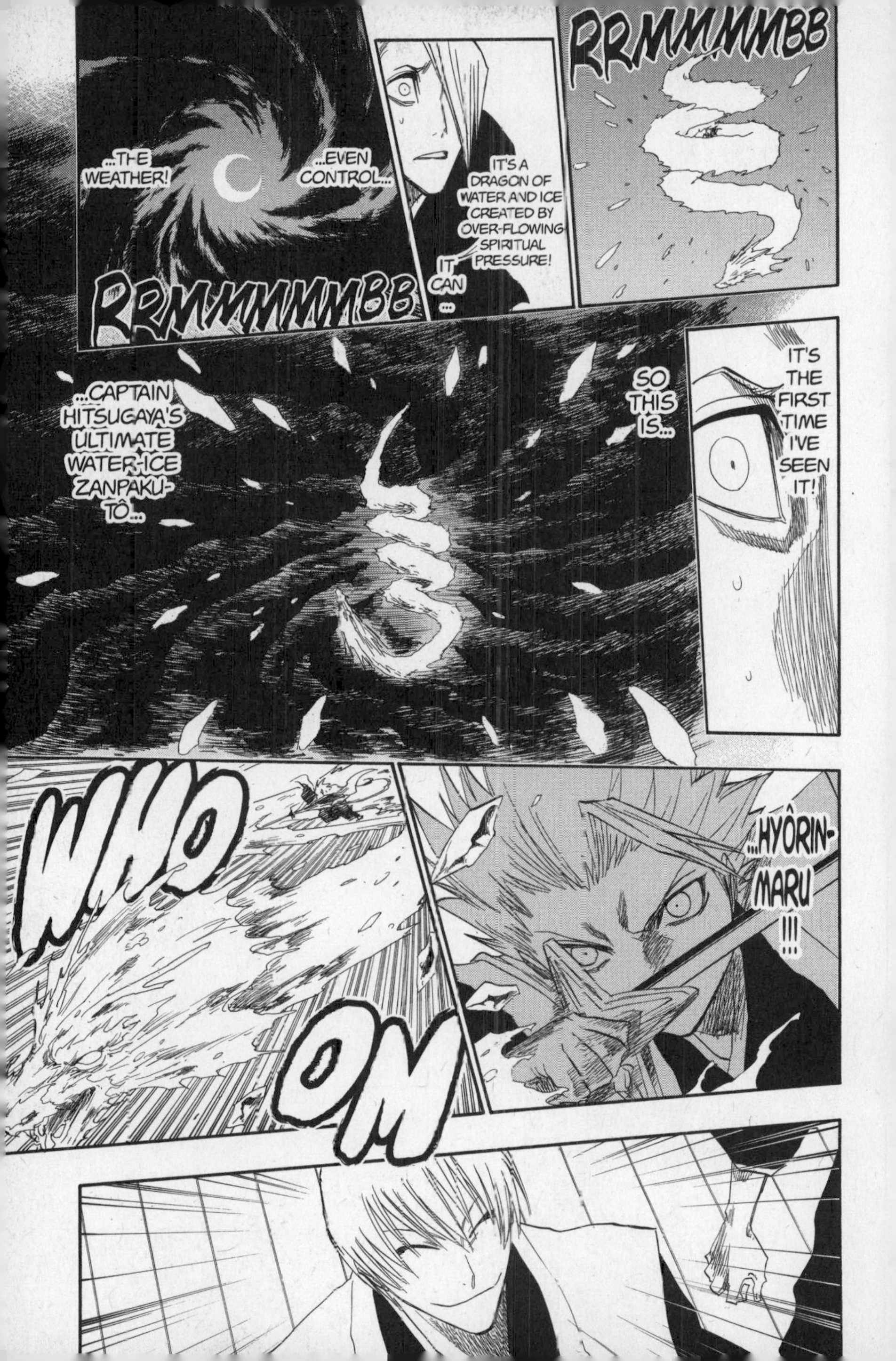
RRMMMMMBB
IT'S A DRAGON OF WATER AND ICE CREATED BY OVER-FLOWING SPIRITUAL PRESSURE!
IT CAN...
...EVEN CONTROL...
...THE WEATHER!
RRMMMMMMBB
IT'S THE FIRST TIME I'VE SEEN IT!
SO THIS IS...
...CAPTAIN HITSUGAYA'S ULTIMATE WATER-ICE ZANPAKU-TÔ...
...HYÔRIN-MARU!!!
WHOOM

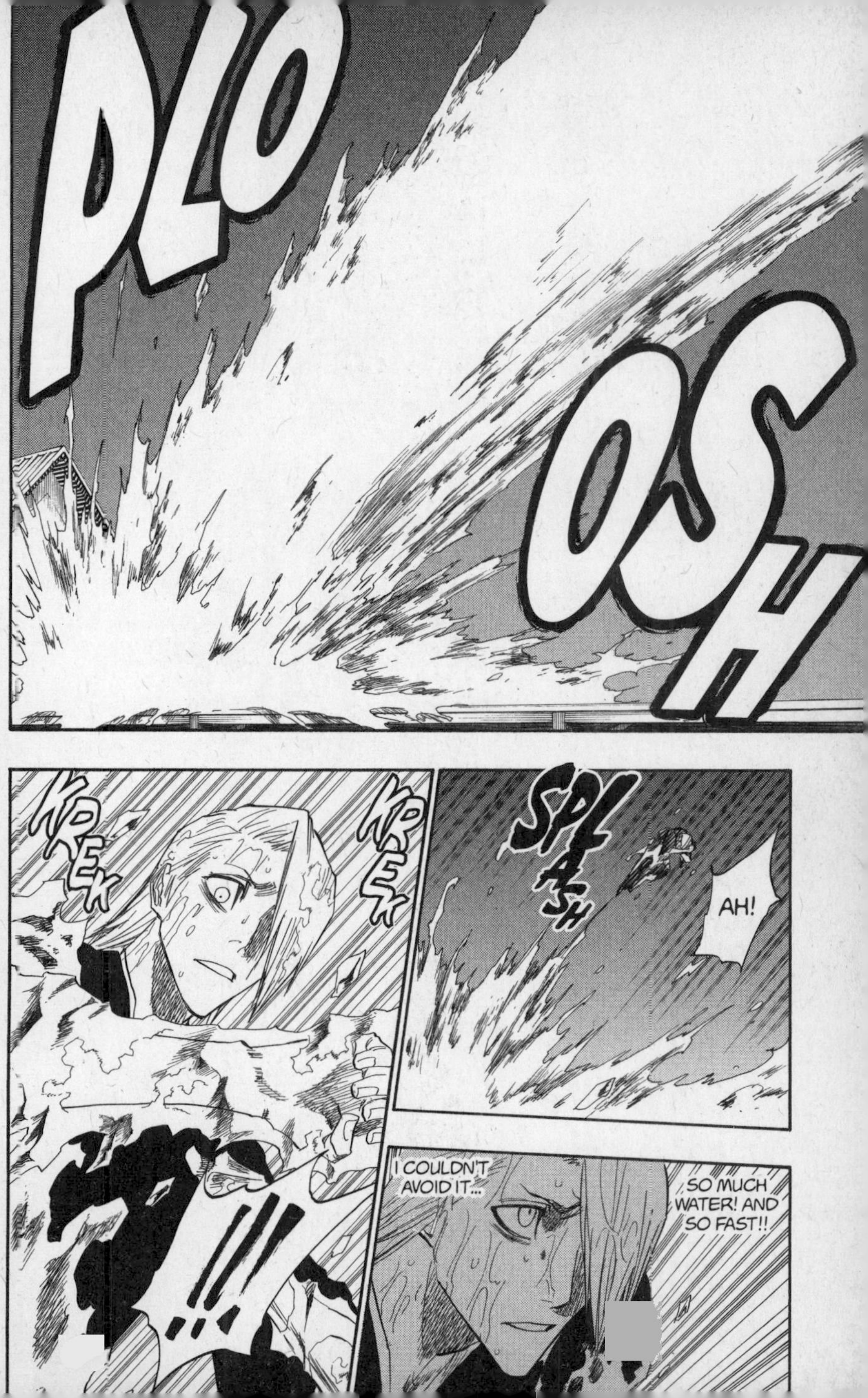
PLOOSH
SPLASH
AH!
SO MUCH WATER! AND SO FAST!!
I COULDN'T AVOID IT...
KREK
KREK
!!!

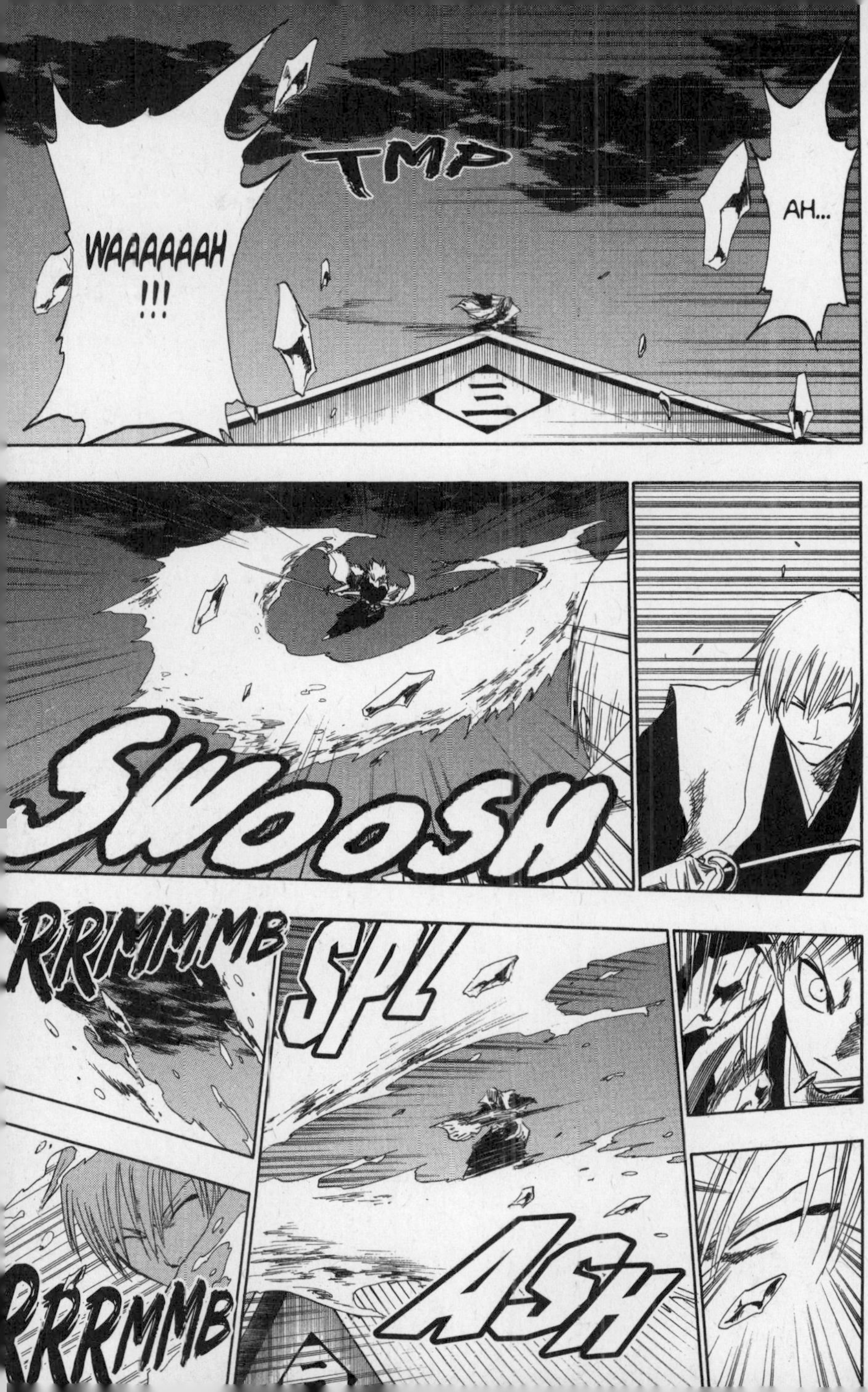
AH...
TMP
WAAAAAAH!!!
SWOOSH
SPL
ASH
RRMMMB
RRRMMMB

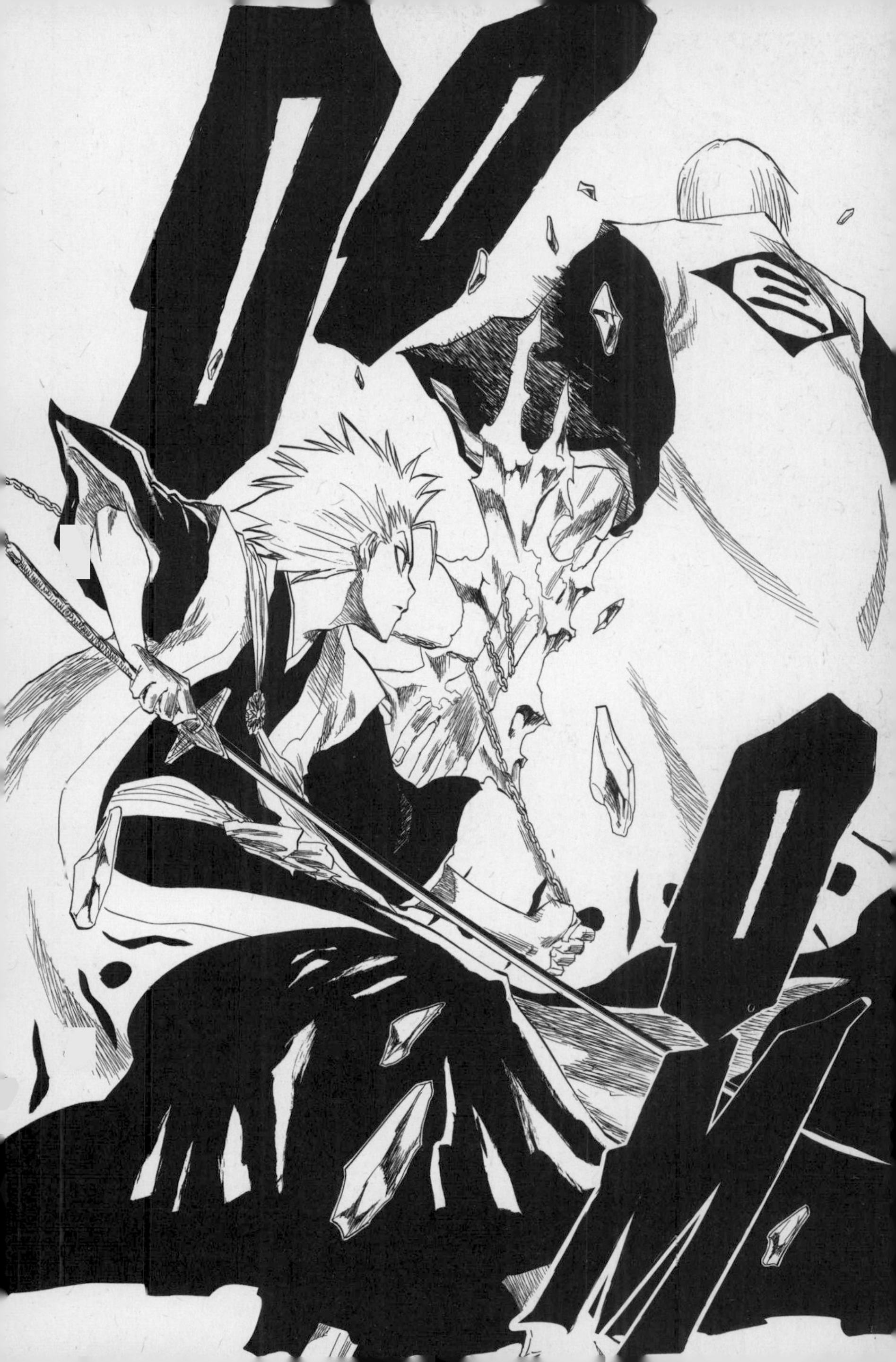

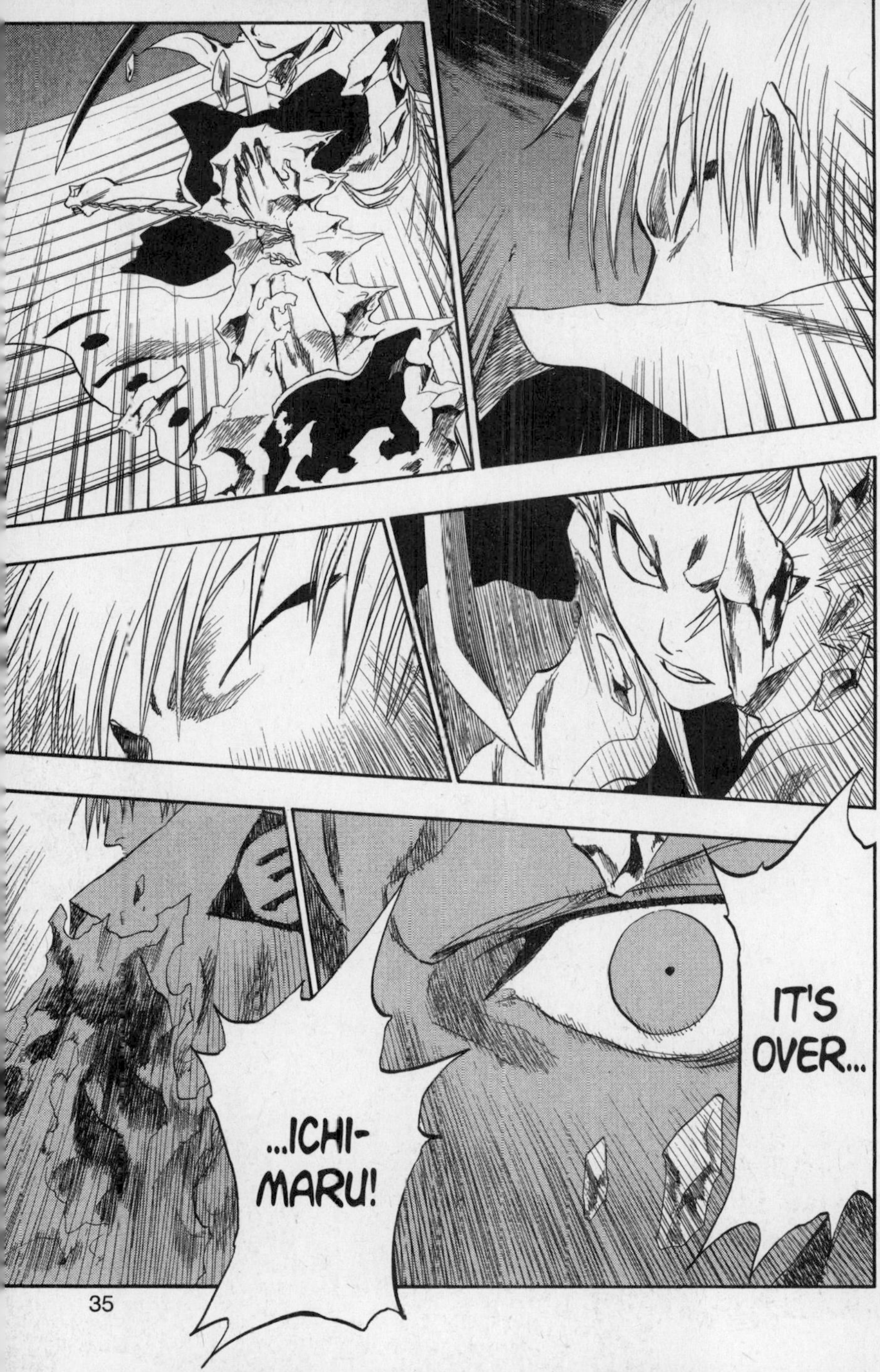
IT'S OVER...
...ICHI-MARU!

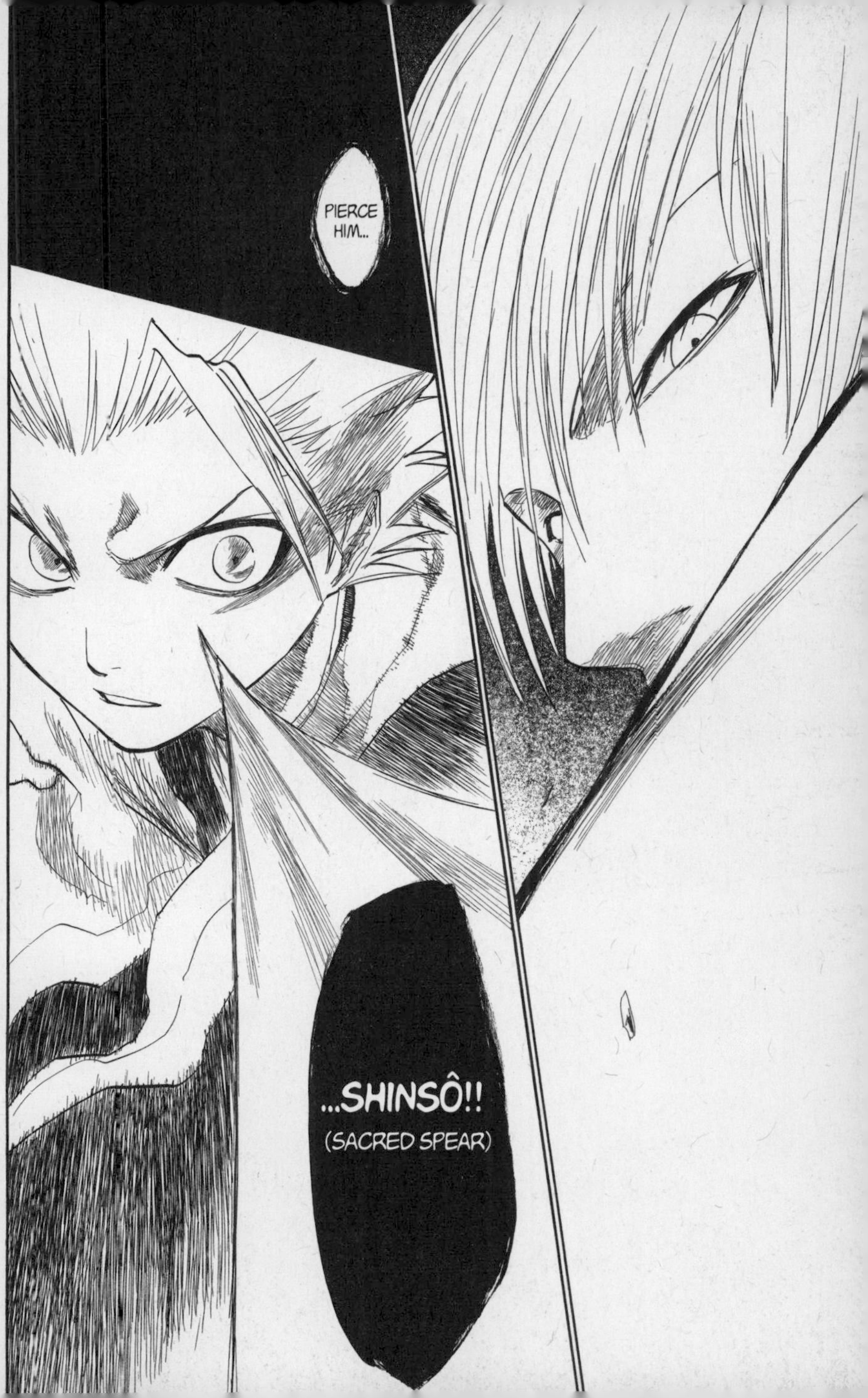
PIERCE HIM...
...SHINSÔ!!
(SACRED SPEAR)

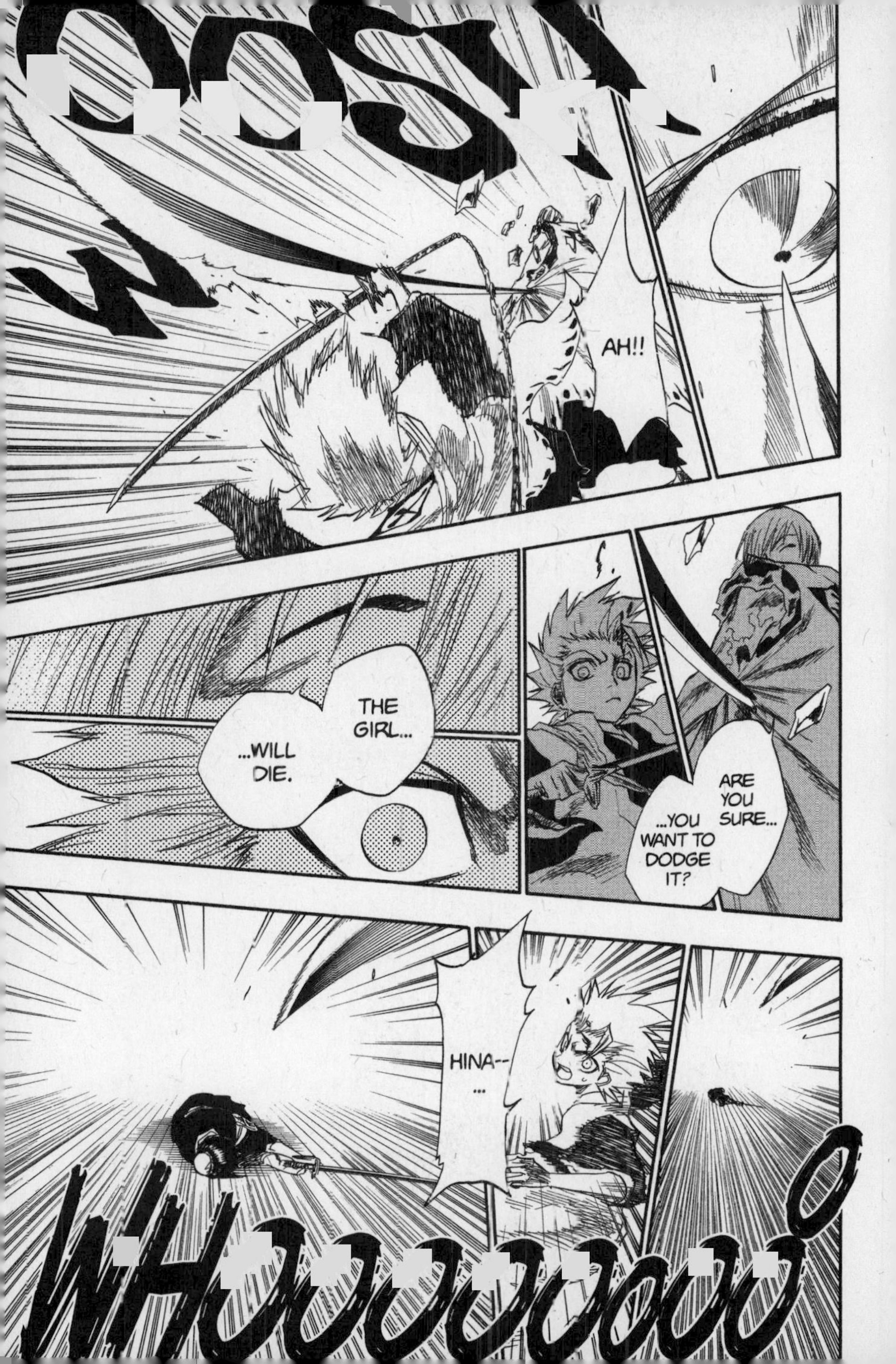
AH!!
ARE YOU SURE... ...YOU WANT TO DODGE IT?
THE GIRL... ...WILL DIE.
HINA-- ...

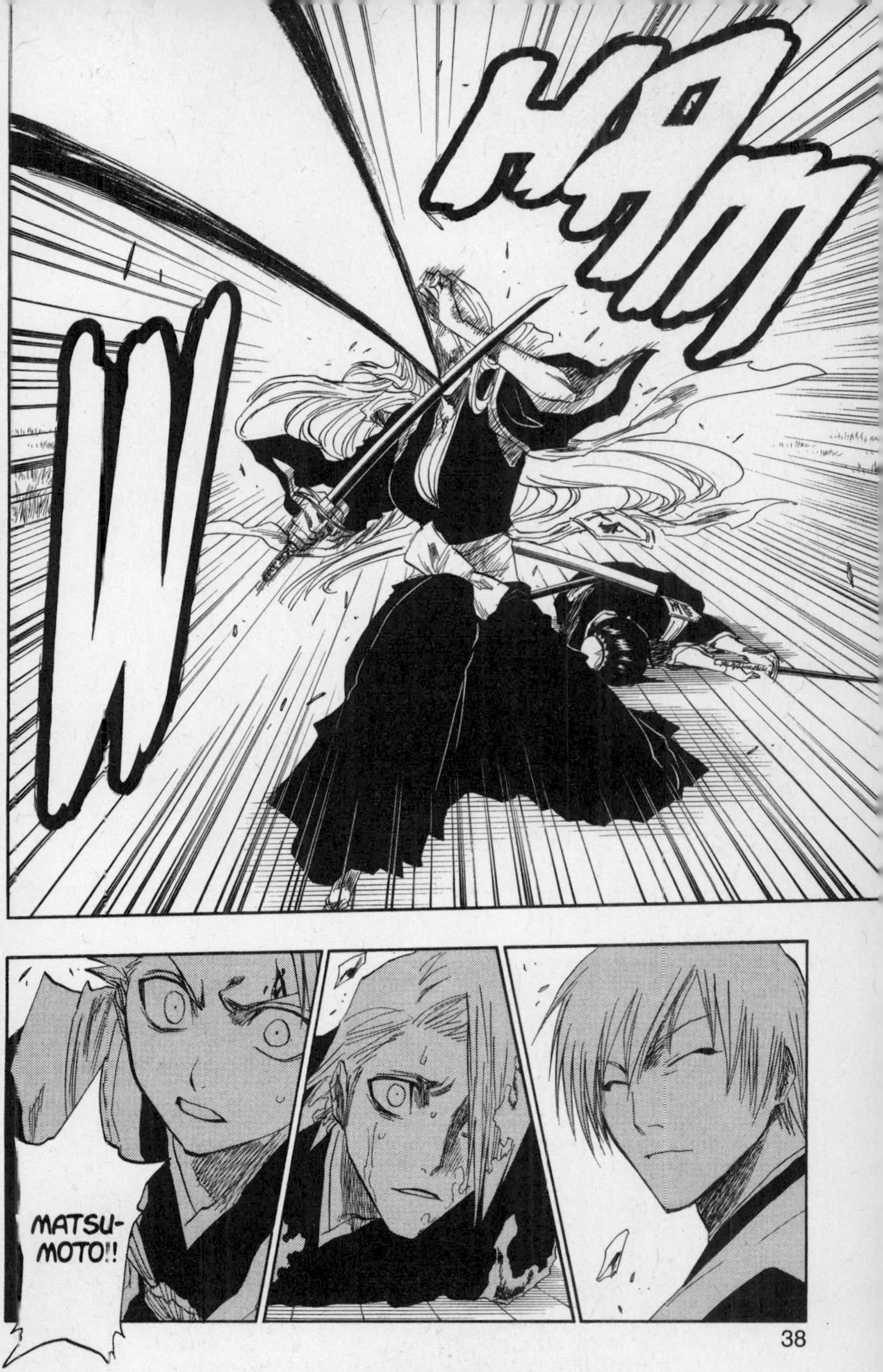
MATSU-
MOTO!!

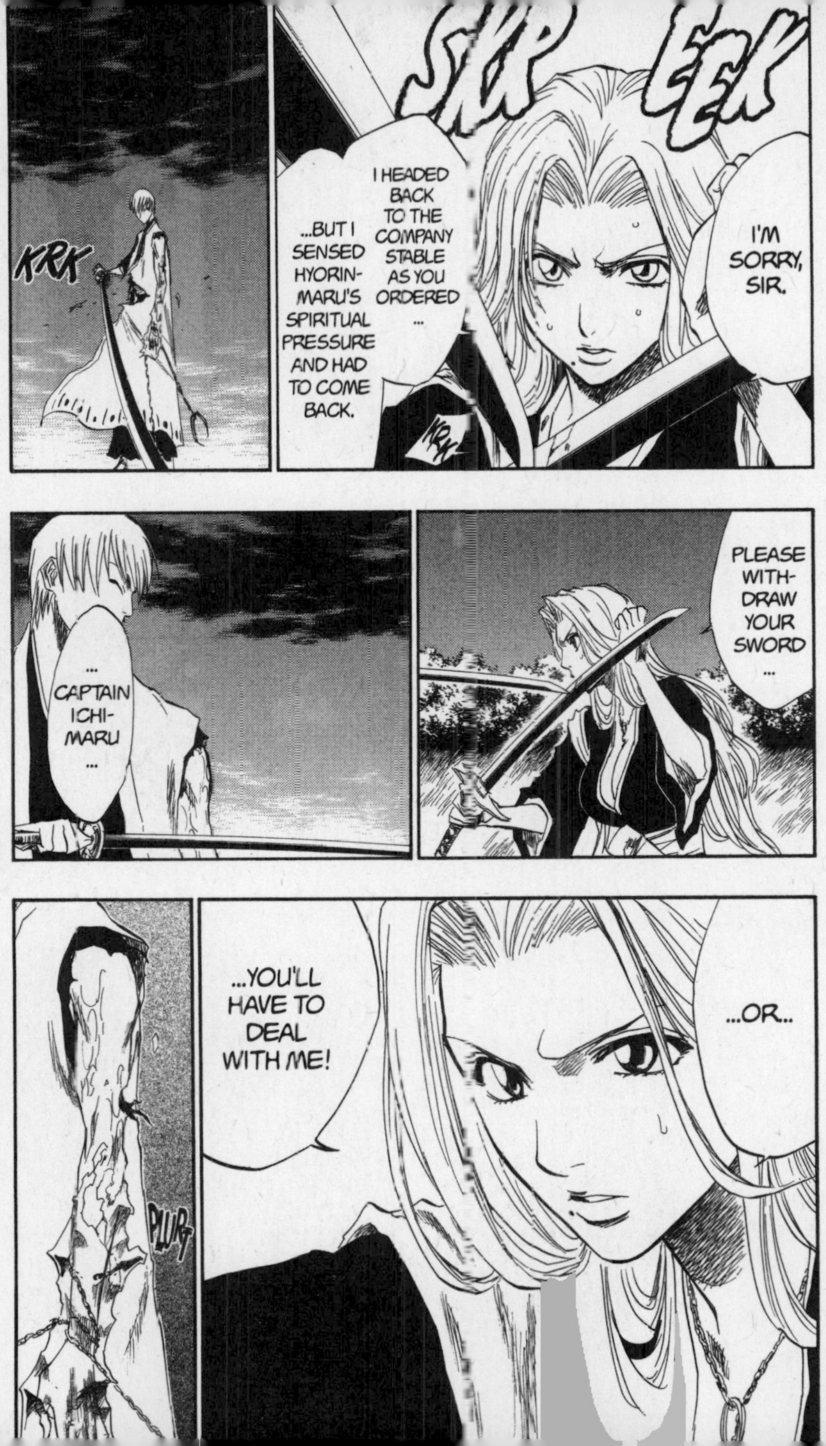
I'M SORRY, SIR.
I HEADED BACK TO THE COMPANY STABLE AS YOU ORDERED...
...BUT I SENSED HYORIN-MARU'S SPIRITUAL PRESSURE AND HAD TO COME BACK.
KRK
KRK
PLEASE WITH-DRAW YOUR SWORD...
...CAPTAIN ICHI-MARU...
...OR...
...YOU'LL HAVE TO DEAL WITH ME!
PLURT

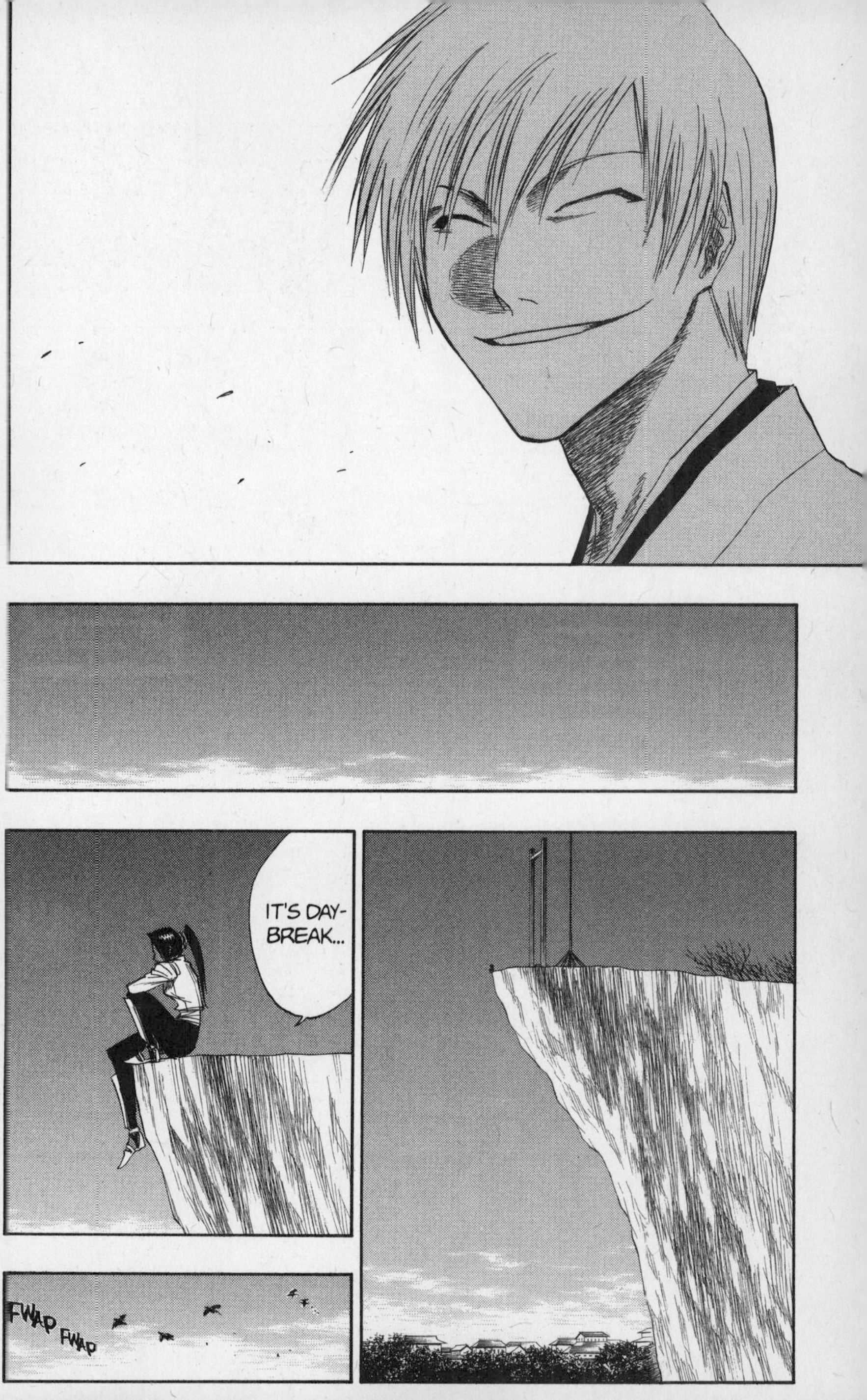
IT'S DAY-
BREAK...
FWAP FWAP

READ THIS WAY

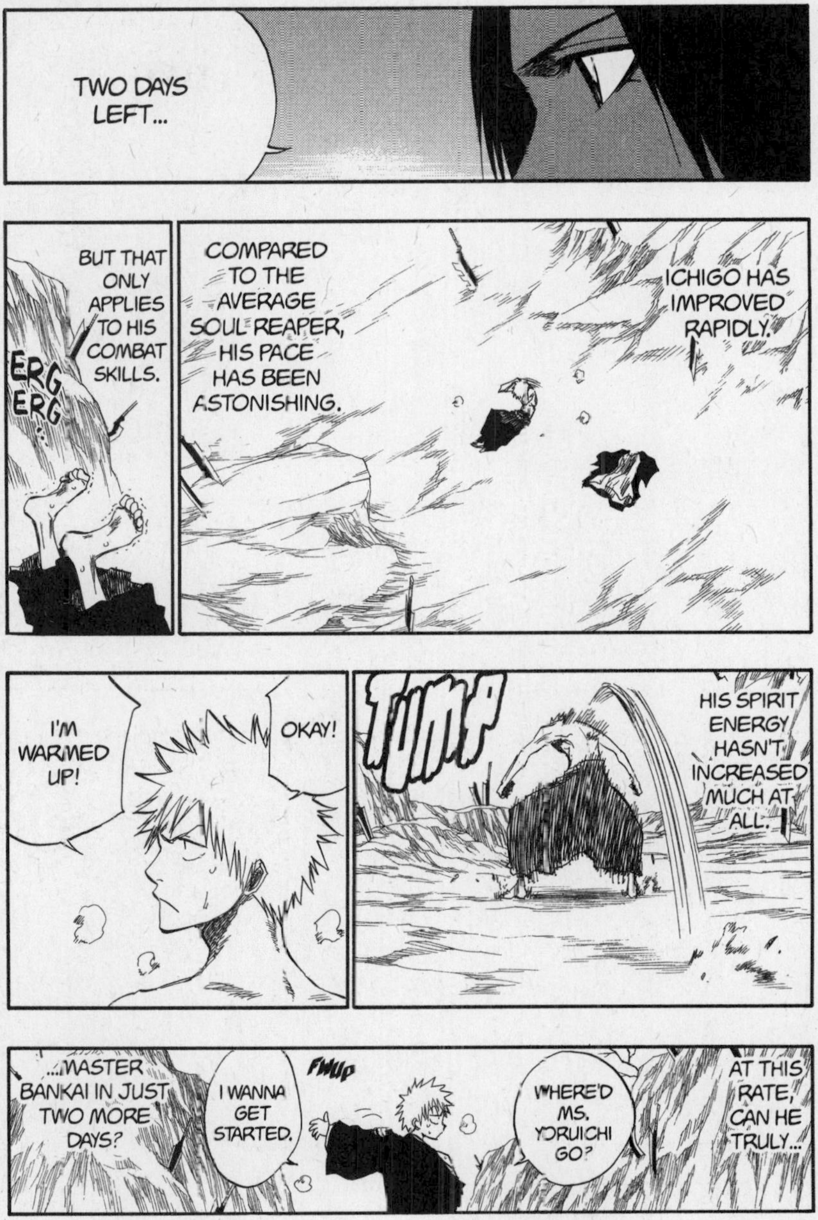
TWO DAYS LEFT...
ICHIGO HAS IMPROVED RAPIDLY.
COMPARED TO THE AVERAGE SOUL REAPER, HIS PACE HAS BEEN ASTONISHING.
BUT THAT ONLY APPLIES TO HIS COMBAT SKILLS.
ERG ERG
TUMP
HIS SPIRIT ENERGY HASN'T INCREASED MUCH AT ALL.
OKAY!
I'M WARMED UP!
AT THIS RATE, CAN HE TRULY...
WHERE'D MS. YORUICHI GO?
FWUP
I WANNA GET STARTED.
...MASTER BANKAI IN JUST TWO MORE DAYS?

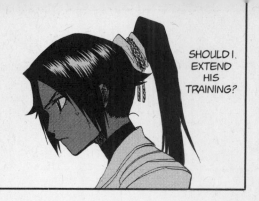

SHOULD I EXTEND HIS TRAINING?
SINCE WE GOT HERE, WE'VE LEARNED THAT RUKIA'S EXECUTION WAS CUT BY FIVE DAYS TO 25.
ORIGINALLY THE TIME-FRAME WOULD HAVE LOOKED LIKE THIS:
World of the Living
Training in World of Living
Time in Senkaimon*
7 Days
10 Days
Rukon District
Kûkaku's House
Seireitei
Bankai Training
To Soul Society via Senkaimon
3 Days
2 Days
1 Day
1 Day
25 days
8 days
Soul Society
*Tunnel World Gate
THAT WOULD HAVE LEFT US ONE DAY TO SAVE RUKIA, ONCE ICHIGO'S TRAINING WAS OVER.
RRMMMB
BUT IT TURNED OUT WE WERE CHASED BY A KÔTOTSU, A CLEANER, INSIDE THE SENKAIMON.
AND THE TIMEFRAME SHIFTED IN OUR FAVOR WHEN WE ENTERED THE SOUL SOCIETY.
World of the Living
7 Days
10 Days
25 days
15 days
Soul Society
SO, EVEN AFTER THREE DAYS OF TRAINING, WE'LL STILL HAVE EIGHT DAYS TO SPARE!

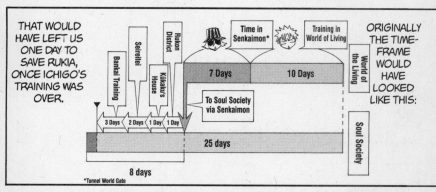

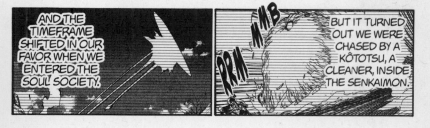

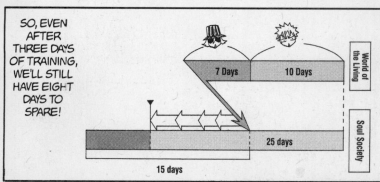

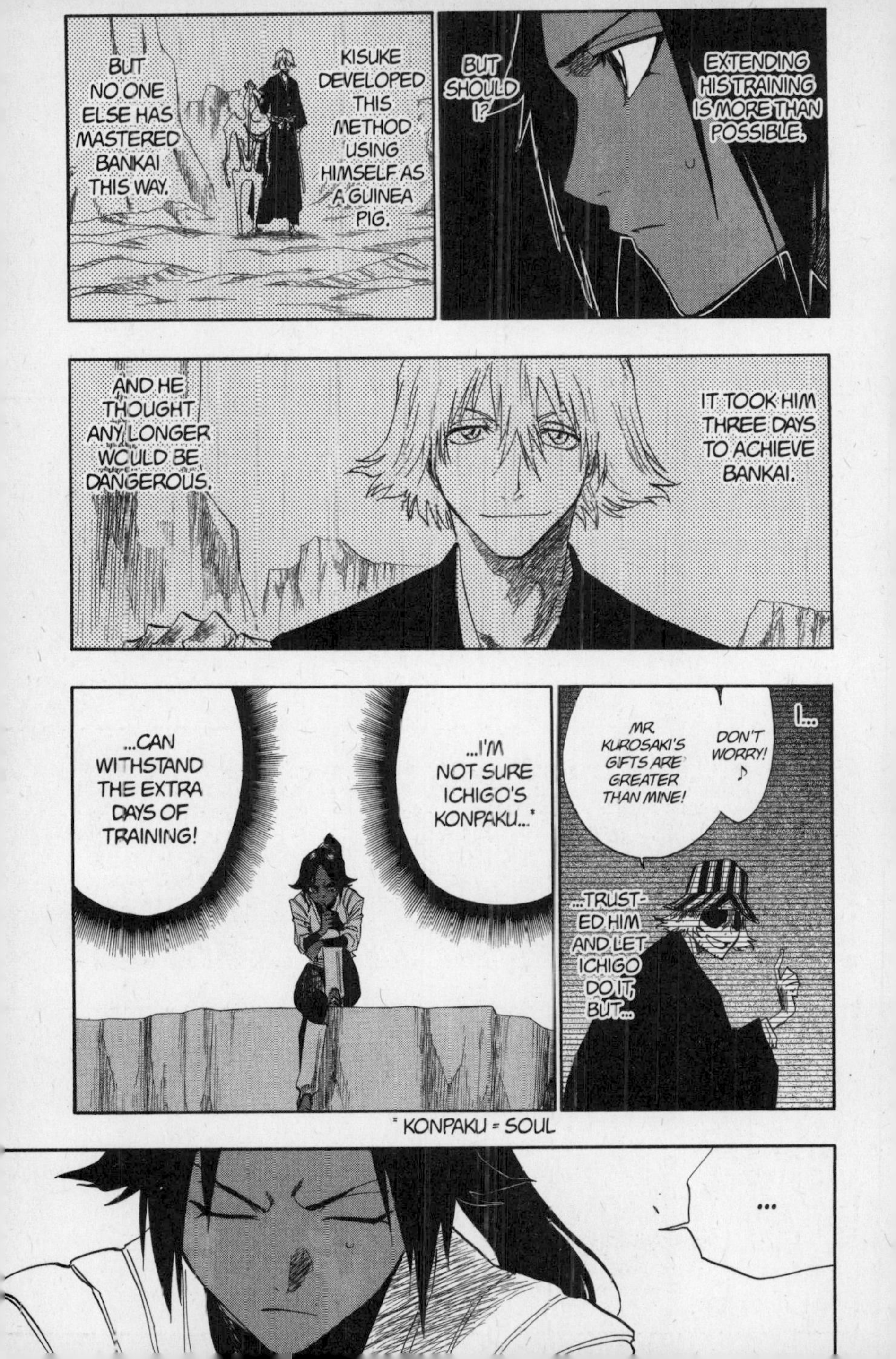
EXTENDING HIS TRAINING IS MORE THAN POSSIBLE.
BUT SHOULD I?
KISUKE DEVELOPED THIS METHOD USING HIMSELF AS A GUINEA PIG.
BUT NO ONE ELSE HAS MASTERED BANKAI THIS WAY.
IT TOOK HIM THREE DAYS TO ACHIEVE BANKAI.
AND HE THOUGHT ANY LONGER WOULD BE DANGEROUS.
I...
DON'T WORRY! ♪
MR. KUROSAKI'S GIFTS ARE GREATER THAN MINE!
...TRUST-ED HIM AND LET ICHIGO DO IT, BUT...
...I'M NOT SURE ICHIGO'S KONPAKU...*
...CAN WITHSTAND THE EXTRA DAYS OF TRAINING!
...

* KONPAKU = SOUL

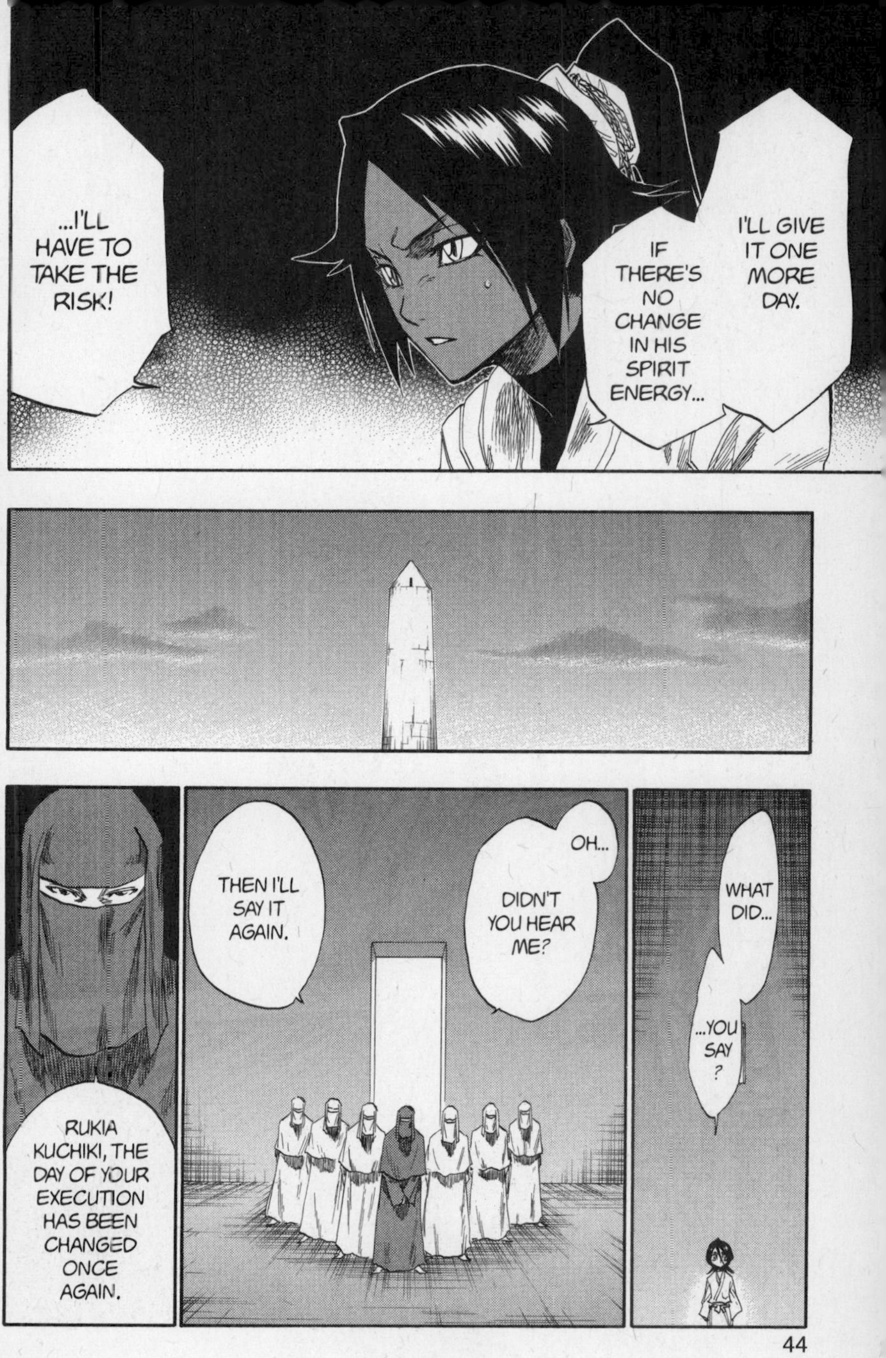
I'LL GIVE IT ONE MORE DAY.
IF THERE'S NO CHANGE IN HIS SPIRIT ENERGY...
...I'LL HAVE TO TAKE THE RISK!
WHAT DID...
...YOU SAY ?
OH...
DIDN'T YOU HEAR ME?
THEN I'LL SAY IT AGAIN.
RUKIA KUCHIKI, THE DAY OF YOUR EXECUTION HAS BEEN CHANGED ONCE AGAIN.

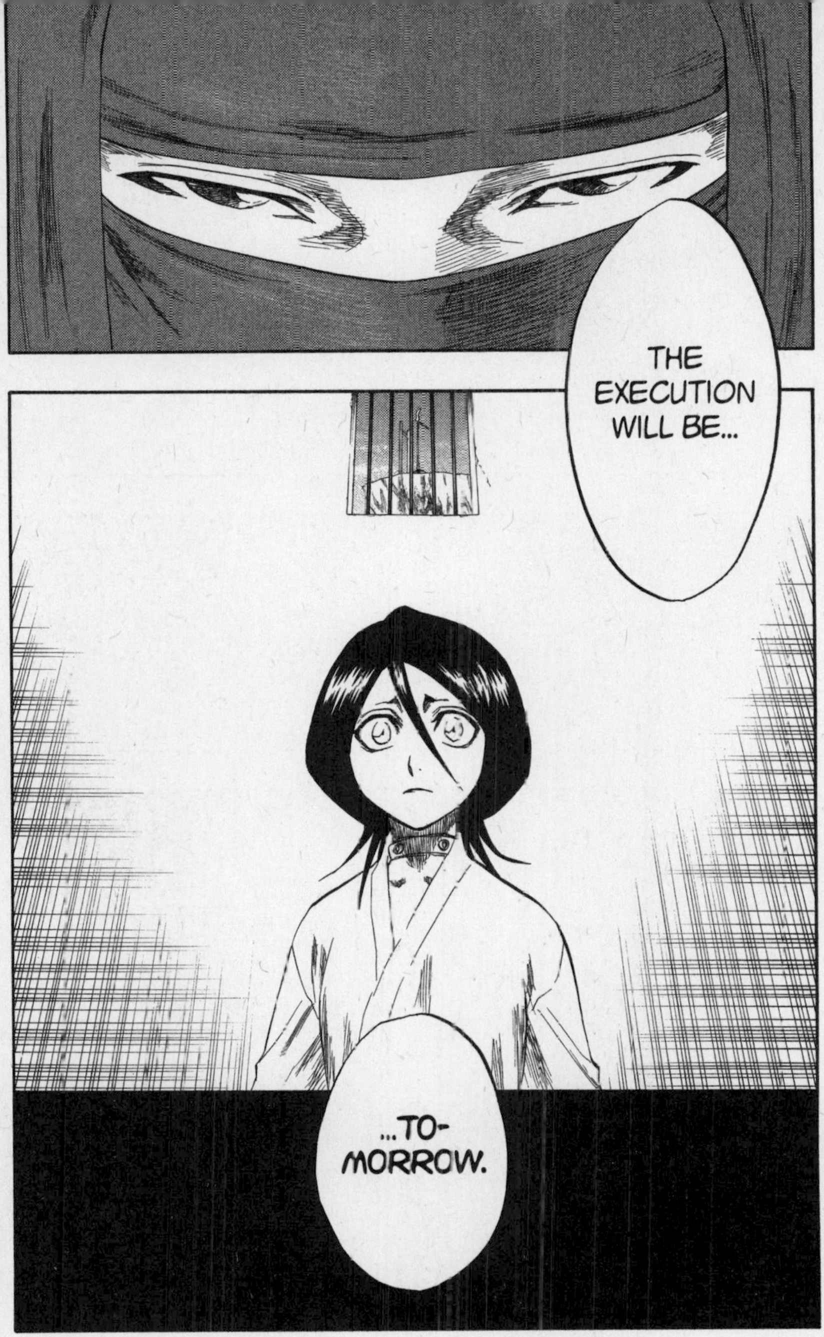
THE EXECUTION WILL BE...
...TO-MORROW.

ICHIGO'S BEEN ACTING WEIRD EVER SINCE HE GOT BACK. ALL HE WANTS TO DO IS WATCH TV SHOWS WITH GIRLS IN BIKINIS. MAYBE THAT'S NORMAL FOR GUYS HIS AGE, BUT IT'S LIKE HE'S TRYING TO AVOID ME.

COME TO THINK OF IT, HE LOOKS KIND OF DIFFERENT.

AUGUST 9, RAINY.

BLEACH ブリーチ

133. memories in the rain 2: Nocturne

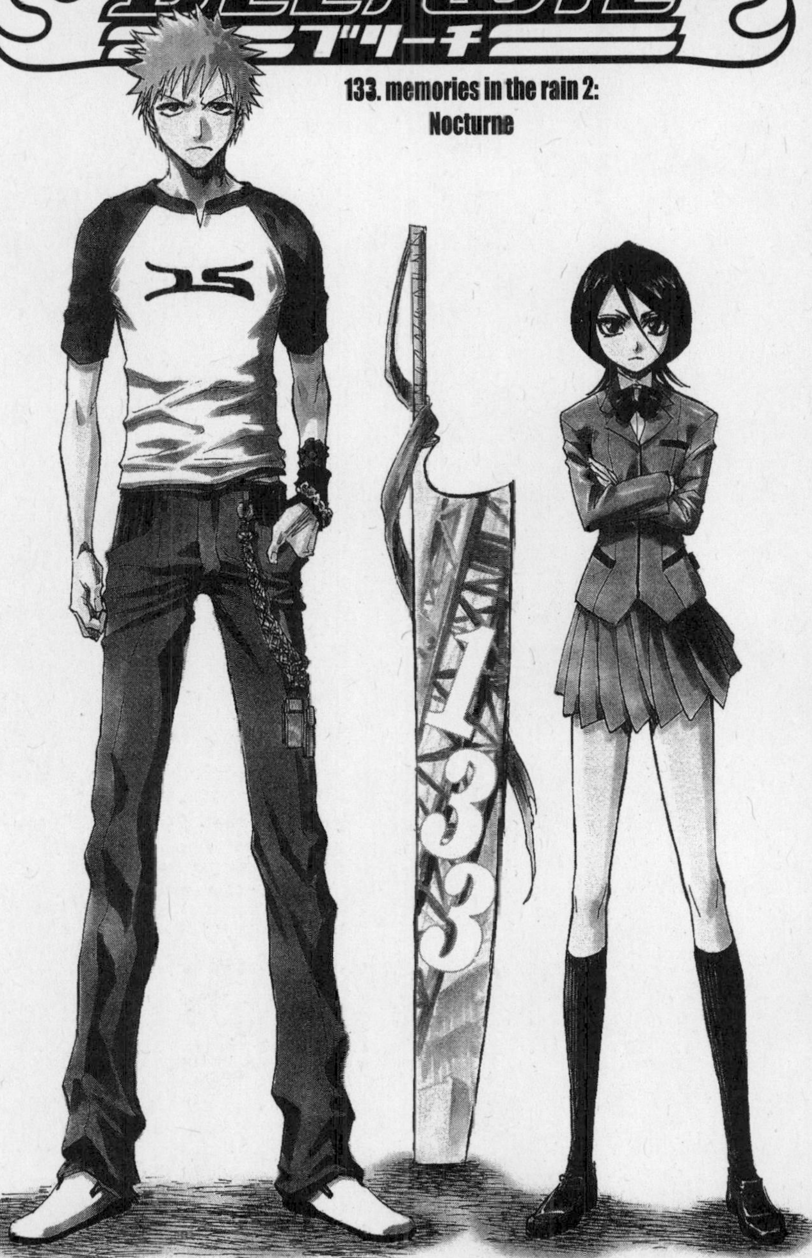
133

BLEACH
ブリーチ

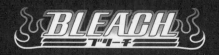

READ THIS WAY

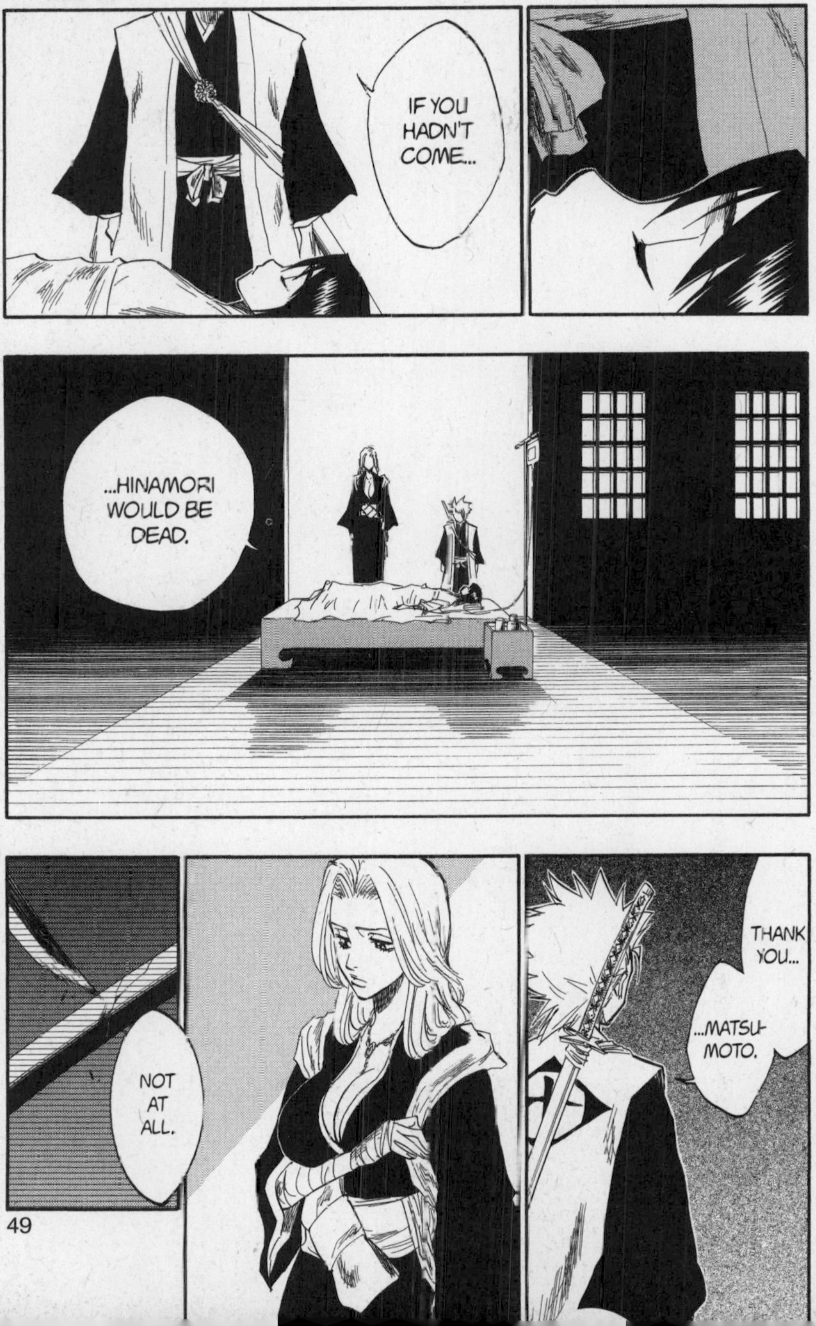

IF YOU HADN'T COME...
...HINAMORI WOULD BE DEAD.
THANK YOU...
...MATSU-MOTO.
NOT AT ALL.

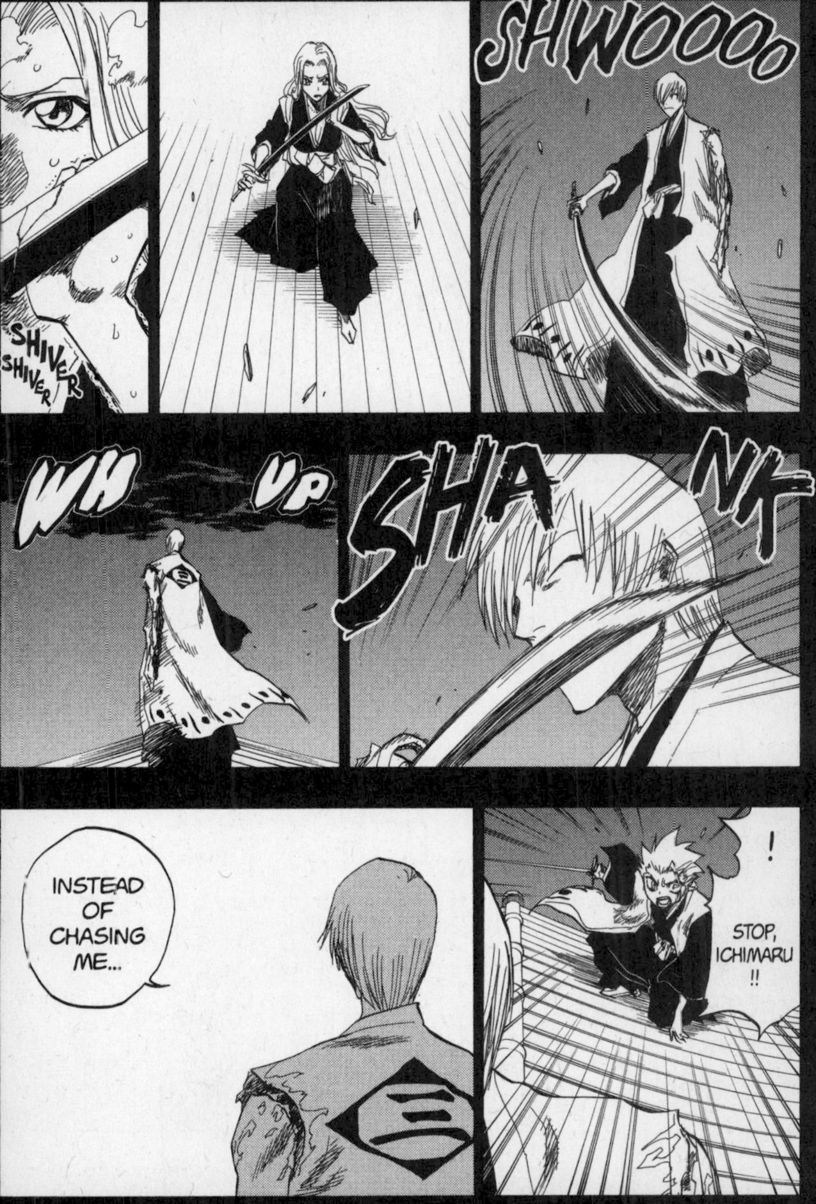
SHWOOOO
SHIVER SHIVER
SHANK
WHUP
!
STOP, ICHIMARU!!
INSTEAD OF CHASING ME...

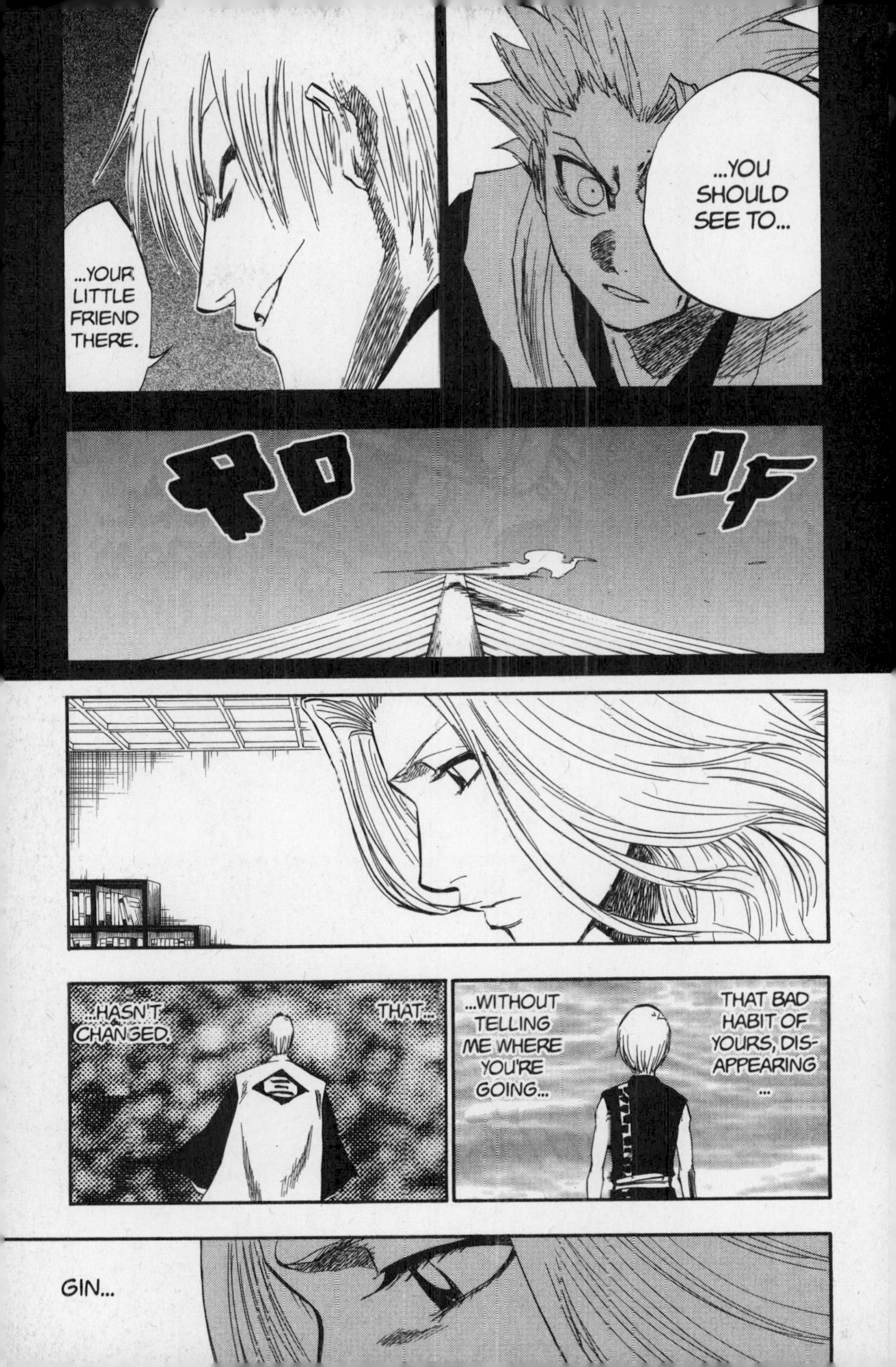
...YOU SHOULD SEE TO...
...YOUR LITTLE FRIEND THERE.
PO
OF
THAT BAD HABIT OF YOURS, DIS-APPEARING ...
...WITHOUT TELLING ME WHERE YOU'RE GOING...
THAT...
...HASN'T CHANGED.
GIN...

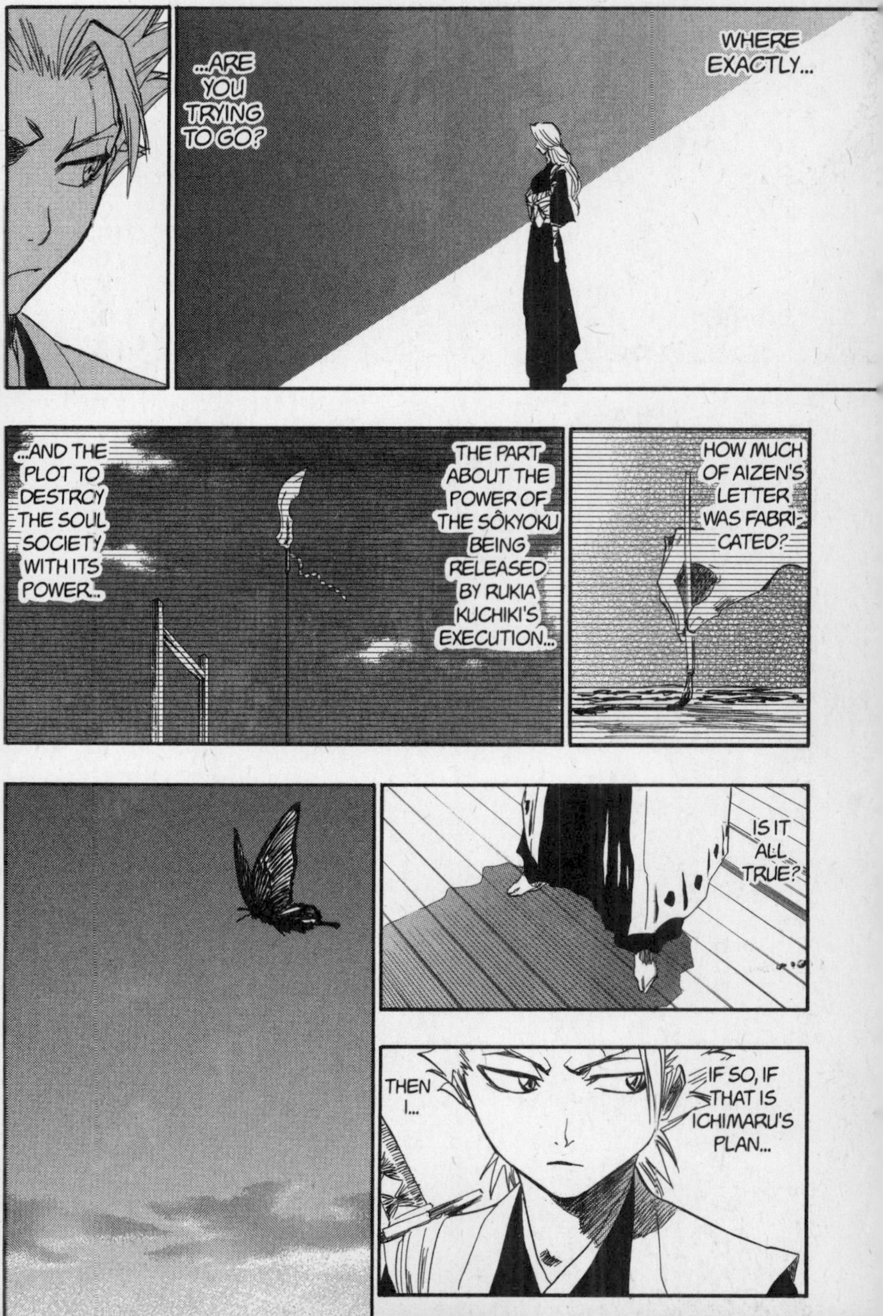
WHERE EXACTLY...
...ARE YOU TRYING TO GO?
HOW MUCH OF AIZEN'S LETTER WAS FABRICATED?
THE PART ABOUT THE POWER OF THE SÔKYOKU BEING RELEASED BY RUKIA KUCHIKI'S EXECUTION...
...AND THE PLOT TO DESTROY THE SOUL SOCIETY WITH ITS POWER..
IS IT ALL TRUE?
IF SO, IF THAT IS ICHIMARU'S PLAN...
THEN I...

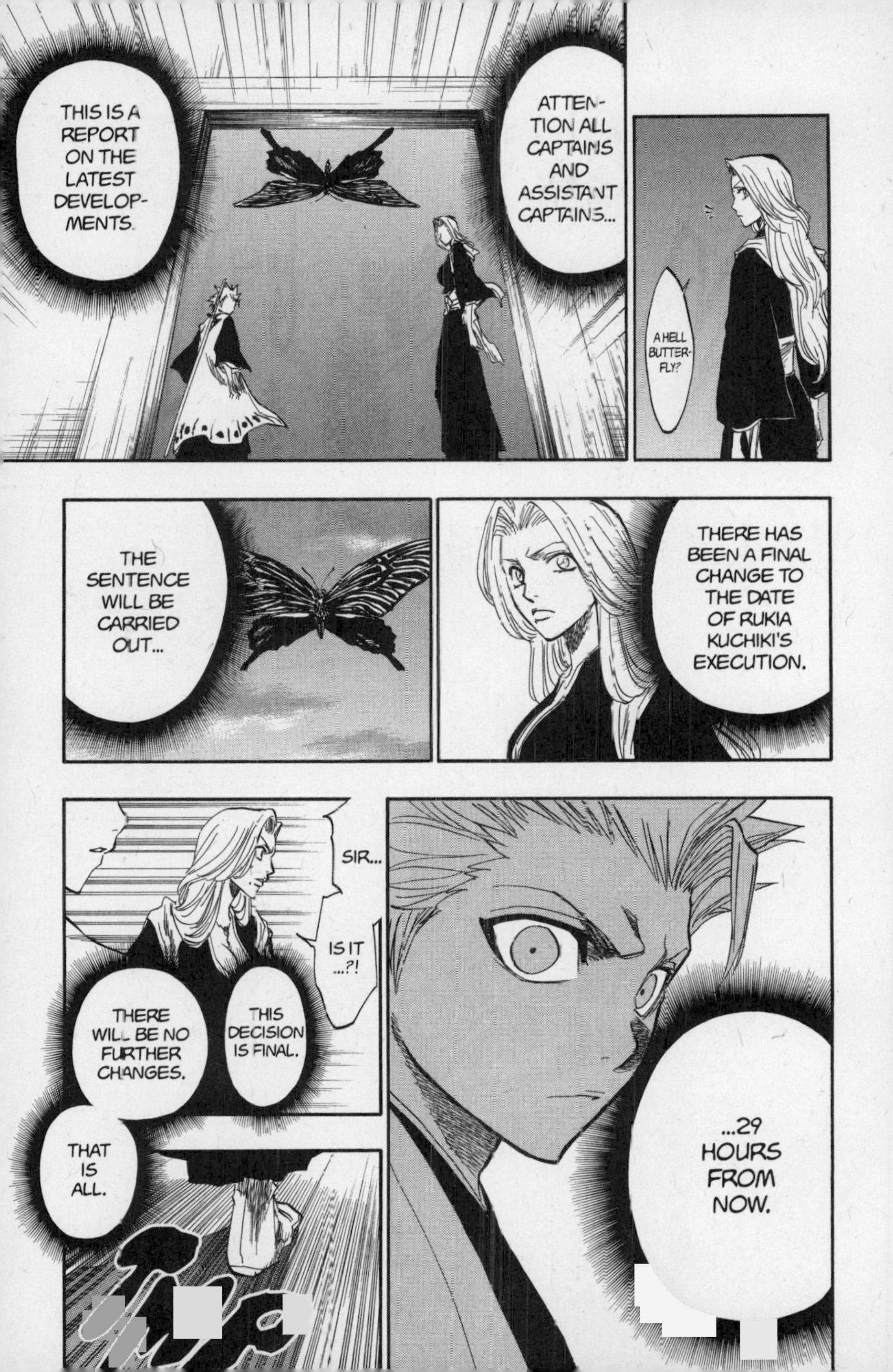
A HELL BUTTER-FLY?
ATTEN-TION ALL CAPTAINS AND ASSISTANT CAPTAINS...
THIS IS A REPORT ON THE LATEST DEVELOP-MENTS.
THERE HAS BEEN A FINAL CHANGE TO THE DATE OF RUKIA KUCHIKI'S EXECUTION.
THE SENTENCE WILL BE CARRIED OUT...
...29 HOURS FROM NOW.
SIR...
IS IT ...?!
THIS DECISION IS FINAL.
THERE WILL BE NO FURTHER CHANGES.
THAT IS ALL.

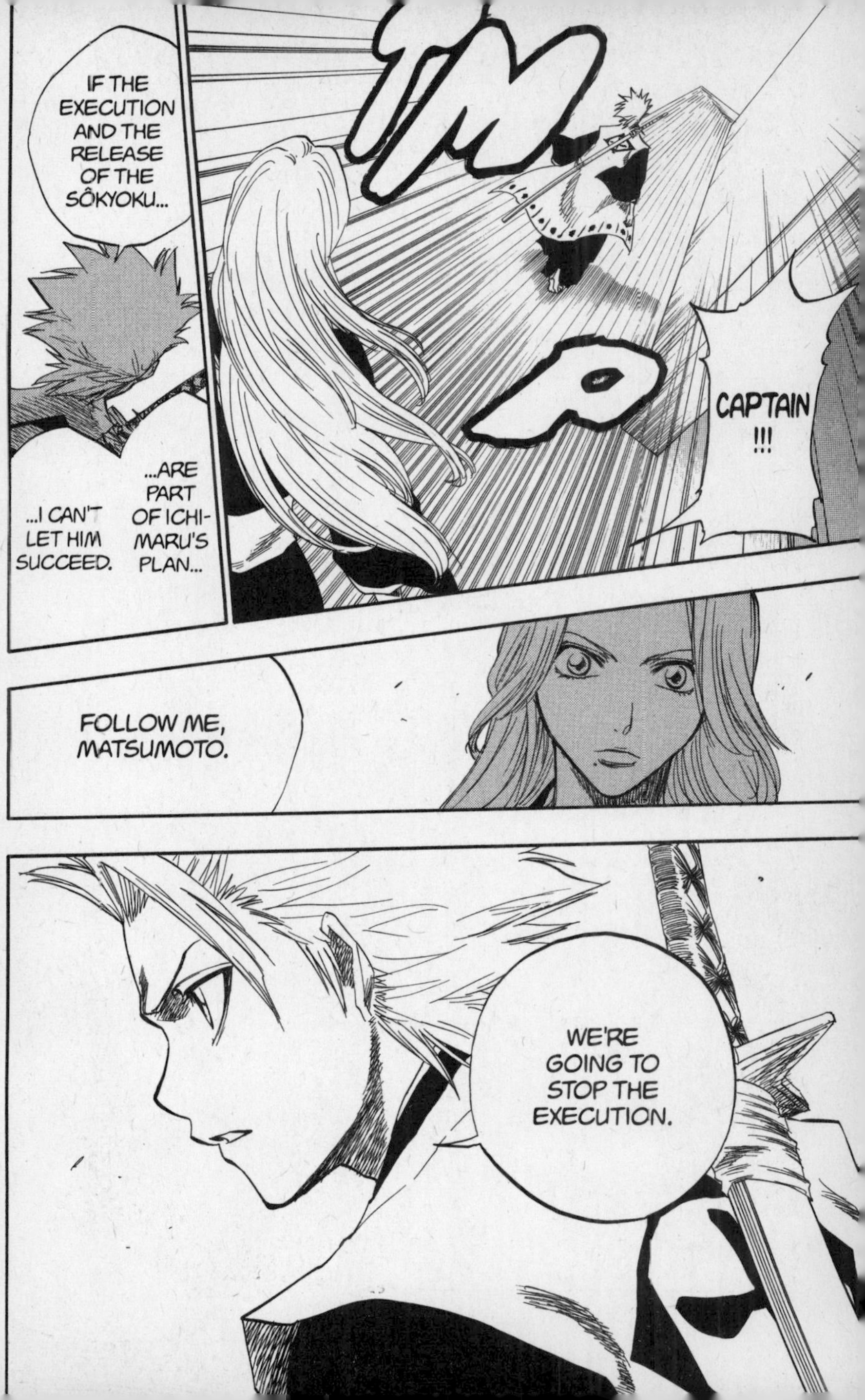
CAPTAIN !!!
IF THE EXECUTION AND THE RELEASE OF THE SÔKYOKU...
...ARE PART OF ICHI-MARU'S PLAN...
...I CAN'T LET HIM SUCCEED.
FOLLOW ME, MATSUMOTO.
WE'RE GOING TO STOP THE EXECUTION.

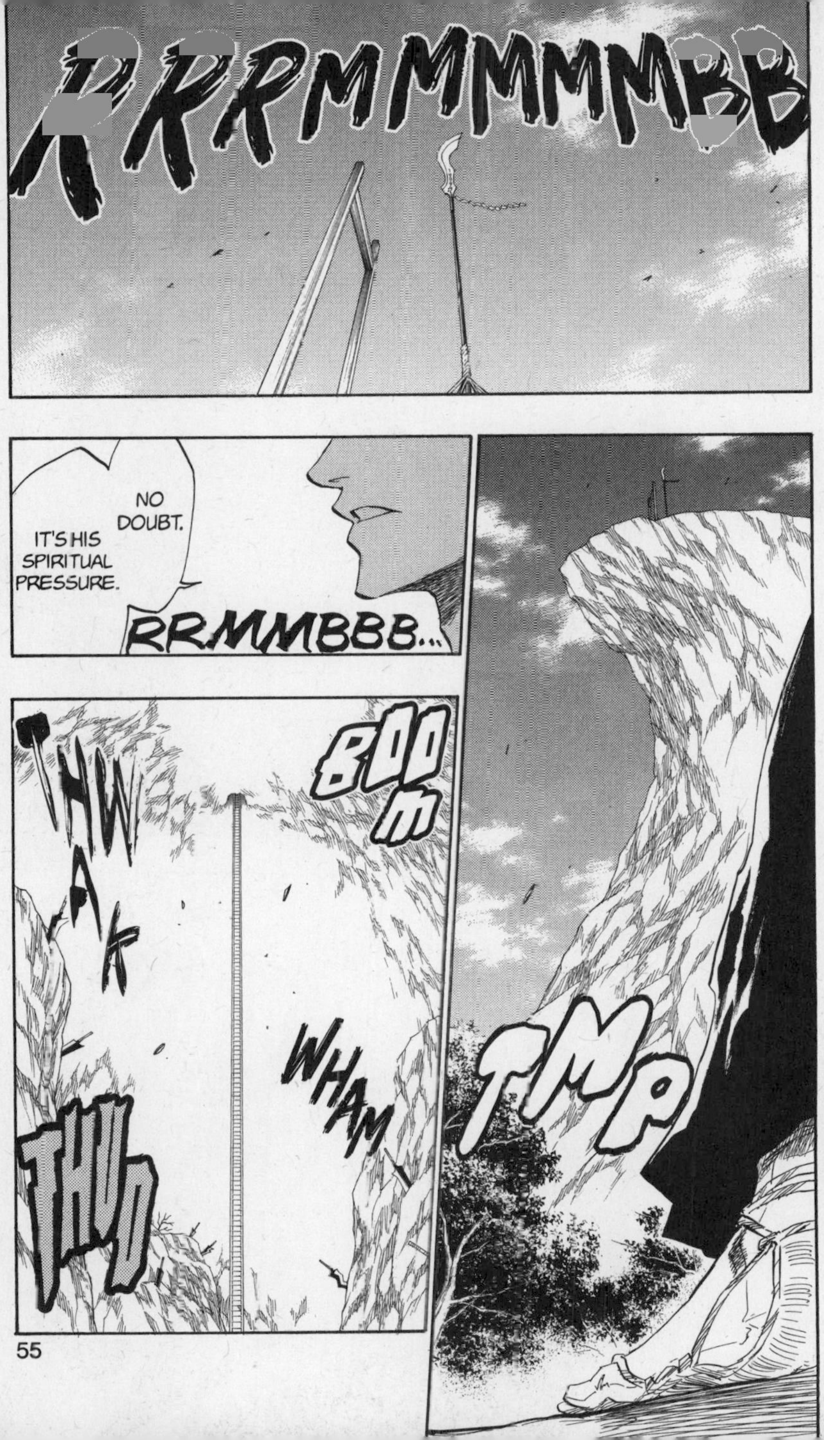
RRRMMMMMBB
TMP
NO DOUBT.
IT'S HIS SPIRITUAL PRESSURE.
RRMMBBB...
BOOM
THWAK
WHAM
THUD

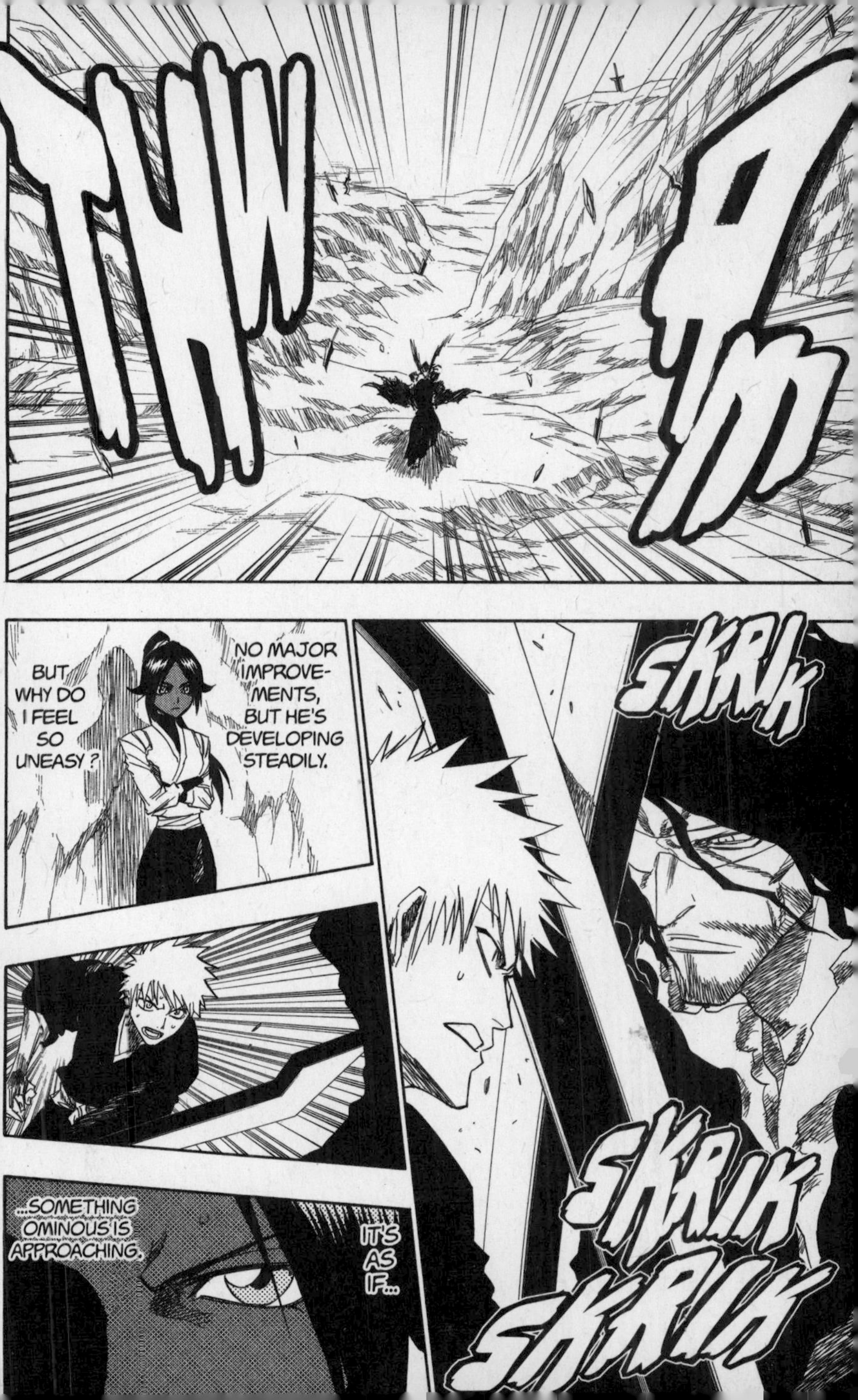
THWAM
SKRIK
SKRIK
SKRIK
NO MAJOR IMPROVEMENTS, BUT HE'S DEVELOPING STEADILY.
BUT WHY DO I FEEL SO UNEASY?
IT'S AS IF...
...SOMETHING OMINOUS IS APPROACHING.

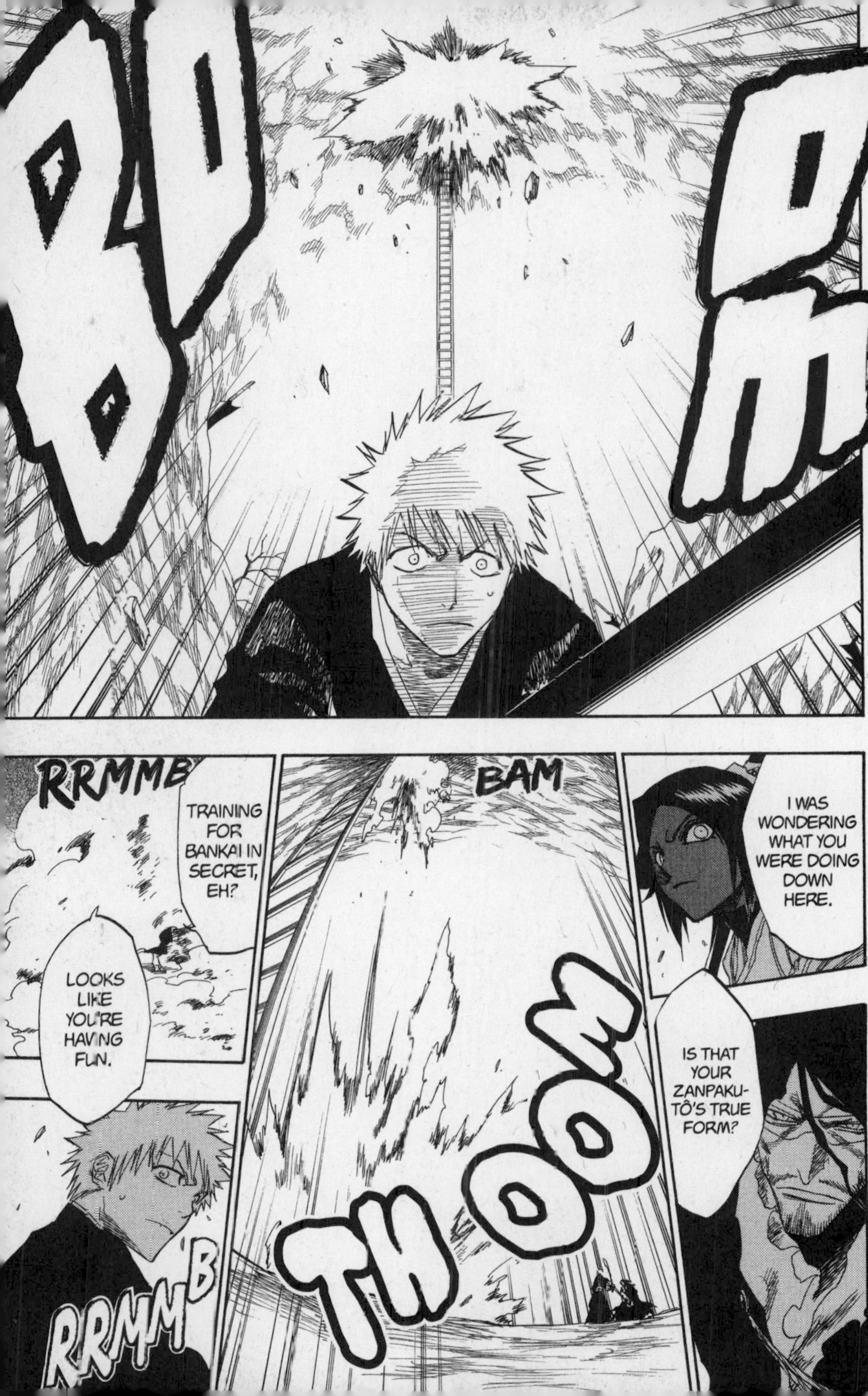
I WAS WONDERING WHAT YOU WERE DOING DOWN HERE.
IS THAT YOUR ZANPAKU-TÔ'S TRUE FORM?
BAM
THOOM
RRMMB
TRAINING FOR BANKAI IN SECRET, EH?
LOOKS LIKE YOU'RE HAVING FUN.
RRMMB

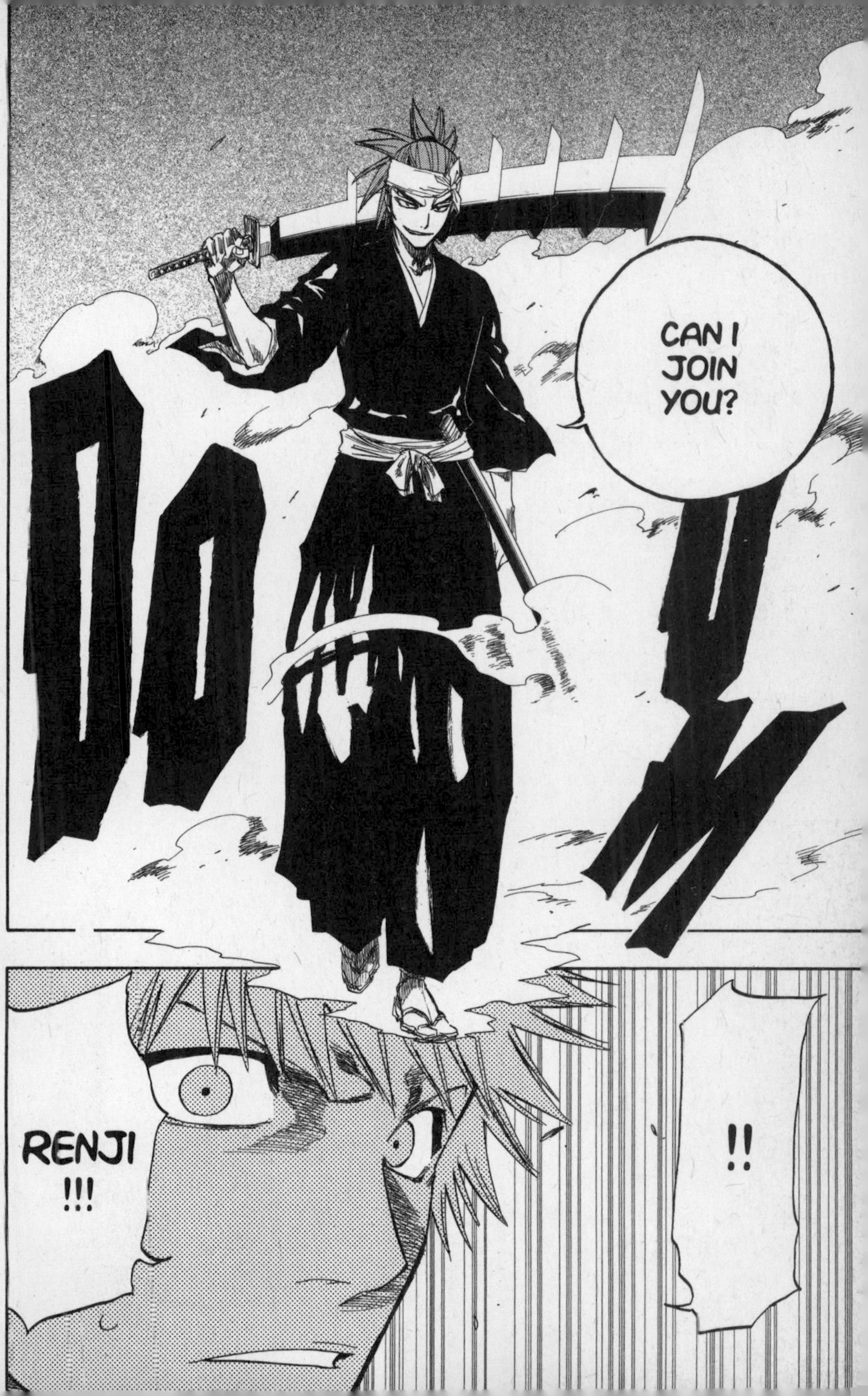
DOOM
CAN I JOIN YOU?
!!
RENJI !!!

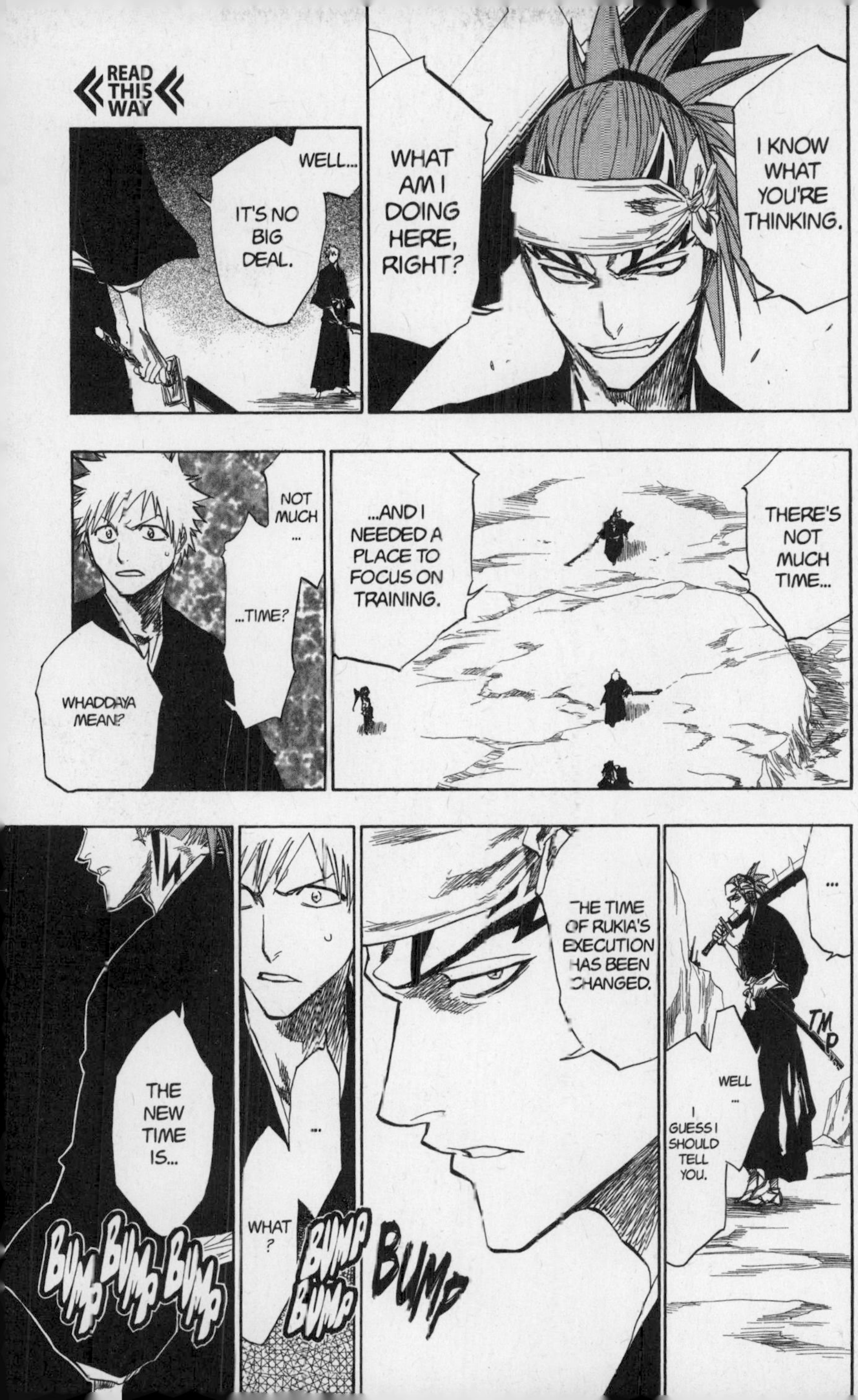
READ THIS WAY
I KNOW WHAT YOU'RE THINKING.
WHAT AM I DOING HERE, RIGHT?
WELL...
IT'S NO BIG DEAL.
THERE'S NOT MUCH TIME...
...AND I NEEDED A PLACE TO FOCUS ON TRAINING.
NOT MUCH ...
...TIME?
WHADDAYA MEAN?
...
TMP
WELL ...
I GUESS I SHOULD TELL YOU.
THE TIME OF RUKIA'S EXECUTION HAS BEEN CHANGED.
BUMP
BUMP BUMP
...
WHAT ?
THE NEW TIME IS...
BUMP BUMP BUMP

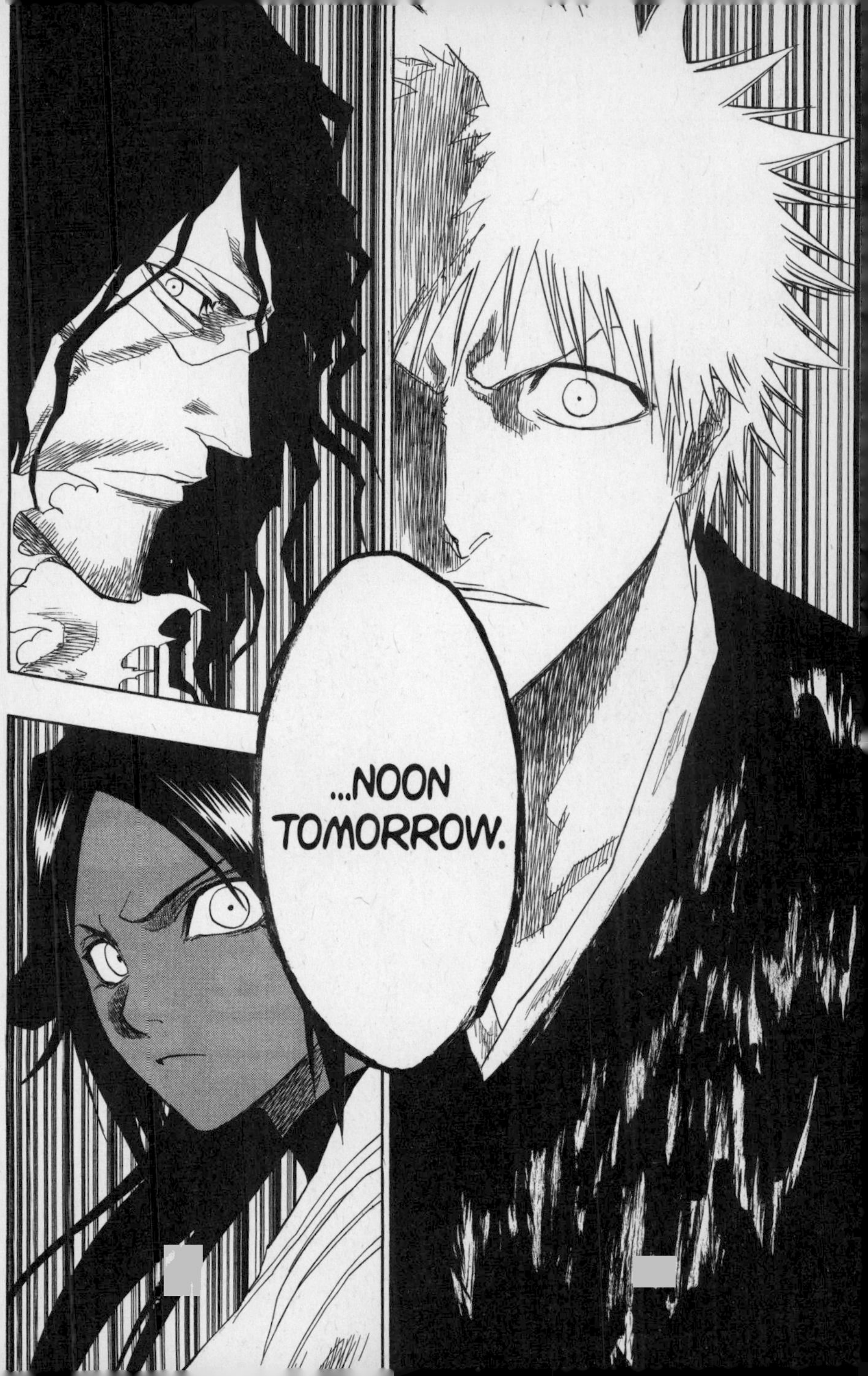
...NOON TOMORROW.

READ THIS WAY

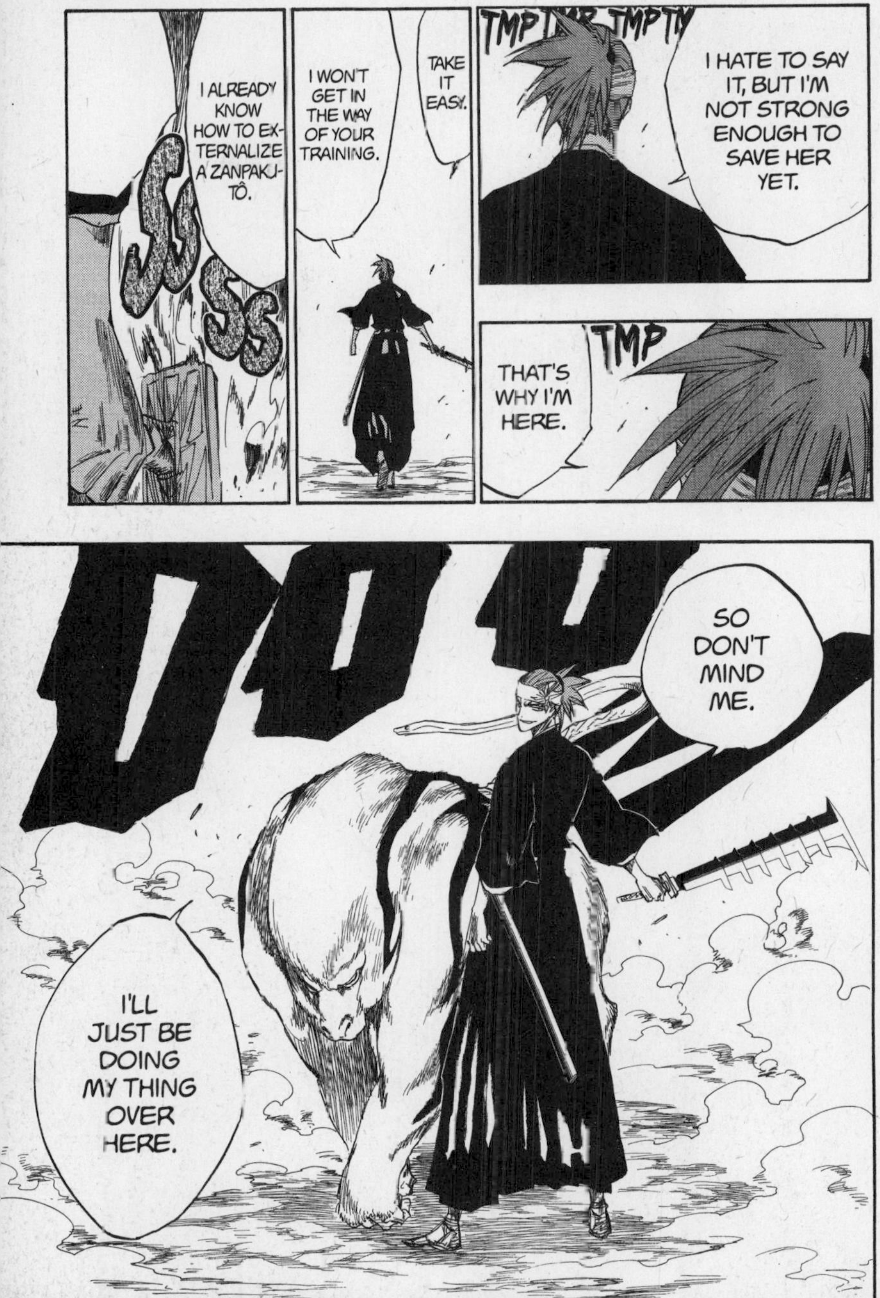

TMP TMP TMP TMP
I HATE TO SAY IT, BUT I'M NOT STRONG ENOUGH TO SAVE HER YET.
TMP
THAT'S WHY I'M HERE.
TAKE IT EASY.
I WON'T GET IN THE WAY OF YOUR TRAINING.
I ALREADY KNOW HOW TO EXTERNALIZE A ZANPAKU-TÔ.
SSS
SO DON'T MIND ME.
I'LL JUST BE DOING MY THING OVER HERE.

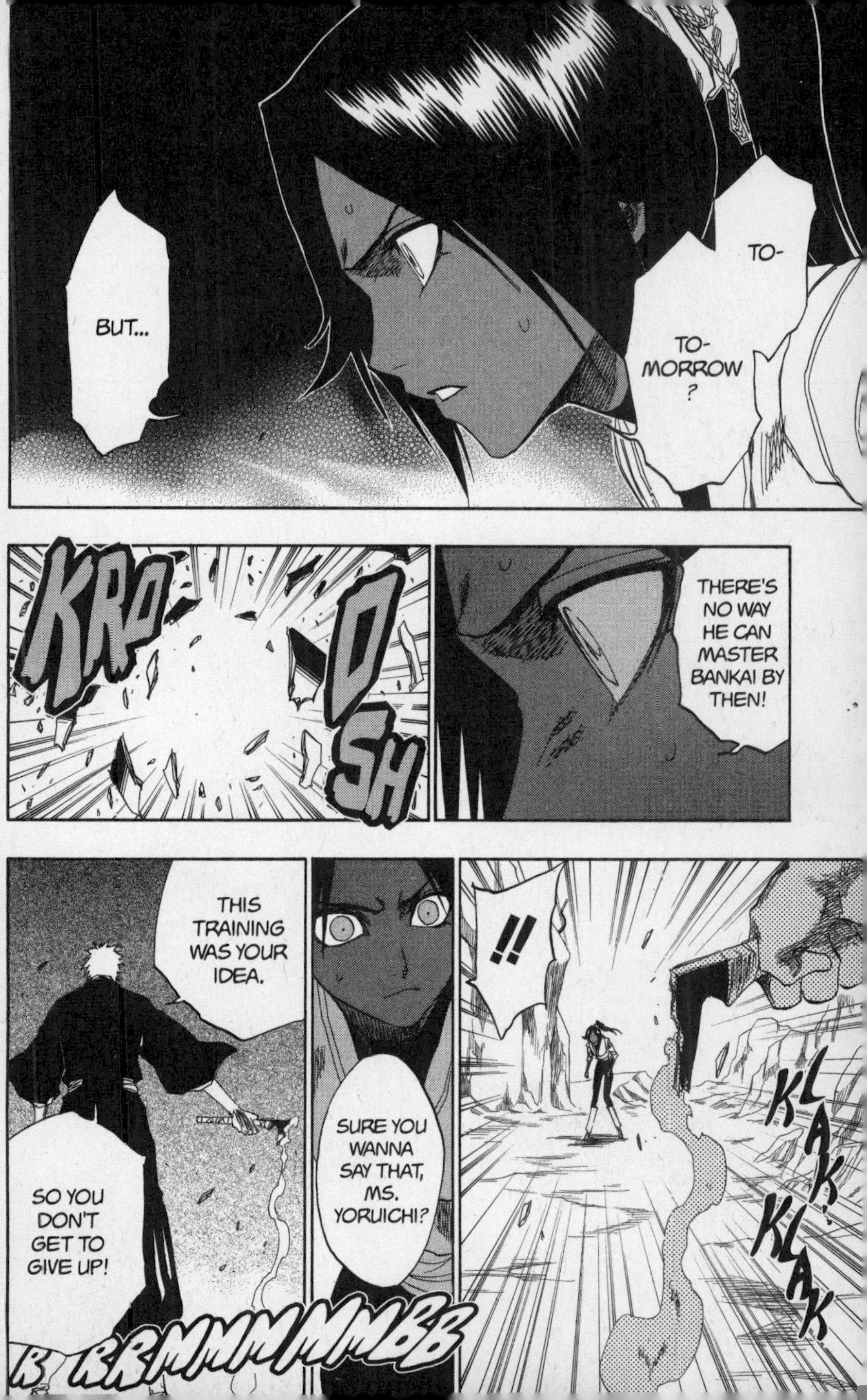
TO-
TO-MORROW?
BUT...
THERE'S NO WAY HE CAN MASTER BANKAI BY THEN!
KRO-OSH
!!
KLAK! KLAK
SURE YOU WANNA SAY THAT, MS. YORUICHI?
THIS TRAINING WAS YOUR IDEA.
SO YOU DON'T GET TO GIVE UP!
BRRMMMMMMMBB

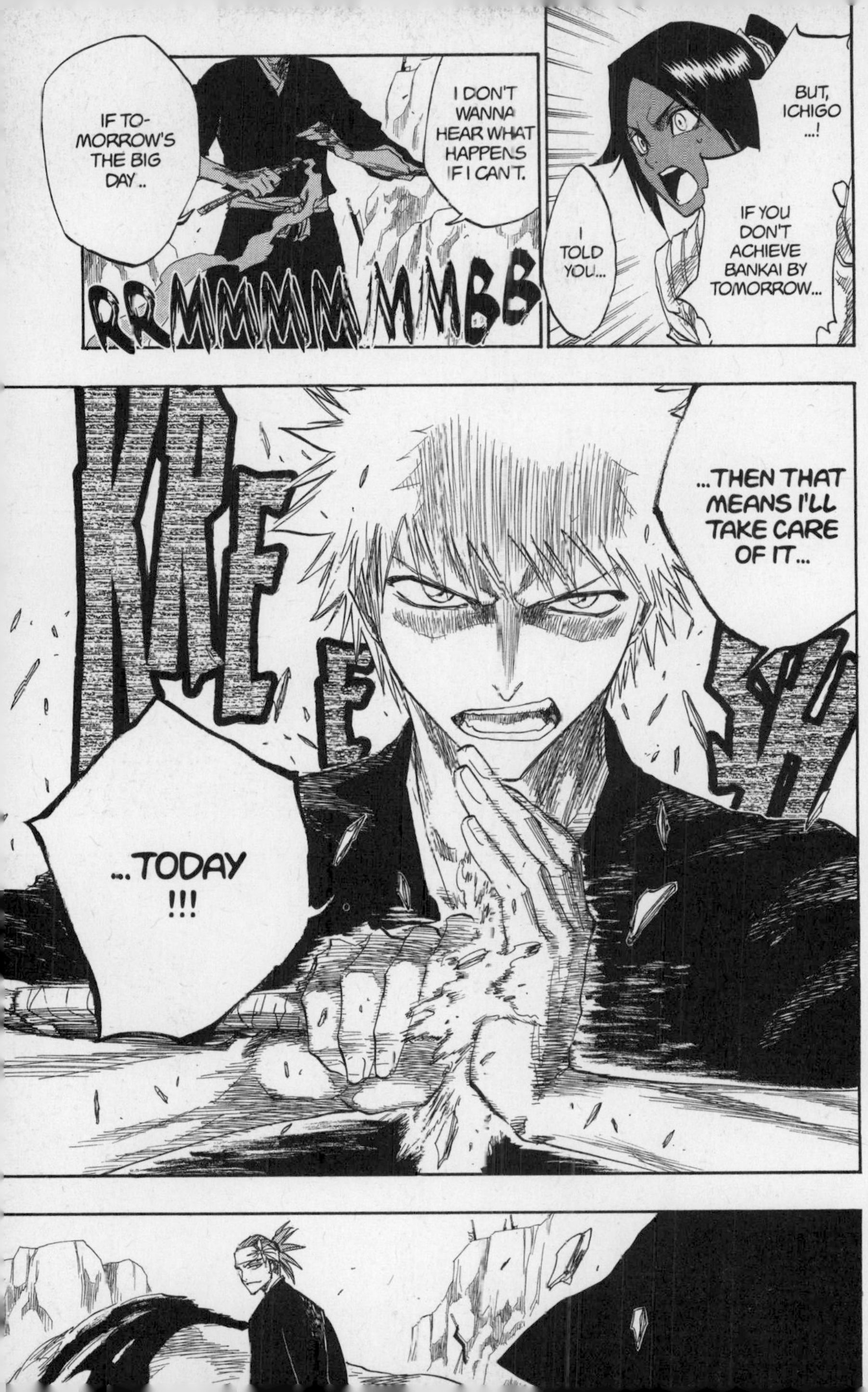
BUT, ICHIGO ...!
IF YOU DON'T ACHIEVE BANKAI BY TOMORROW...
I TOLD YOU...
I DON'T WANNA HEAR WHAT HAPPENS IF I CAN'T.
IF TO-MORROW'S THE BIG DAY..
RRMMMMMMMMBB
...THEN THAT MEANS I'LL TAKE CARE OF IT...
...TODAY !!!

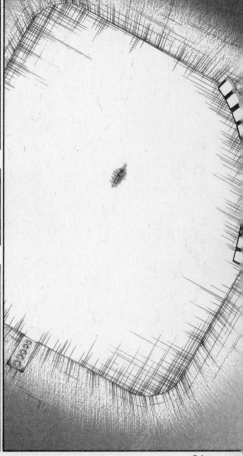

THE EXECUTION IS TOMORROW.

HMM...

BUT...

...BEFORE THE EXECUTION...

..I'LL ASK THEM TO RETURN ICHIGO AND THE OTHERS SAFELY TO THE WORLD OF THE LIVING.

READ THIS WAY

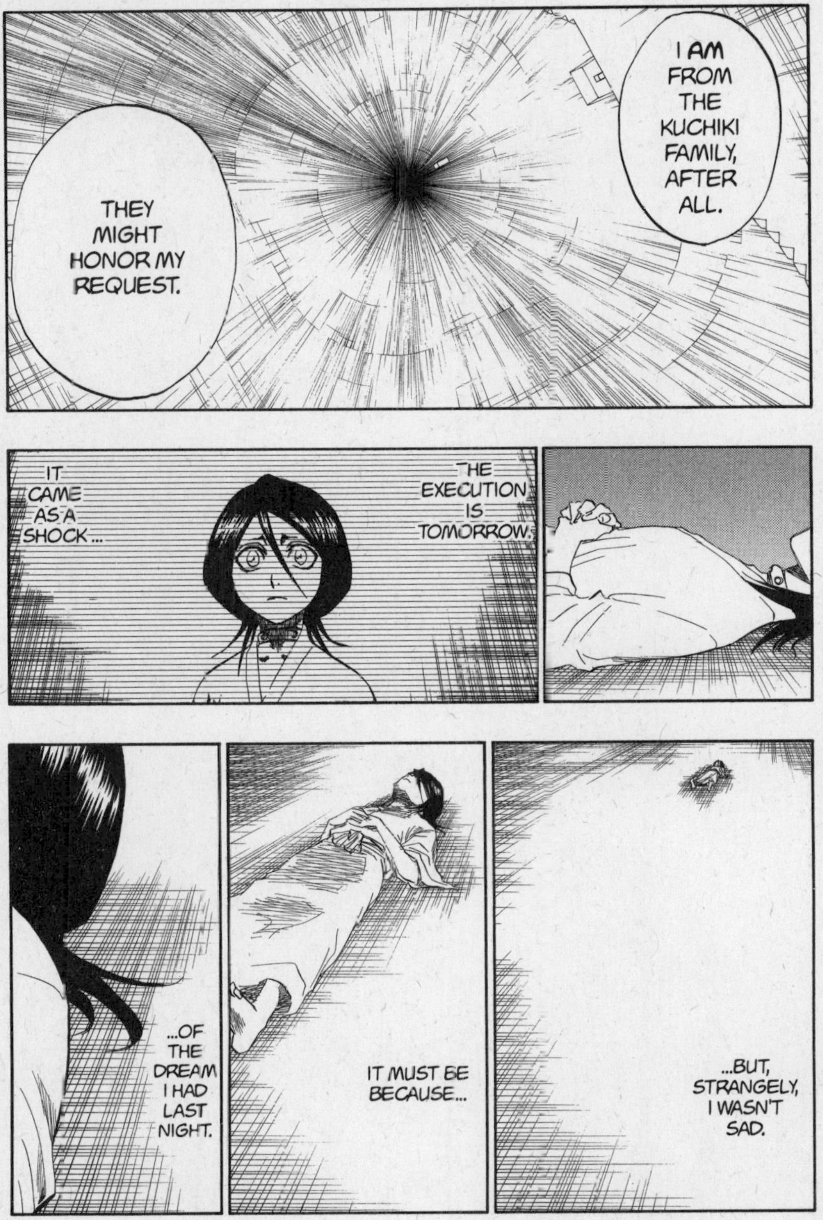
I AM FROM THE KUCHIKI FAMILY, AFTER ALL.
THEY MIGHT HONOR MY REQUEST.
THE EXECUTION IS TOMORROW.
IT CAME AS A SHOCK...
...BUT, STRANGELY, I WASN'T SAD.
IT MUST BE BECAUSE...
...OF THE DREAM I HAD LAST NIGHT.

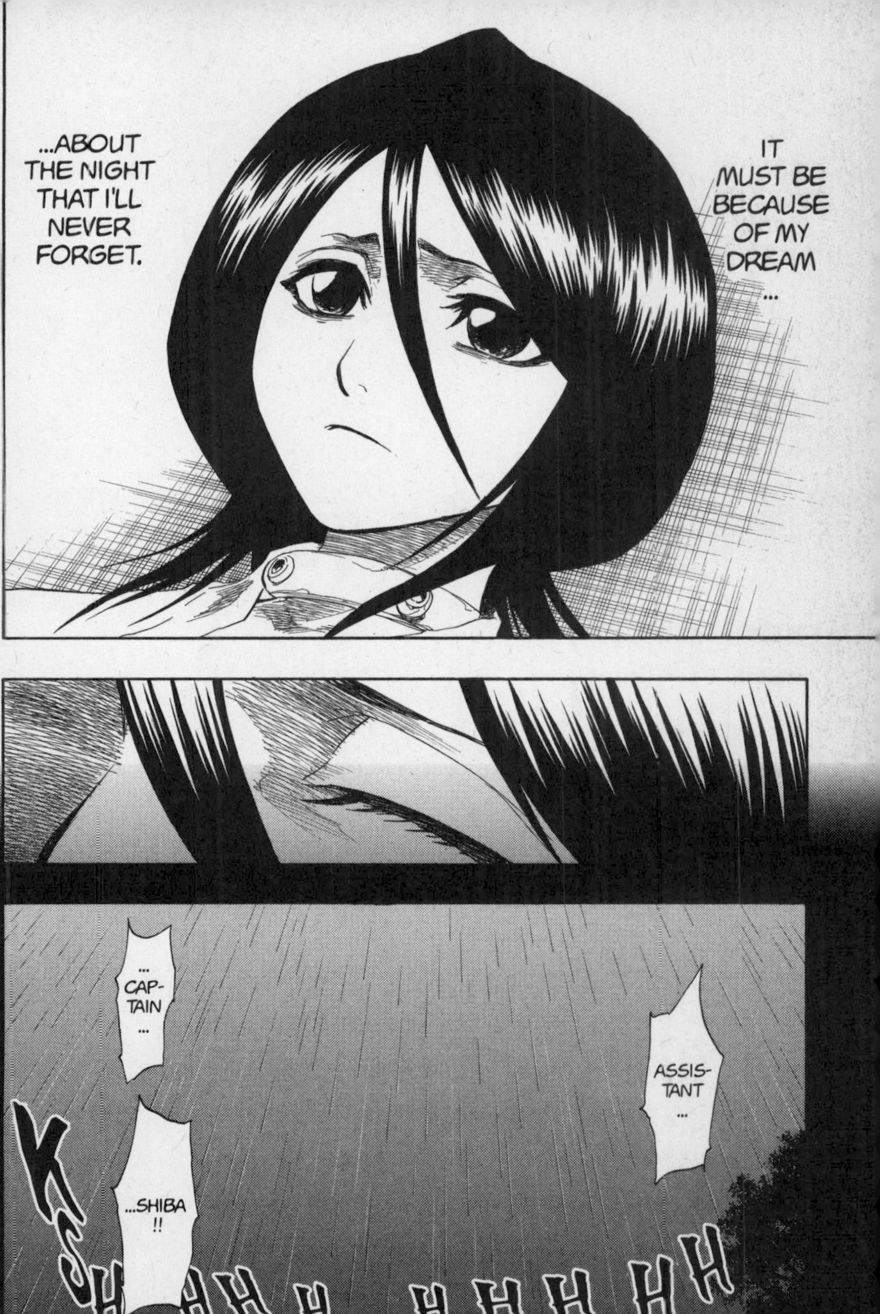
IT MUST BE BECAUSE OF MY DREAM ...
...ABOUT THE NIGHT THAT I'LL NEVER FORGET.
ASSISTANT ...
... CAPTAIN ...
...SHIBA !!
KSHHHH H HHHHHH

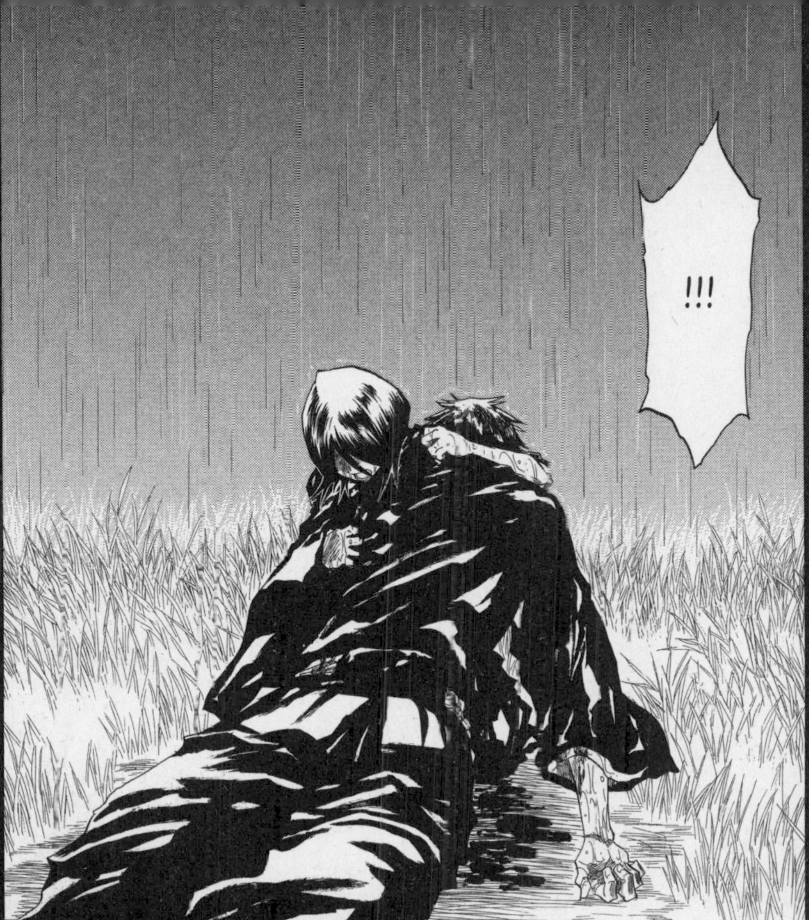
!!!
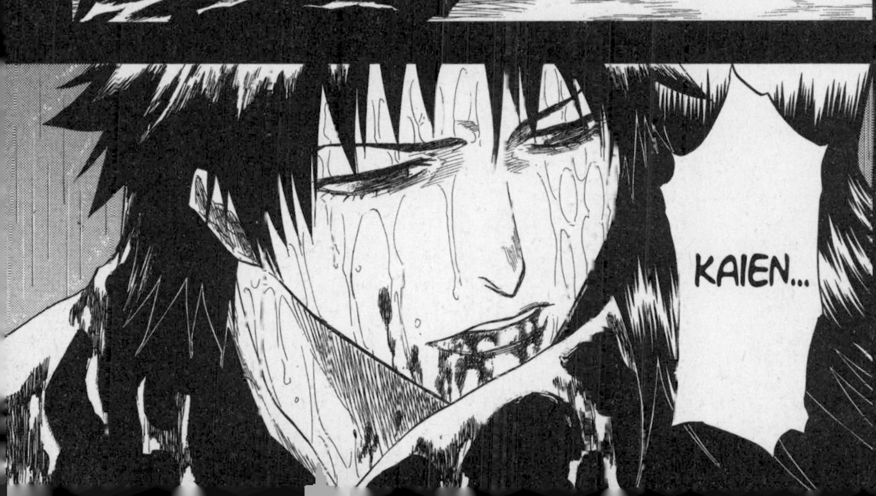
KAIEN...

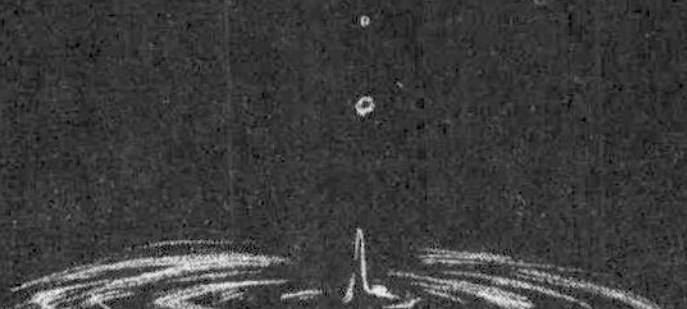

134. memories in the rain 2, op. 2:
Longing for Sanctuary

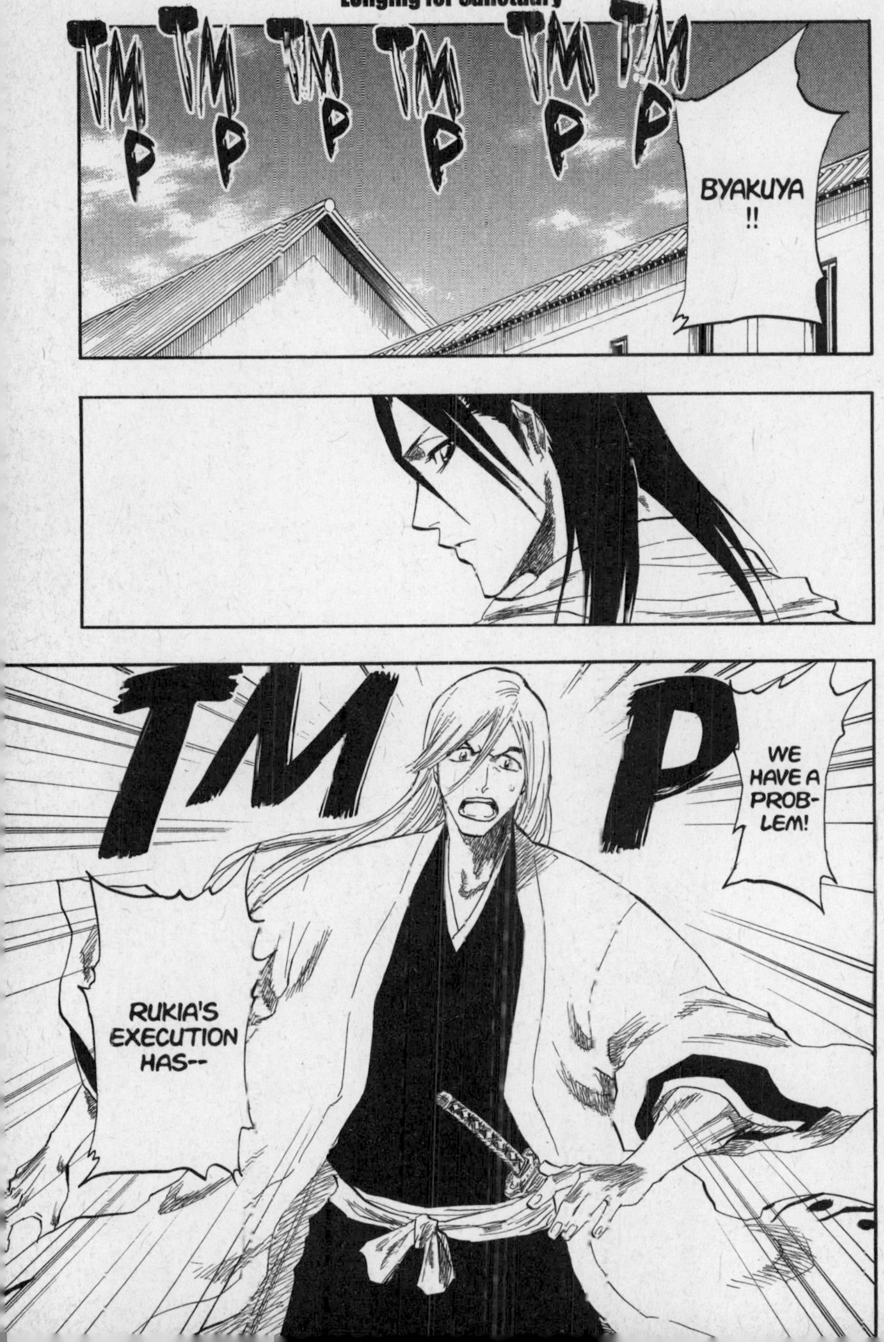
TMP TMP TMP TMP TMP TMP
BYAKUYA !!
TMP
WE HAVE A PROB-LEM!
RUKIA'S EXECUTION HAS--

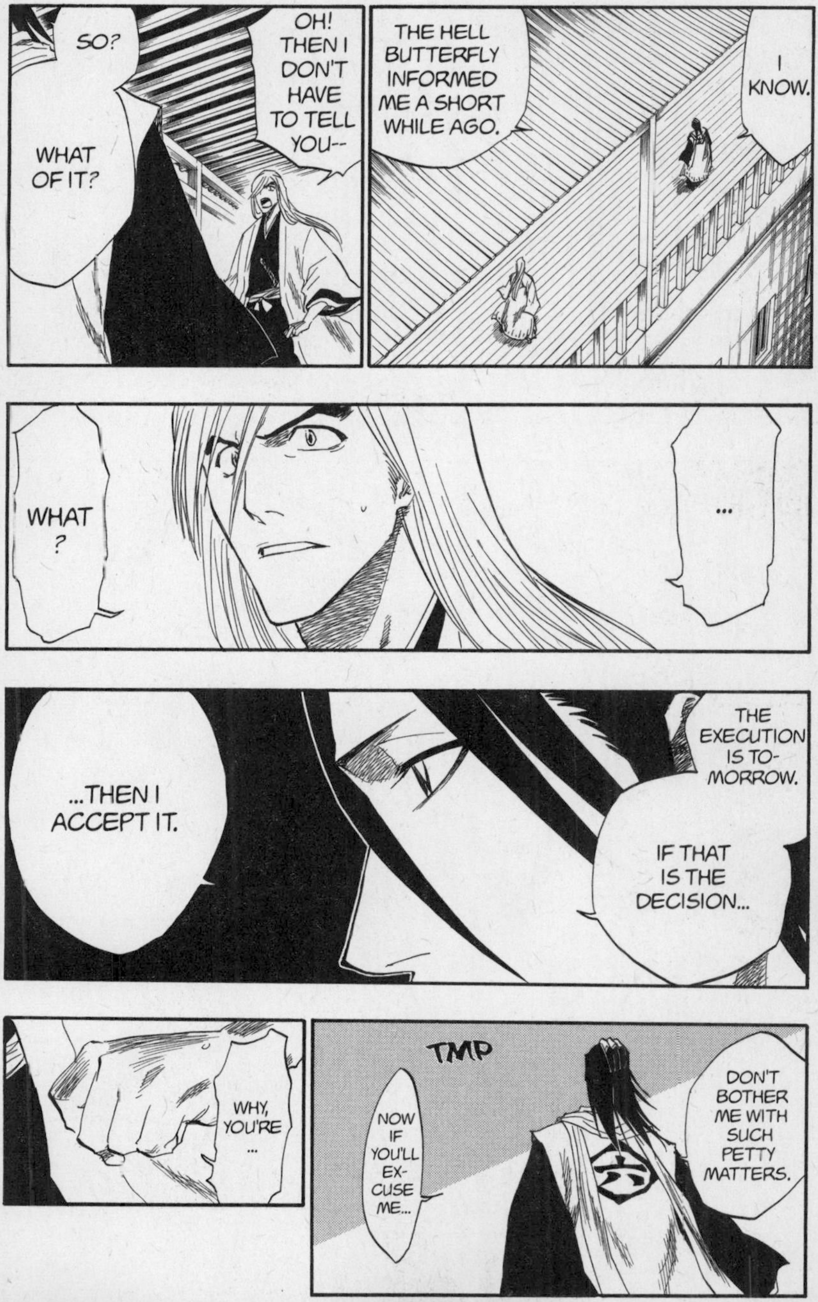
I KNOW.
THE HELL BUTTERFLY INFORMED ME A SHORT WHILE AGO.
OH! THEN I DON'T HAVE TO TELL YOU--
SO? WHAT OF IT?
...
WHAT?
THE EXECUTION IS TOMORROW.
IF THAT IS THE DECISION...
...THEN I ACCEPT IT.
DON'T BOTHER ME WITH SUCH PETTY MATTERS.
TMP
NOW IF YOU'LL EXCUSE ME...
WHY, YOU'RE ...

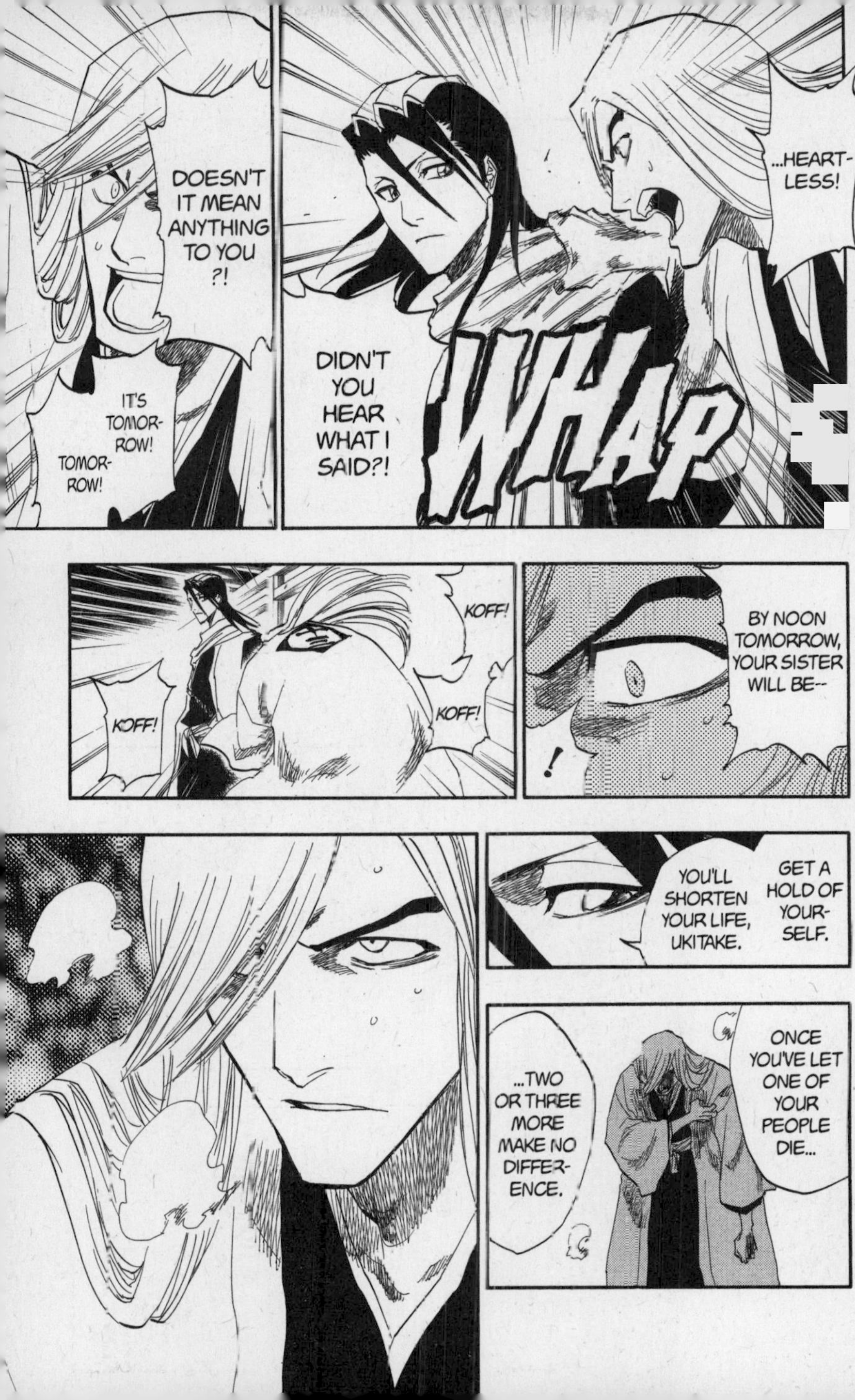
...HEART-LESS!
WHAP
DIDN'T YOU HEAR WHAT I SAID?!
DOESN'T IT MEAN ANYTHING TO YOU ?!
IT'S TOMOR-ROW!
TOMOR-ROW!
BY NOON TOMORROW, YOUR SISTER WILL BE--
!
KOFF!
KOFF!
KOFF!
GET A HOLD OF YOUR-SELF.
YOU'LL SHORTEN YOUR LIFE, UKITAKE.
ONCE YOU'VE LET ONE OF YOUR PEOPLE DIE...
...TWO OR THREE MORE MAKE NO DIFFER-ENCE.

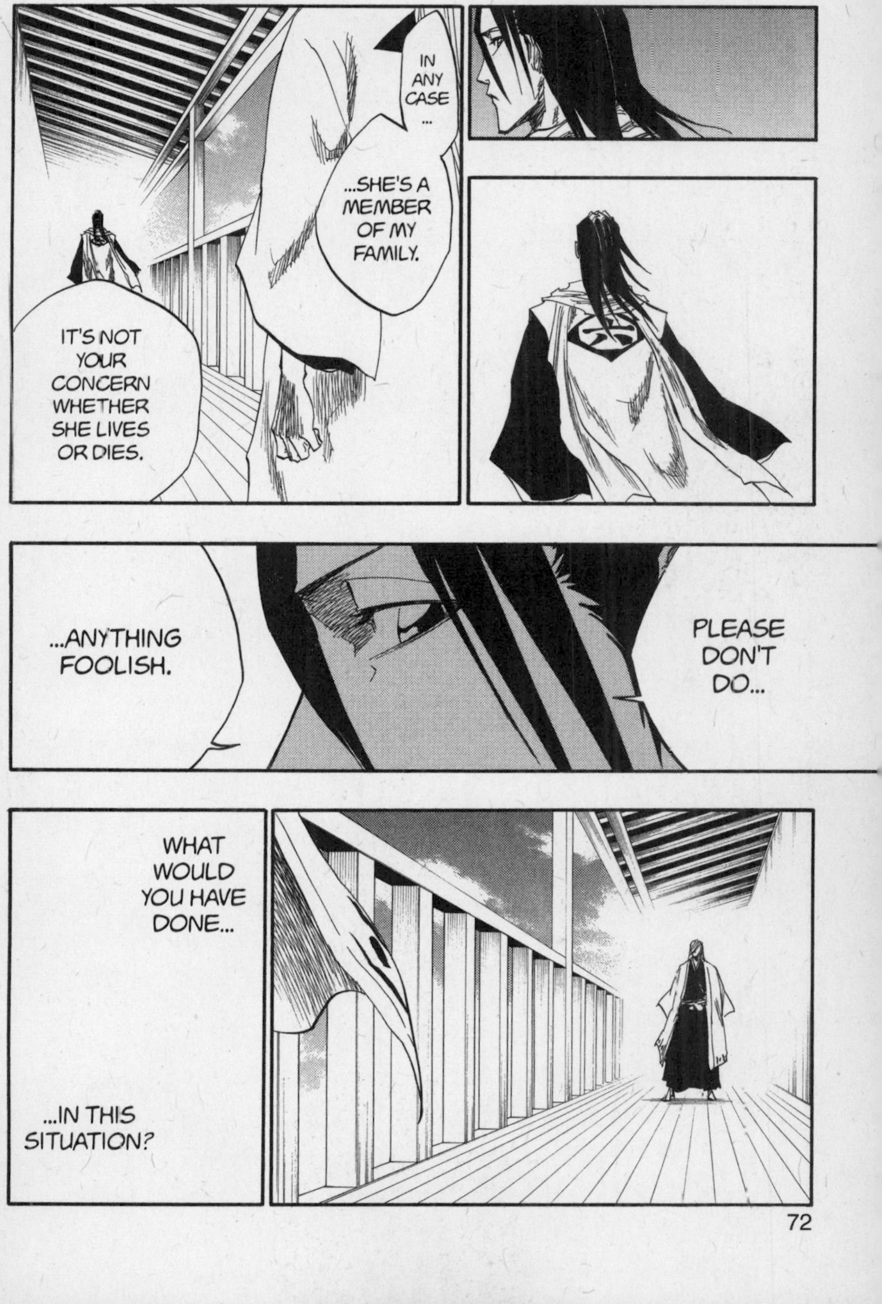
IN ANY CASE ...
...SHE'S A MEMBER OF MY FAMILY.
IT'S NOT YOUR CONCERN WHETHER SHE LIVES OR DIES.
PLEASE DON'T DO...
...ANYTHING FOOLISH.
WHAT WOULD YOU HAVE DONE...
...IN THIS SITUATION?

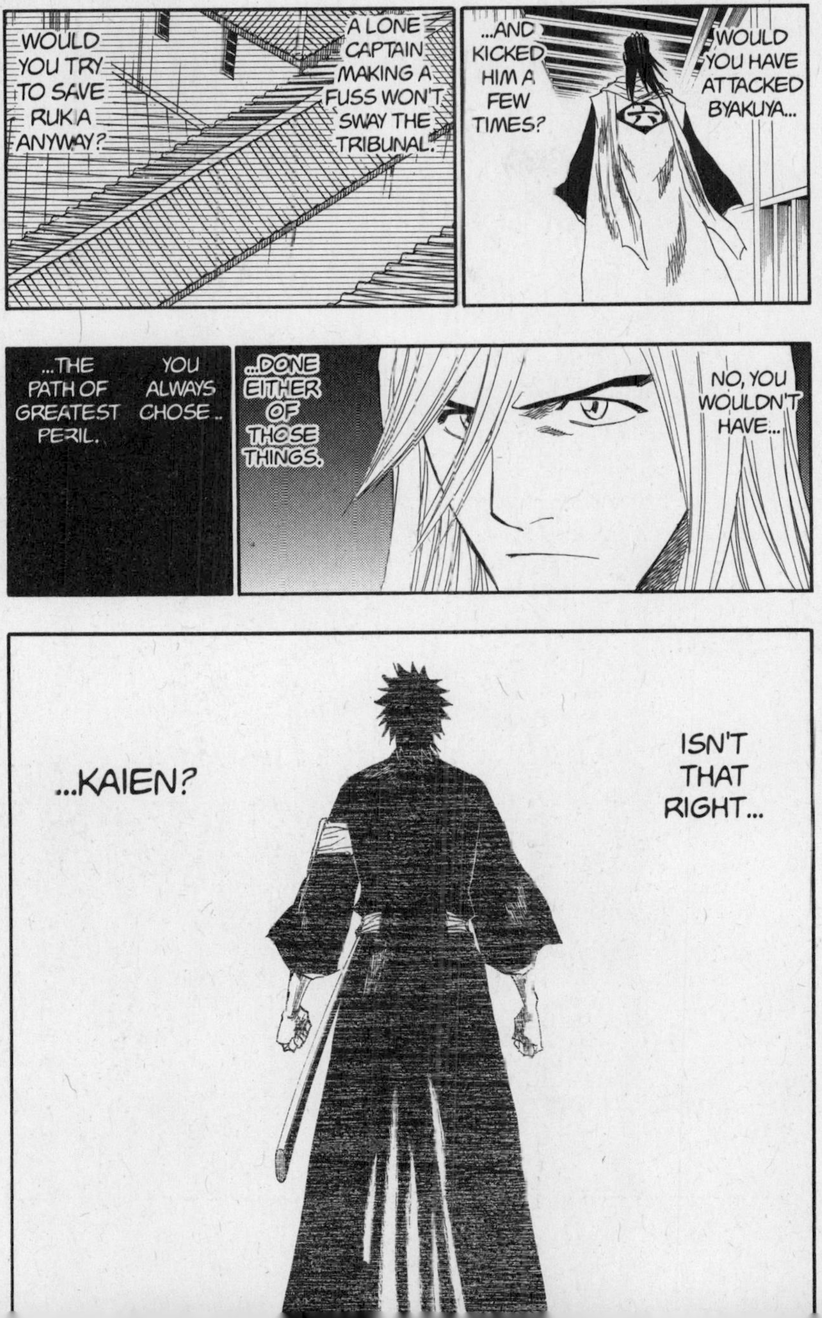
WOULD YOU HAVE ATTACKED BYAKUYA...
...AND KICKED HIM A FEW TIMES?
A LONE CAPTAIN MAKING A FUSS WON'T SWAY THE TRIBUNAL.
WOULD YOU TRY TO SAVE RUKIA ANYWAY?
NO, YOU WOULDN'T HAVE...
...DONE EITHER OF THOSE THINGS.
YOU ALWAYS CHOSE...
...THE PATH OF GREATEST PERIL.
ISN'T THAT RIGHT...
...KAIEN?

134. memories in the rain 2, op. 2: Longing for Sanctuary

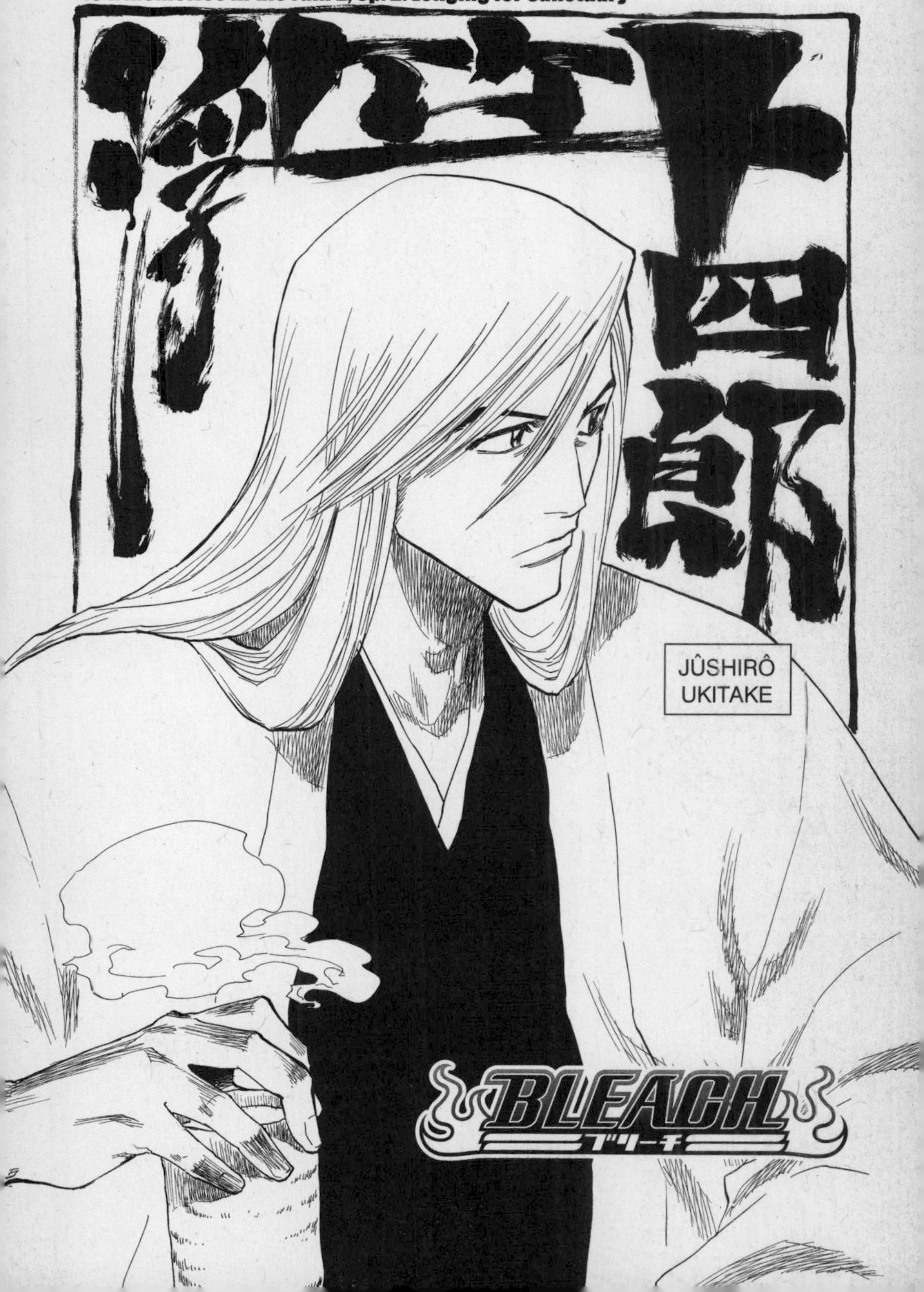
浮竹十四郎
JÛSHIRÔ
UKITAKE
BLEACH
ブリーチ

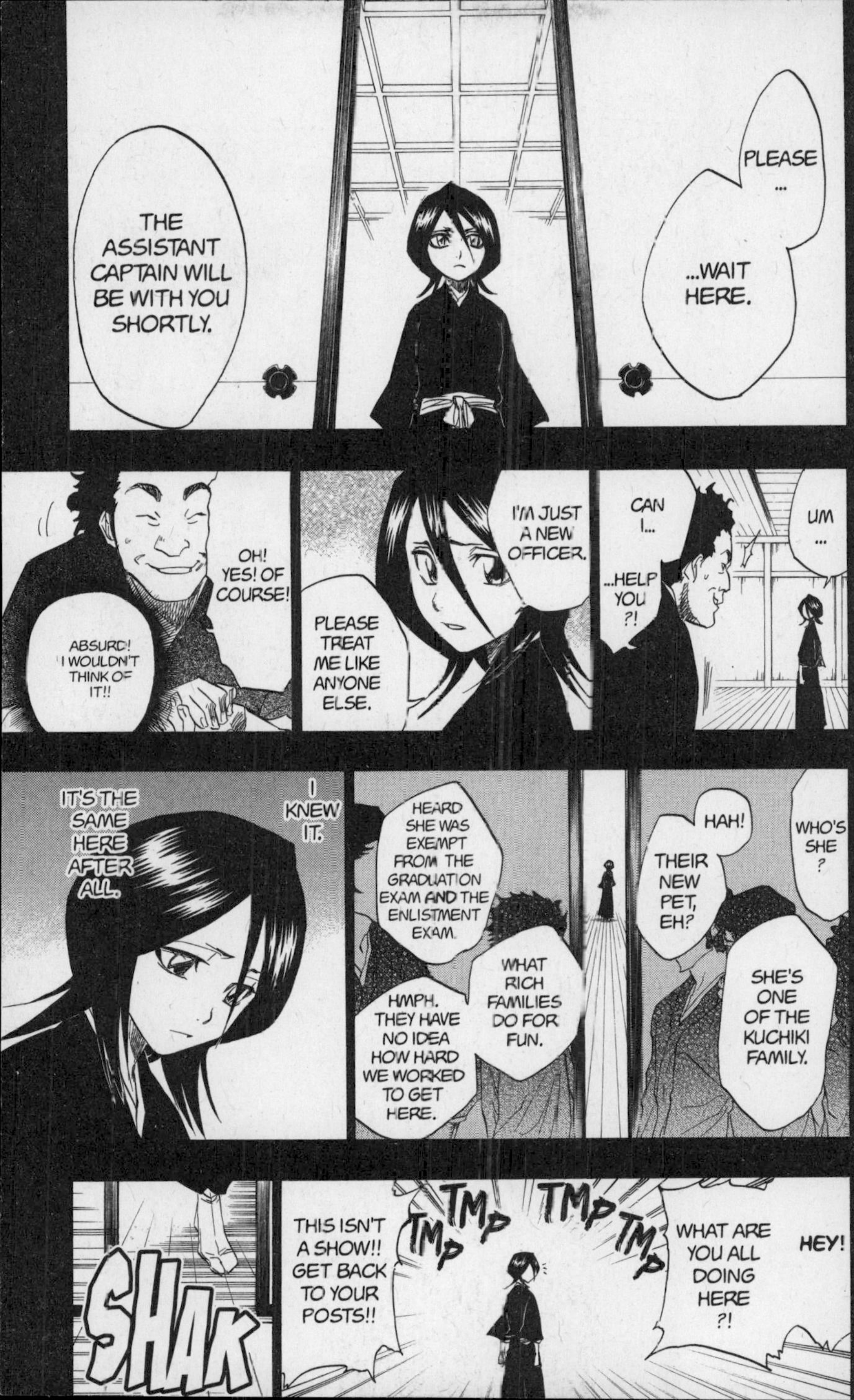
PLEASE ...
...WAIT HERE.
THE ASSISTANT CAPTAIN WILL BE WITH YOU SHORTLY.
UM ...
CAN I...
...HELP YOU ?!
I'M JUST A NEW OFFICER.
PLEASE TREAT ME LIKE ANYONE ELSE.
OH! YES! OF COURSE!
ABSURD! I WOULDN'T THINK OF IT!!
WHO'S SHE ?
HAH!
THEIR NEW PET, EH?
SHE'S ONE OF THE KUCHIKI FAMILY.
HEARD SHE WAS EXEMPT FROM THE GRADUATION EXAM AND THE ENLISTMENT EXAM.
WHAT RICH FAMILIES DO FOR FUN.
HMPH. THEY HAVE NO IDEA HOW HARD WE WORKED TO GET HERE.
I KNEW IT.
IT'S THE SAME HERE AFTER ALL.
HEY!
WHAT ARE YOU ALL DOING HERE ?!
TMP TMP
TMP TMP
THIS ISN'T A SHOW!! GET BACK TO YOUR POSTS!!
SHAK

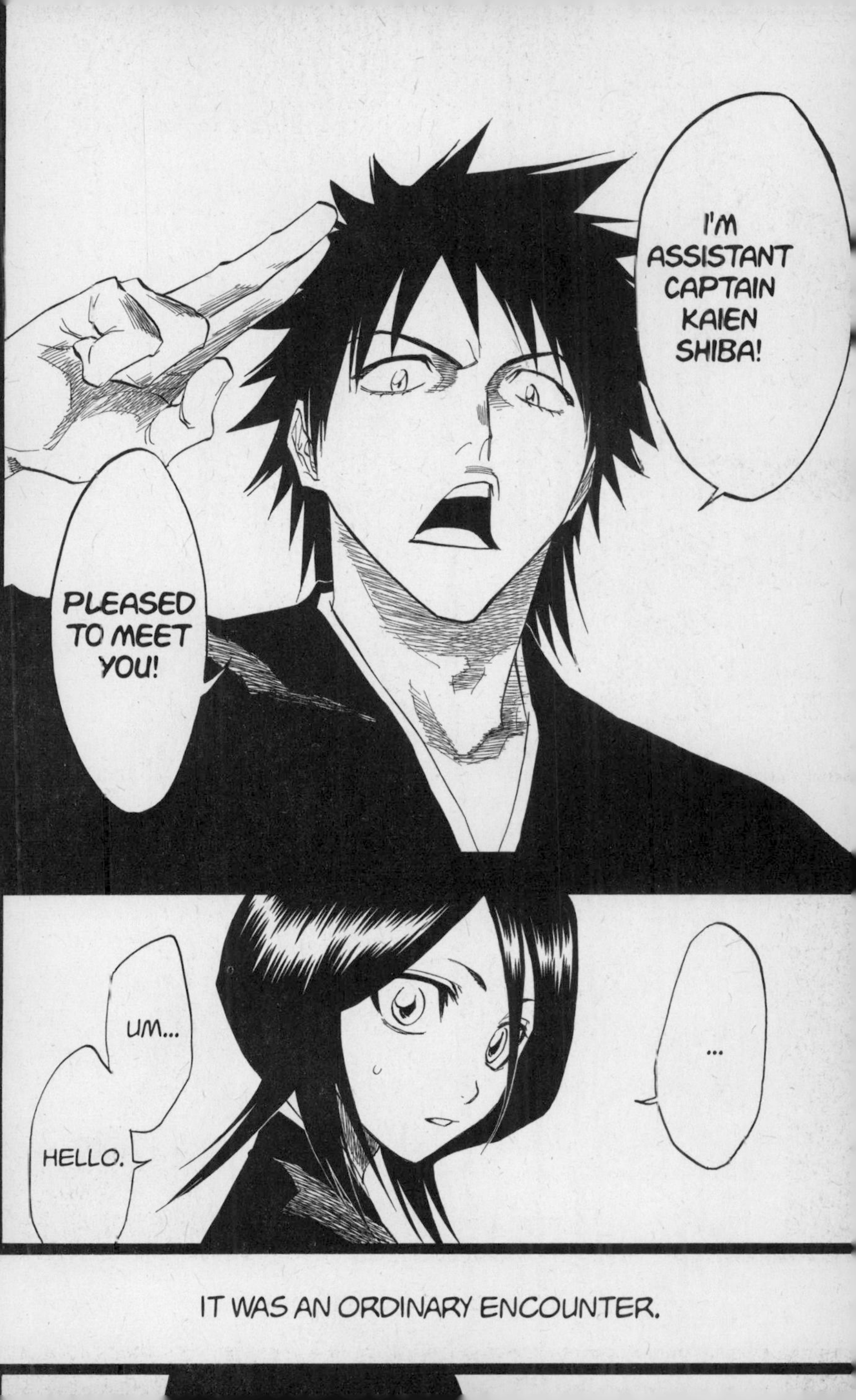
I'M ASSISTANT CAPTAIN KAIEN SHIBA!
PLEASED TO MEET YOU!
...
UM...
HELLO.
IT WAS AN ORDINARY ENCOUNTER.

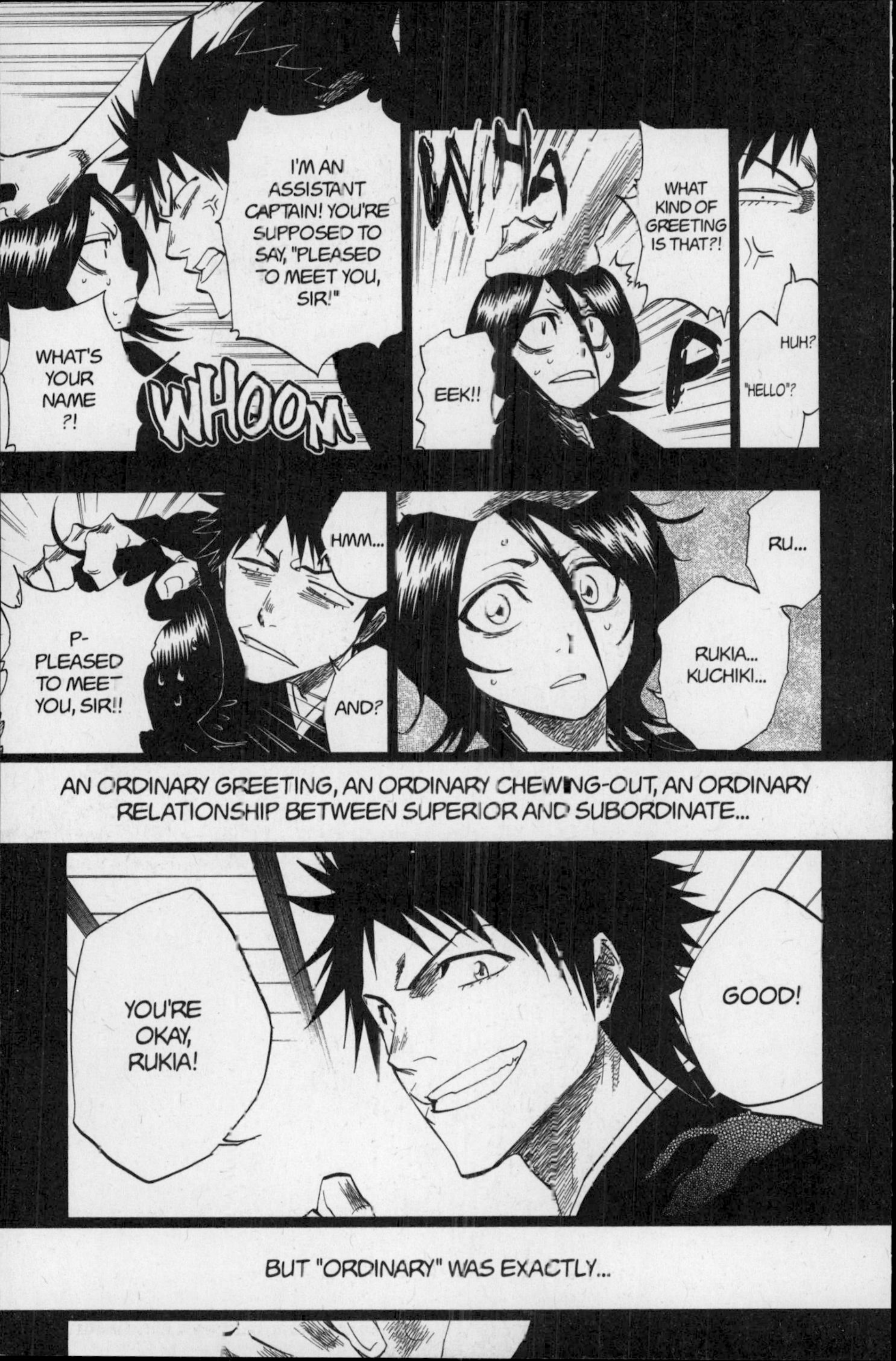
HUH?
"HELLO"?
WHAP
WHAT KIND OF GREETING IS THAT?!
EEK!!
I'M AN ASSISTANT CAPTAIN! YOU'RE SUPPOSED TO SAY, "PLEASED TO MEET YOU, SIR!"
WHOOM
WHAT'S YOUR NAME?!
RU...
RUKIA... KUCHIKI...
HMM...
AND?
P- PLEASED TO MEET YOU, SIR!!
AN ORDINARY GREETING, AN ORDINARY CHEWING-OUT, AN ORDINARY RELATIONSHIP BETWEEN SUPERIOR AND SUBORDINATE...
GOOD!
YOU'RE OKAY, RUKIA!
BUT "ORDINARY" WAS EXACTLY...

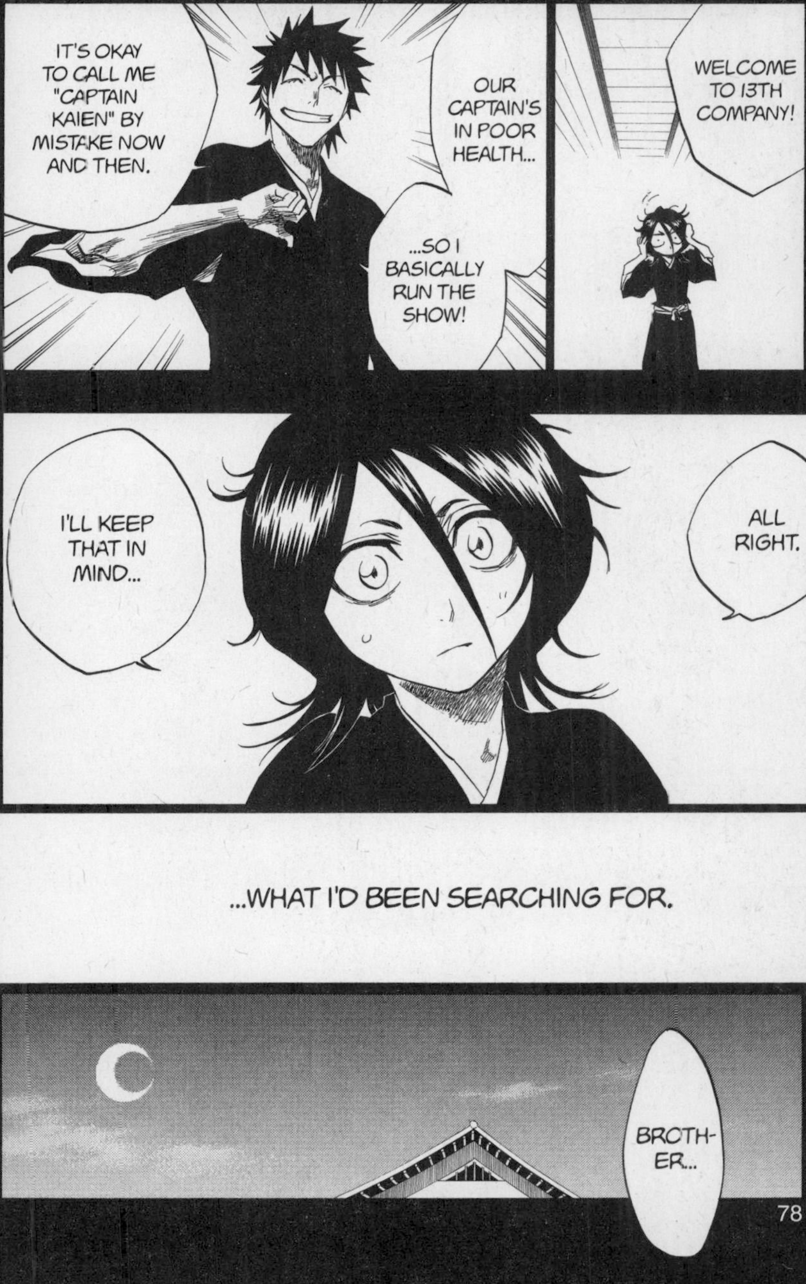
WELCOME TO 13TH COMPANY!
OUR CAPTAIN'S IN POOR HEALTH...
...SO I BASICALLY RUN THE SHOW!
IT'S OKAY TO CALL ME "CAPTAIN KAIEN" BY MISTAKE NOW AND THEN.
ALL RIGHT.
I'LL KEEP THAT IN MIND...
...WHAT I'D BEEN SEARCHING FOR.
BROTH-ER...

READ THIS WAY

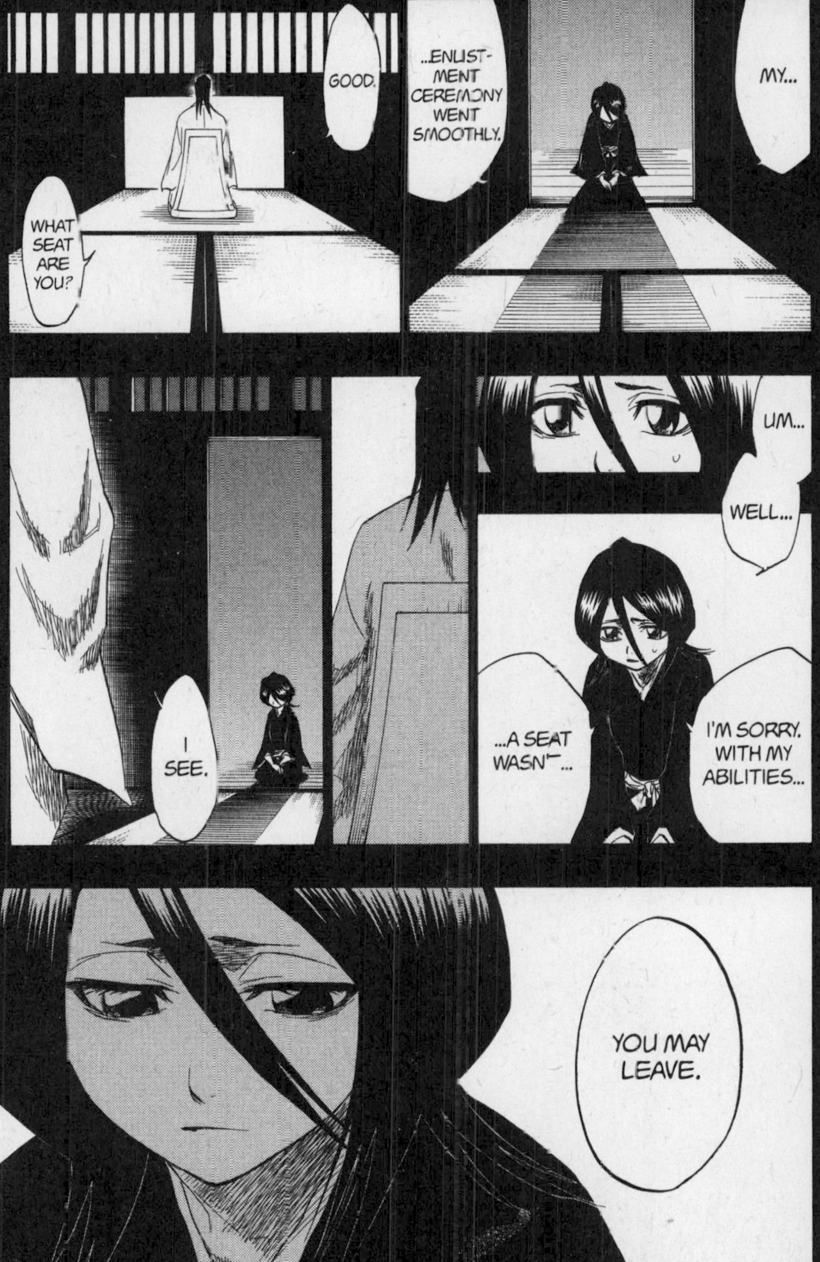
MY...
...ENLISTMENT CEREMONY WENT SMOOTHLY.
GOOD.
WHAT SEAT ARE YOU?
UM...
WELL...
I'M SORRY. WITH MY ABILITIES...
...A SEAT WASN'T...
I SEE.
YOU MAY LEAVE.

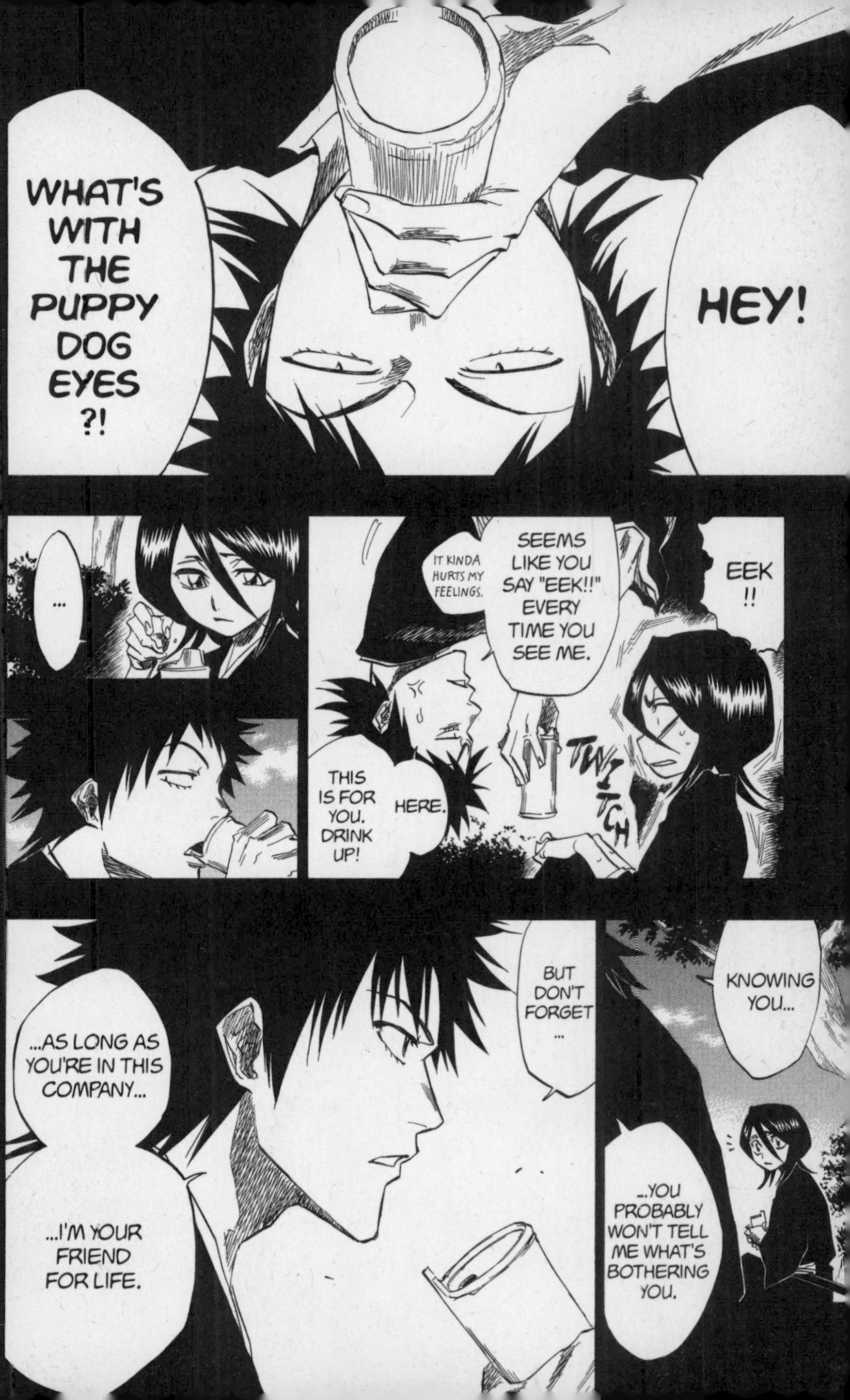
HEY!
WHAT'S WITH THE PUPPY DOG EYES ?!
EEK !!
TWITCH
SEEMS LIKE YOU SAY "EEK!!" EVERY TIME YOU SEE ME.
IT KINDA HURTS MY FEELINGS.
HERE.
THIS IS FOR YOU. DRINK UP!
...
KNOWING YOU...
...YOU PROBABLY WON'T TELL ME WHAT'S BOTHERING YOU.
BUT DON'T FORGET ...
...AS LONG AS YOU'RE IN THIS COMPANY...
...I'M YOUR FRIEND FOR LIFE.

READ THIS WAY

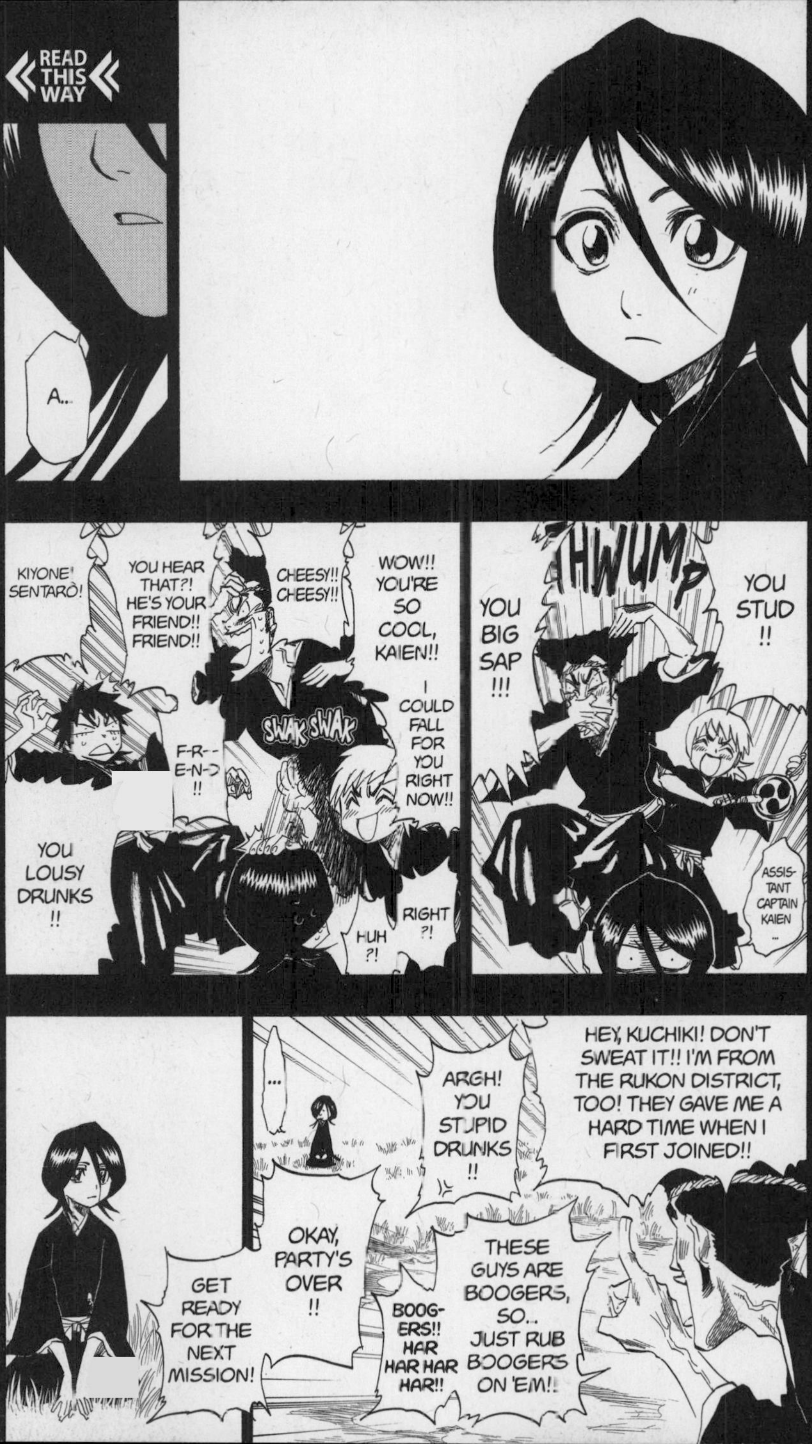
A...
THWUMP
YOU STUD!!
YOU BIG SAP!!!
ASSISTANT CAPTAIN KAIEN...
WOW!! YOU'RE SO COOL, KAIEN!!
I COULD FALL FOR YOU RIGHT NOW!!
CHEESY!! CHEESY!!
YOU HEAR THAT?! HE'S YOUR FRIEND!! FRIEND!!
KIYONE! SENTARŌ!
SWAK SWAK
F-R--E-N-D!!
RIGHT?!
HUH?!
YOU LOUSY DRUNKS!!
HEY, KUCHIKI! DON'T SWEAT IT!! I'M FROM THE RUKON DISTRICT, TOO! THEY GAVE ME A HARD TIME WHEN I FIRST JOINED!!
ARGH! YOU STUPID DRUNKS!!
THESE GUYS ARE BOOGERS, SO... JUST RUB BOOGERS ON 'EM!!
BOOGERS!! HAR HAR HAR HAR!!
OKAY, PARTY'S OVER!!
GET READY FOR THE NEXT MISSION!
...

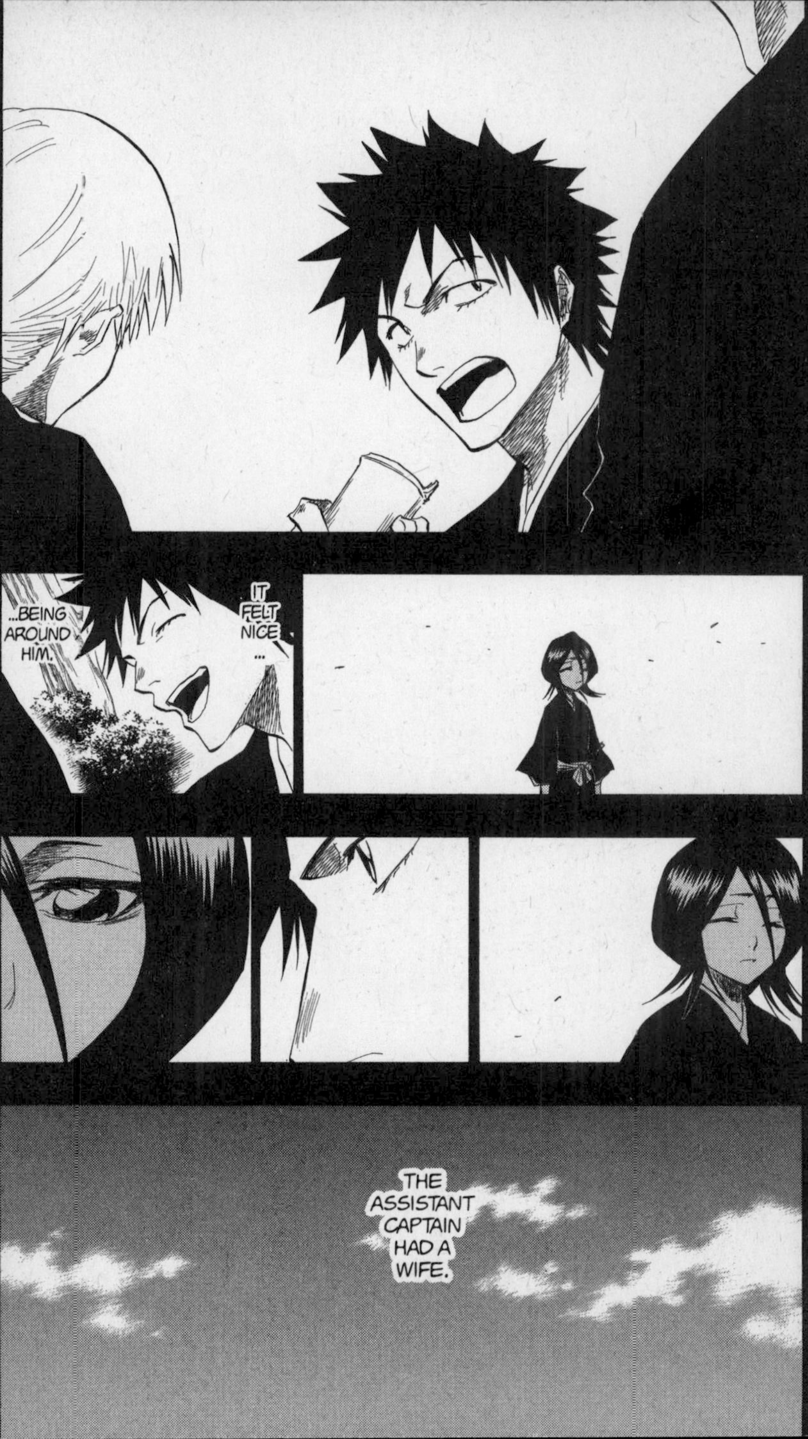
IT FELT NICE ...
...BEING AROUND HIM.
THE ASSISTANT CAPTAIN HAD A WIFE.

READ THIS WAY

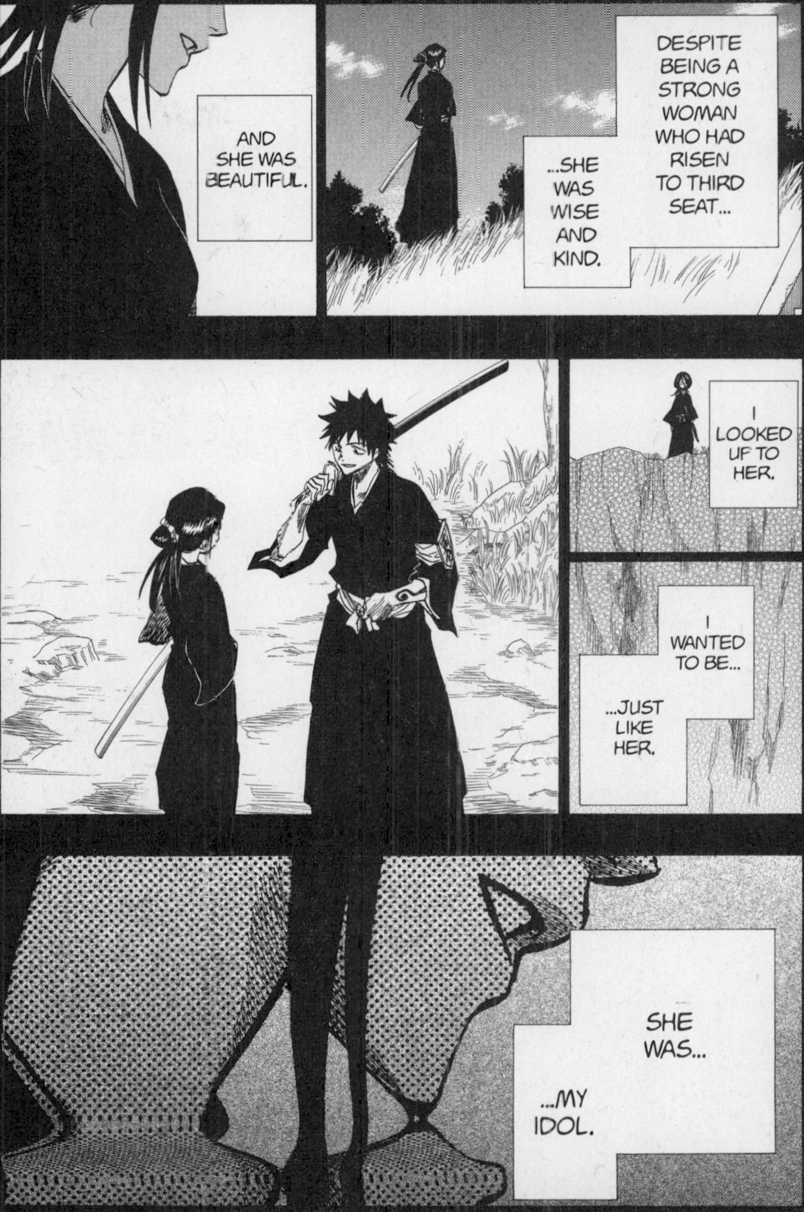

DESPITE BEING A STRONG WOMAN WHO HAD RISEN TO THIRD SEAT...
...SHE WAS WISE AND KIND.
AND SHE WAS BEAUTIFUL.
I LOOKED UP TO HER.
I WANTED TO BE...
...JUST LIKE HER.
SHE WAS...
...MY IDOL.

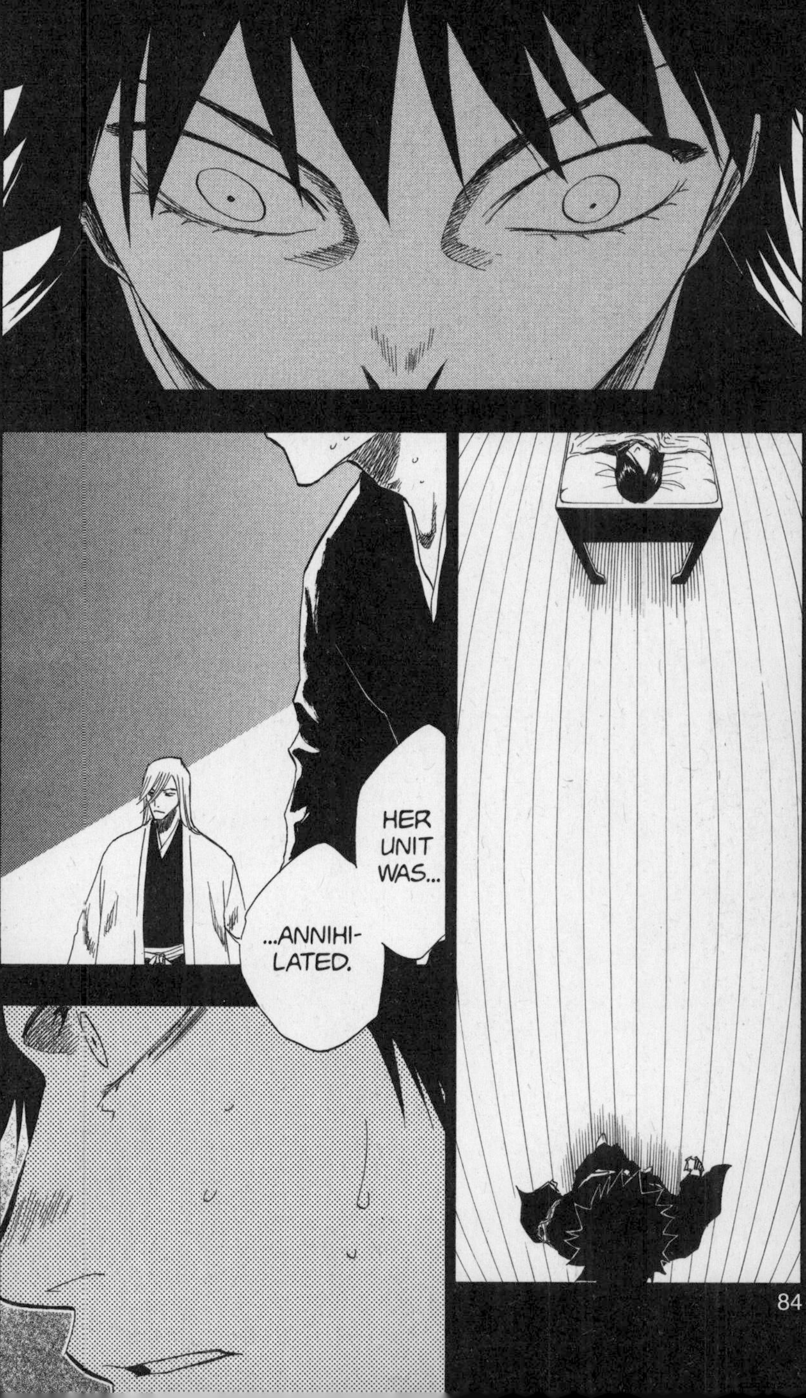
HER UNIT WAS...
...ANNIHI-LATED.

READ THIS WAY

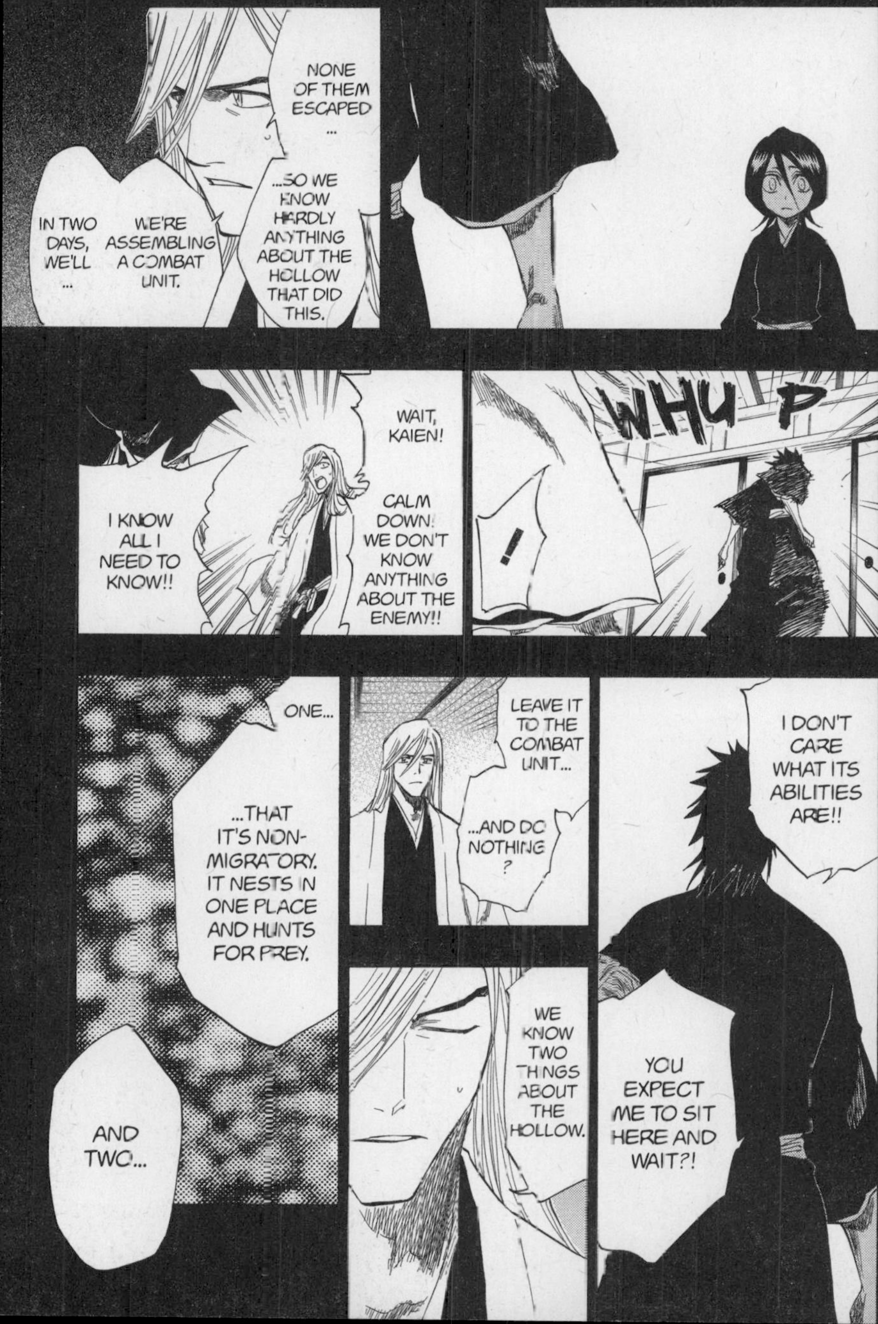
NONE OF THEM ESCAPED ...
...SO WE KNOW HARDLY ANYTHING ABOUT THE HOLLOW THAT DID THIS.
WE'RE ASSEMBLING A COMBAT UNIT.
IN TWO DAYS, WE'LL ...
WHUP
!
WAIT, KAIEN!
CALM DOWN! WE DON'T KNOW ANYTHING ABOUT THE ENEMY!!
I KNOW ALL I NEED TO KNOW!!
I DON'T CARE WHAT ITS ABILITIES ARE!!
YOU EXPECT ME TO SIT HERE AND WAIT?!
LEAVE IT TO THE COMBAT UNIT...
...AND DO NOTHING ?
WE KNOW TWO THINGS ABOUT THE HOLLOW.
ONE...
...THAT IT'S NON-MIGRATORY. IT NESTS IN ONE PLACE AND HUNTS FOR PREY.
AND TWO...

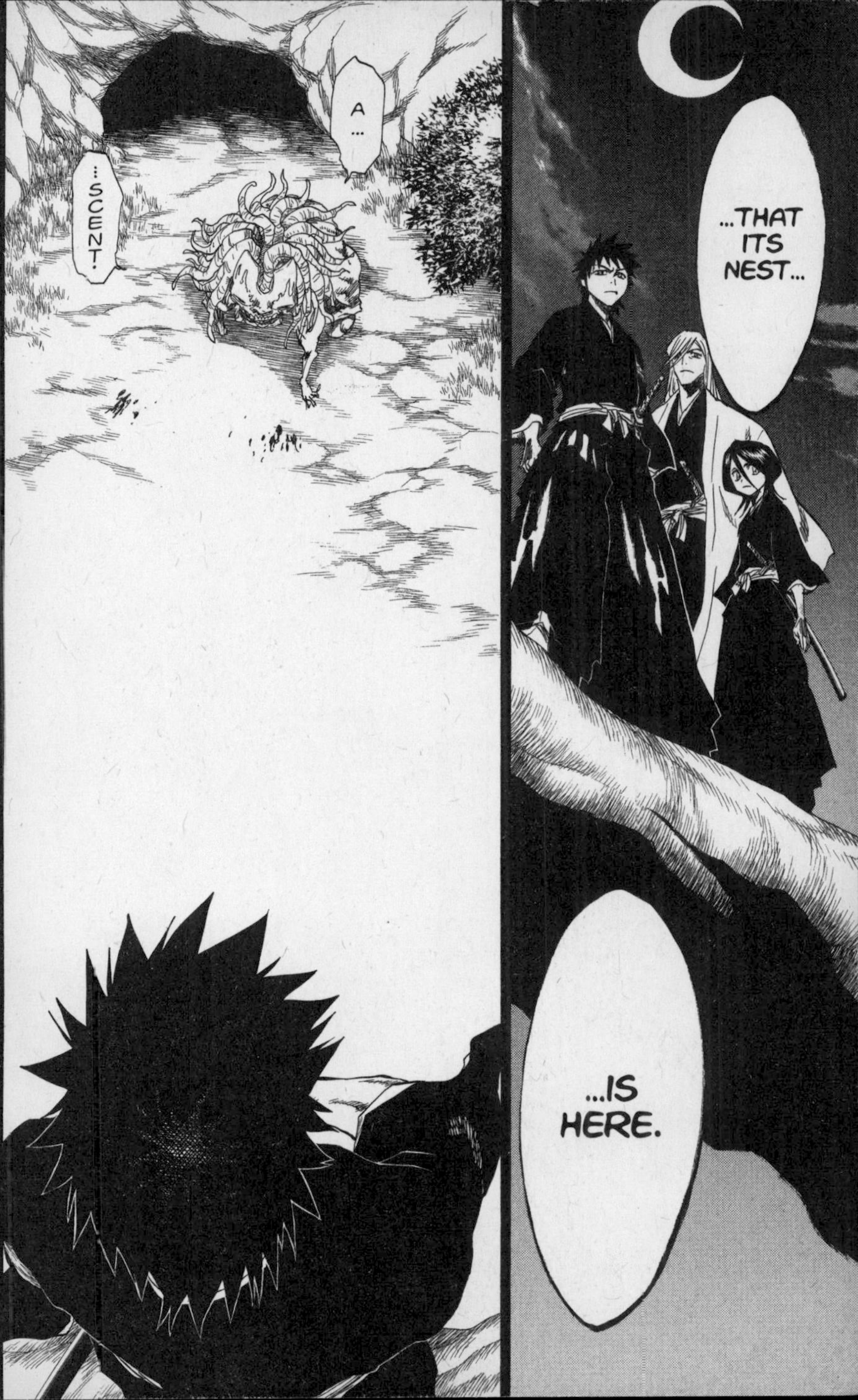
...THAT ITS NEST...
...IS HERE.
A...
...SCENT!

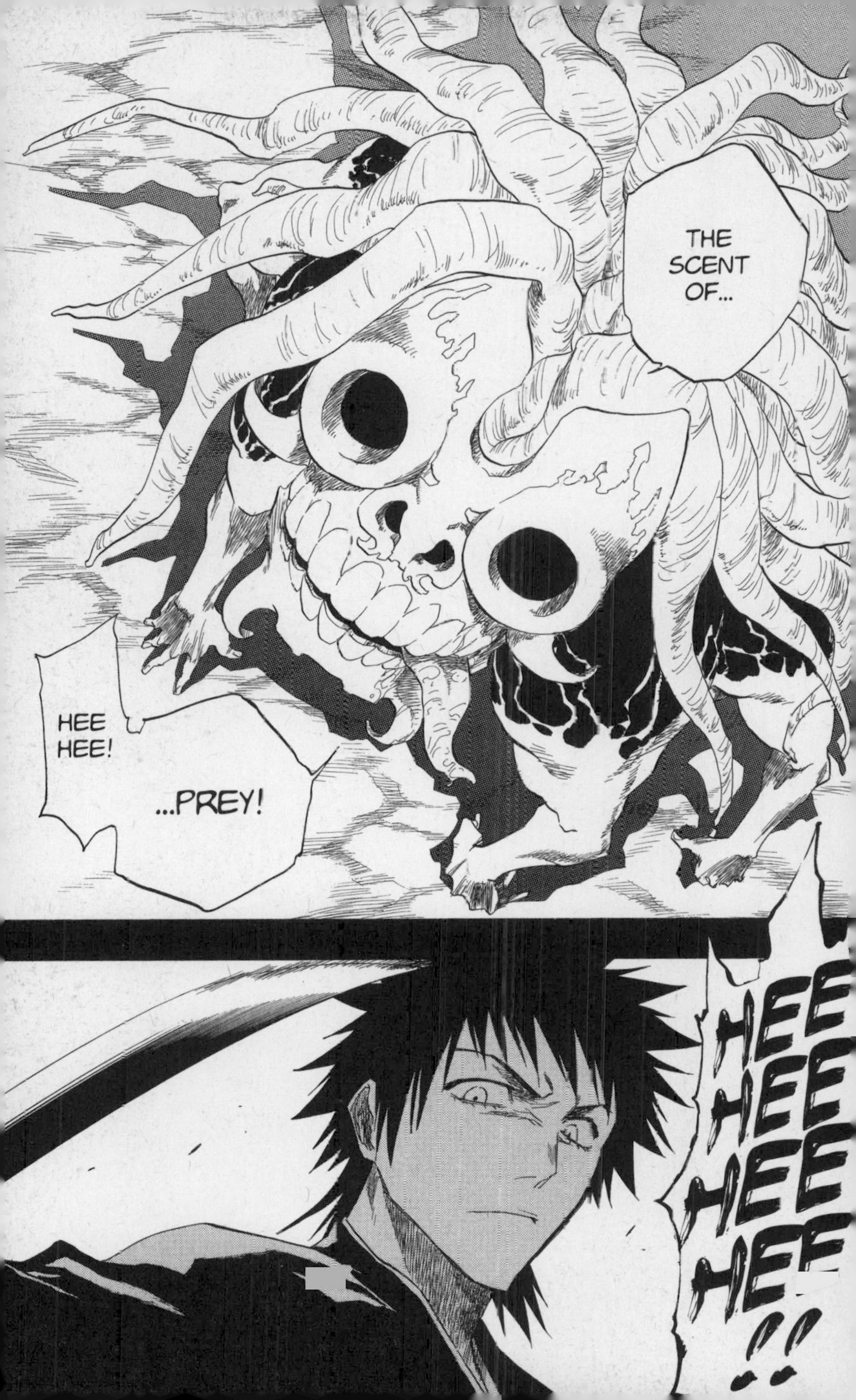
THE SCENT OF...
HEE HEE!
...PREY!
HEE HEE HEE HEE HEE!!

134. memories in the rain 2, op. 2: Affected by the Night

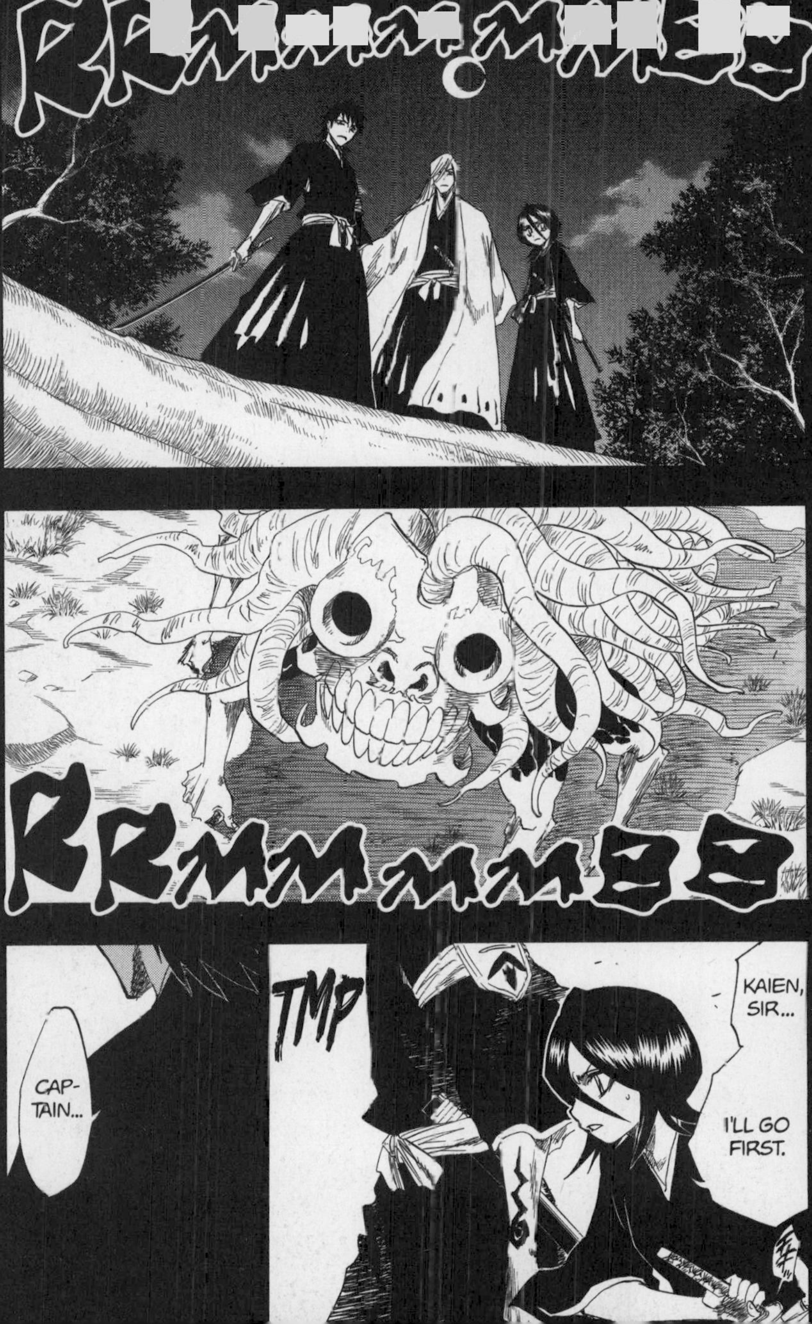
KAIEN, SIR...
I'LL GO FIRST.
TMP
CAP-TAIN...

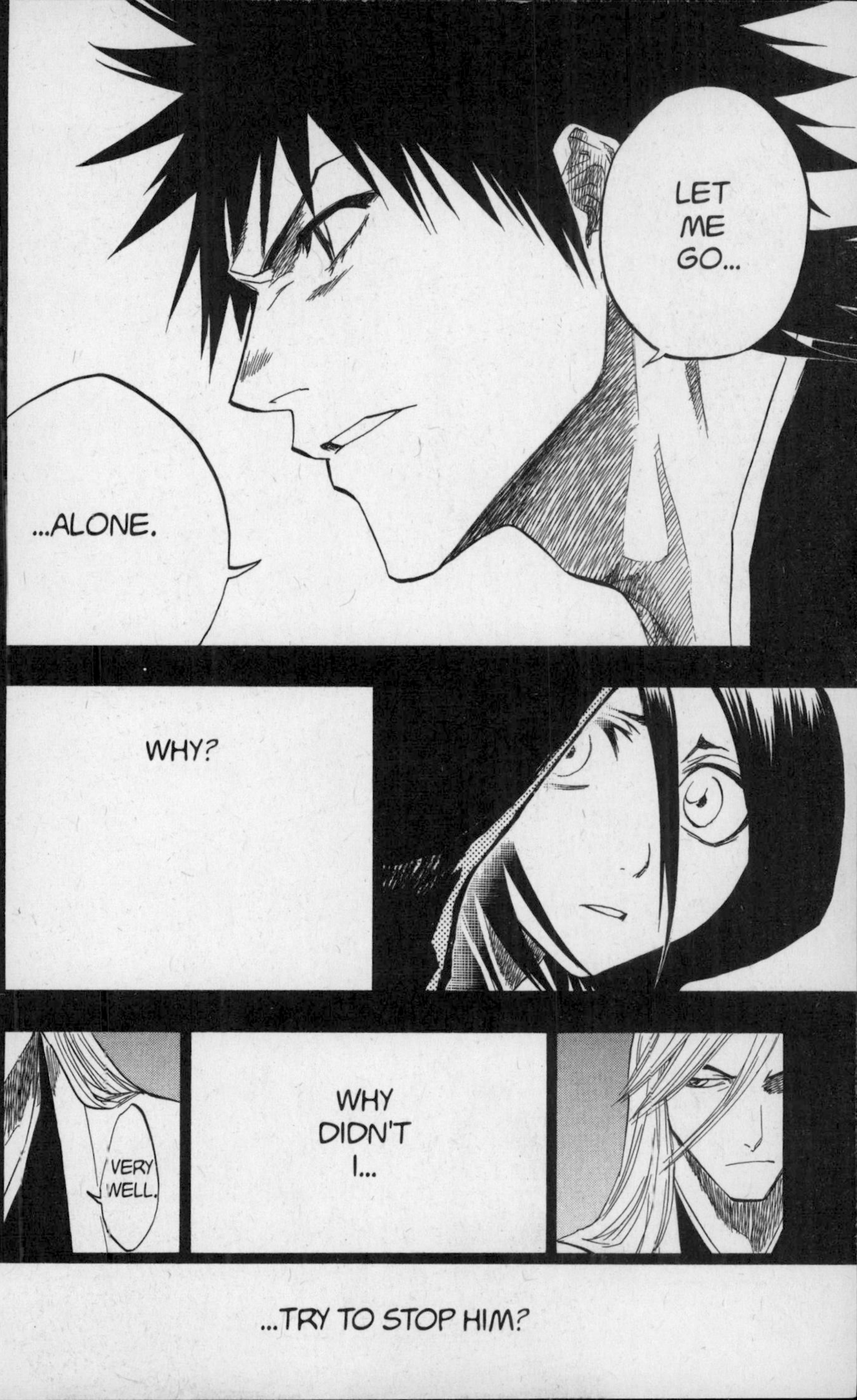
LET ME GO...
...ALONE.
WHY?
WHY DIDN'T I...
VERY WELL.
...TRY TO STOP HIM?

135. memories in the rain 2, op. 3: Affected by the Night

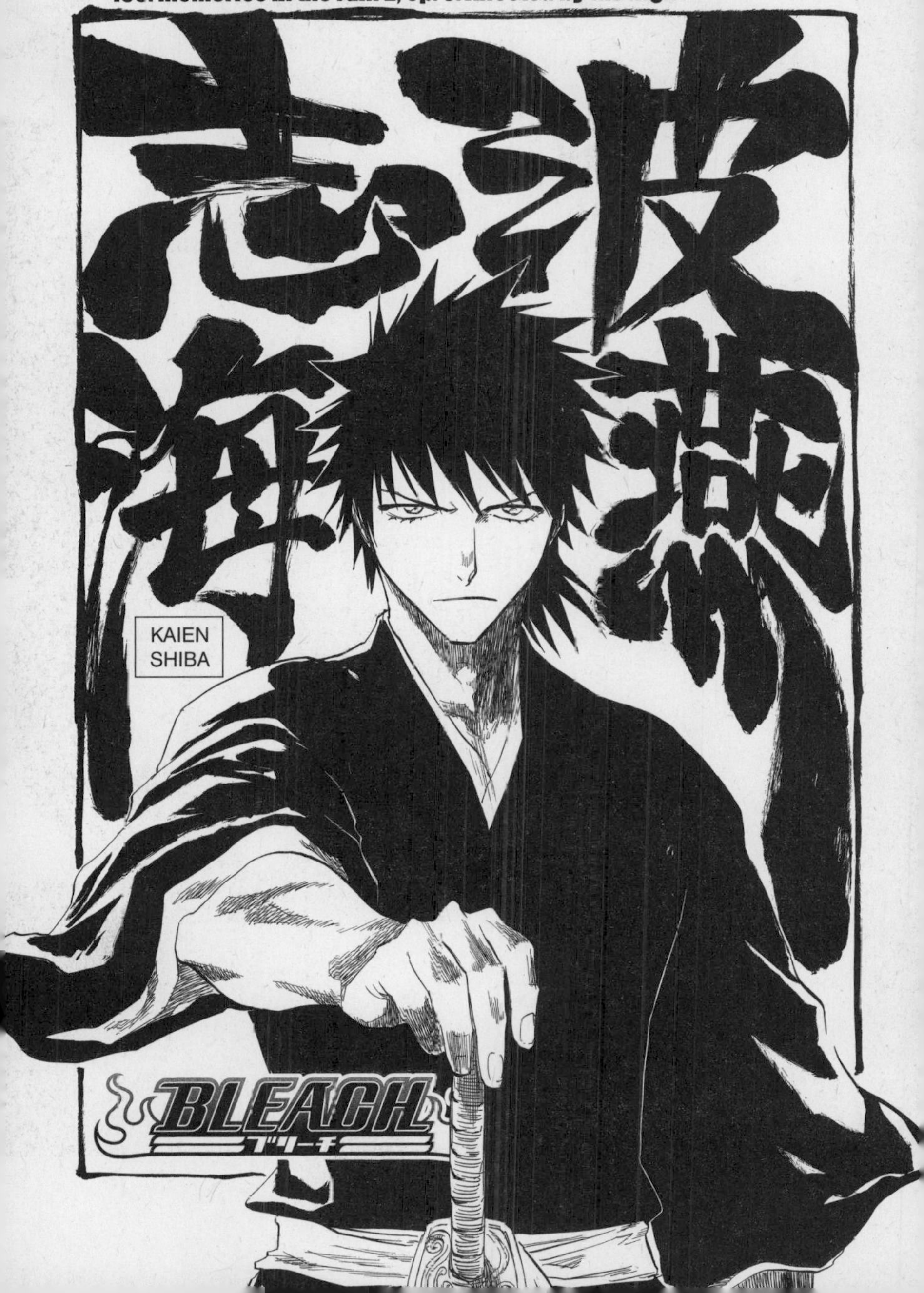
KAIEN
SHIBA
BLEACH
ブリーチ

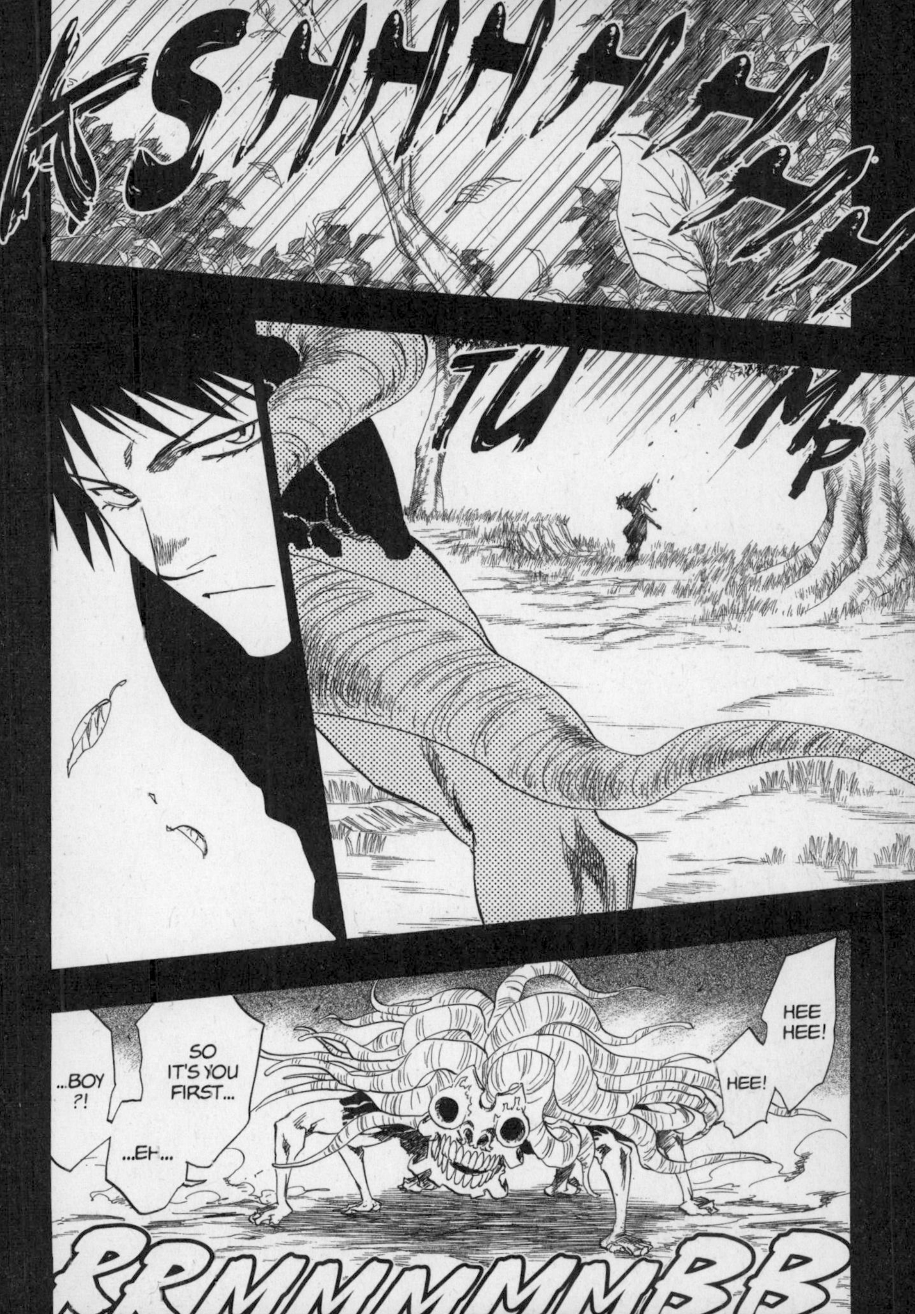
KSHHHHHHHHH
TUMP
HEE HEE!
HEE!
SO IT'S YOU FIRST...
...BOY ?!
...EH...
RRMMMMMBB

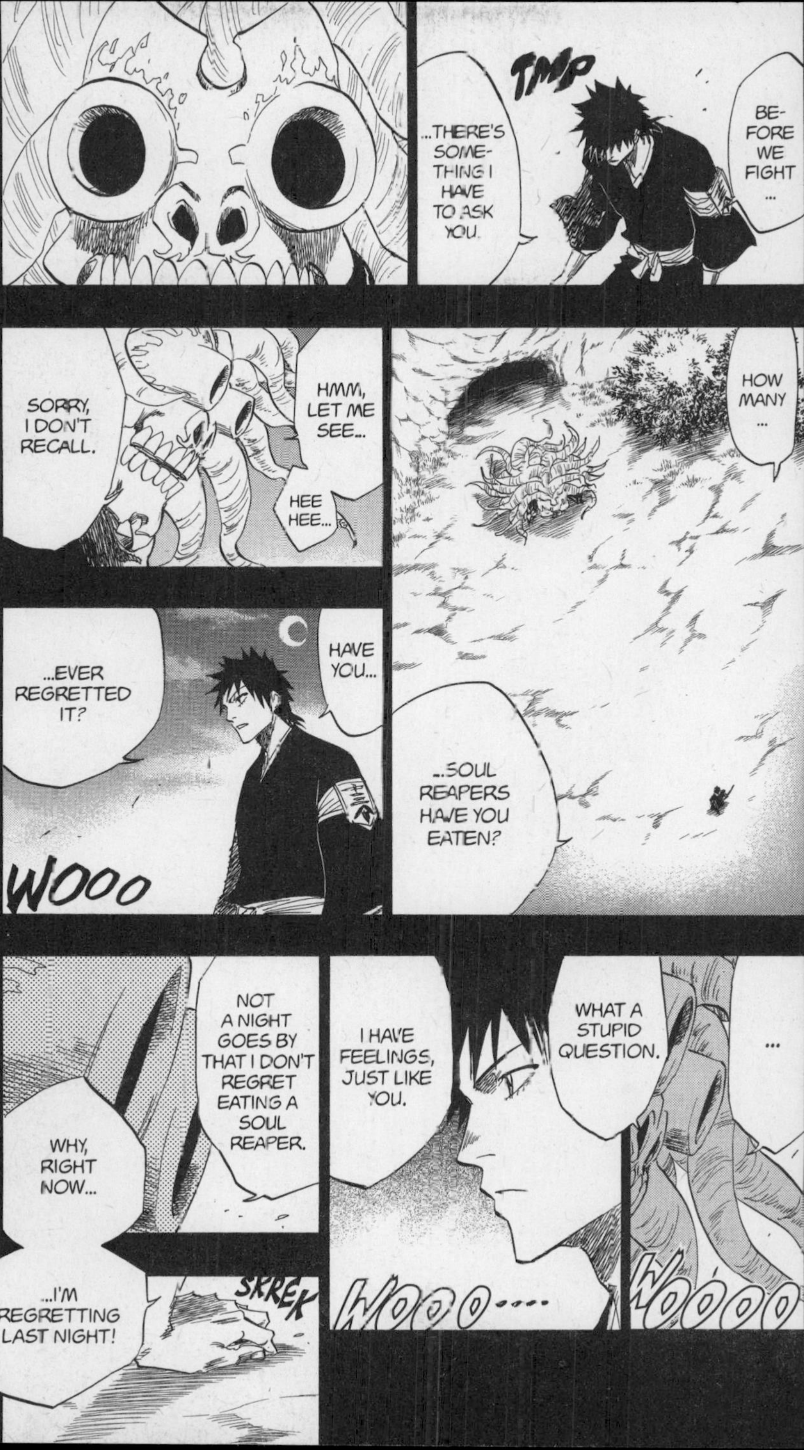
BE-FORE WE FIGHT ...
TMP
...THERE'S SOME-THING I HAVE TO ASK YOU.
HOW MANY ...
...SOUL REAPERS HAVE YOU EATEN?
HMM, LET ME SEE...
HEE HEE...
SORRY, I DON'T RECALL.
HAVE YOU...
...EVER REGRETTED IT?
WOOO
...
WOOOOO
WHAT A STUPID QUESTION.
I HAVE FEELINGS, JUST LIKE YOU.
WOOO....
NOT A NIGHT GOES BY THAT I DON'T REGRET EATING A SOUL REAPER.
WHY, RIGHT NOW...
...I'M REGRETTING LAST NIGHT!
SKREK

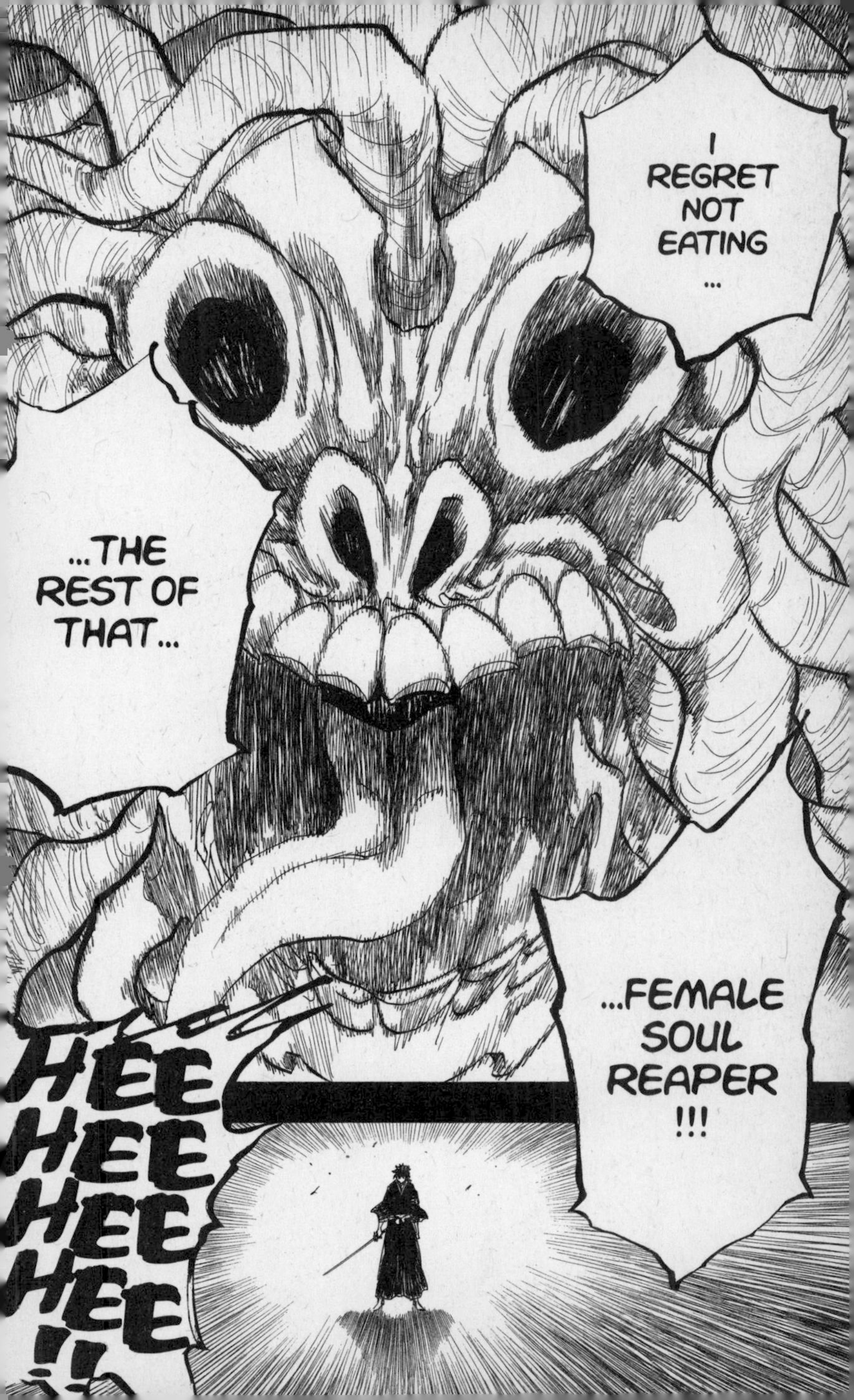
I REGRET NOT EATING ...
...THE REST OF THAT...
...FEMALE SOUL REAPER !!!
HEE HEE HEE HEE !!

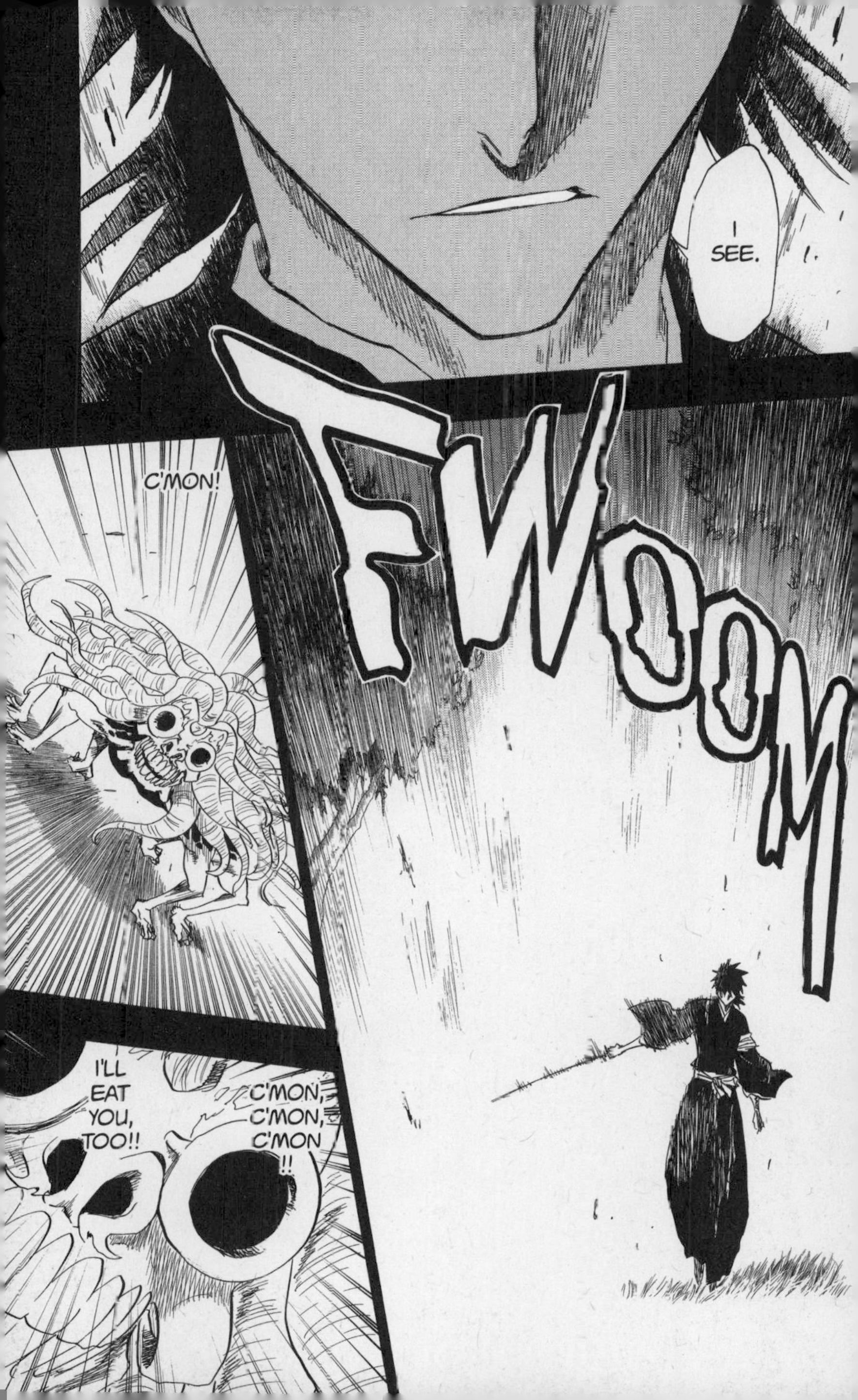
I SEE.
FWOOOM
C'MON!
C'MON, C'MON, C'MON!!
I'LL EAT YOU, TOO!!

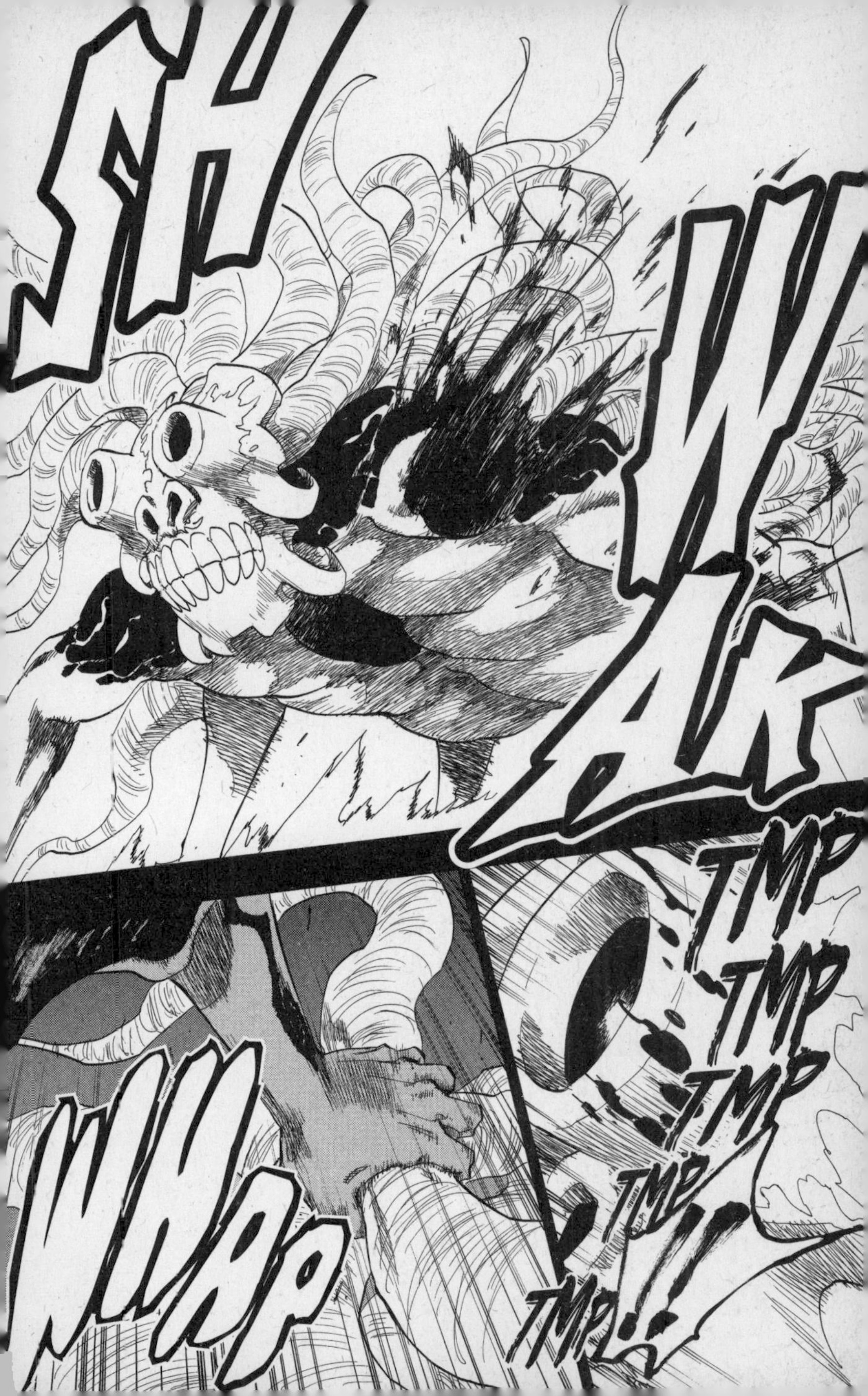
SHWAK
TMP TMP TMP TMP TMP!!
WHAP

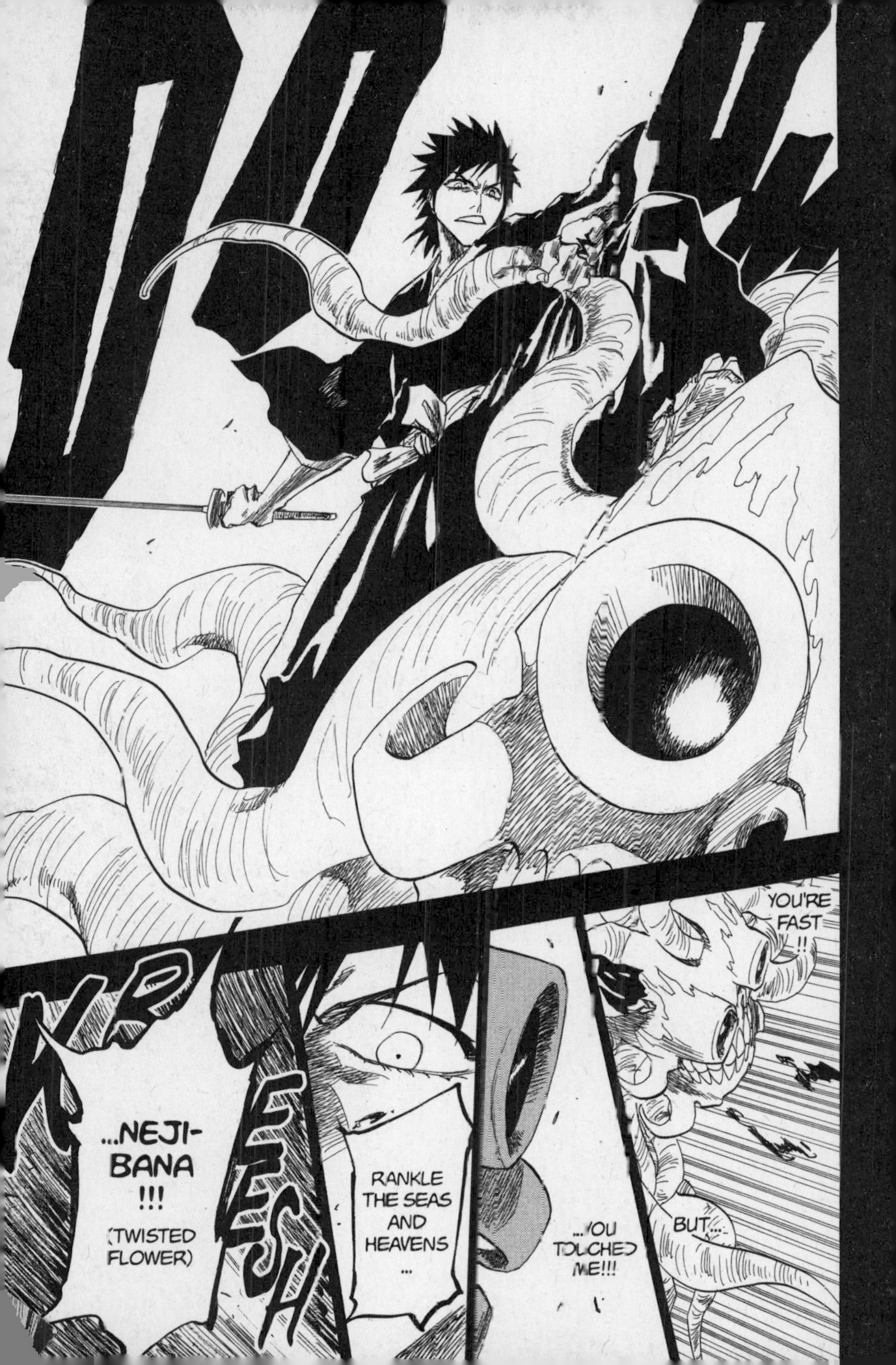
YOU'RE FAST!!
BUT...
...YOU TOUCHED ME!!!
RANKLE THE SEAS AND HEAVENS ...
...NEJI-BANA!!! (TWISTED FLOWER)

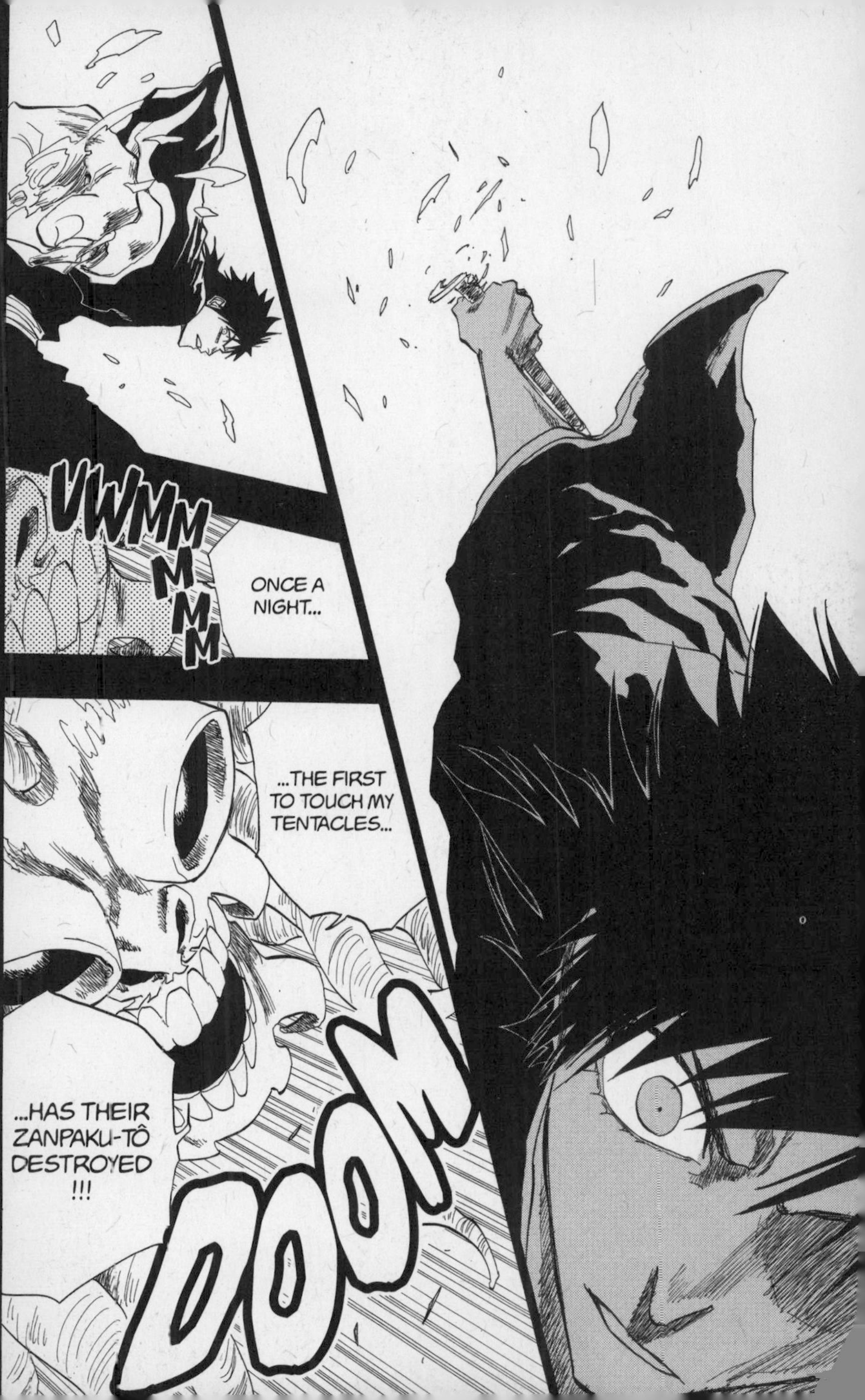
ONCE A NIGHT...
VWMMMMMMM
...THE FIRST TO TOUCH MY TENTACLES...
...HAS THEIR ZANPAKU-TÔ DESTROYED !!!
DOOM

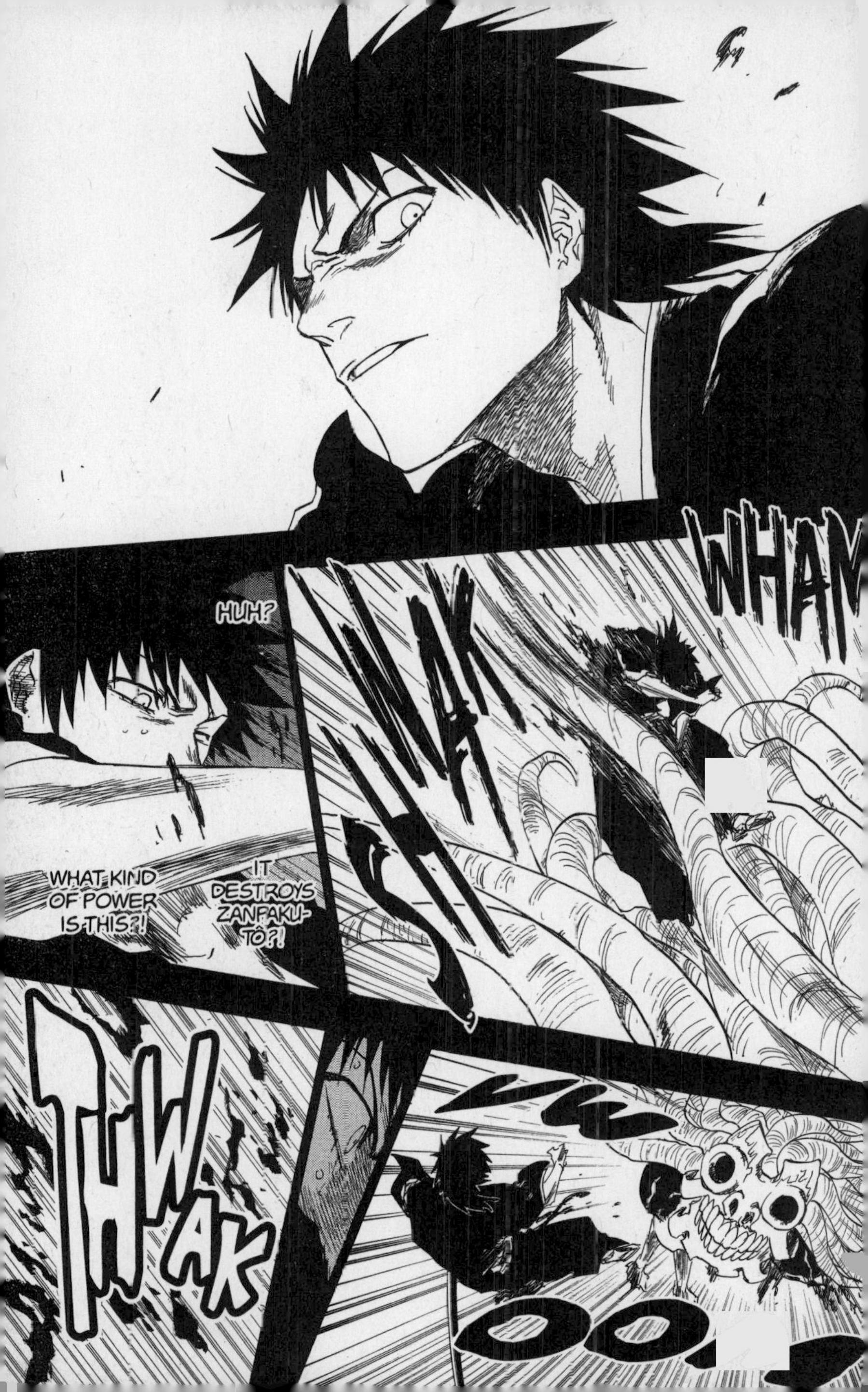
WHAM
HUH?
IT DESTROYS ZANPAKU-TÔ?!
WHAT KIND OF POWER IS THIS?!
THWAK

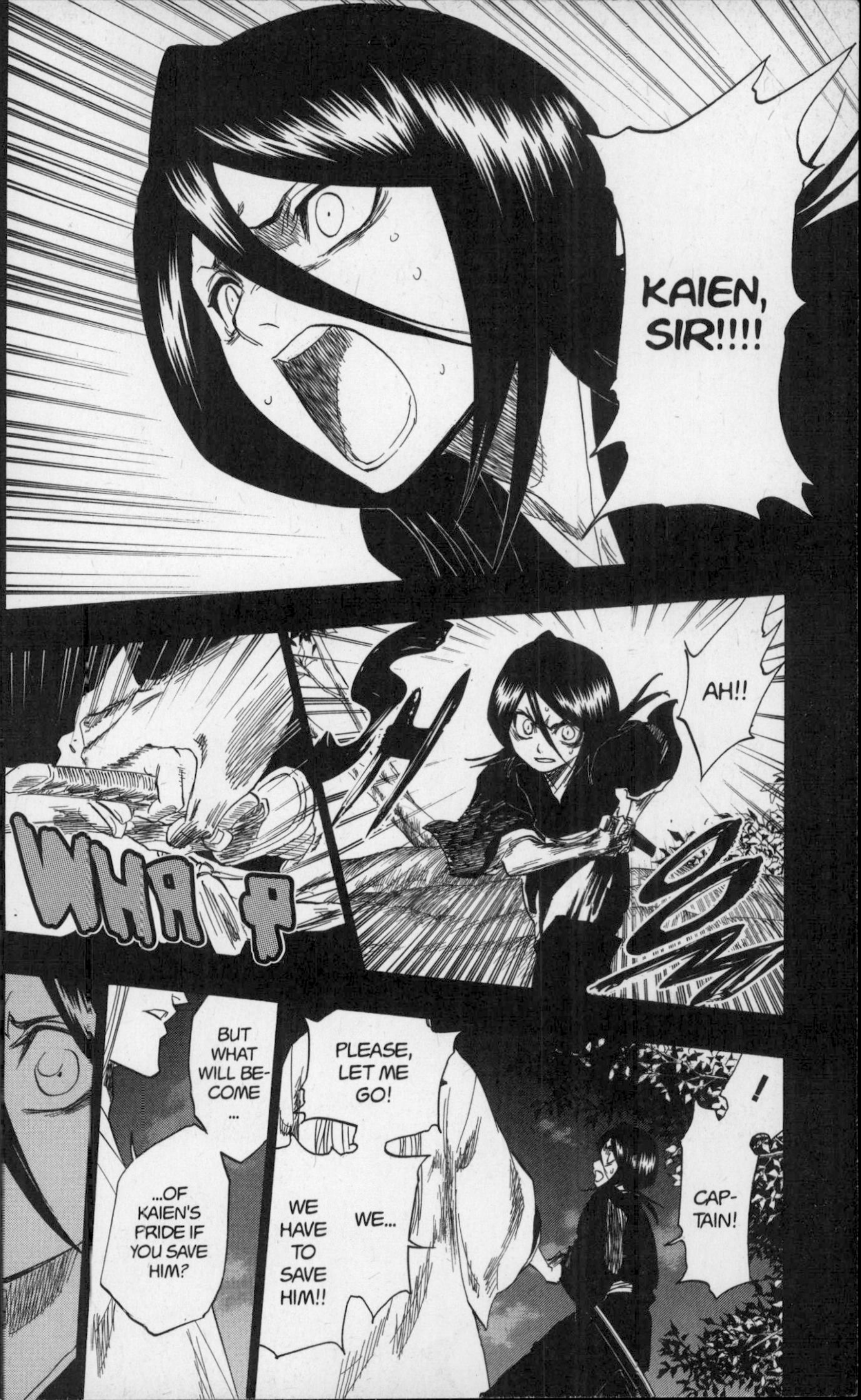
KAIEN, SIR!!!!
AH!!
WHAP
!
CAPTAIN!
PLEASE, LET ME GO!
WE...
WE HAVE TO SAVE HIM!!
BUT WHAT WILL BECOME...
...OF KAIEN'S PRIDE IF YOU SAVE HIM?

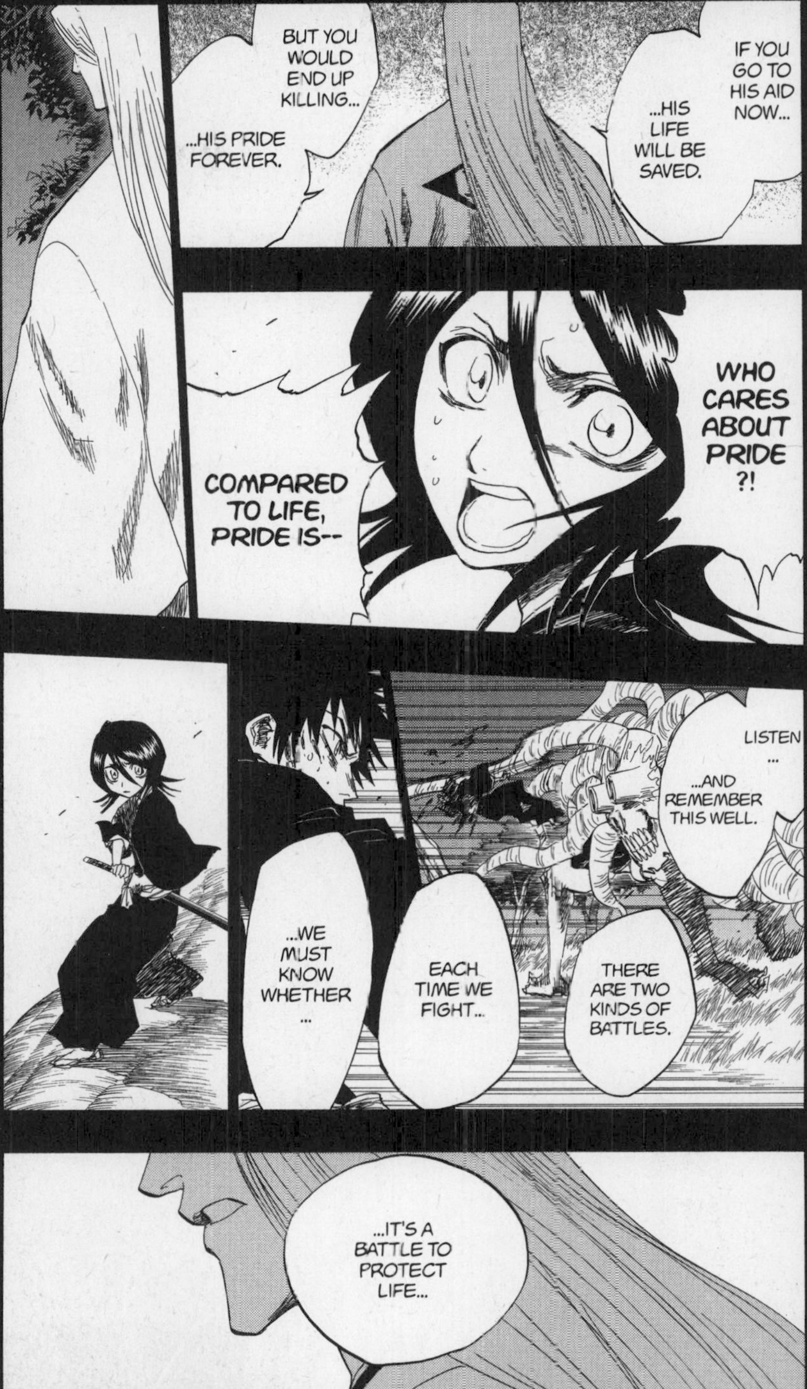
IF YOU GO TO HIS AID NOW...
...HIS LIFE WILL BE SAVED.
BUT YOU WOULD END UP KILLING...
...HIS PRIDE FOREVER.
WHO CARES ABOUT PRIDE ?!
COMPARED TO LIFE, PRIDE IS--
LISTEN ...
...AND REMEMBER THIS WELL.
THERE ARE TWO KINDS OF BATTLES.
EACH TIME WE FIGHT...
...WE MUST KNOW WHETHER ...
...IT'S A BATTLE TO PROTECT LIFE...

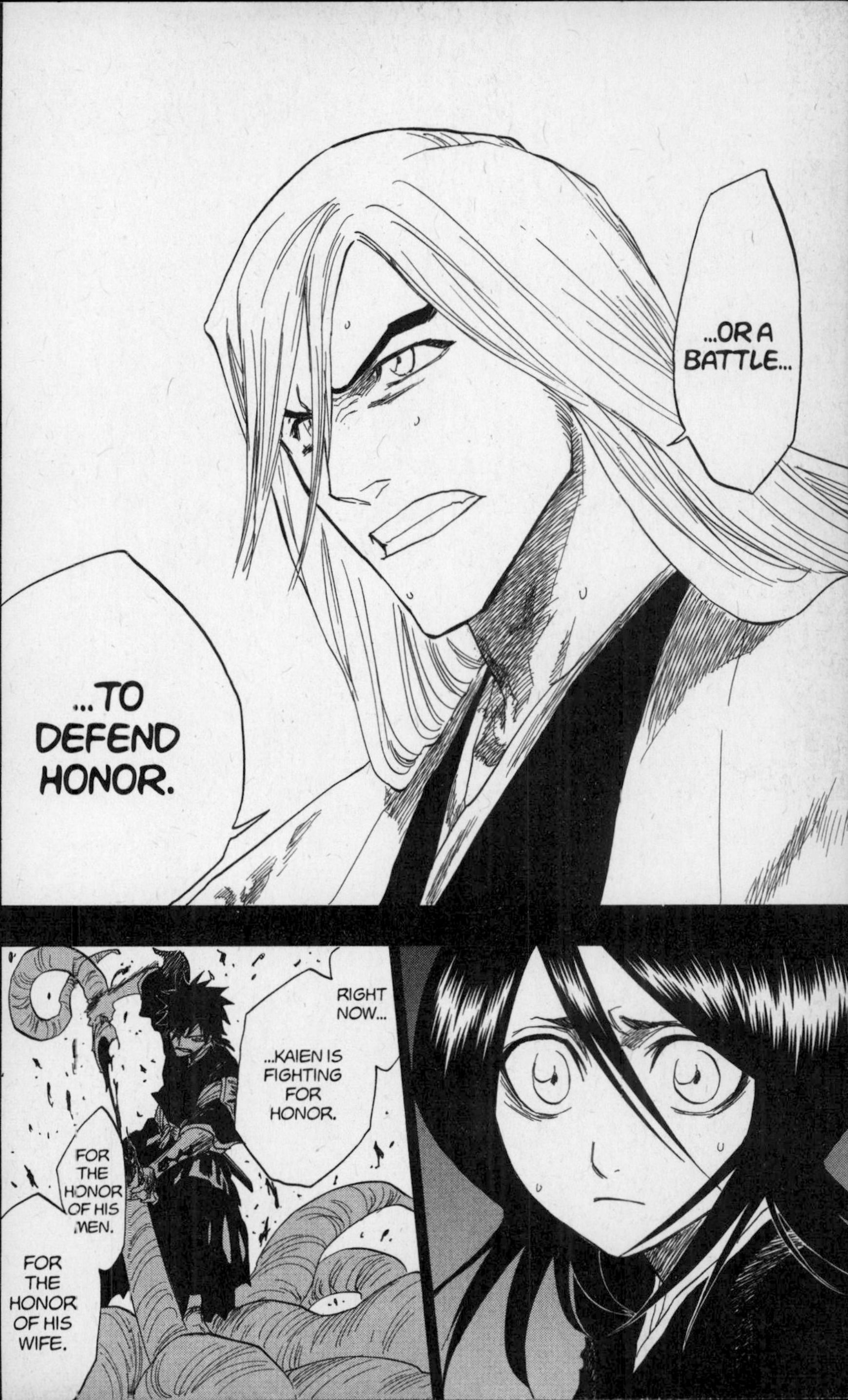
...OR A BATTLE...
...TO DEFEND HONOR.
RIGHT NOW...
...KAIEN IS FIGHTING FOR HONOR.
FOR THE HONOR OF HIS MEN.
FOR THE HONOR OF HIS WIFE.

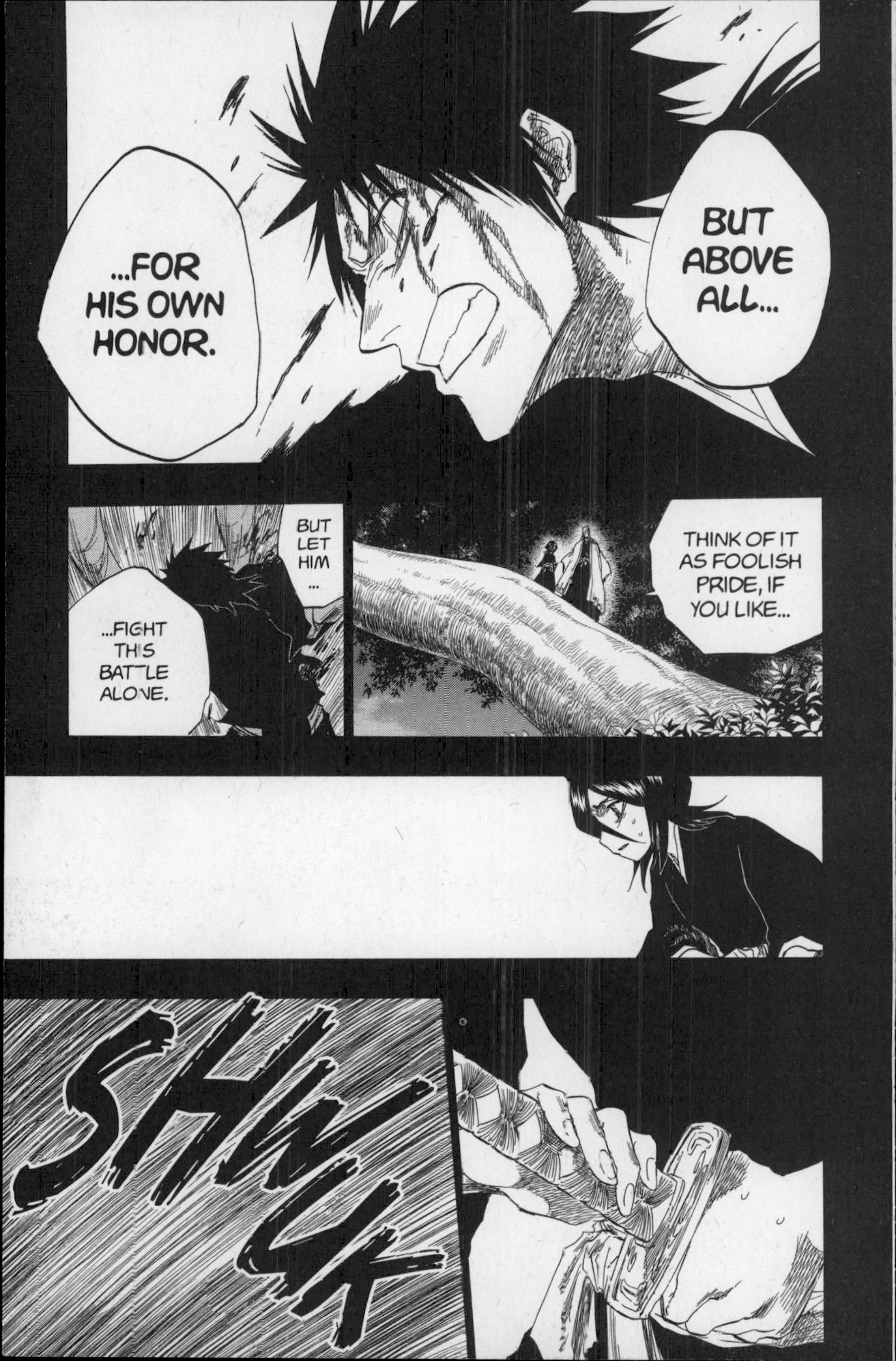
BUT ABOVE ALL...
...FOR HIS OWN HONOR.
THINK OF IT AS FOOLISH PRIDE, IF YOU LIKE...
BUT LET HIM ...
...FIGHT THIS BATTLE ALONE.
SHINK

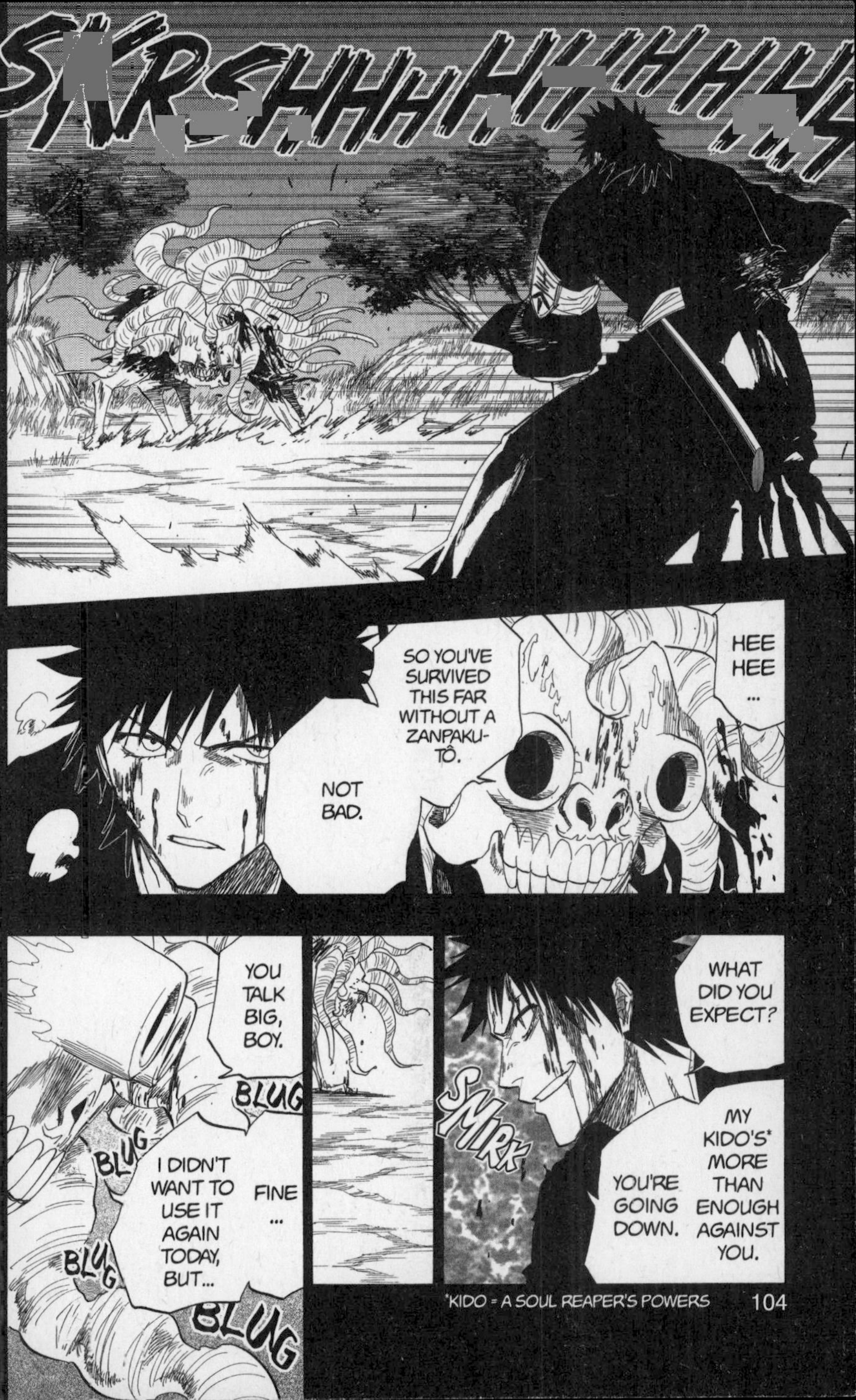
HEE HEE ...
SO YOU'VE SURVIVED THIS FAR WITHOUT A ZANPAKU-TÔ.
NOT BAD.
WHAT DID YOU EXPECT?
MY KIDO'S* MORE THAN ENOUGH AGAINST YOU.
YOU'RE GOING DOWN.
SMIRK
FINE ...
YOU TALK BIG, BOY.
BLUG
BLUG
I DIDN'T WANT TO USE IT AGAIN TODAY, BUT...
BLUG
BLUG

*KIDO = A SOUL REAPER'S POWERS

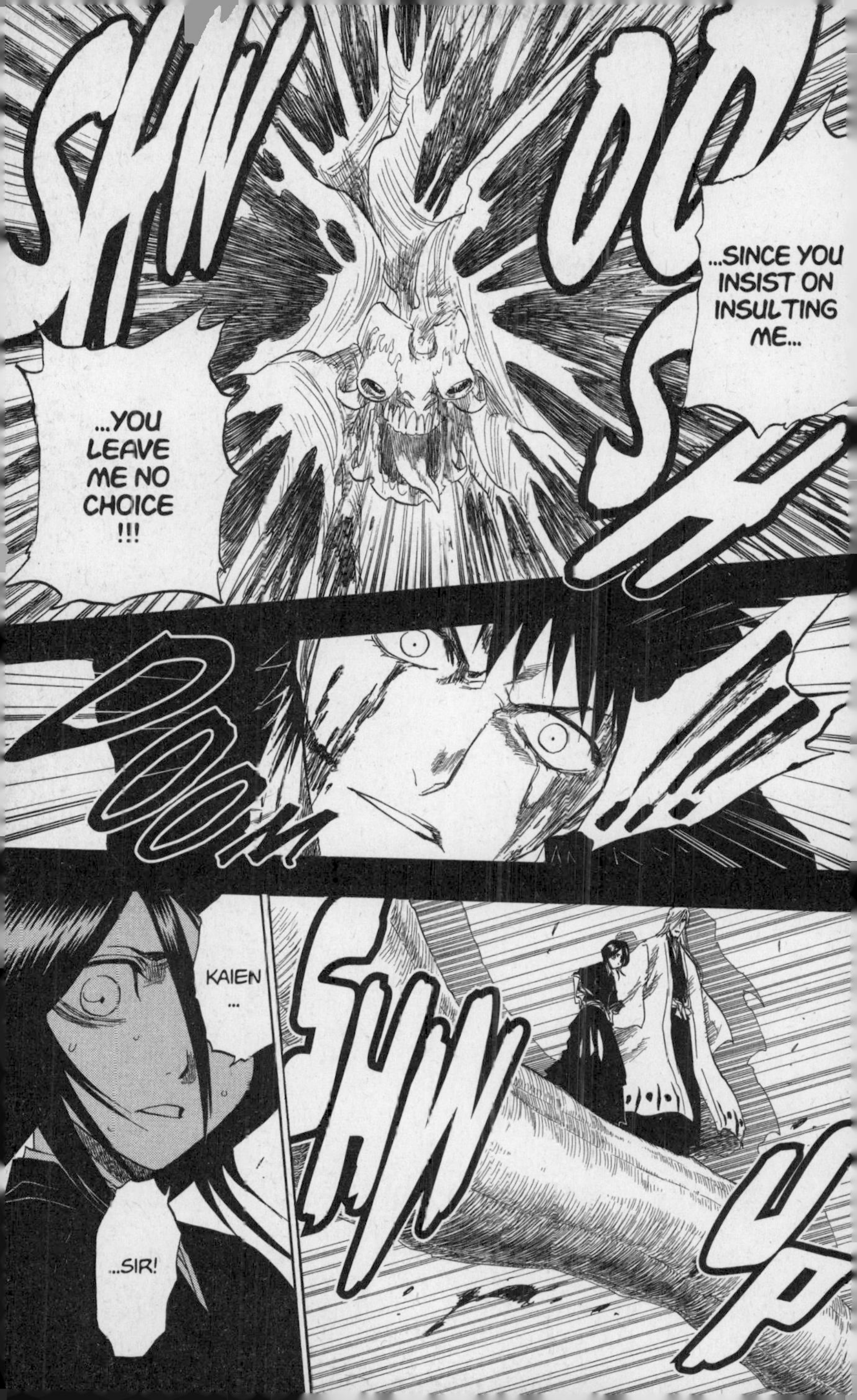
...SINCE YOU INSIST ON INSULTING ME...
...YOU LEAVE ME NO CHOICE !!!
KAIEN ...
...SIR!

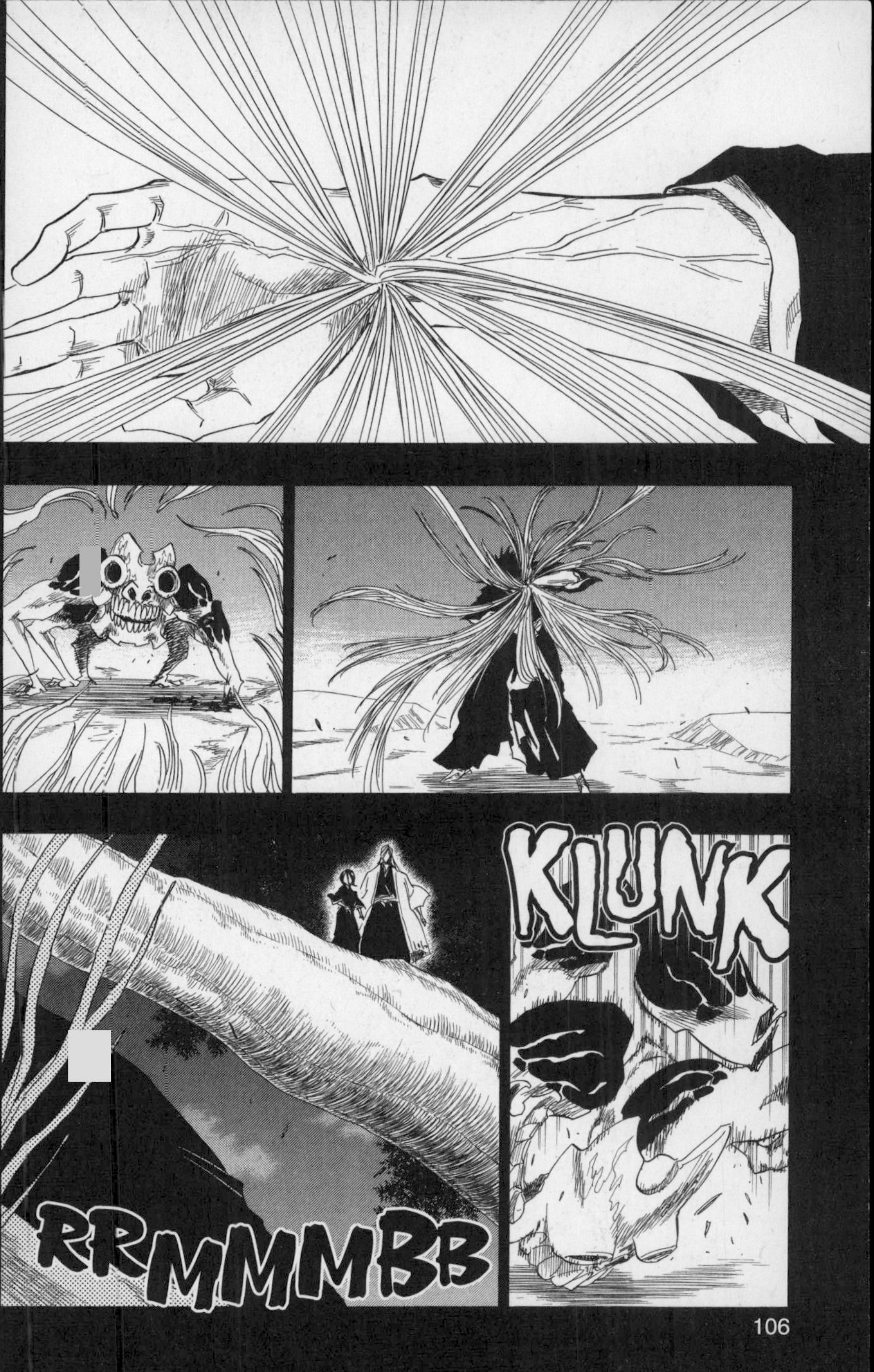
KLUNK
RRMMMBB

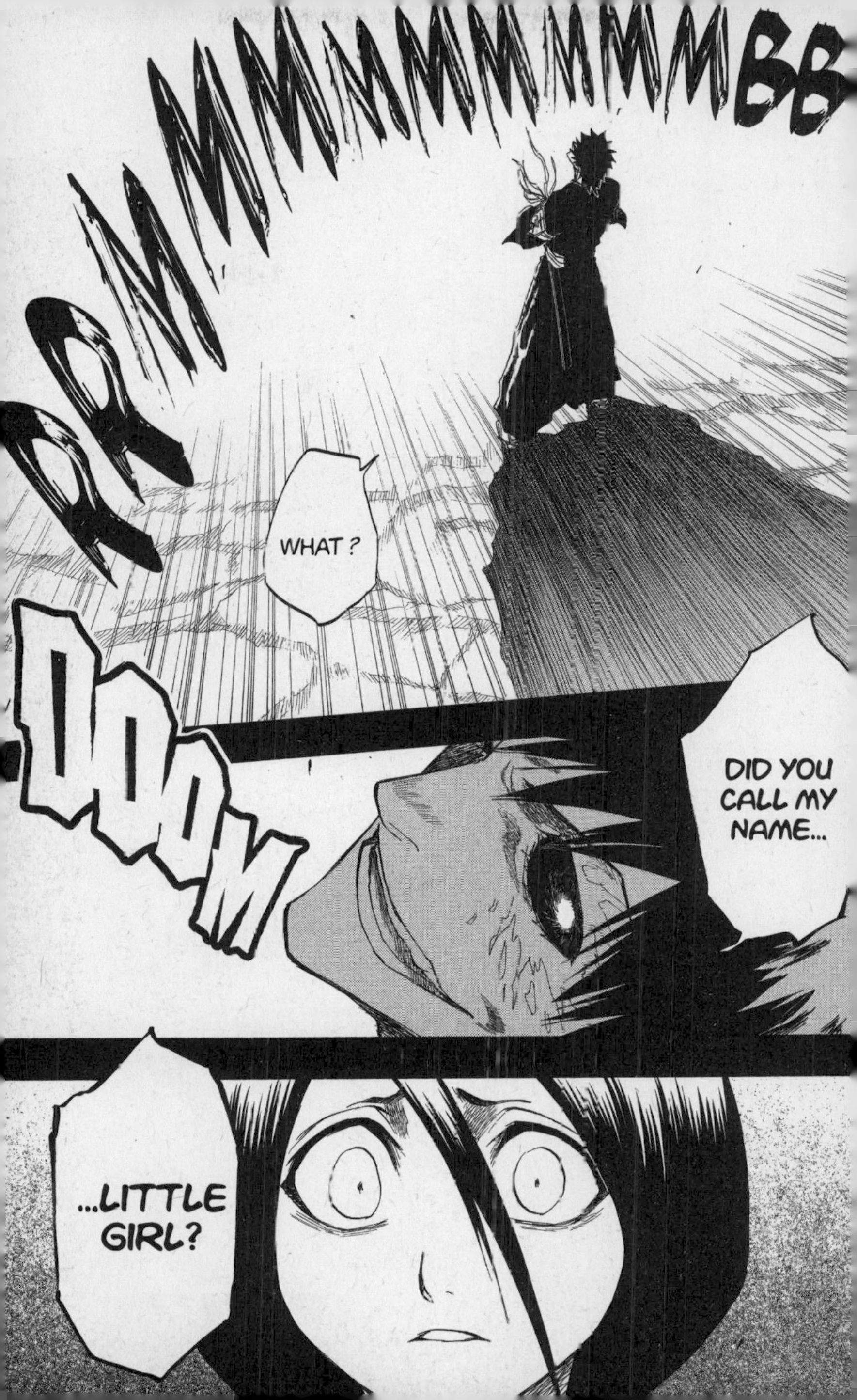
WHAT?
DOOM
DID YOU CALL MY NAME...
...LITTLE GIRL?

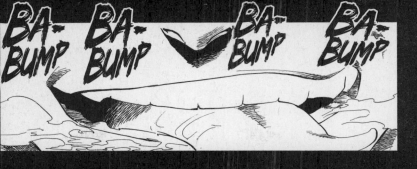

BA-BUMP BA-BUMP BA-BUMP BA-BUMP

BA-BUMP BA-BUMP BA-BUMP BA-BUMP

K...

TMP

WHY...

...DO YOU KEEP SAYING MY NAME LIKE THAT?

RRMMBB

KAIEN...

SIR...?

RRMMM BB

**136. memories in the rain 2, op.4:
Night of Wijnruit**

AM I THAT...

ARE YOU THAT WORRIED ABOUT ME, LITTLE GIRL?

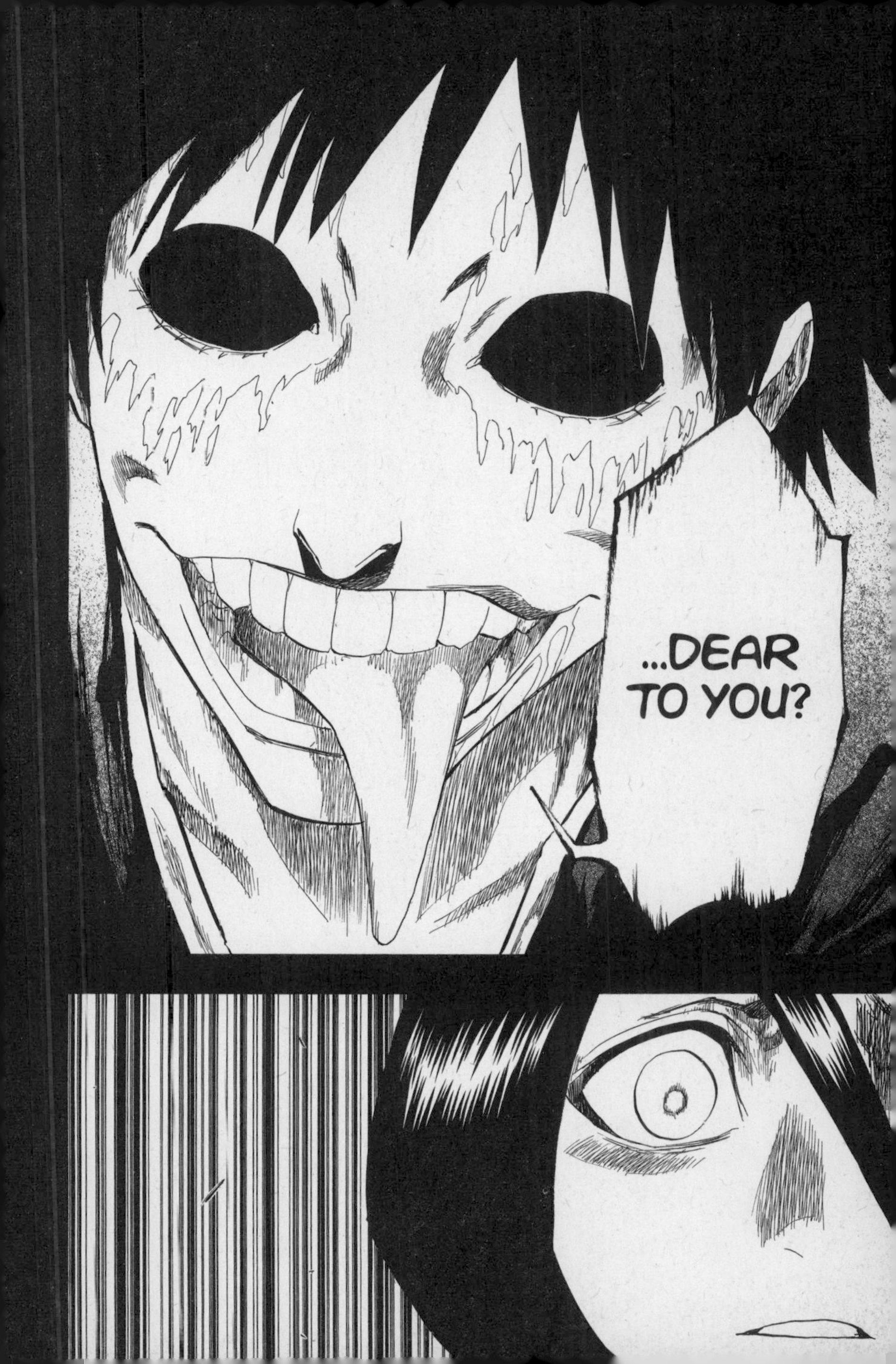
...DEAR TO YOU?

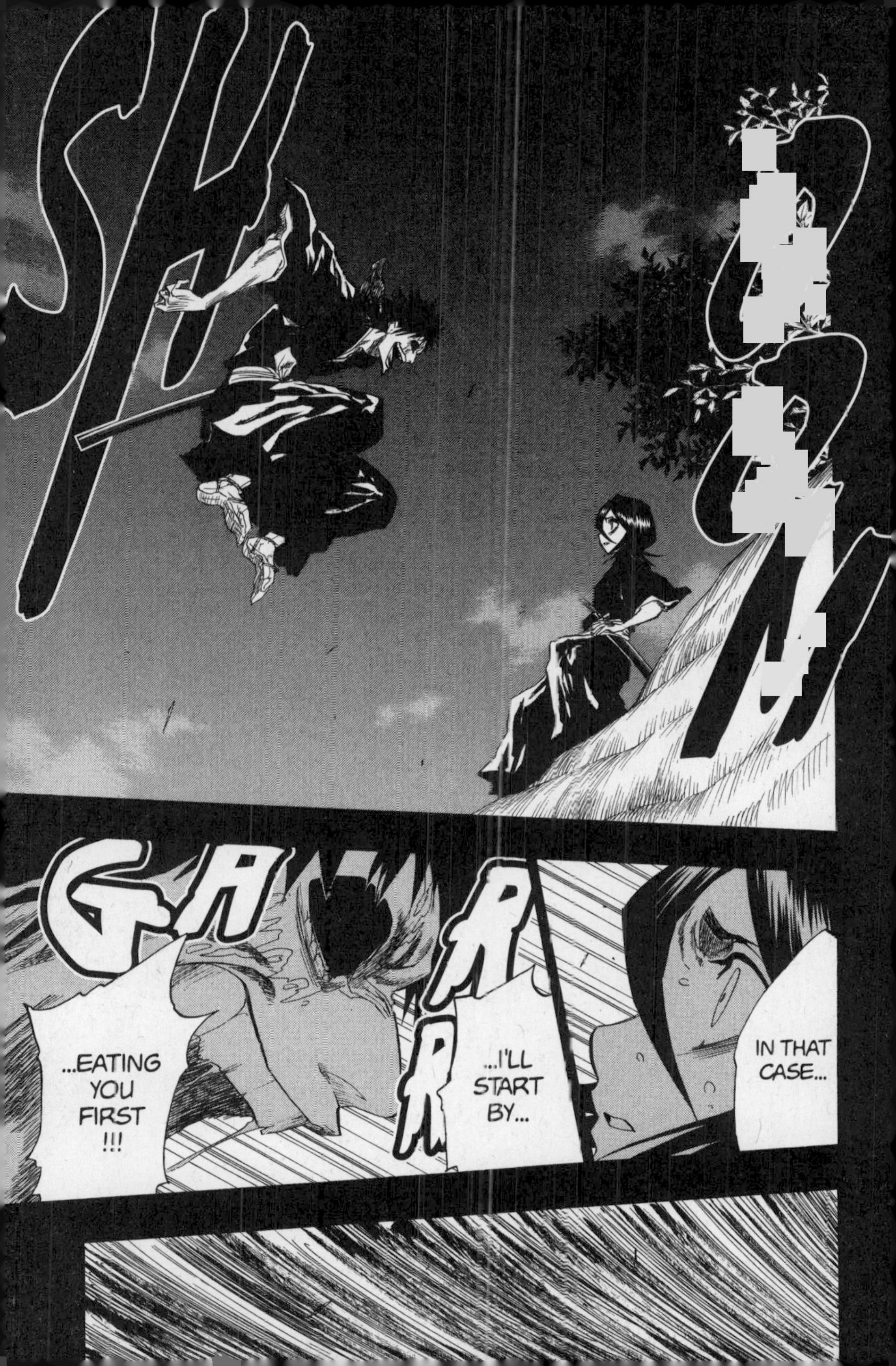
IN THAT CASE...
...I'LL START BY...
...EATING YOU FIRST !!!

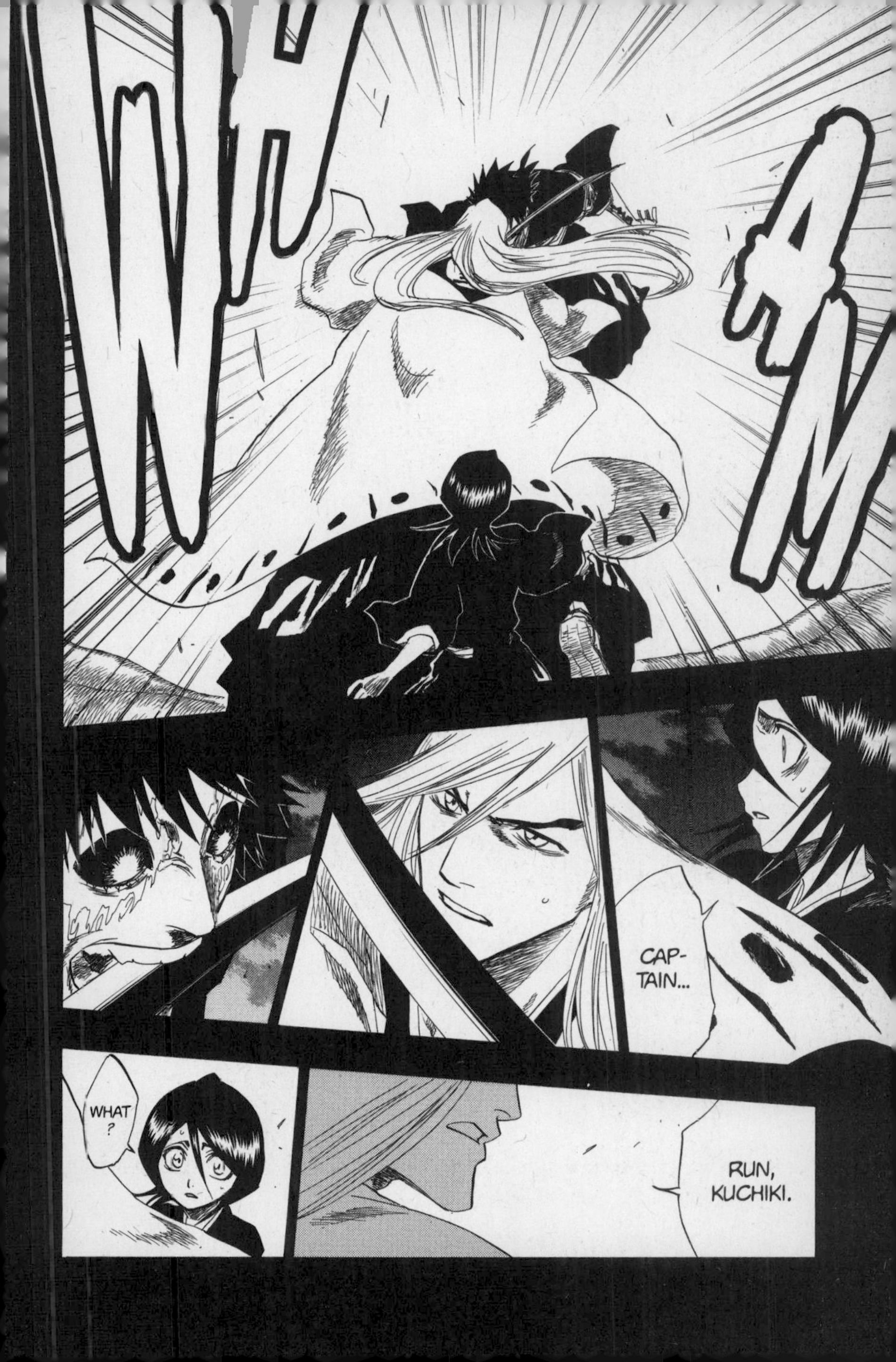
WHAM
CAP-
TAIN...
RUN,
KUCHIKI.
WHAT
?

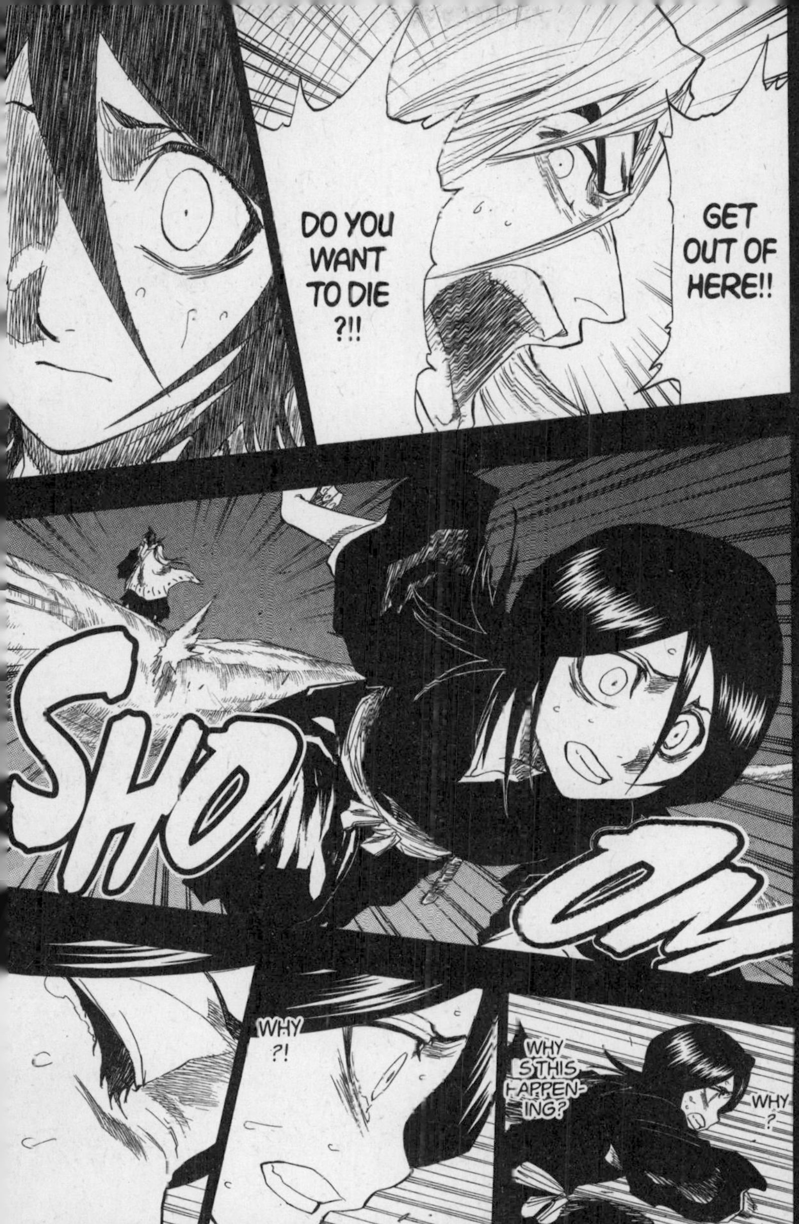
GET OUT OF HERE!!
DO YOU WANT TO DIE ?!!
SHOOM
WHY ?
WHY IS THIS HAPPENING?
WHY ?!

ASSISTANT CAPTAIN KAIEN!!

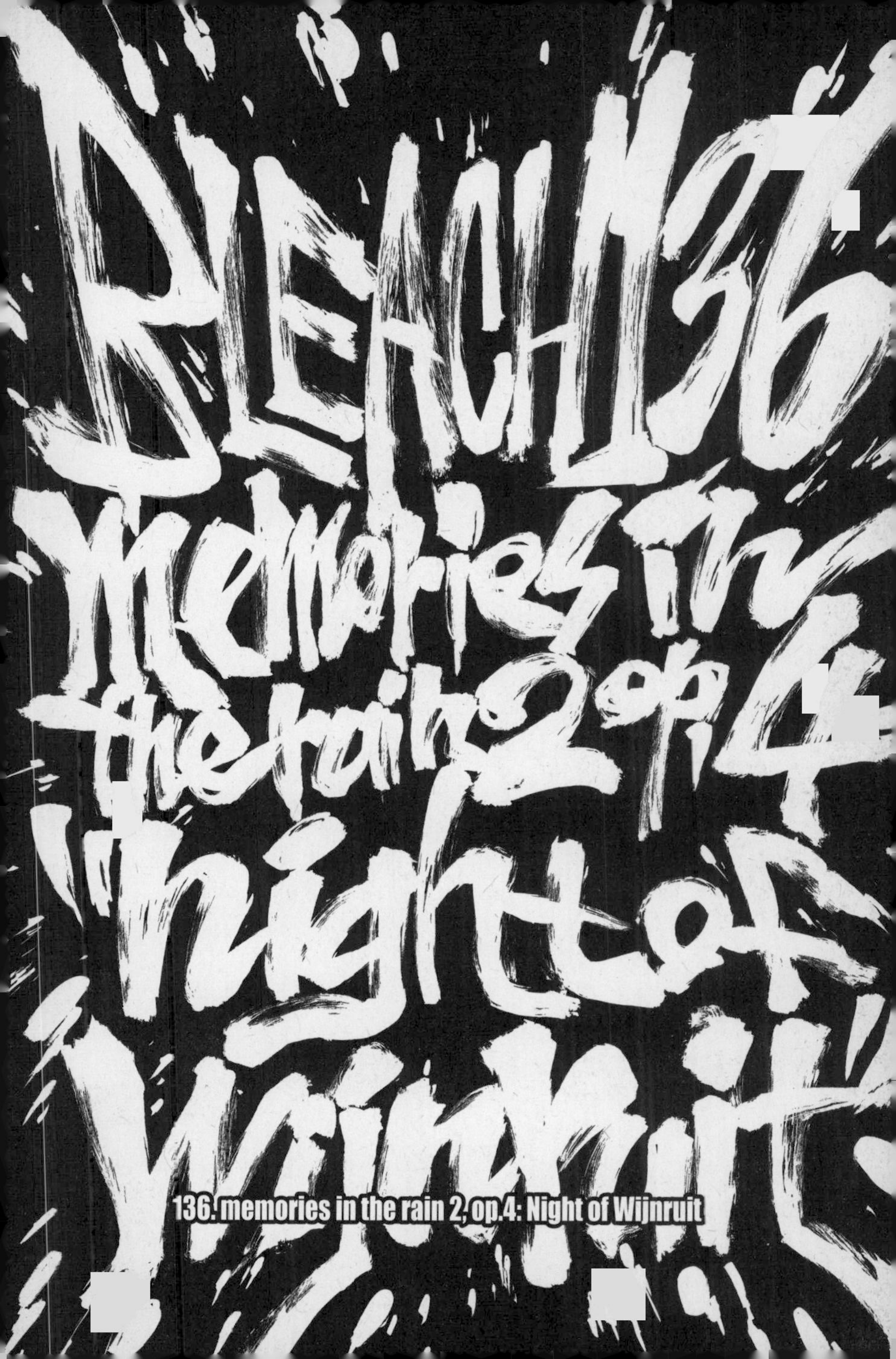
BLEACH 136
memories in the rain 2 op.4
Night of Wijnruit

136. memories in the rain 2, op.4: Night of Wijnruit

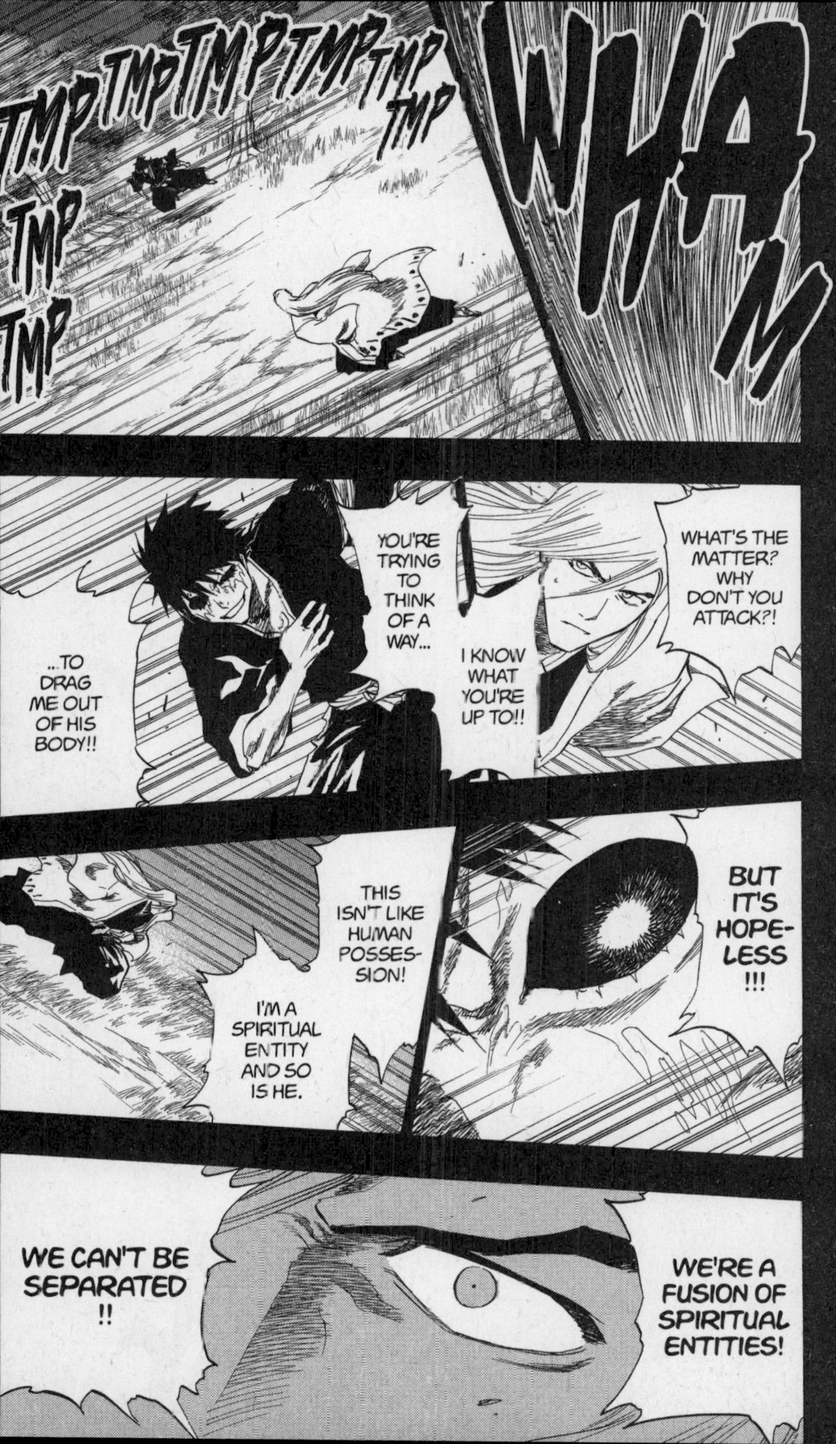
WHAM
TMP TMP TMP TMP TMP
TMP
TMP
TMP
TMP
WHAT'S THE MATTER? WHY DON'T YOU ATTACK?!
YOU'RE TRYING TO THINK OF A WAY...
I KNOW WHAT YOU'RE UP TO!!
...TO DRAG ME OUT OF HIS BODY!!
BUT IT'S HOPELESS!!!
THIS ISN'T LIKE HUMAN POSSESSION!
I'M A SPIRITUAL ENTITY AND SO IS HE.
WE'RE A FUSION OF SPIRITUAL ENTITIES!
WE CAN'T BE SEPARATED!!

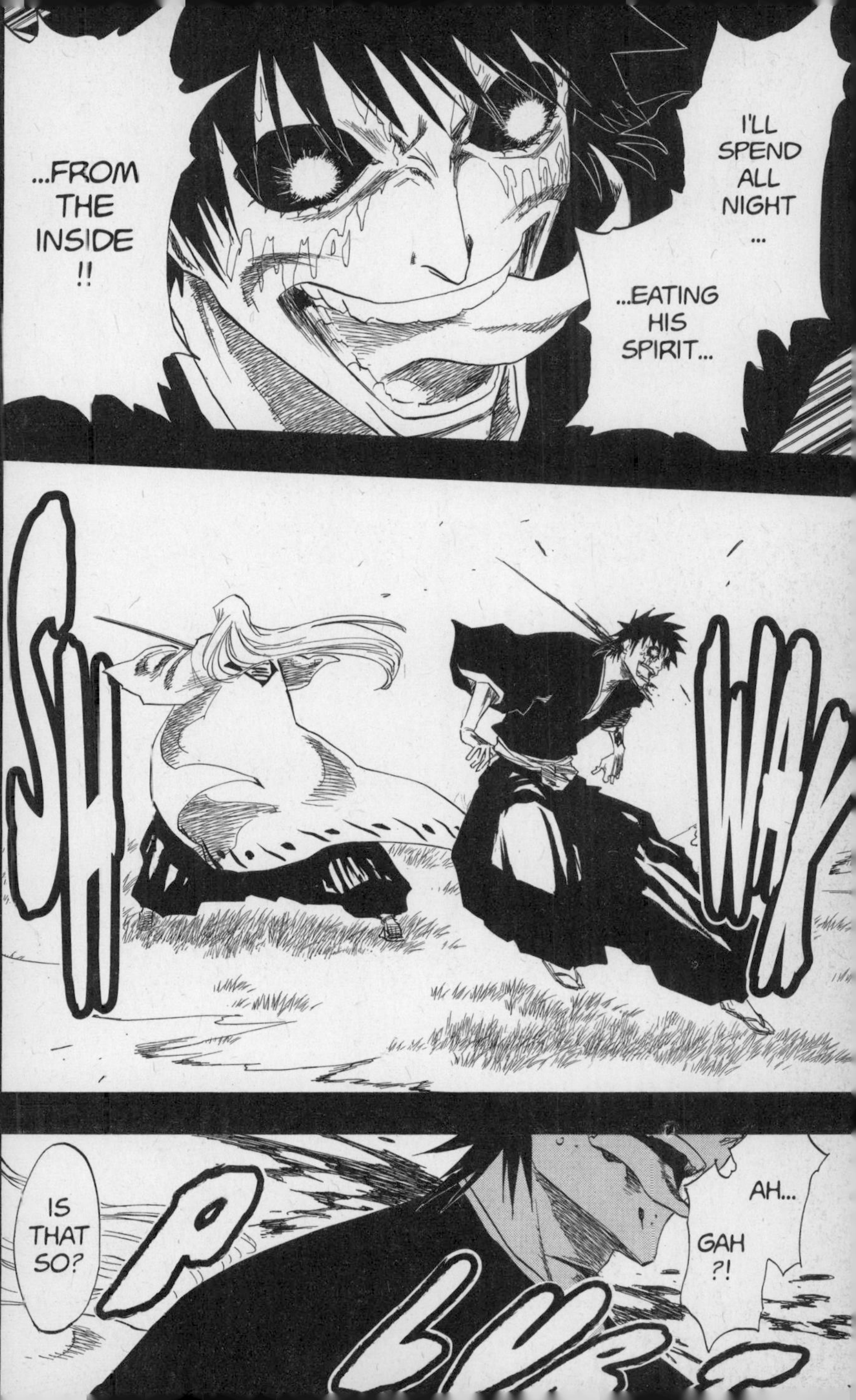
I'LL SPEND ALL NIGHT ...
...EATING HIS SPIRIT...
...FROM THE INSIDE !!
SHWAK
AH...
GAH ?!
IS THAT SO?

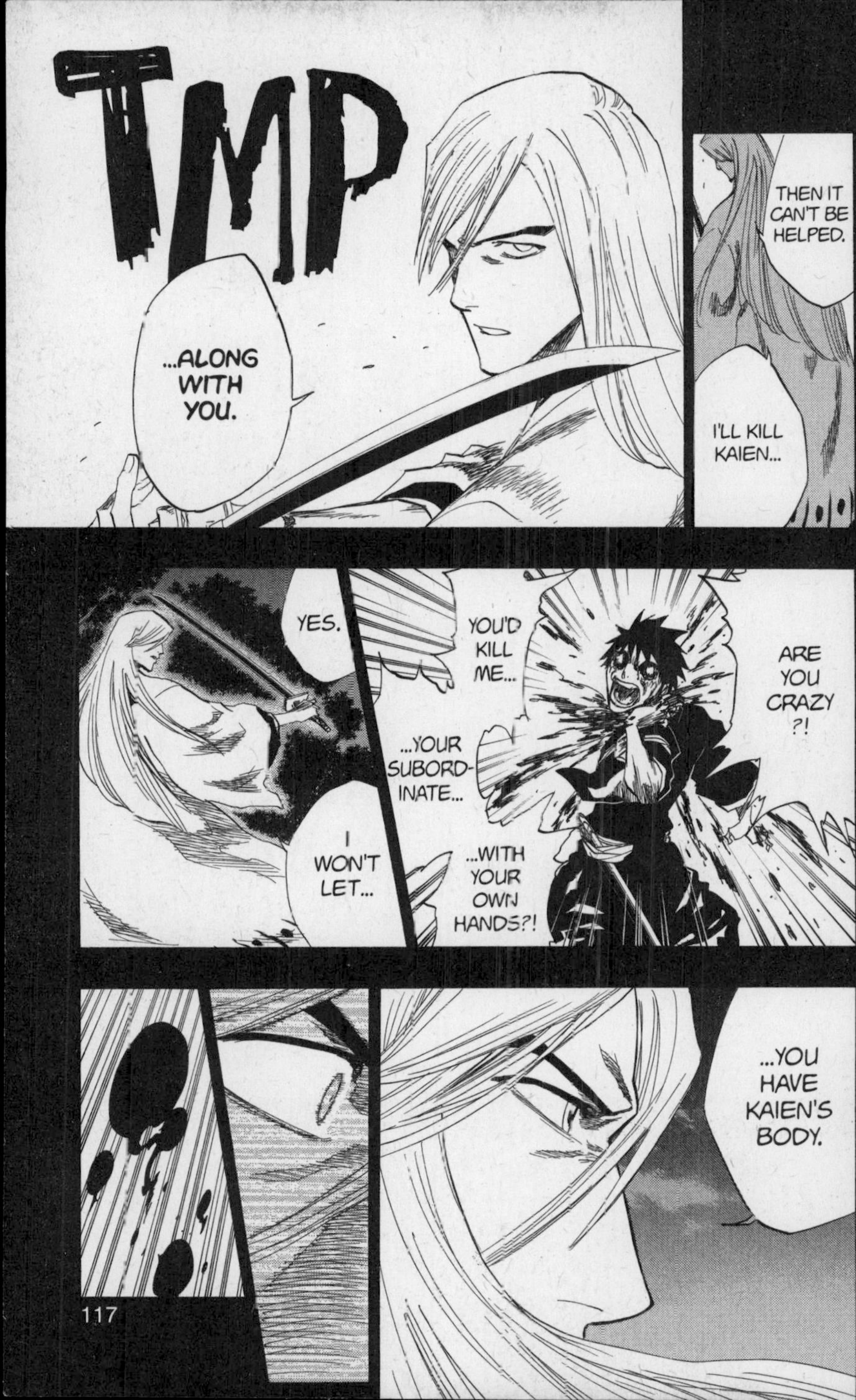
THEN IT CAN'T BE HELPED.
I'LL KILL KAIEN...
TMP
...ALONG WITH YOU.
ARE YOU CRAZY?!
YOU'D KILL ME...
...YOUR SUBORDINATE...
...WITH YOUR OWN HANDS?!
YES.
I WON'T LET...
...YOU HAVE KAIEN'S BODY.

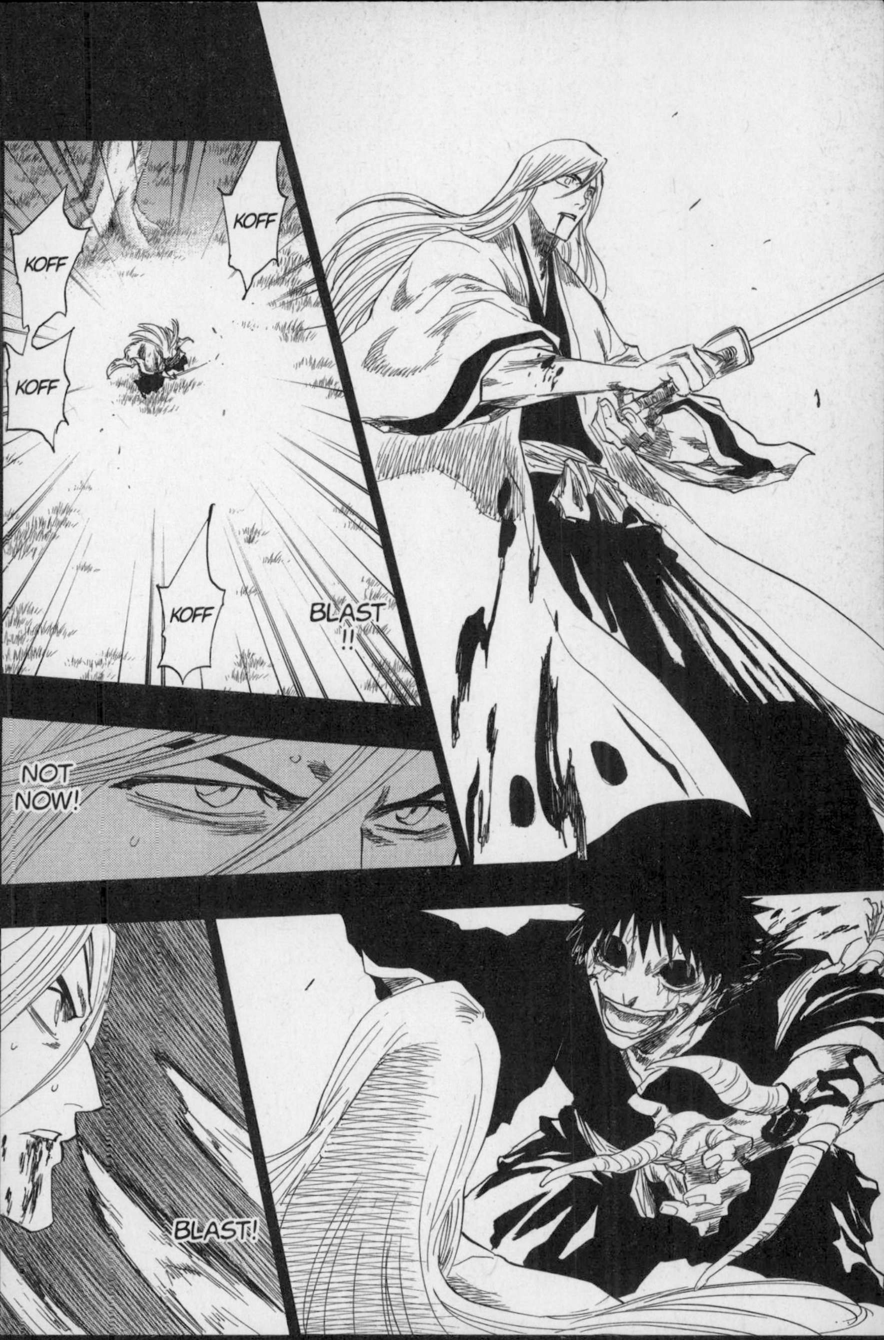
KOFF
KOFF
KOFF
BLAST !!
KOFF
NOT NOW!
BLAST!

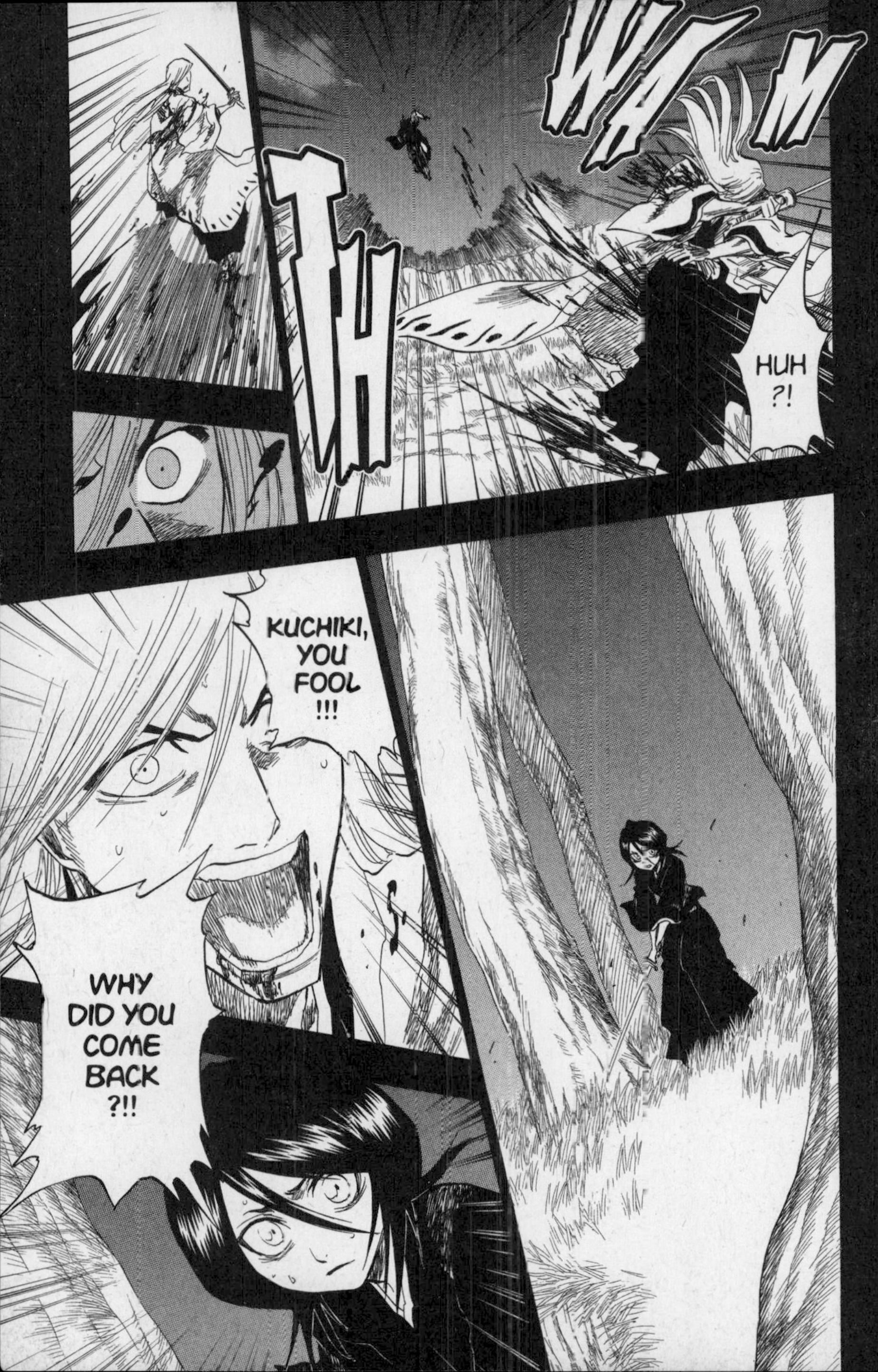
HUH ?!
KUCHIKI, YOU FOOL !!!
WHY DID YOU COME BACK ?!!

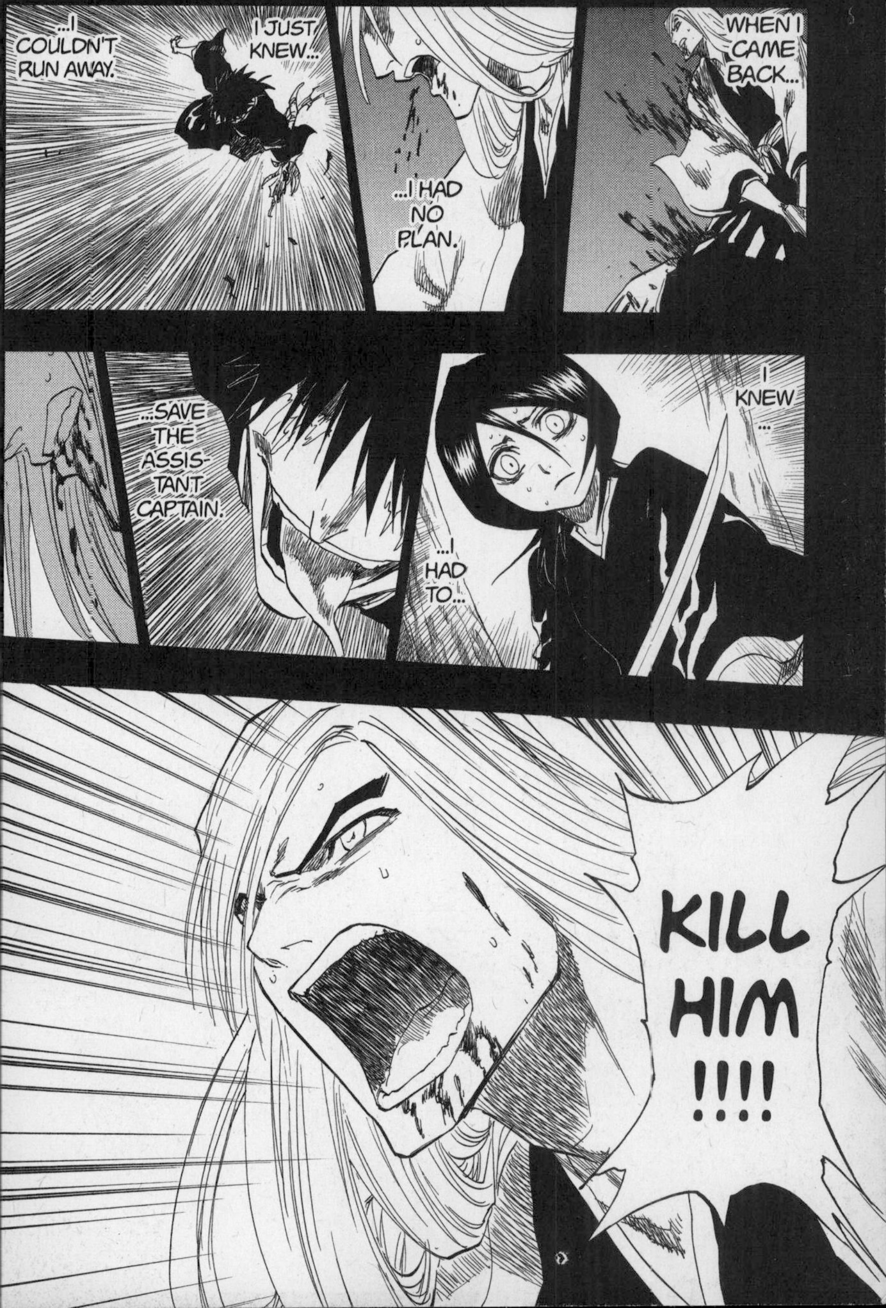
WHEN I CAME BACK...
...I HAD NO PLAN.
I JUST KNEW...
...I COULDN'T RUN AWAY.
I KNEW ...
...I HAD TO...
...SAVE THE ASSIS-TANT CAPTAIN.
KILL HIM !!!!

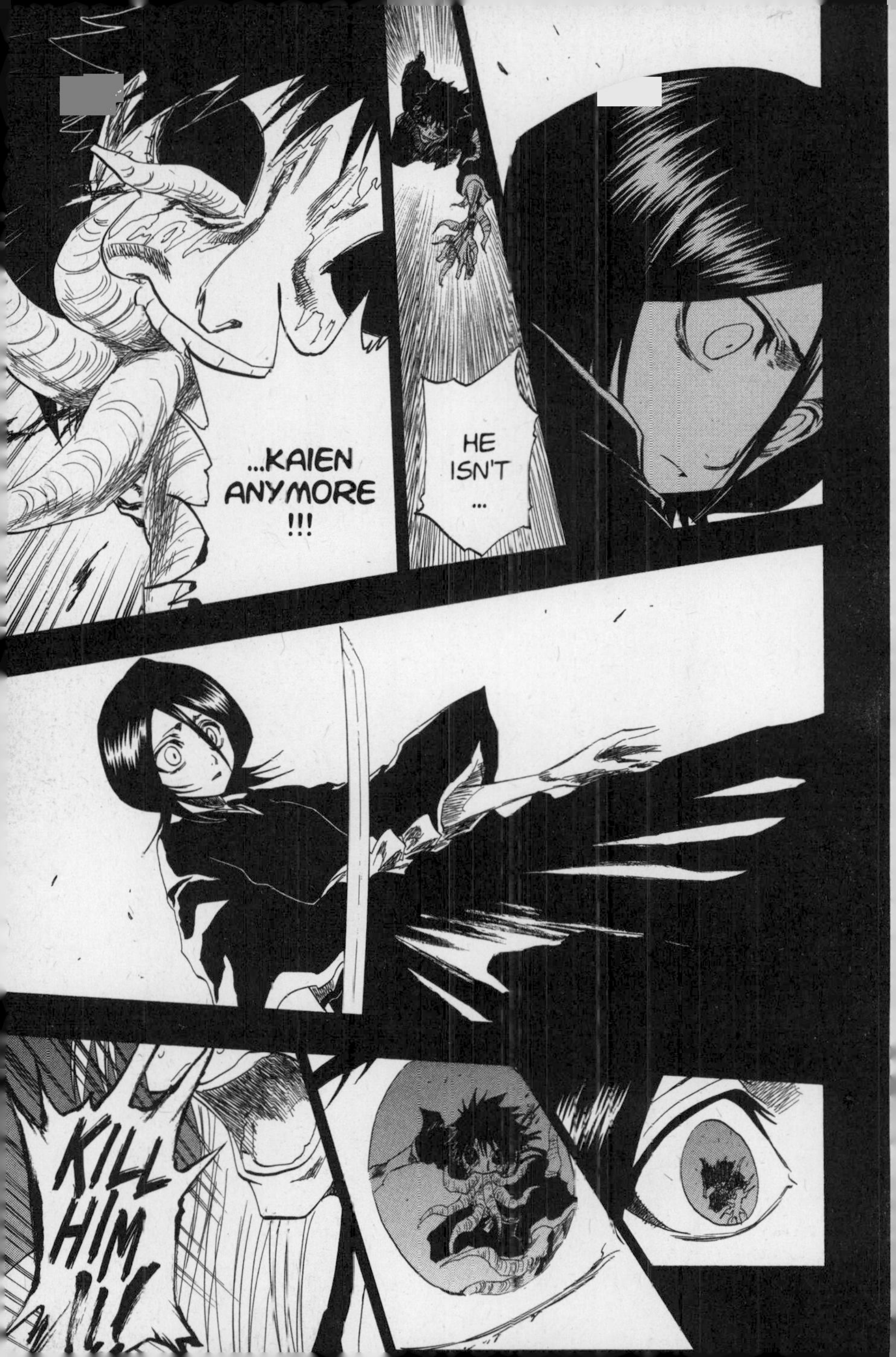
HE ISN'T ...
...KAIEN ANYMORE !!!
KILL HIM !!

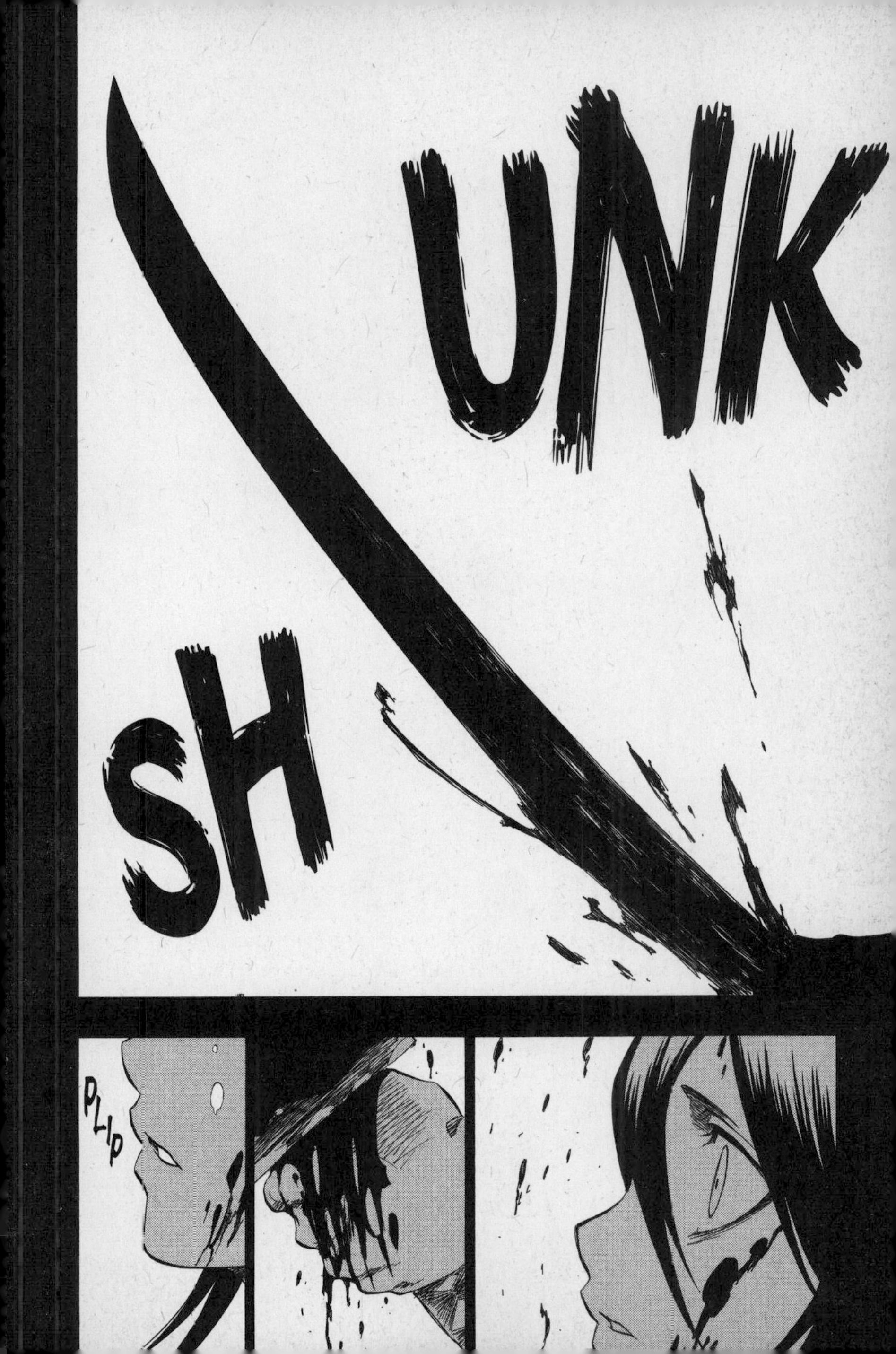
SH
UNK
PLIP

« READ THIS WAY «

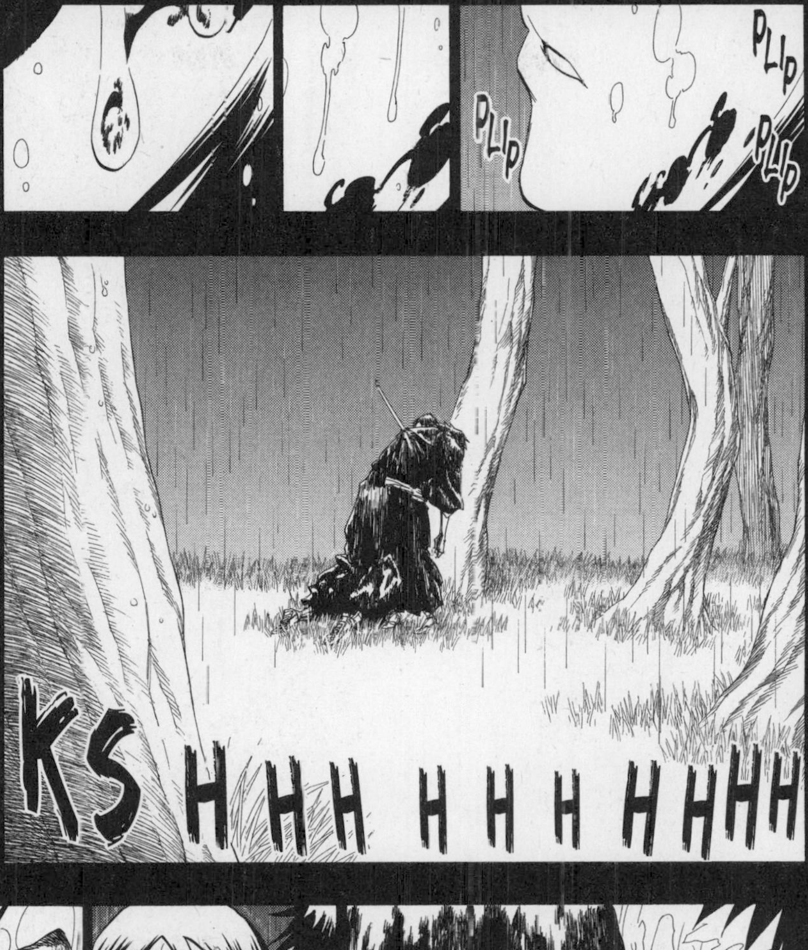
PLIP
PLIP
PLIP
KSHHHHHHHHHH
PLIP...
PLIP...
PLIP...
...
CAPTAIN...

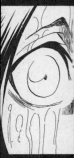

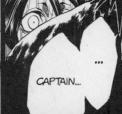

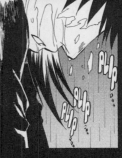

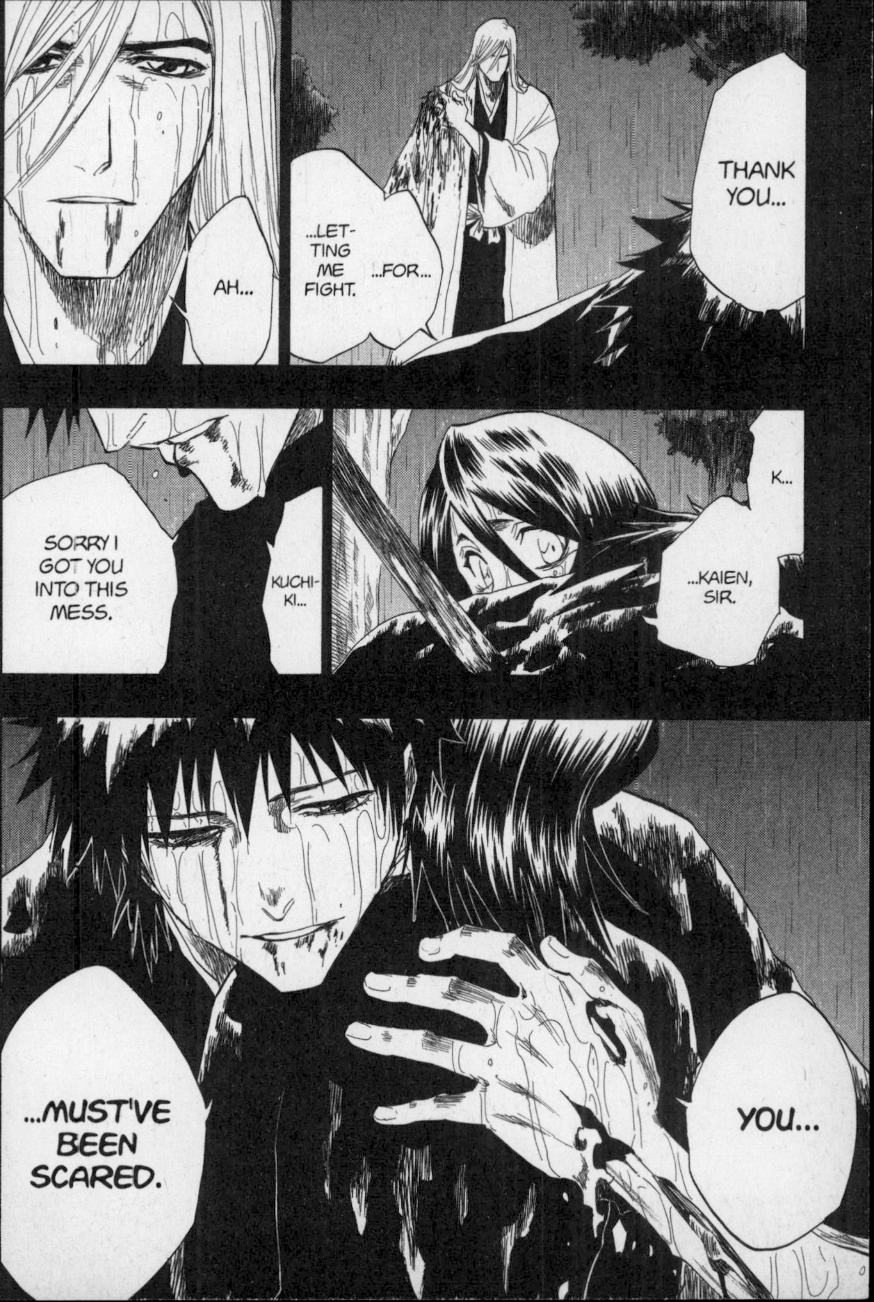
THANK YOU...
...FOR...
...LETTING ME FIGHT.
AH...
K...
...KAIEN, SIR.
KUCHIKI...
SORRY I GOT YOU INTO THIS MESS.
YOU...
...MUST'VE BEEN SCARED.

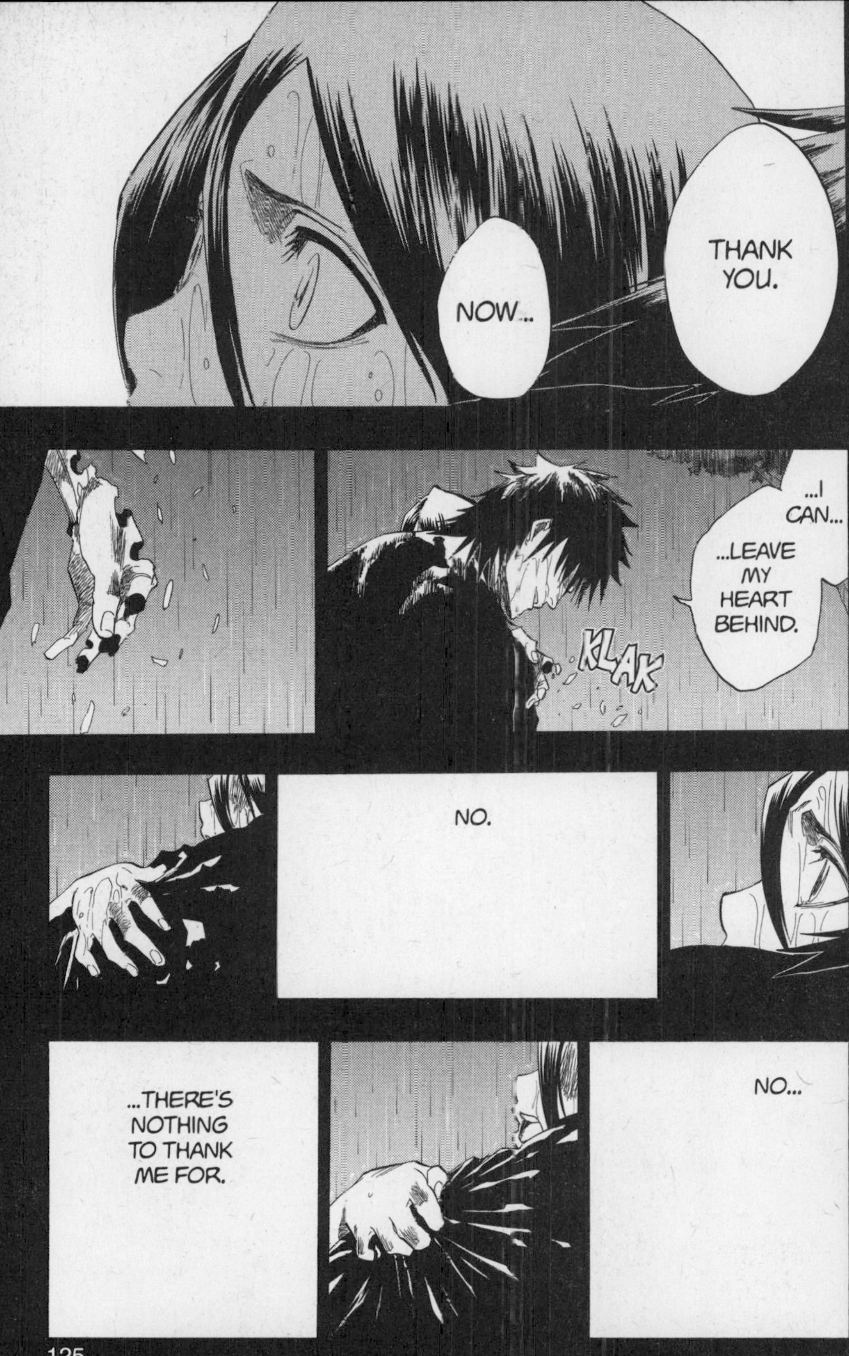
THANK YOU.
NOW...
...I CAN...
...LEAVE MY HEART BEHIND.
KLAK
NO.
NO...
...THERE'S NOTHING TO THANK ME FOR.

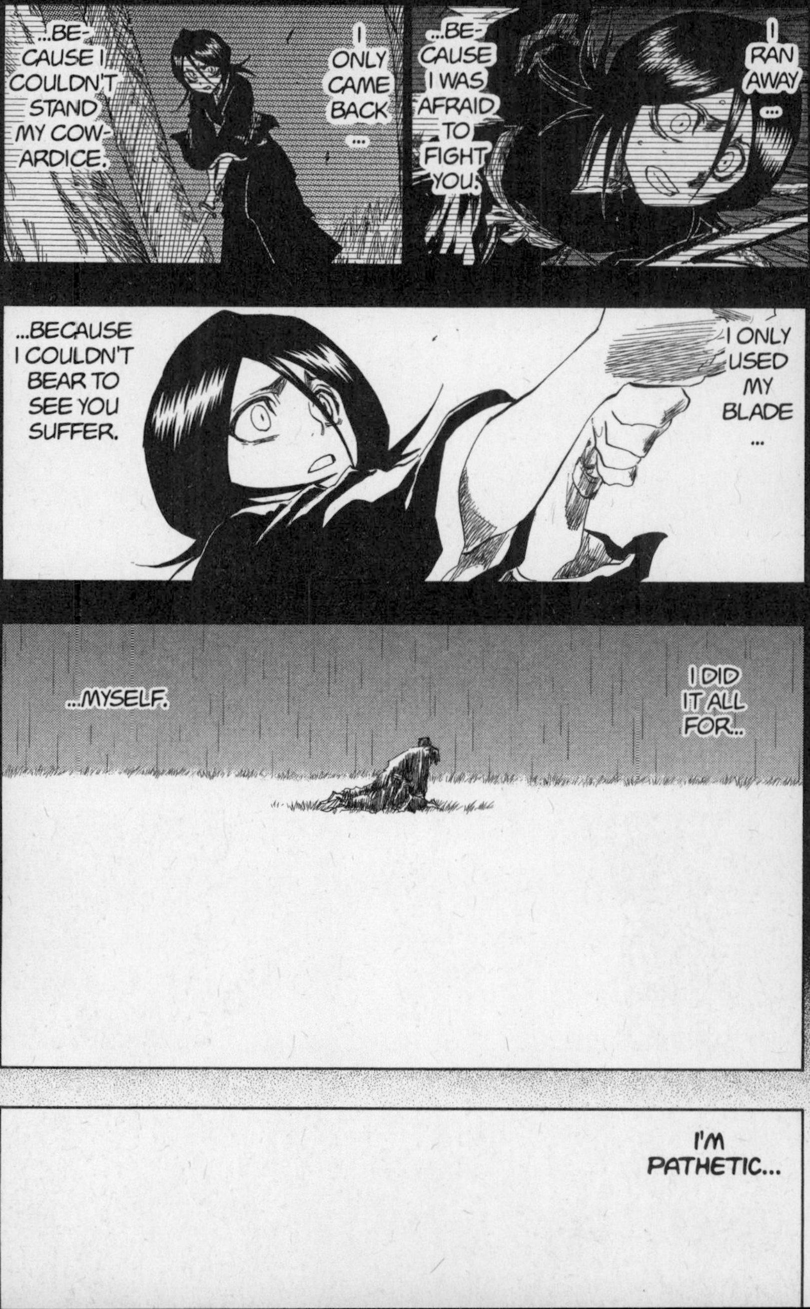
I RAN AWAY ...
...BE-CAUSE I WAS AFRAID TO FIGHT YOU.
I ONLY CAME BACK ...
...BE-CAUSE I COULDN'T STAND MY COW-ARDICE.
I ONLY USED MY BLADE ...
...BECAUSE I COULDN'T BEAR TO SEE YOU SUFFER.
I DID IT ALL FOR...
...MYSELF.
I'M PATHETIC...

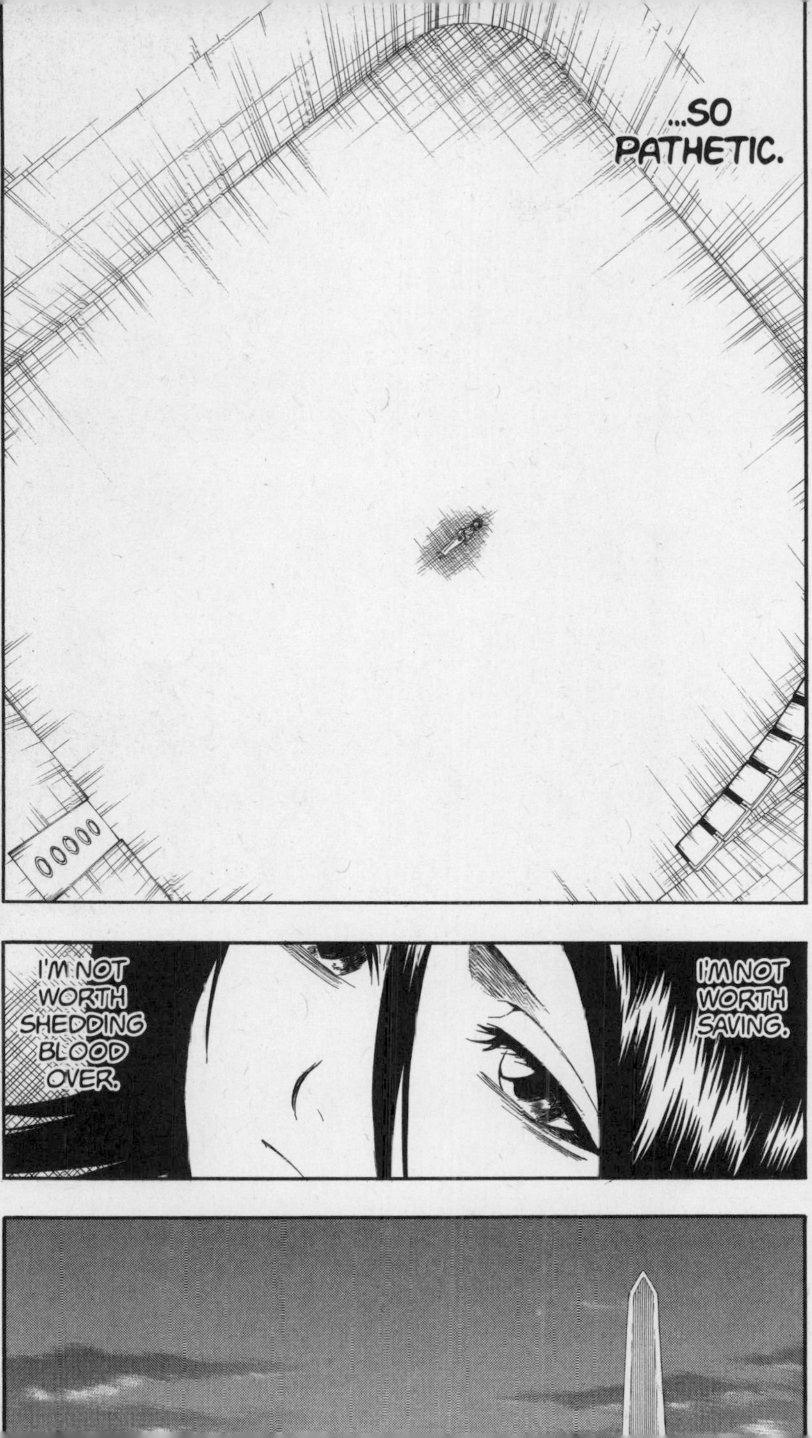
...SO PATHETIC.
I'M NOT WORTH SAVING.
I'M NOT WORTH SHEDDING BLOOD OVER.

137. Surrounding Clutch

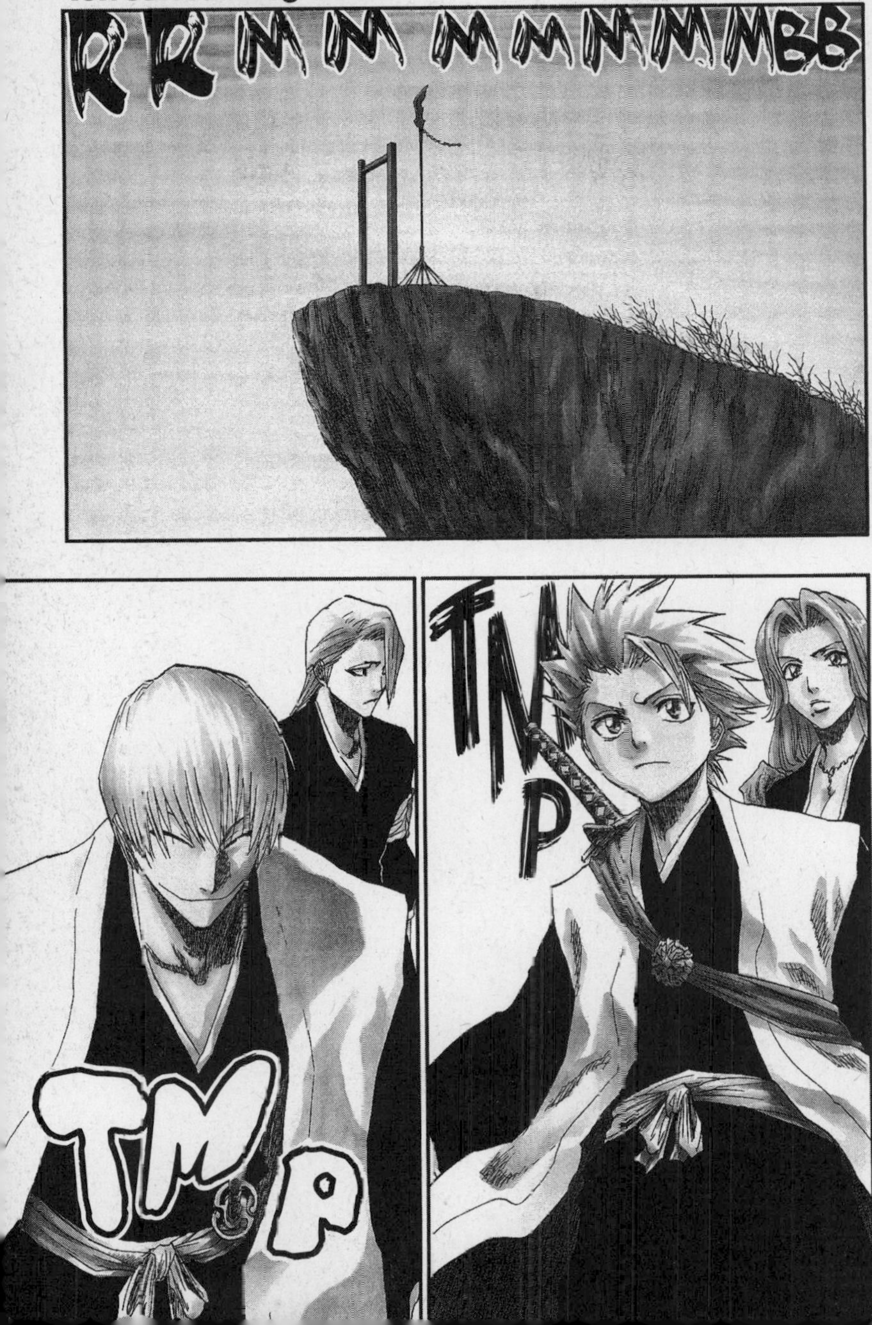
RRMMMMMMMMBB
TMP
TMP

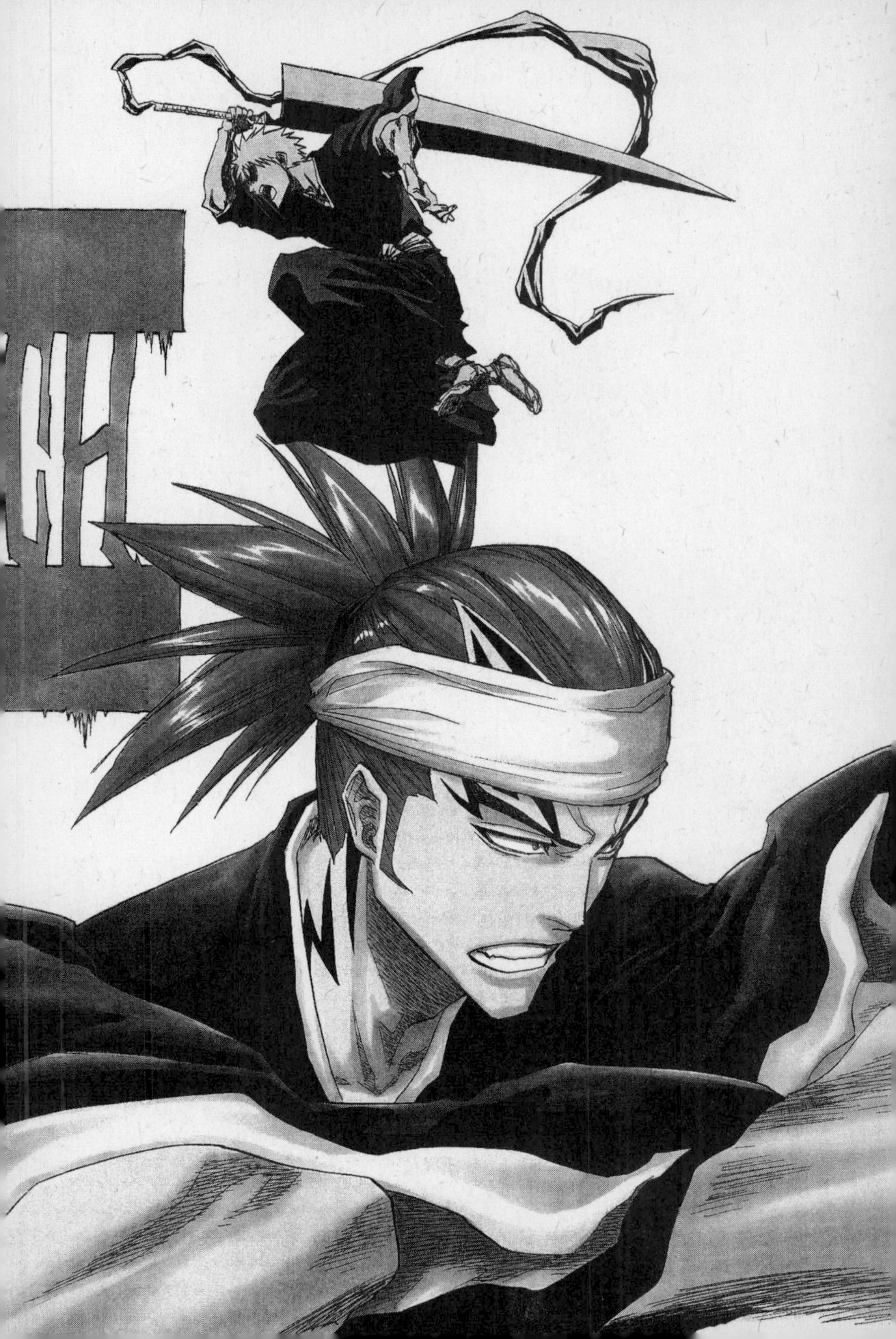

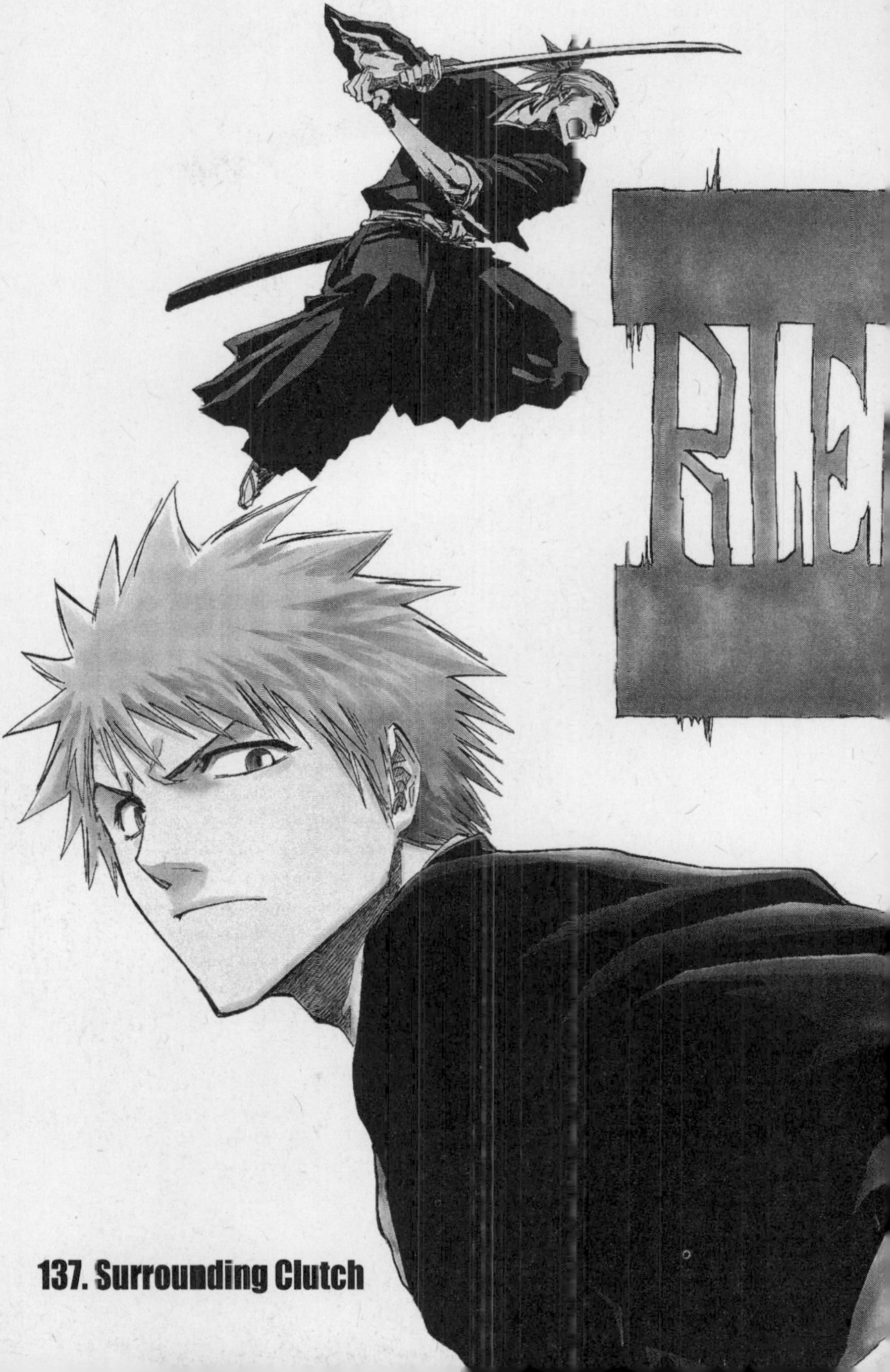

137. Surrounding Clutch

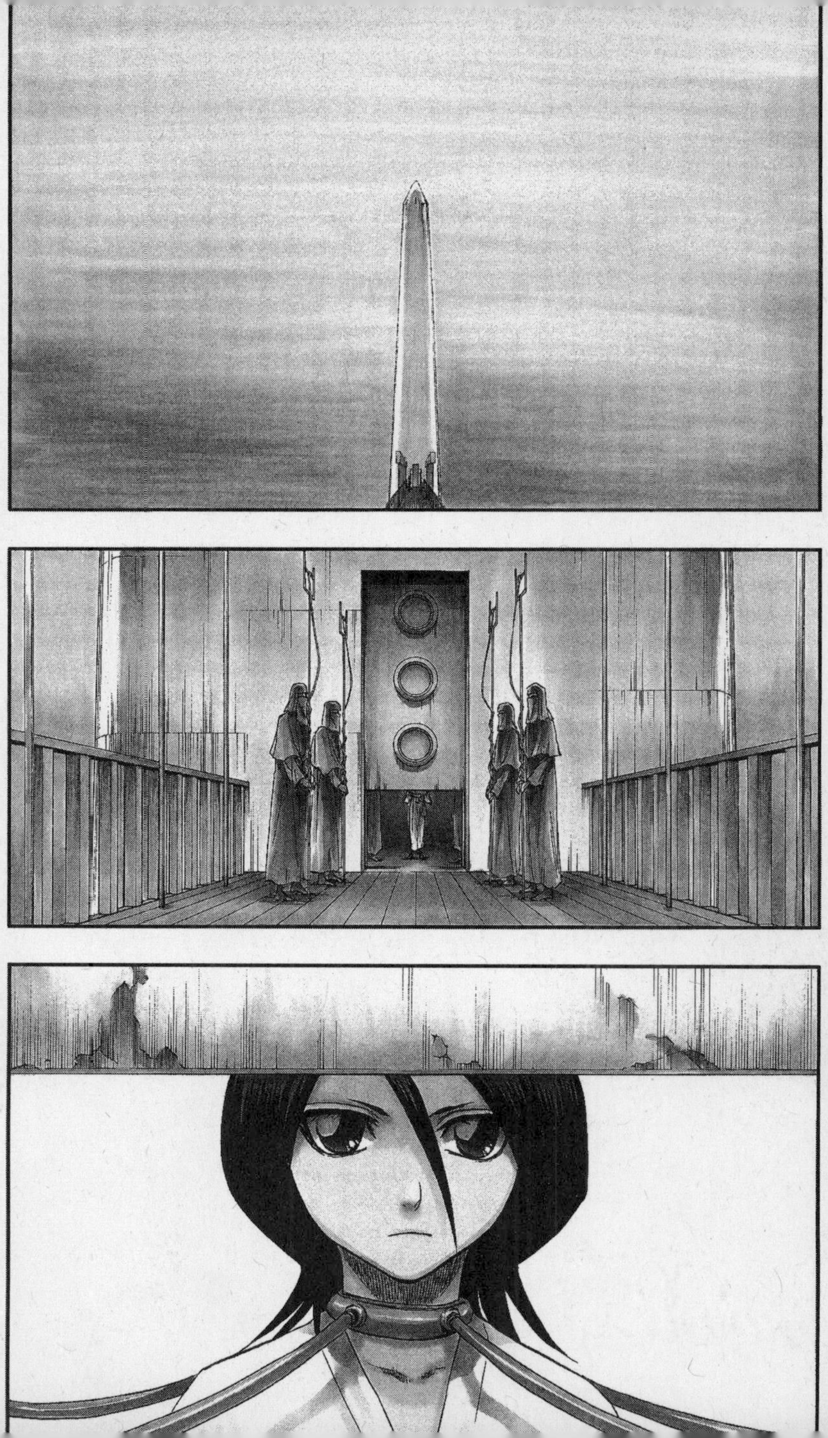

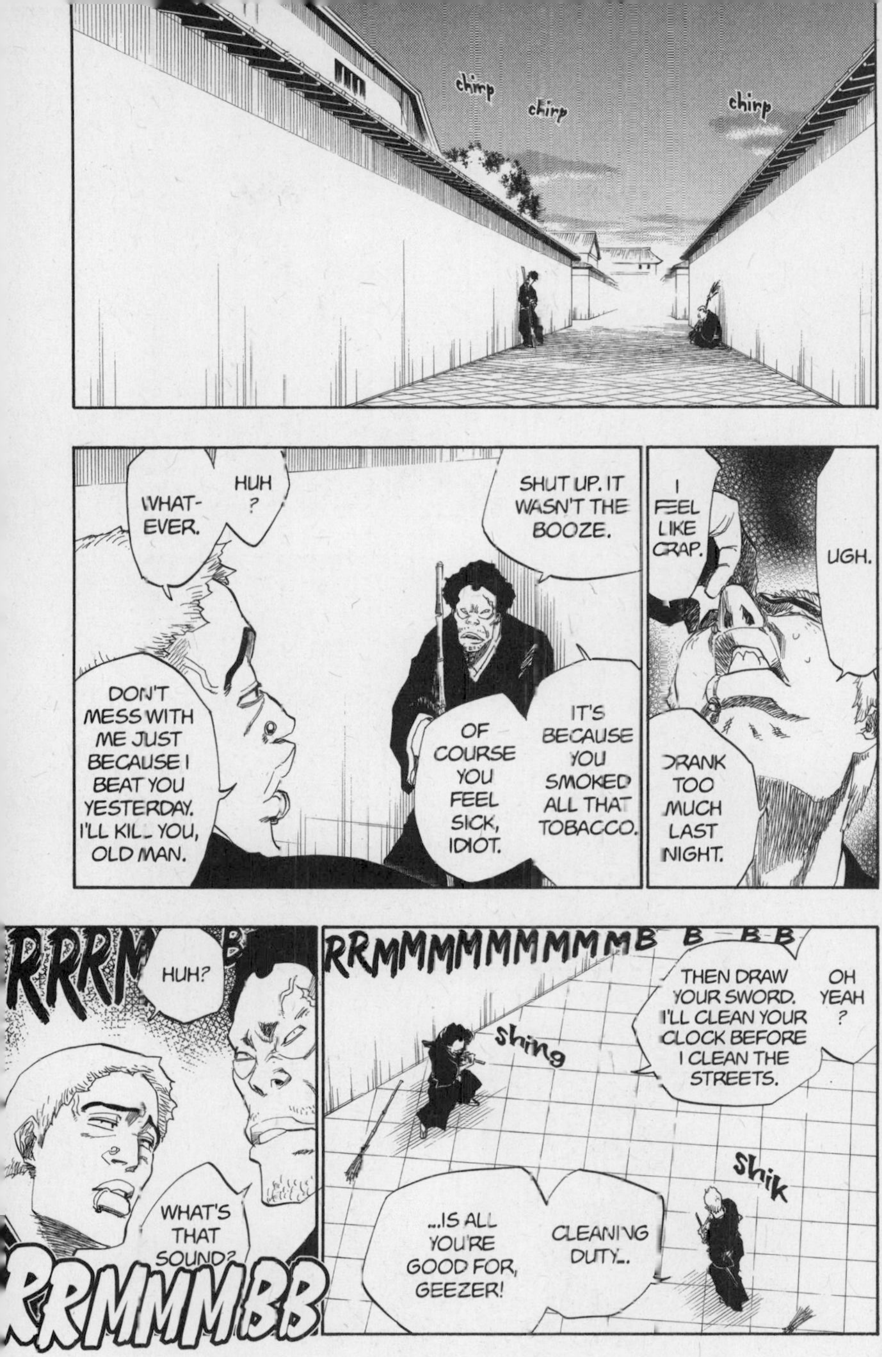
chirp
chirp
chirp
UGH.
I FEEL LIKE CRAP.
DRANK TOO MUCH LAST NIGHT.
SHUT UP. IT WASN'T THE BOOZE.
IT'S BECAUSE YOU SMOKED ALL THAT TOBACCO.
OF COURSE YOU FEEL SICK, IDIOT.
HUH?
WHAT-EVER.
DON'T MESS WITH ME JUST BECAUSE I BEAT YOU YESTERDAY. I'LL KILL YOU, OLD MAN.
RRMMMMMMMMMB B B-B
OH YEAH?
THEN DRAW YOUR SWORD. I'LL CLEAN YOUR CLOCK BEFORE I CLEAN THE STREETS.
Shing
Shik
CLEANING DUTY...
...IS ALL YOU'RE GOOD FOR, GEEZER!
RRRM
B
HUH?
WHAT'S THAT SOUND?
RRMMMBB

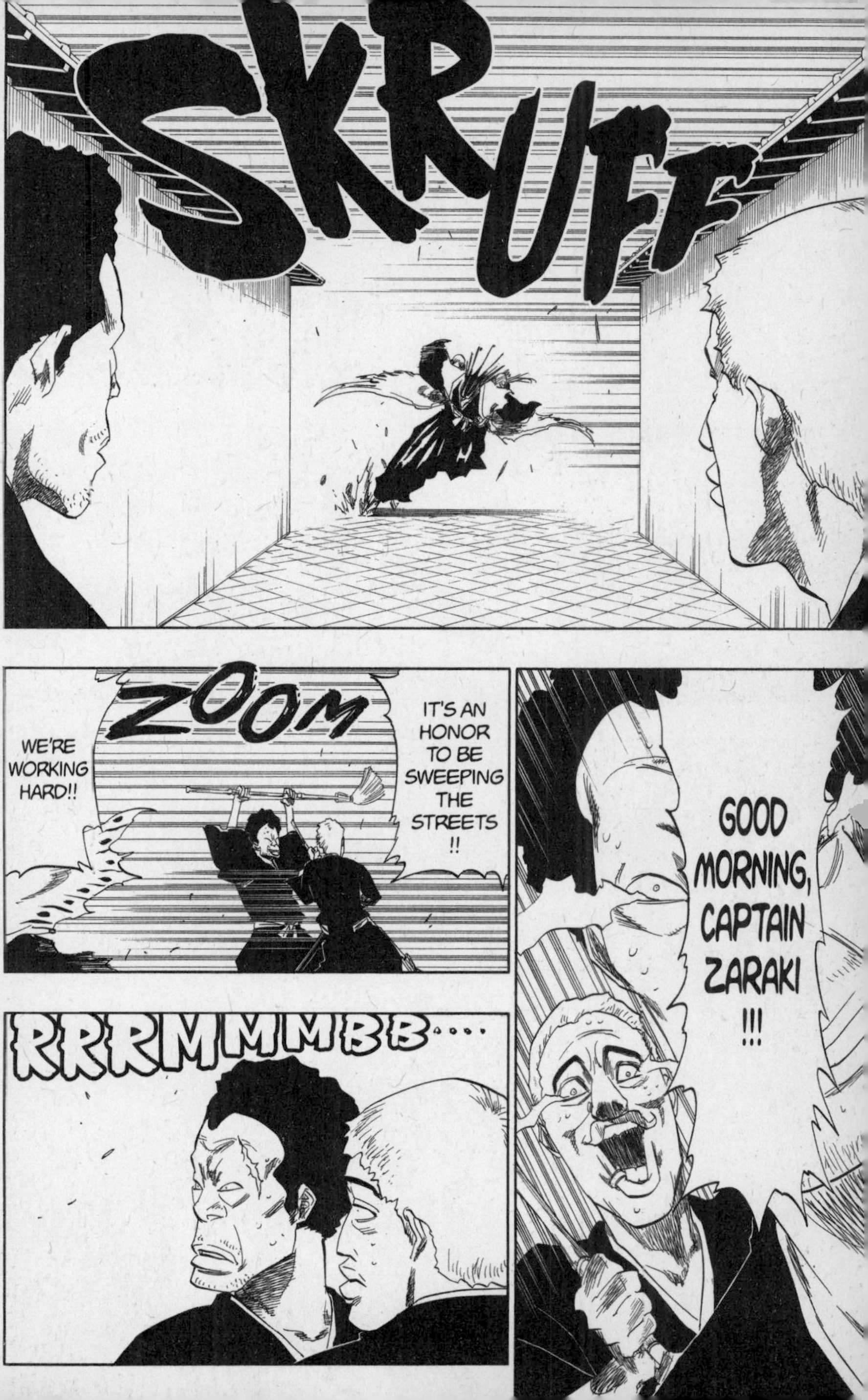
SKRUFF
GOOD MORNING, CAPTAIN ZARAKI!!!
ZOOM
IT'S AN HONOR TO BE SWEEPING THE STREETS!!
WE'RE WORKING HARD!!
RRRMMMBB...

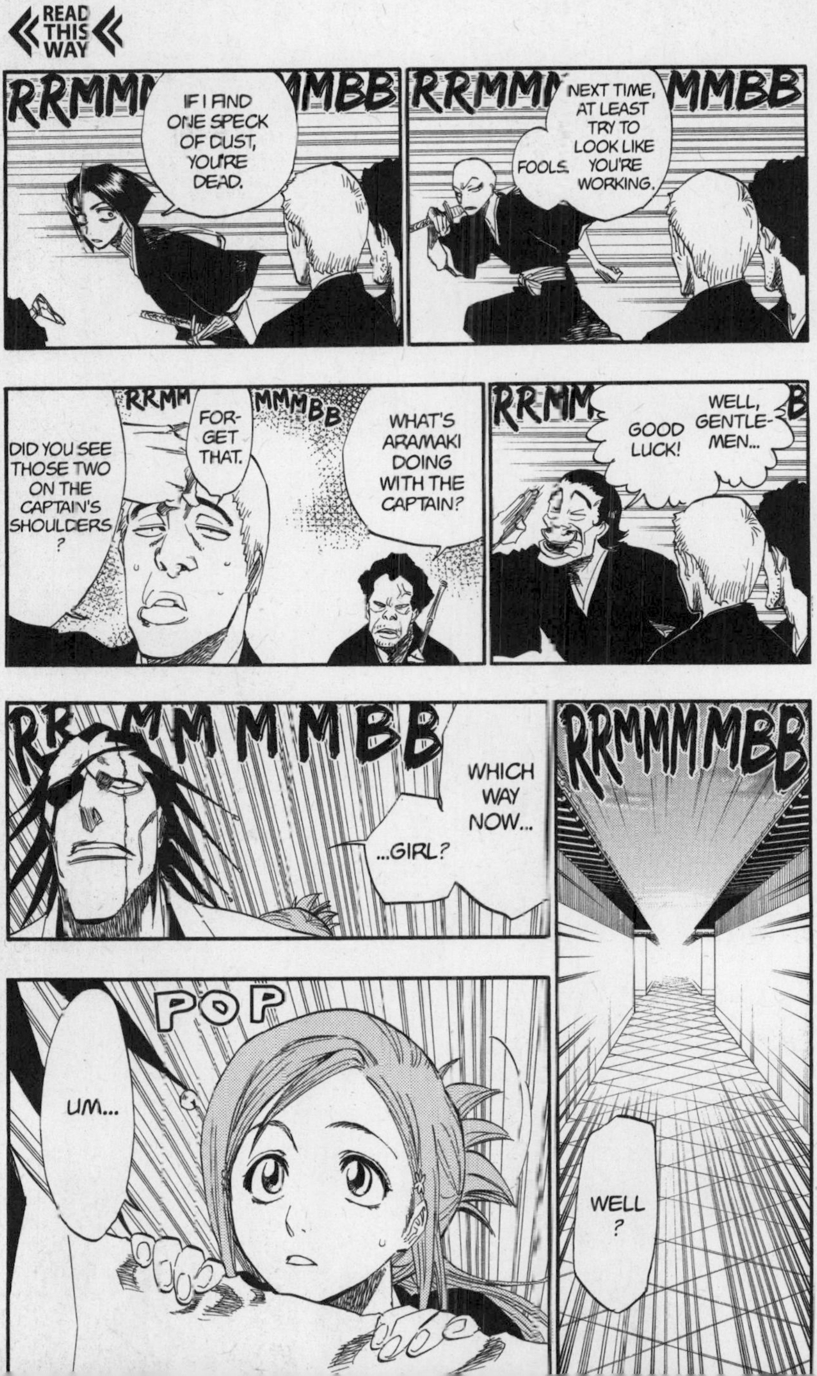
READ THIS WAY
RRMMMMMBB
FOOLS.
NEXT TIME, AT LEAST TRY TO LOOK LIKE YOU'RE WORKING.
RRMMMMMBB
IF I FIND ONE SPECK OF DUST, YOU'RE DEAD.
RRMMMB
WELL, GENTLEMEN...
GOOD LUCK!
RRMMMMMBB
WHAT'S ARAMAKI DOING WITH THE CAPTAIN?
FOR-GET THAT.
DID YOU SEE THOSE TWO ON THE CAPTAIN'S SHOULDERS?
RRMMMMBB
WELL?
RRMMMMMBB
WHICH WAY NOW...
...GIRL?
POP
UM...

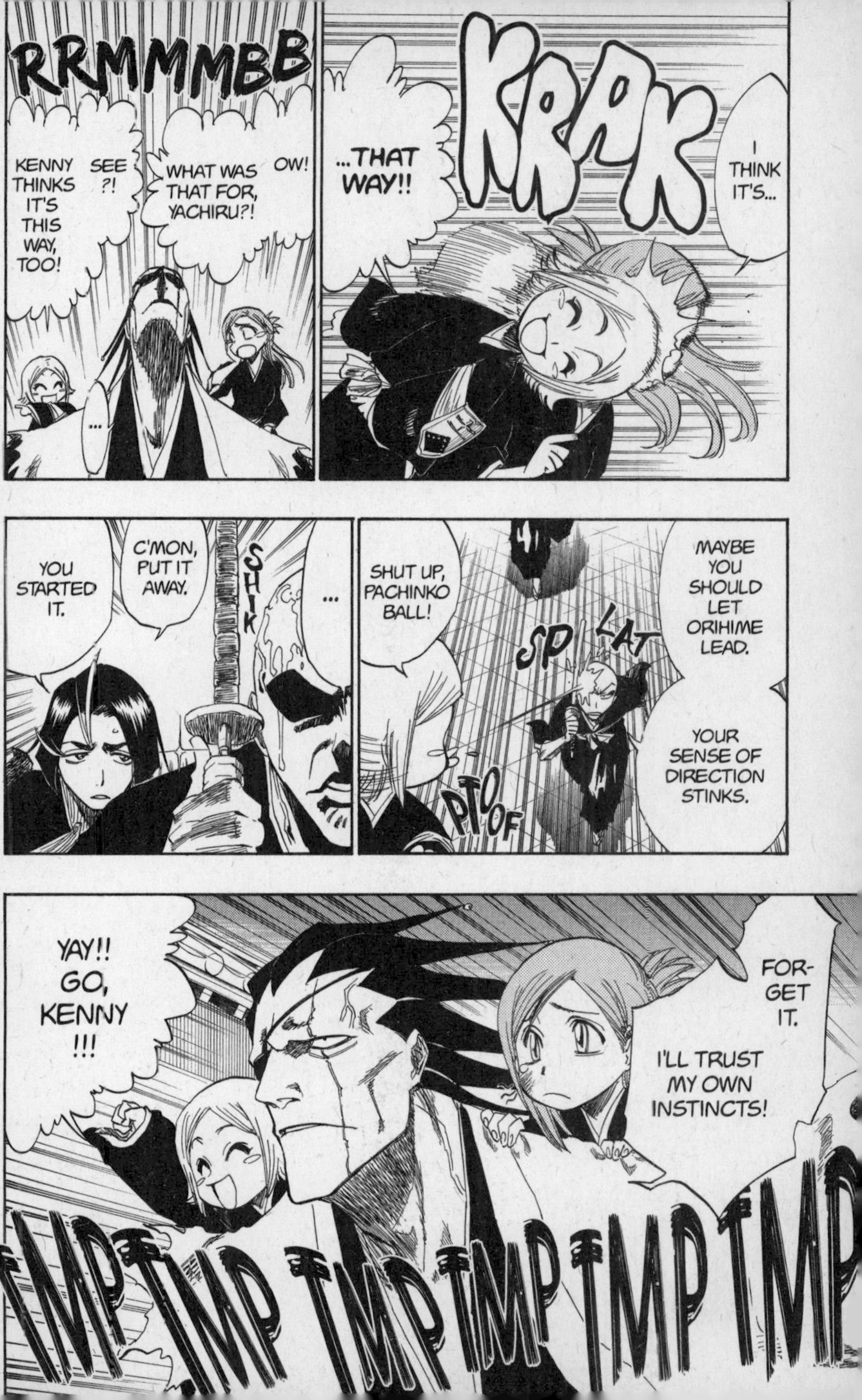
I THINK IT'S...
KRAK
...THAT WAY!!
OW! WHAT WAS THAT FOR, YACHIRU?!
RRMMMBB
SEE?!
KENNY THINKS IT'S THIS WAY, TOO!
...
MAYBE YOU SHOULD LET ORIHIME LEAD.
YOUR SENSE OF DIRECTION STINKS.
SPLAT
SHUT UP, PACHINKO BALL!
PTOOF
...
SHIK
C'MON, PUT IT AWAY.
YOU STARTED IT.
FOR-GET IT.
I'LL TRUST MY OWN INSTINCTS!
YAY!! GO, KENNY!!!
TMP TMP TMP TMP TMP TMP TMP

READ THIS WAY

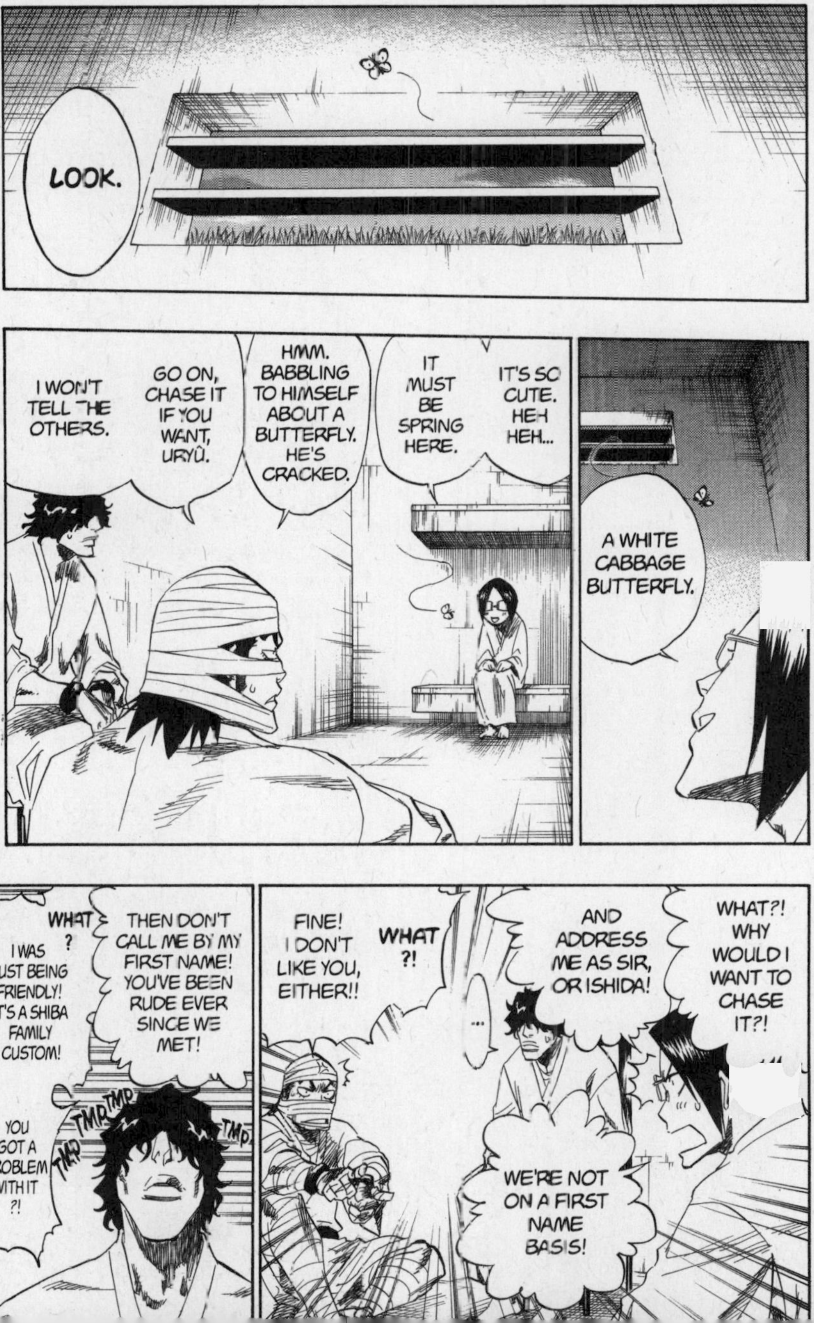
LOOK.
A WHITE CABBAGE BUTTERFLY.
IT'S SO CUTE. HEH HEH...
IT MUST BE SPRING HERE.
HMM. BABBLING TO HIMSELF ABOUT A BUTTERFLY. HE'S CRACKED.
GO ON, CHASE IT IF YOU WANT, URYÛ.
I WON'T TELL THE OTHERS.
WHAT?! WHY WOULD I WANT TO CHASE IT?!
AND ADDRESS ME AS SIR, OR ISHIDA!
WE'RE NOT ON A FIRST NAME BASIS!
...
WHAT?!
FINE! I DON'T LIKE YOU, EITHER!!
THEN DON'T CALL ME BY MY FIRST NAME! YOU'VE BEEN RUDE EVER SINCE WE MET!
WHAT?
I WAS JUST BEING FRIENDLY! IT'S A SHIBA FAMILY CUSTOM!
TMP TMP TMP TMP
YOU GOT A PROBLEM WITH IT?!

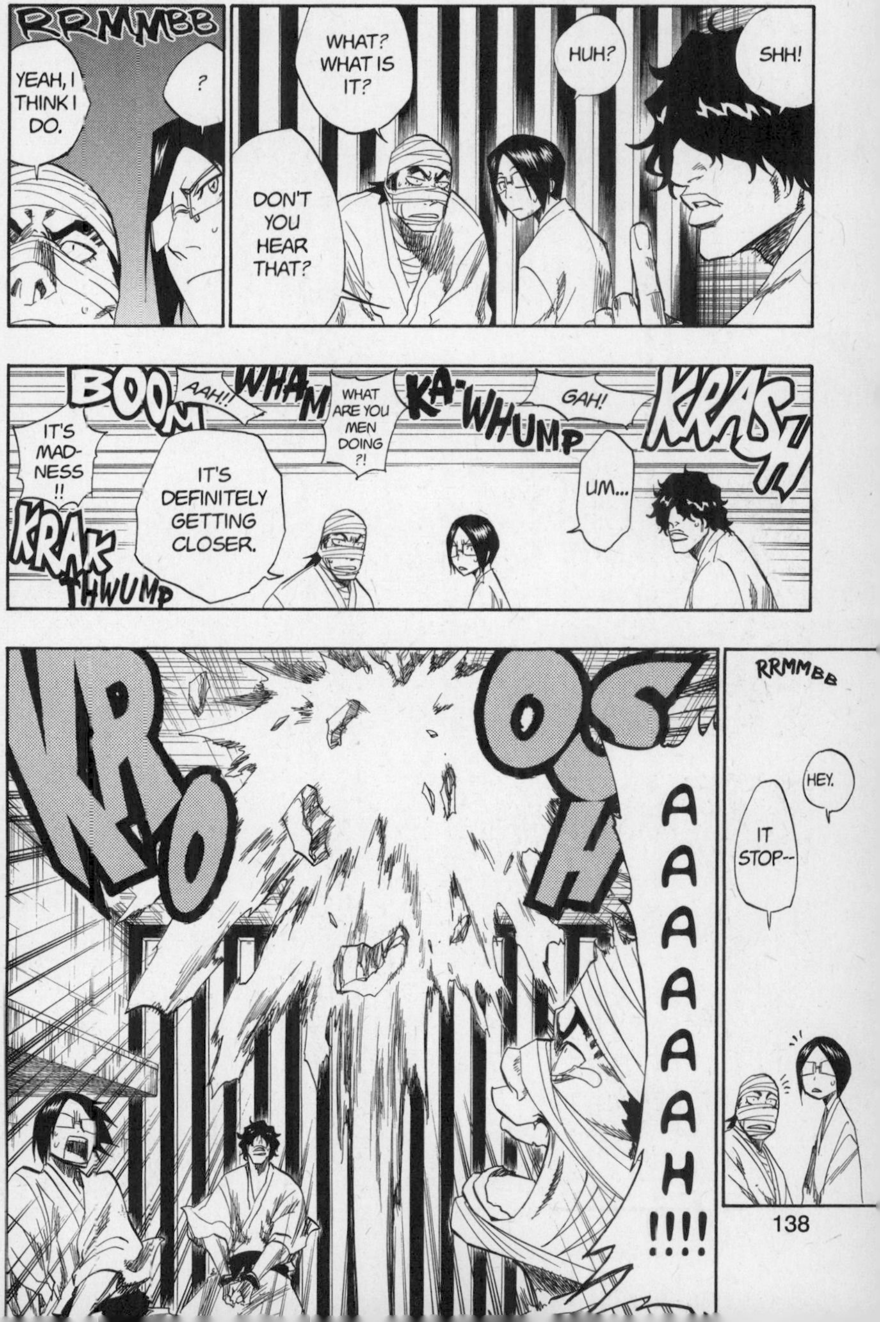
SHH!
HUH?
WHAT? WHAT IS IT?
DON'T YOU HEAR THAT?
RRMMBB
?
YEAH, I THINK I DO.
KRASH
GAH!
KA-WHUMP
WHAT ARE YOU MEN DOING?!
WHAM
AAH!!
BOOM
UM...
IT'S DEFINITELY GETTING CLOSER.
IT'S MADNESS!!
KRAK
THWUMP
RRMMBB
HEY.
IT STOP--
VROOOSH
AAAAAAH!!!!

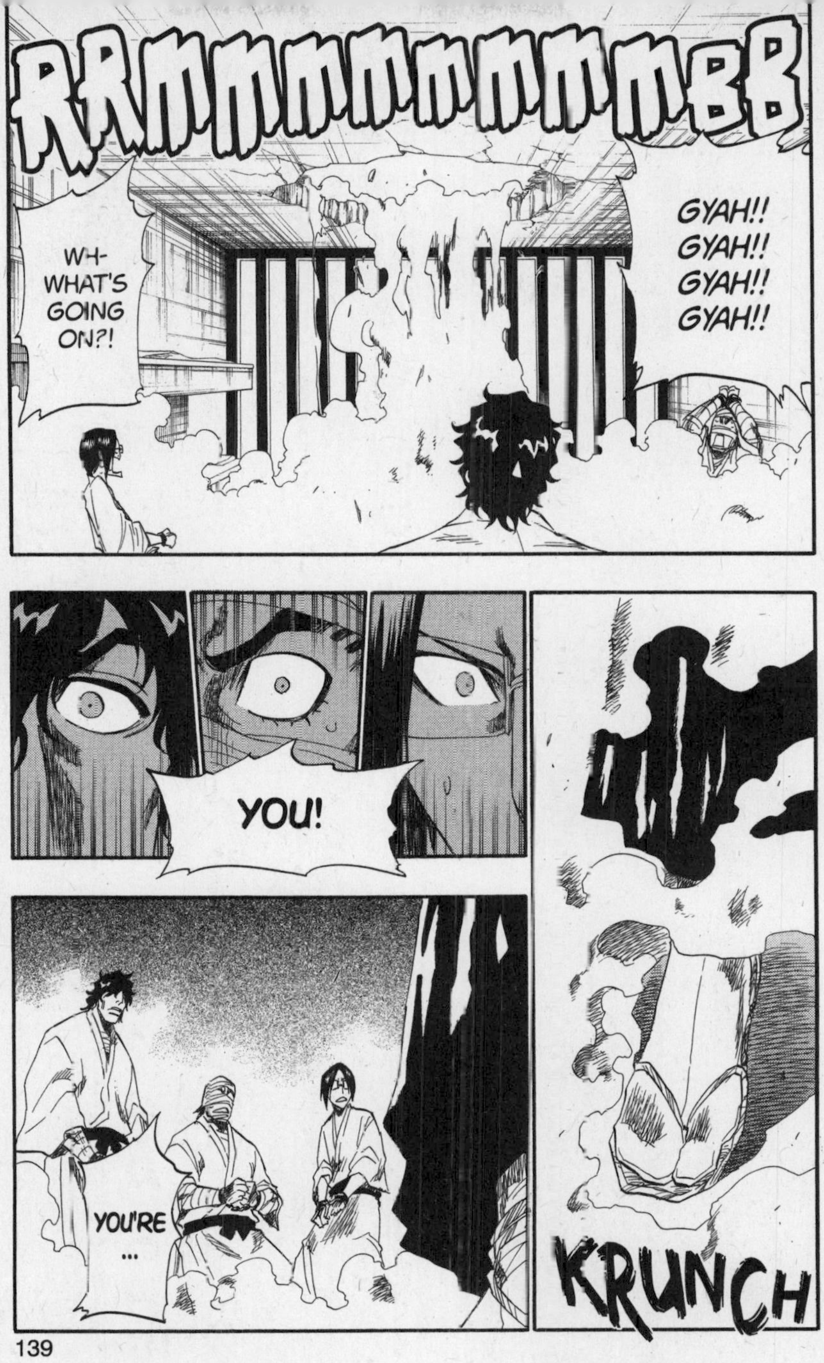
RRMMMMMMMMBB
GYAH!! GYAH!! GYAH!! GYAH!!
WH-WHAT'S GOING ON?!
KRUNCH
YOU!
YOU'RE ...

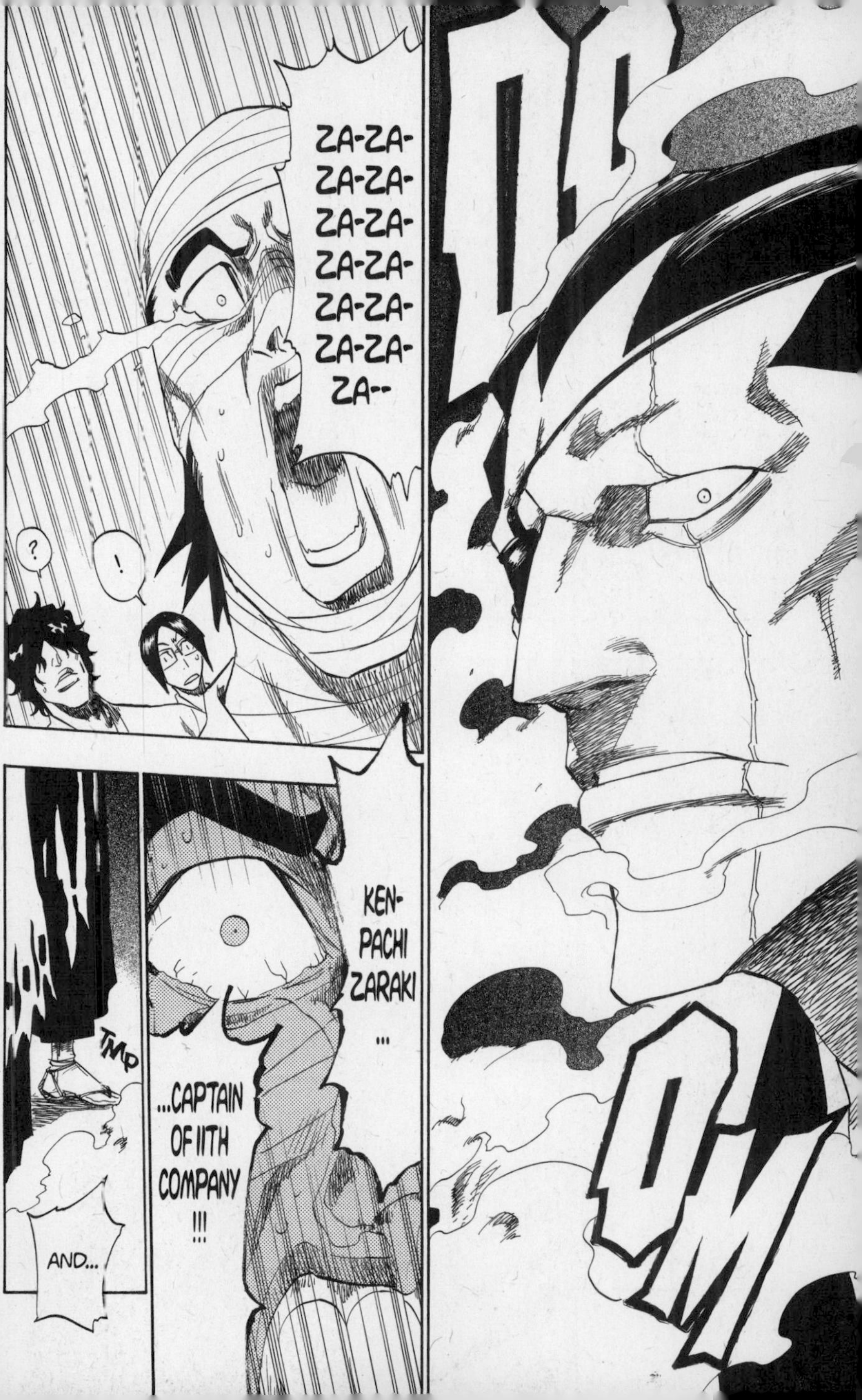
ZA-ZA-
ZA-ZA-
ZA-ZA-
ZA-ZA-
ZA-ZA-
ZA-ZA-
ZA--
?
!
KEN-PACHI ZARAKI ...
...CAPTAIN OF 11TH COMPANY !!!
TMP
AND...

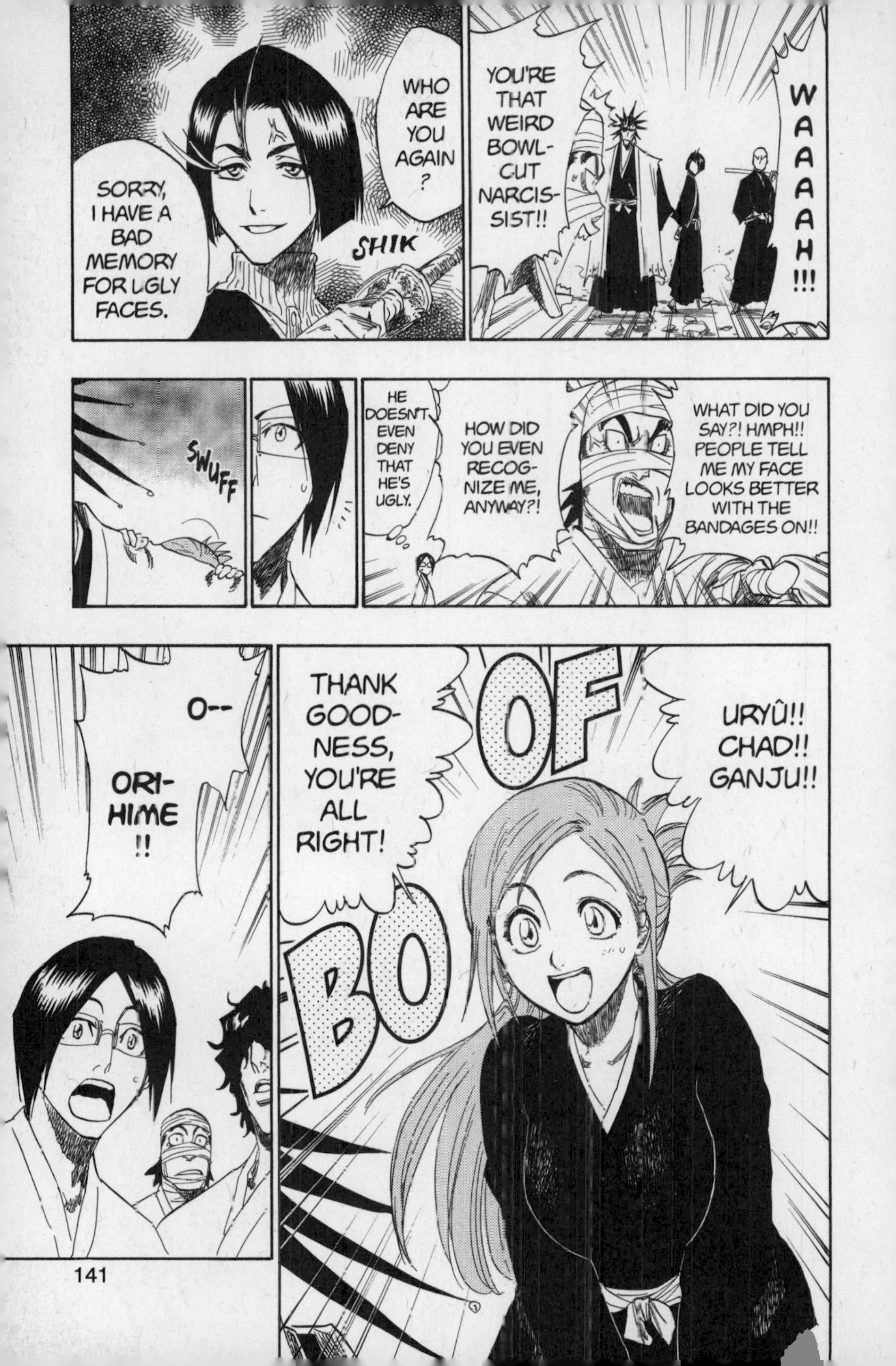
WAAAAH!!!
YOU'RE THAT WEIRD BOWL-CUT NARCISSIST!!
WHO ARE YOU AGAIN?
SHIK
SORRY, I HAVE A BAD MEMORY FOR UGLY FACES.
WHAT DID YOU SAY?! HMPH!! PEOPLE TELL ME MY FACE LOOKS BETTER WITH THE BANDAGES ON!!
HOW DID YOU EVEN RECOGNIZE ME, ANYWAY?!
HE DOESN'T EVEN DENY THAT HE'S UGLY.
SWUFF
URYÛ!! CHAD!! GANJU!!
BOOF
THANK GOODNESS, YOU'RE ALL RIGHT!
O--
ORIHIME!!

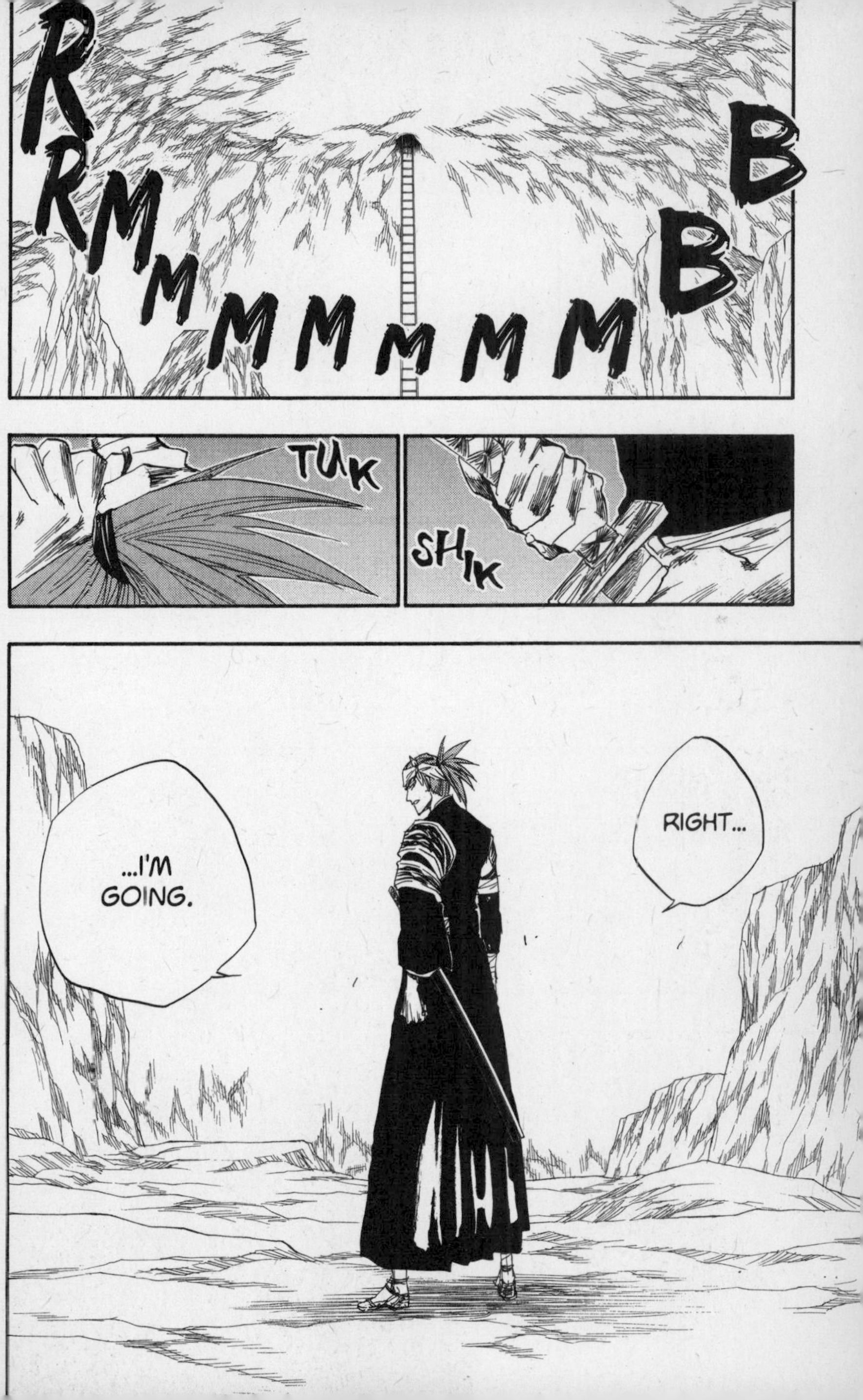
RRMMMMMMMBB
SHIK
TUK
RIGHT...
...I'M GOING.

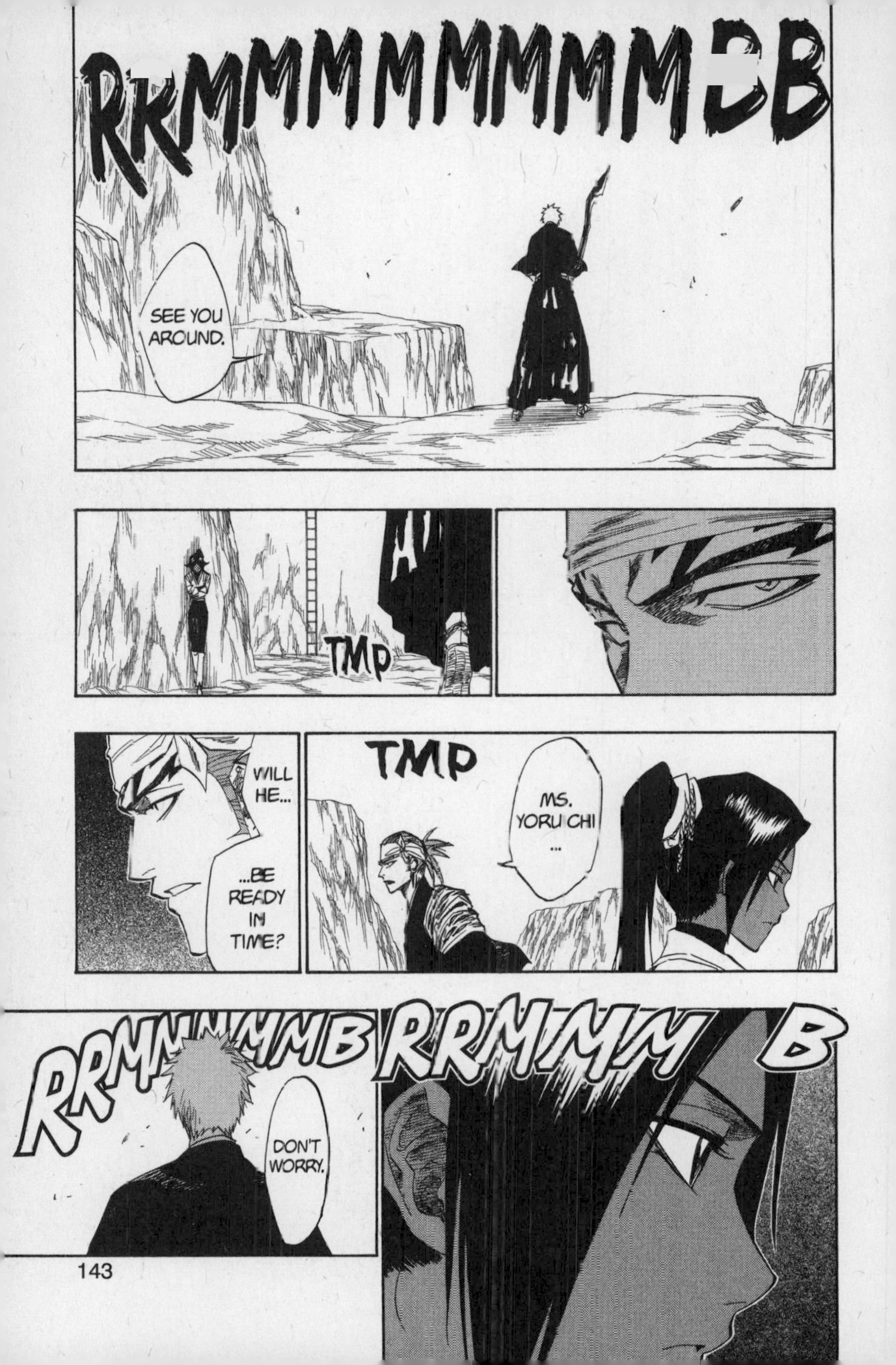
SEE YOU AROUND.
TMP
TMP
MS. YORUICHI ...
WILL HE...
...BE READY IN TIME?
RRMMMM B
RRMMMMMB
DON'T WORRY.

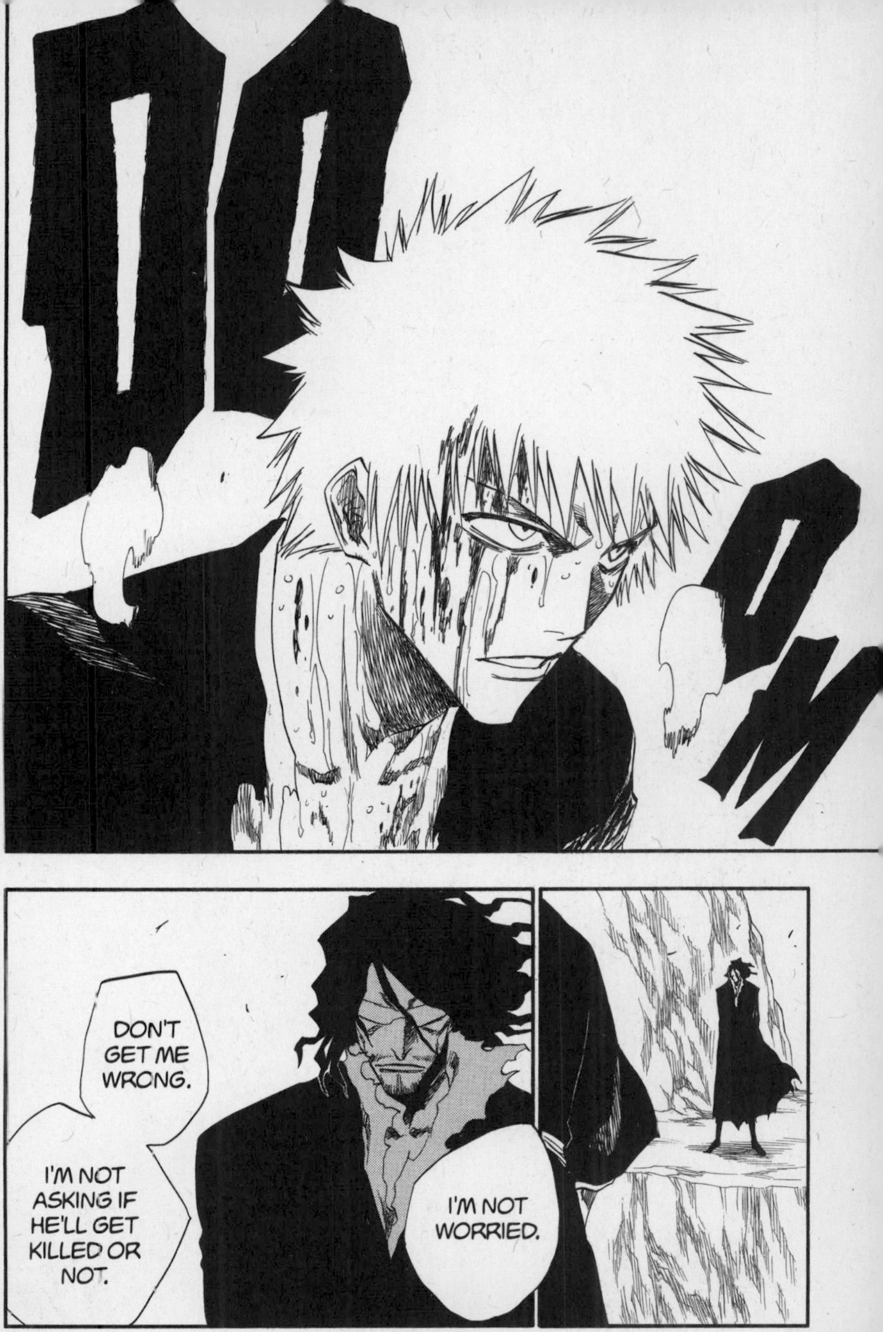
DOOM
I'M NOT WORRIED.
DON'T GET ME WRONG.
I'M NOT ASKING IF HE'LL GET KILLED OR NOT.

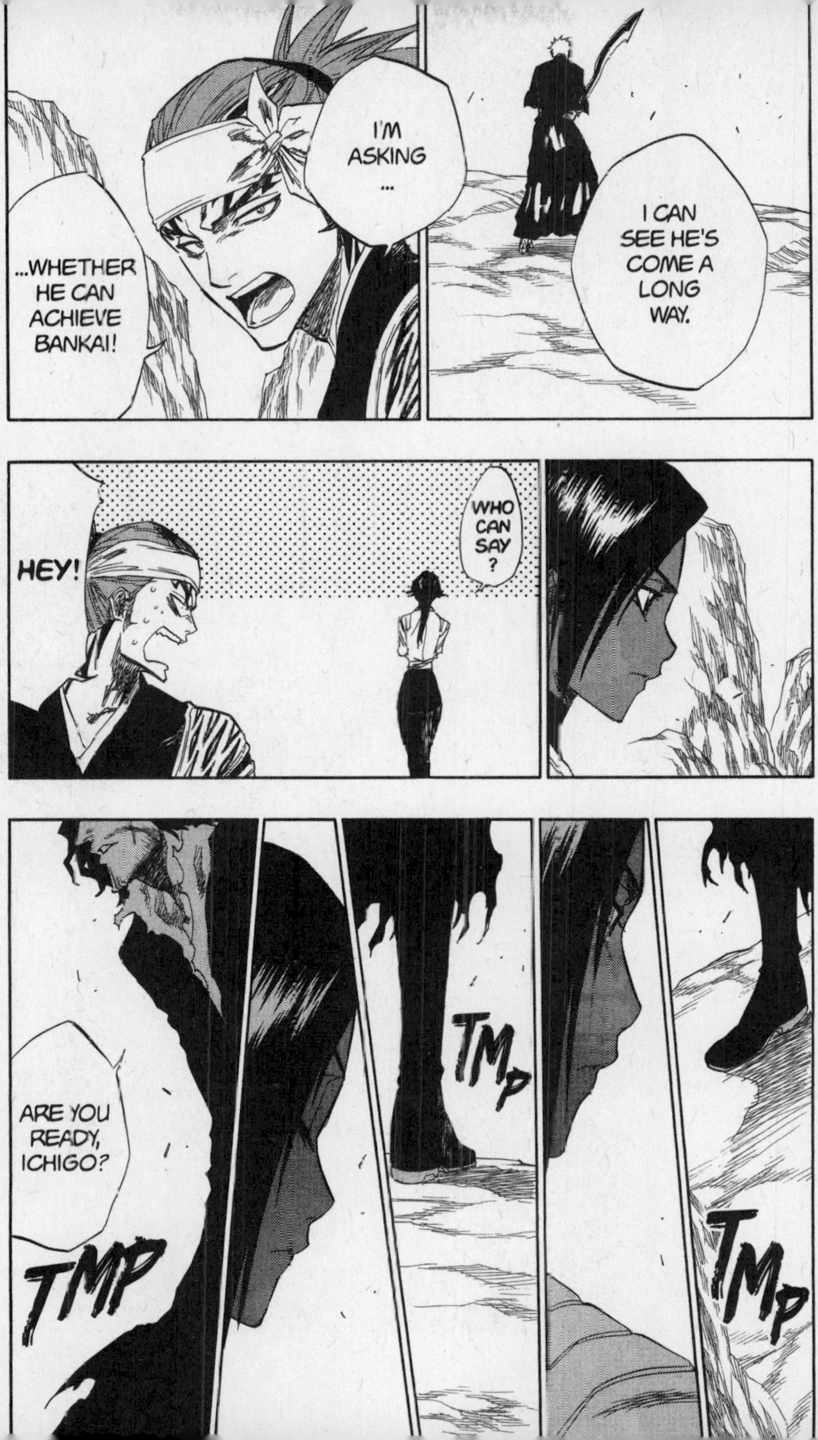
I CAN SEE HE'S COME A LONG WAY.
I'M ASKING ...
...WHETHER HE CAN ACHIEVE BANKAI!
WHO CAN SAY?
HEY!
TMP
TMP
ARE YOU READY, ICHIGO?
TMP

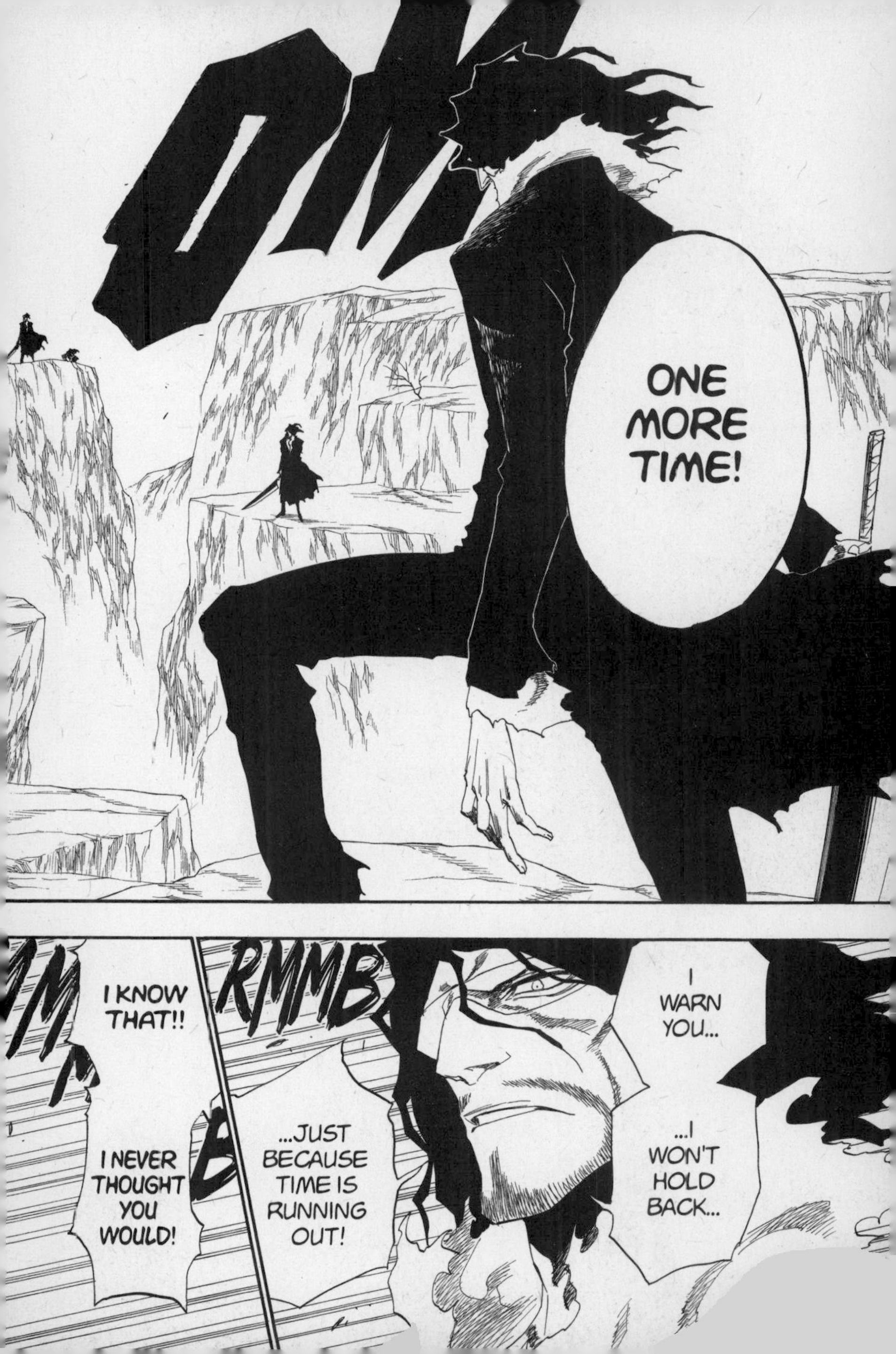
ONE MORE TIME!
RMMB
I WARN YOU...
...I WON'T HOLD BACK...
...JUST BECAUSE TIME IS RUNNING OUT!
I KNOW THAT!!
I NEVER THOUGHT YOU WOULD!

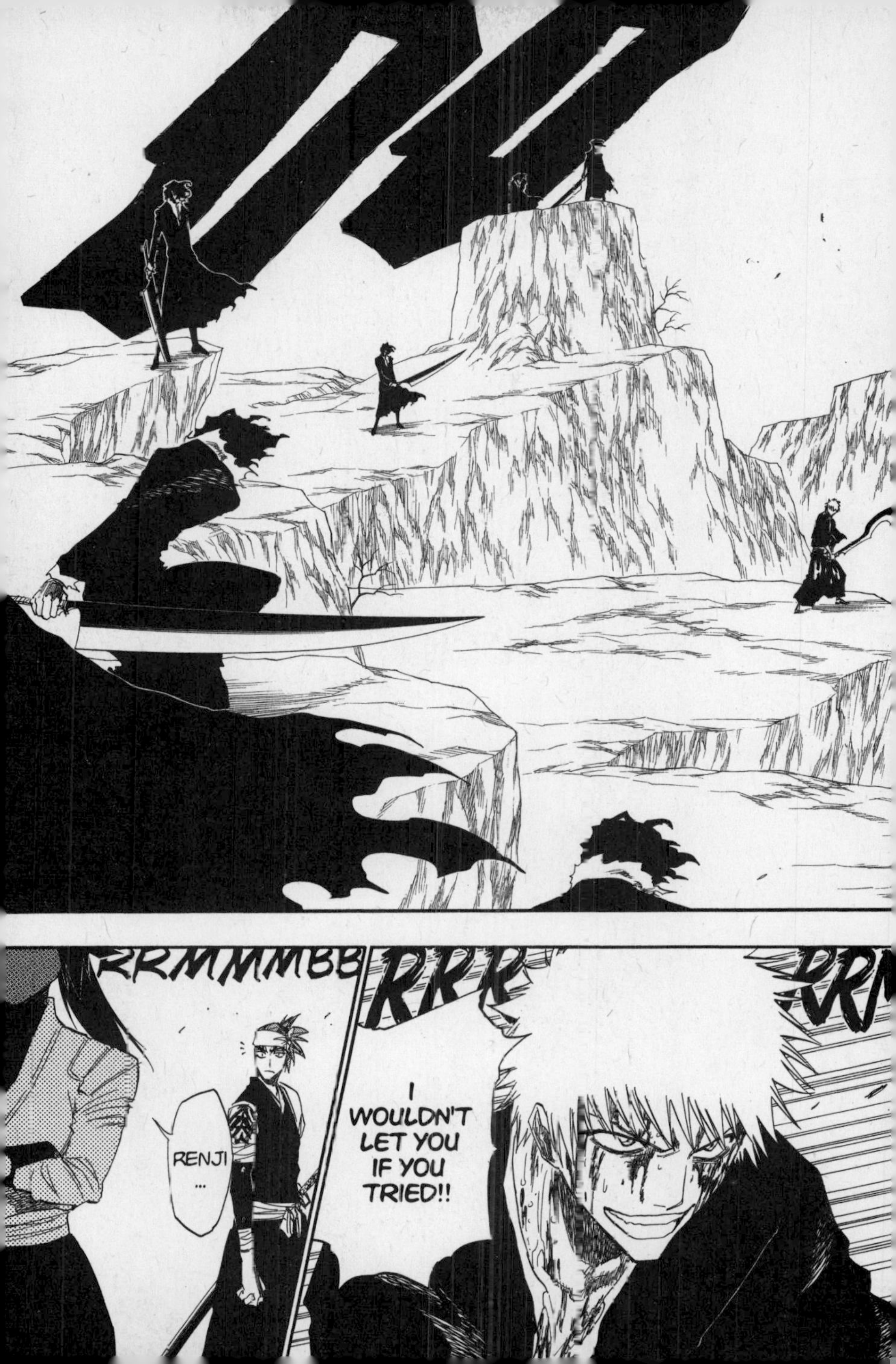
RRM
RRR
I WOULDN'T LET YOU IF YOU TRIED!!
RRMMMMBB
RENJI ...

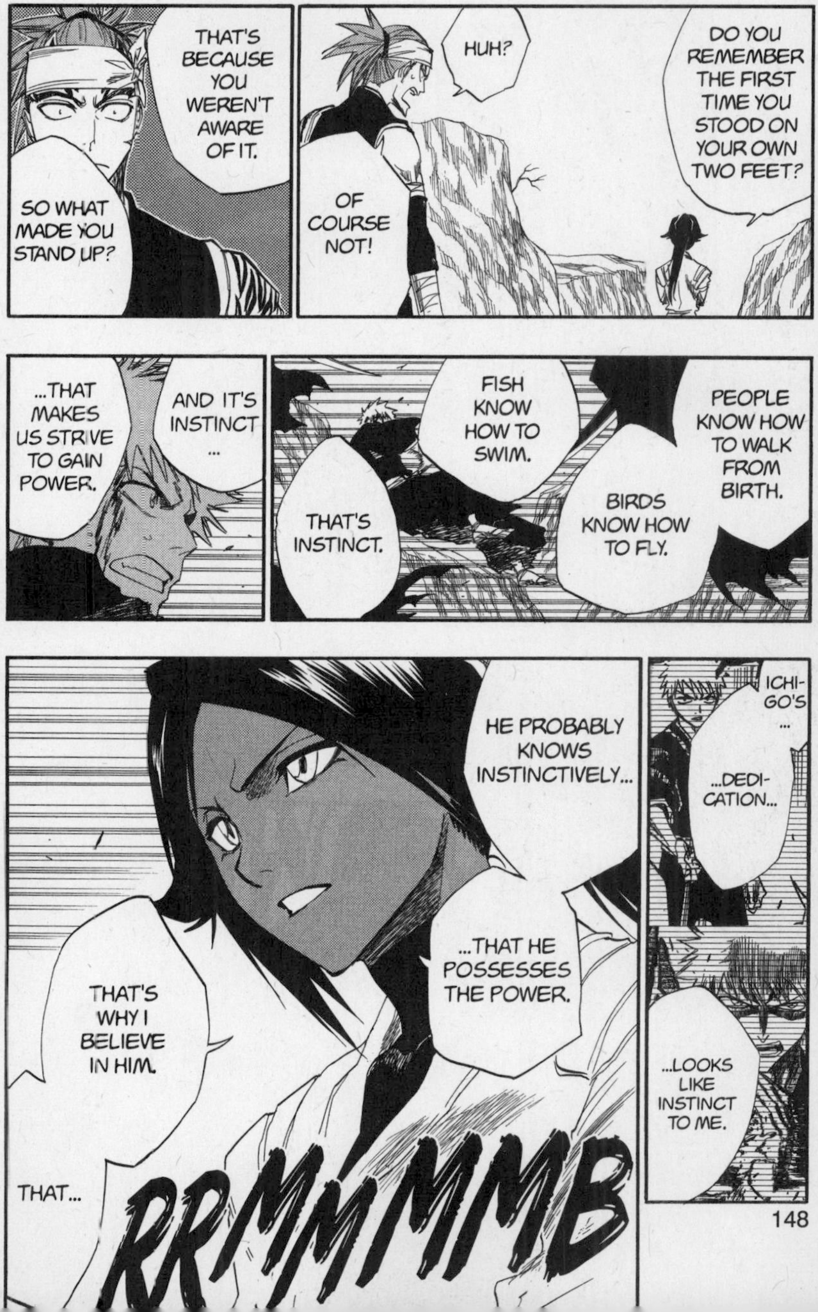
DO YOU REMEMBER THE FIRST TIME YOU STOOD ON YOUR OWN TWO FEET?
HUH?
OF COURSE NOT!
THAT'S BECAUSE YOU WEREN'T AWARE OF IT.
SO WHAT MADE YOU STAND UP?
PEOPLE KNOW HOW TO WALK FROM BIRTH.
FISH KNOW HOW TO SWIM.
BIRDS KNOW HOW TO FLY.
THAT'S INSTINCT.
AND IT'S INSTINCT ...
...THAT MAKES US STRIVE TO GAIN POWER.
ICHI-GO'S ...
...DEDI-CATION...
...LOOKS LIKE INSTINCT TO ME.
HE PROBABLY KNOWS INSTINCTIVELY...
...THAT HE POSSESSES THE POWER.
THAT'S WHY I BELIEVE IN HIM.
THAT...
RRMMMMB

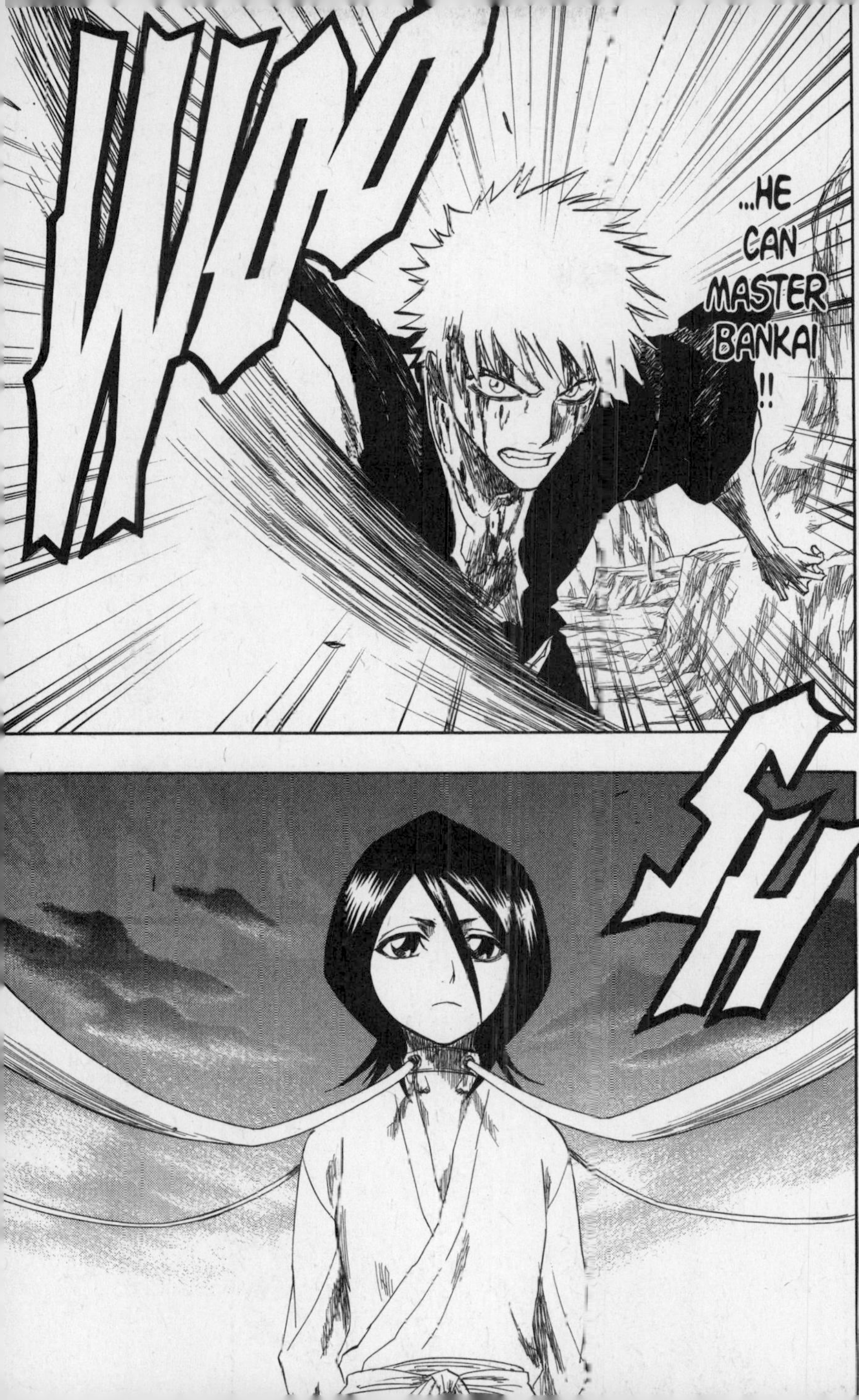
...HE CAN MASTER BANKAI !!

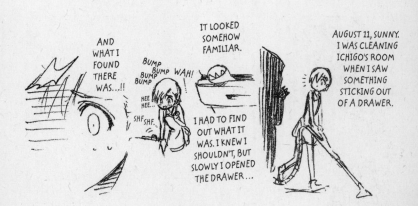

AUGUST 11, SUNNY. I WAS CLEANING ICHIGO'S ROOM WHEN I SAW SOMETHING STICKING OUT OF A DRAWER.
IT LOOKED SOMEHOW FAMILIAR.
I HAD TO FIND OUT WHAT IT WAS. I KNEW I SHOULDN'T, BUT SLOWLY I OPENED THE DRAWER...
WAH!
BUMP BUMP BUMP BUMP
HEE HEE...
SHF SHF...
AND WHAT I FOUND THERE WAS...!!

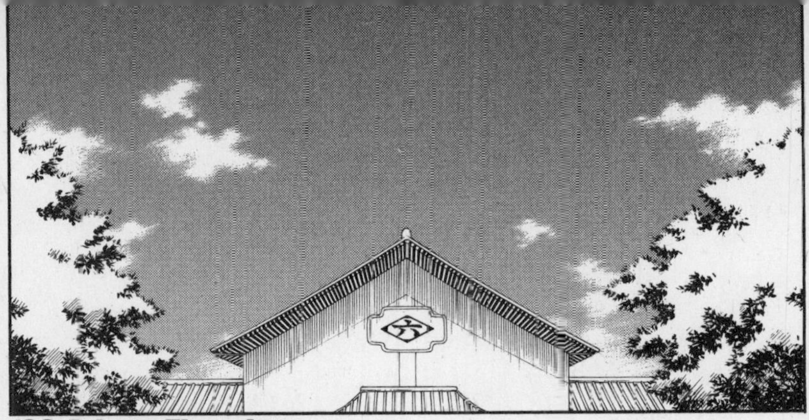

138. Private Thoughts

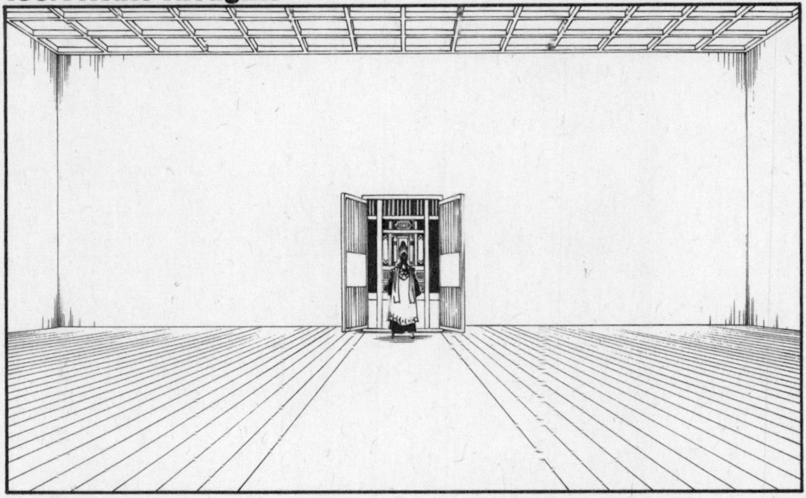

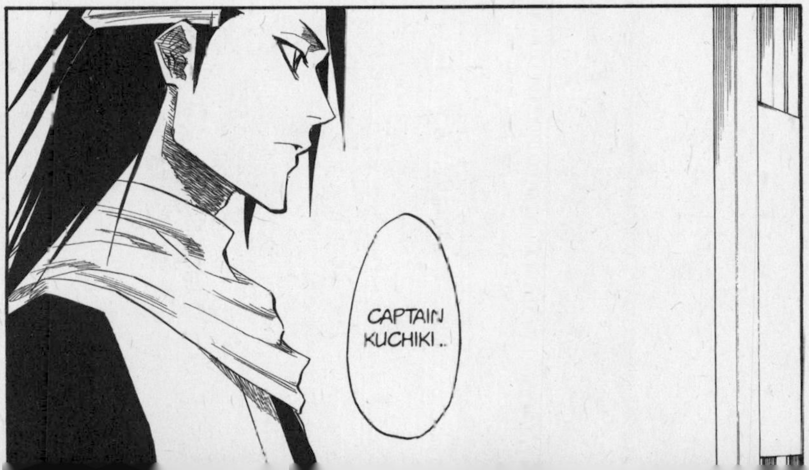
CAPTAIN KUCHIKI..

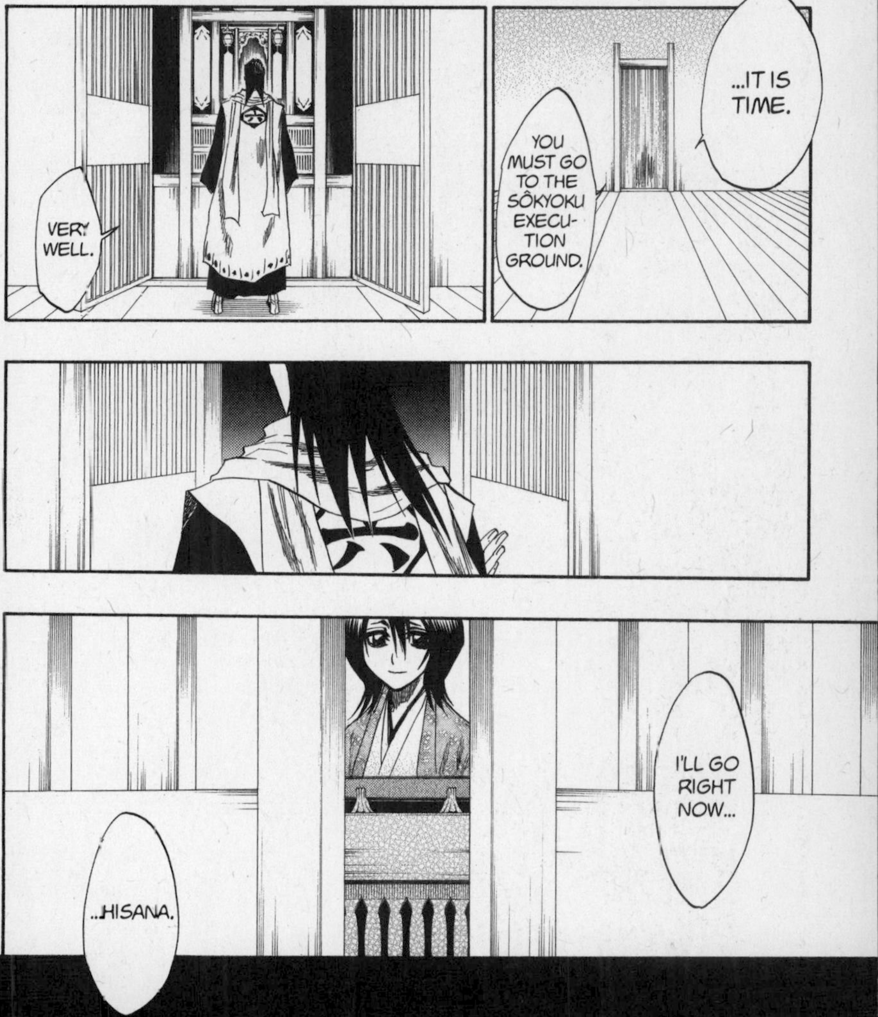
...IT IS TIME.
YOU MUST GO TO THE SÔKYOKU EXECUTION GROUND.
VERY WELL.
I'LL GO RIGHT NOW...
...HISANA.

138. Private Thoughts

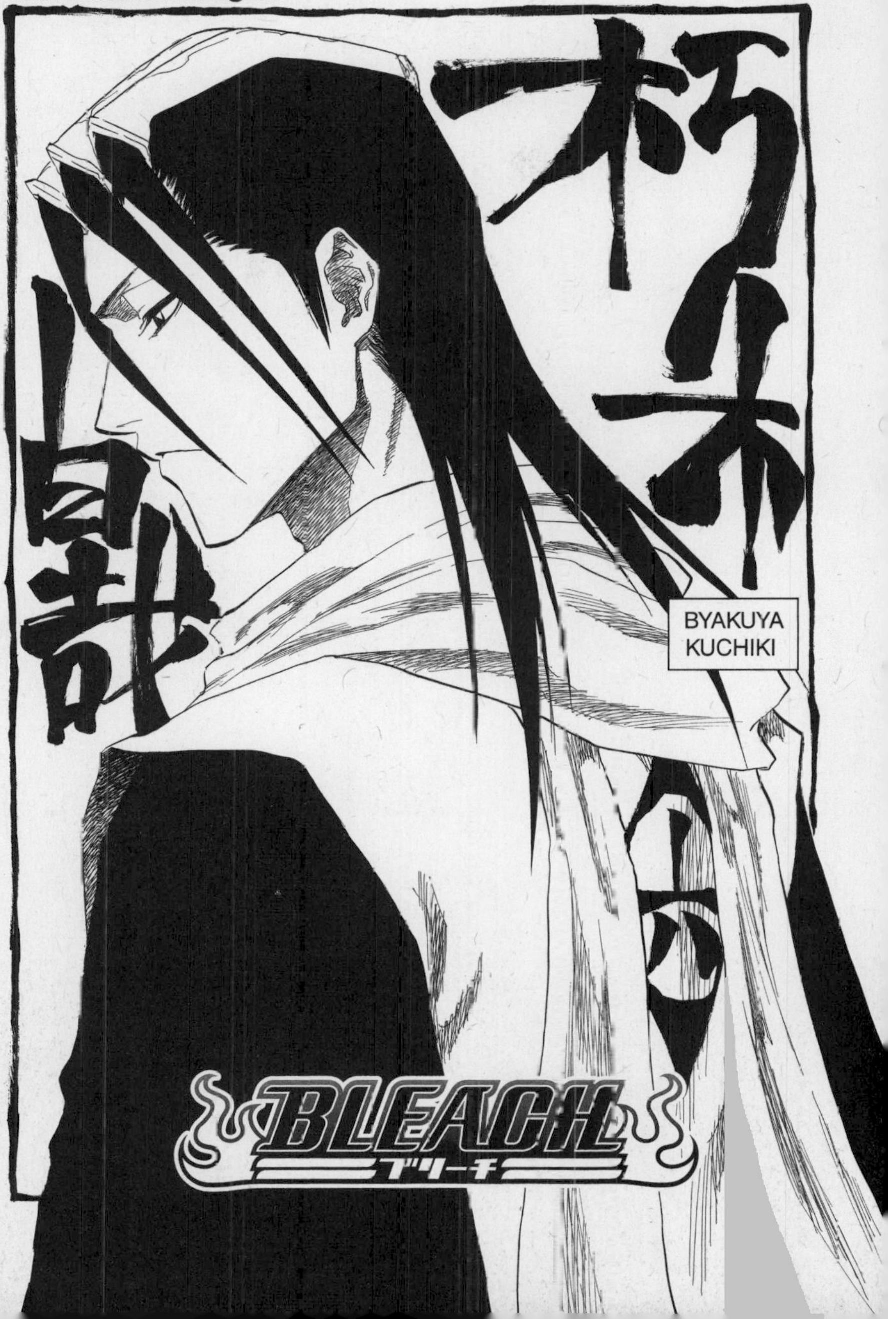
BYAKUYA
KUCHIKI
BLEACH
ブリーチ

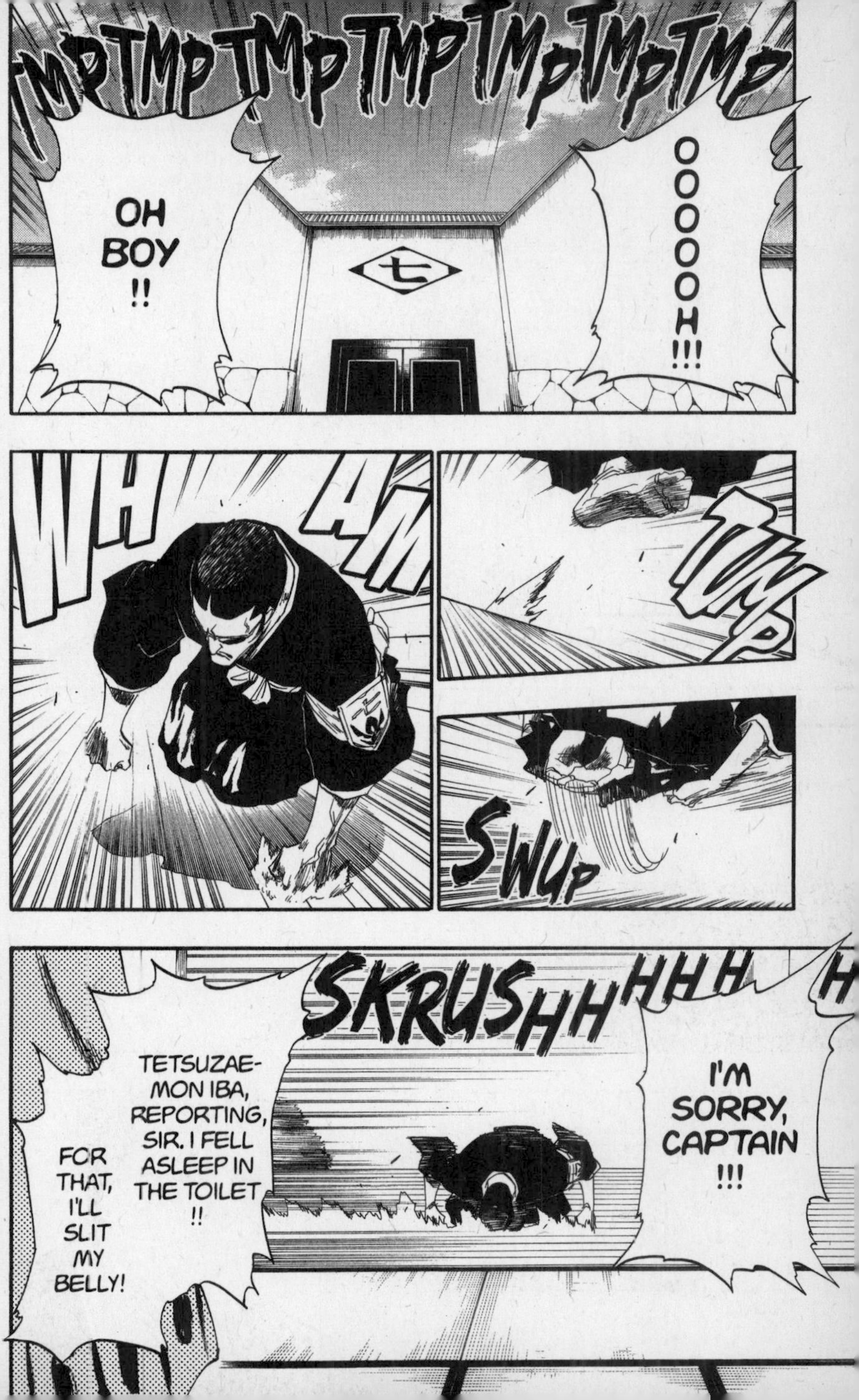
TMP TMP TMP TMP TMP TMP TMP
OOOOOH!!!
OH BOY!!
TMP
SWUP
WHAM
SKRUSHHHHHH
I'M SORRY, CAPTAIN!!!
TETSUZAE-MON IBA, REPORTING, SIR. I FELL ASLEEP IN THE TOILET!!
FOR THAT, I'LL SLIT MY BELLY!

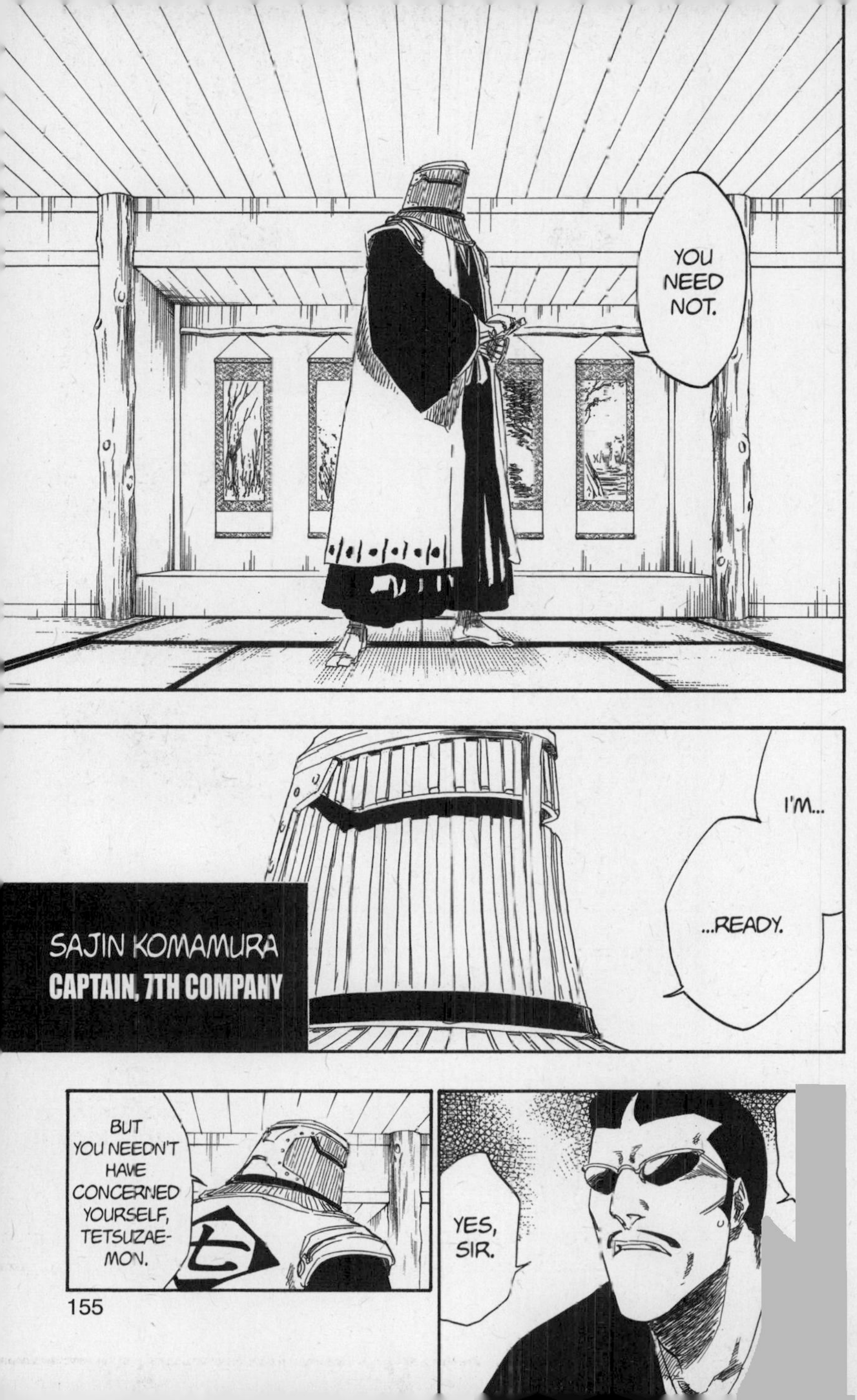
YOU NEED NOT.
I'M...
...READY.
SAJIN KOMAMURA
CAPTAIN, 7TH COMPANY
YES, SIR.
BUT YOU NEEDN'T HAVE CONCERNED YOURSELF, TETSUZAEMON.

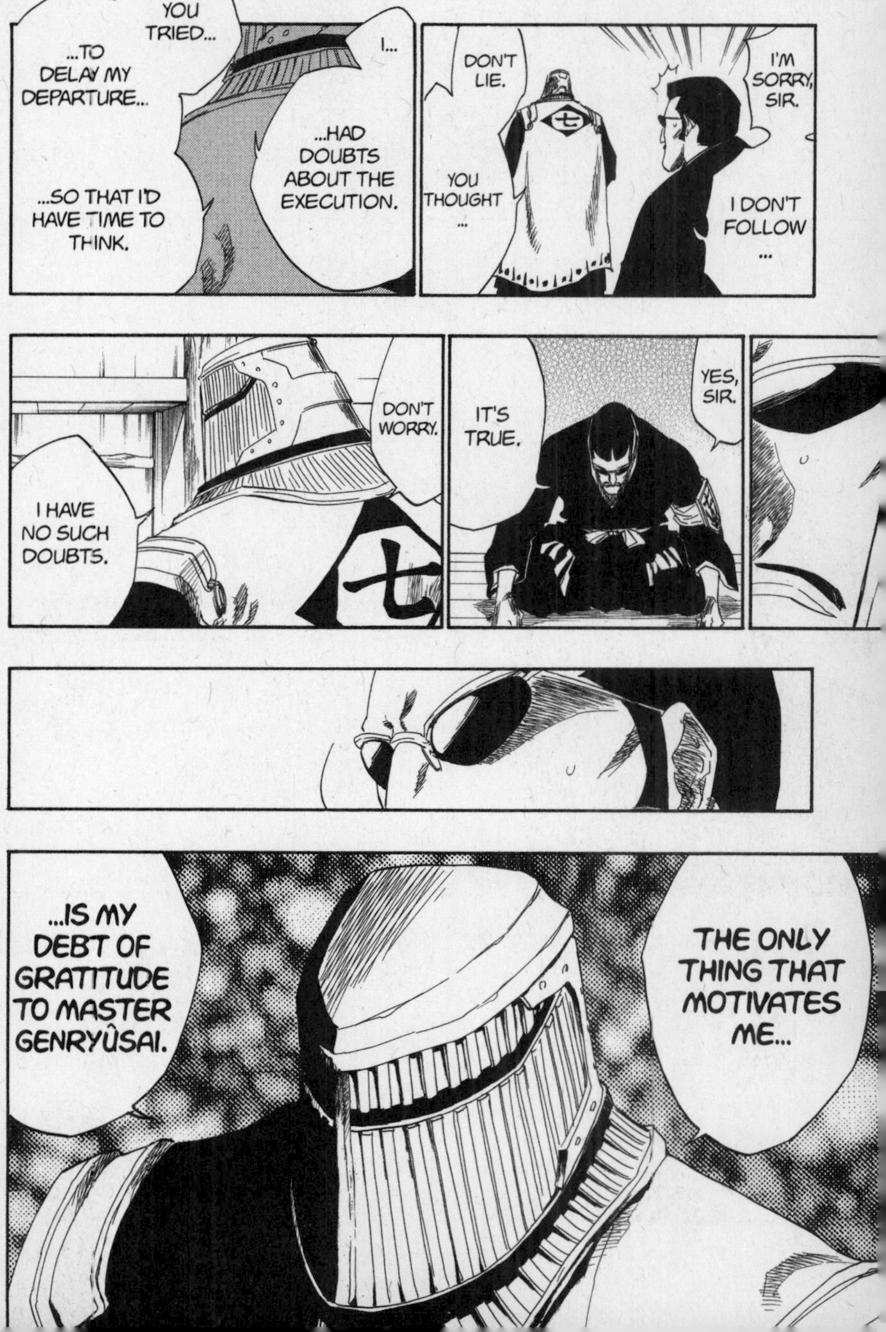
I'M SORRY, SIR.
I DON'T FOLLOW...
DON'T LIE.
YOU THOUGHT...
I...
...HAD DOUBTS ABOUT THE EXECUTION.
YOU TRIED...
...TO DELAY MY DEPARTURE...
...SO THAT I'D HAVE TIME TO THINK.
YES, SIR.
IT'S TRUE.
DON'T WORRY.
I HAVE NO SUCH DOUBTS.
THE ONLY THING THAT MOTIVATES ME...
...IS MY DEBT OF GRATITUDE TO MASTER GENRYÛSAI.

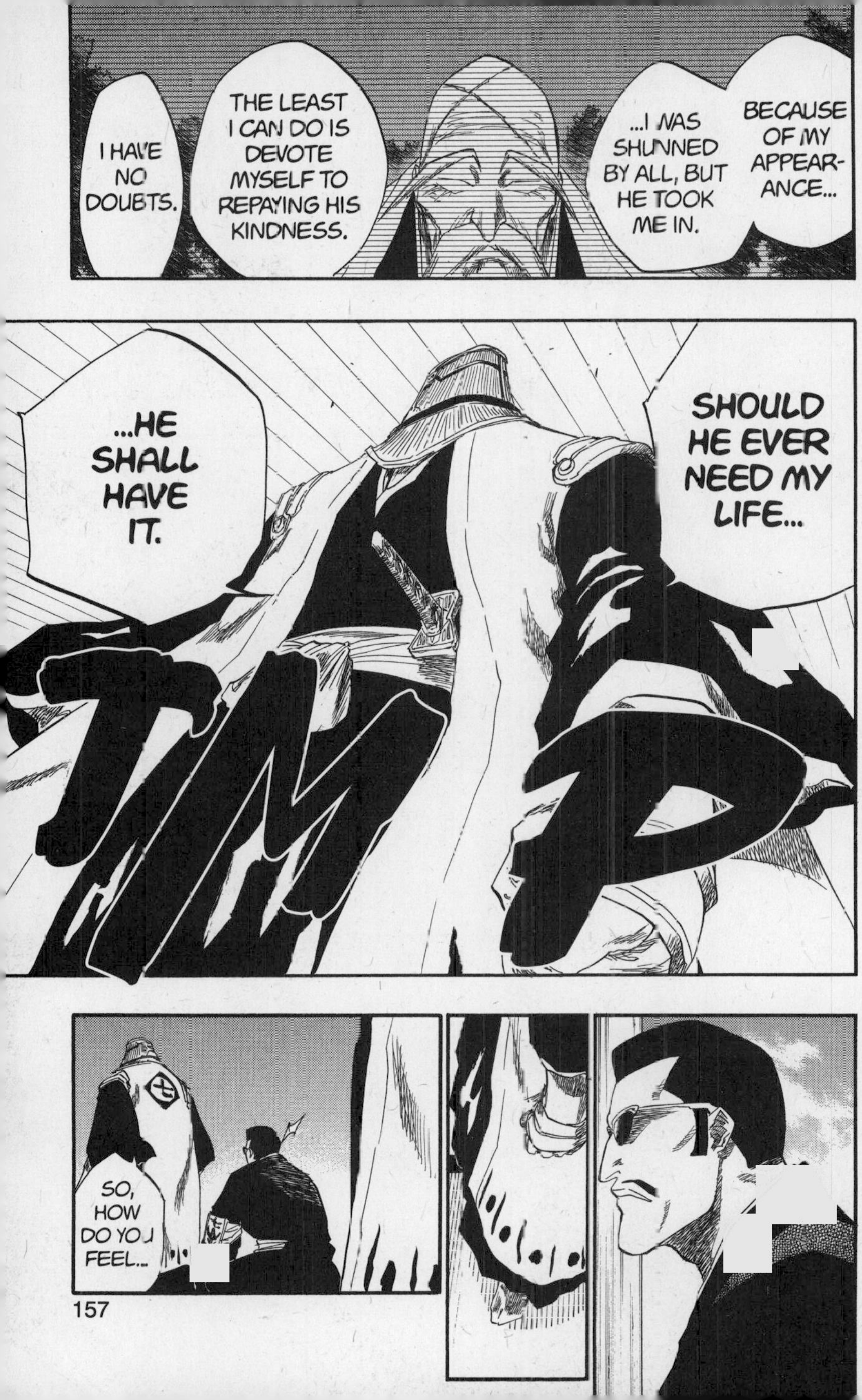
BECAUSE OF MY APPEARANCE...
...I WAS SHUNNED BY ALL, BUT HE TOOK ME IN.
THE LEAST I CAN DO IS DEVOTE MYSELF TO REPAYING HIS KINDNESS.
I HAVE NO DOUBTS.
SHOULD HE EVER NEED MY LIFE...
...HE SHALL HAVE IT.
TMP
SO, HOW DO YOU FEEL...

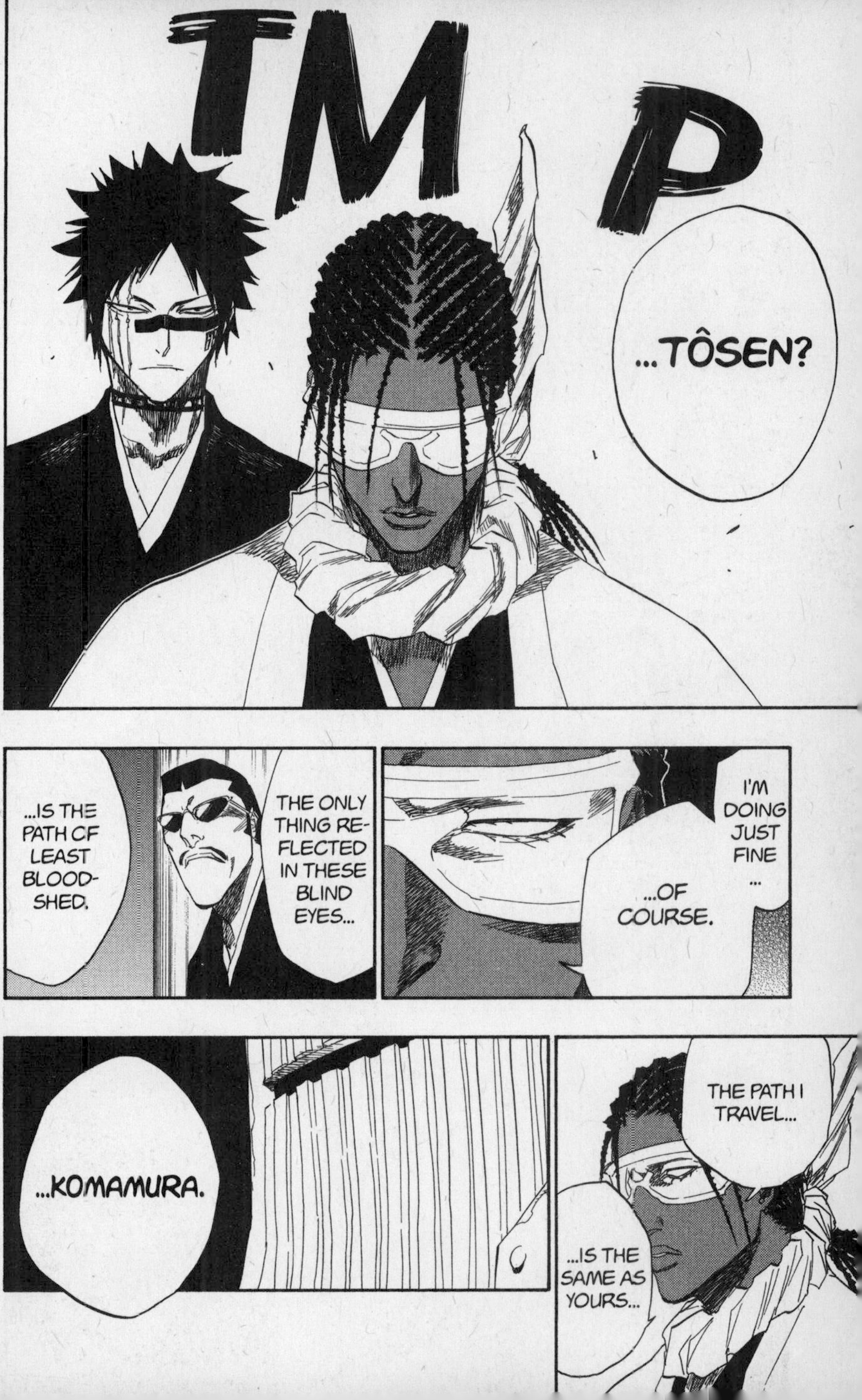
TMP
...TÔSEN?
I'M DOING JUST FINE ...
...OF COURSE.
THE ONLY THING RE-FLECTED IN THESE BLIND EYES...
...IS THE PATH OF LEAST BLOOD-SHED.
THE PATH I TRAVEL...
...IS THE SAME AS YOURS...
...KOMAMURA.

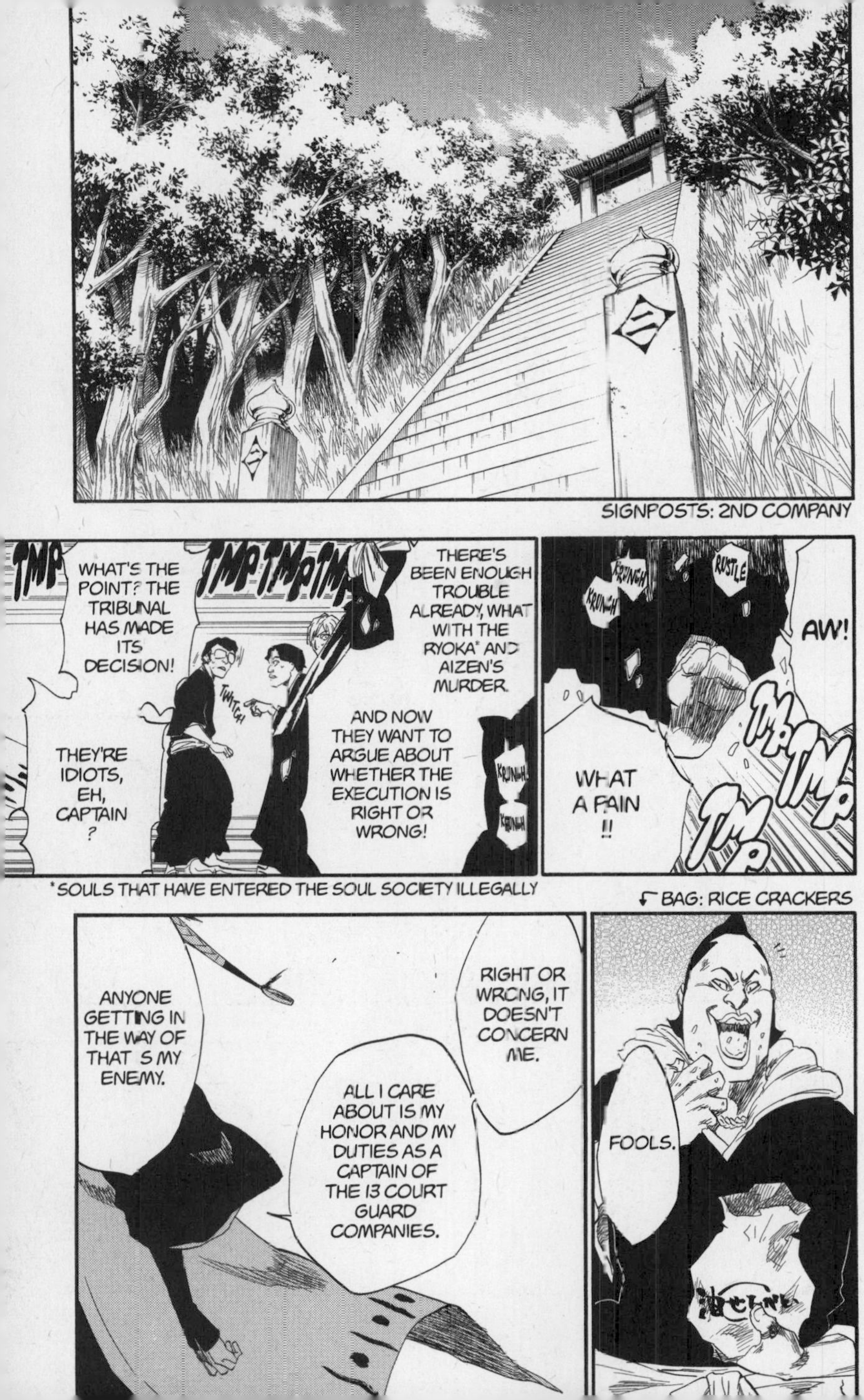
SIGNPOSTS: 2ND COMPANY
KRUNCH
KRUNCH
RUSTLE
AW!
TMP TMP TMP
WHAT A PAIN!!
TMP
WHAT'S THE POINT? THE TRIBUNAL HAS MADE ITS DECISION!
TMP TMP TMP
THERE'S BEEN ENOUGH TROUBLE ALREADY, WHAT WITH THE RYOKA* AND AIZEN'S MURDER.
TWITCH
AND NOW THEY WANT TO ARGUE ABOUT WHETHER THE EXECUTION IS RIGHT OR WRONG!
THEY'RE IDIOTS, EH, CAPTAIN?
KRUNCH
KRUNCH
*SOULS THAT HAVE ENTERED THE SOUL SOCIETY ILLEGALLY
BAG: RICE CRACKERS
FOOLS.
油せんべい
RIGHT OR WRONG, IT DOESN'T CONCERN ME.
ALL I CARE ABOUT IS MY HONOR AND MY DUTIES AS A CAPTAIN OF THE 13 COURT GUARD COMPANIES.
ANYONE GETTING IN THE WAY OF THAT IS MY ENEMY.

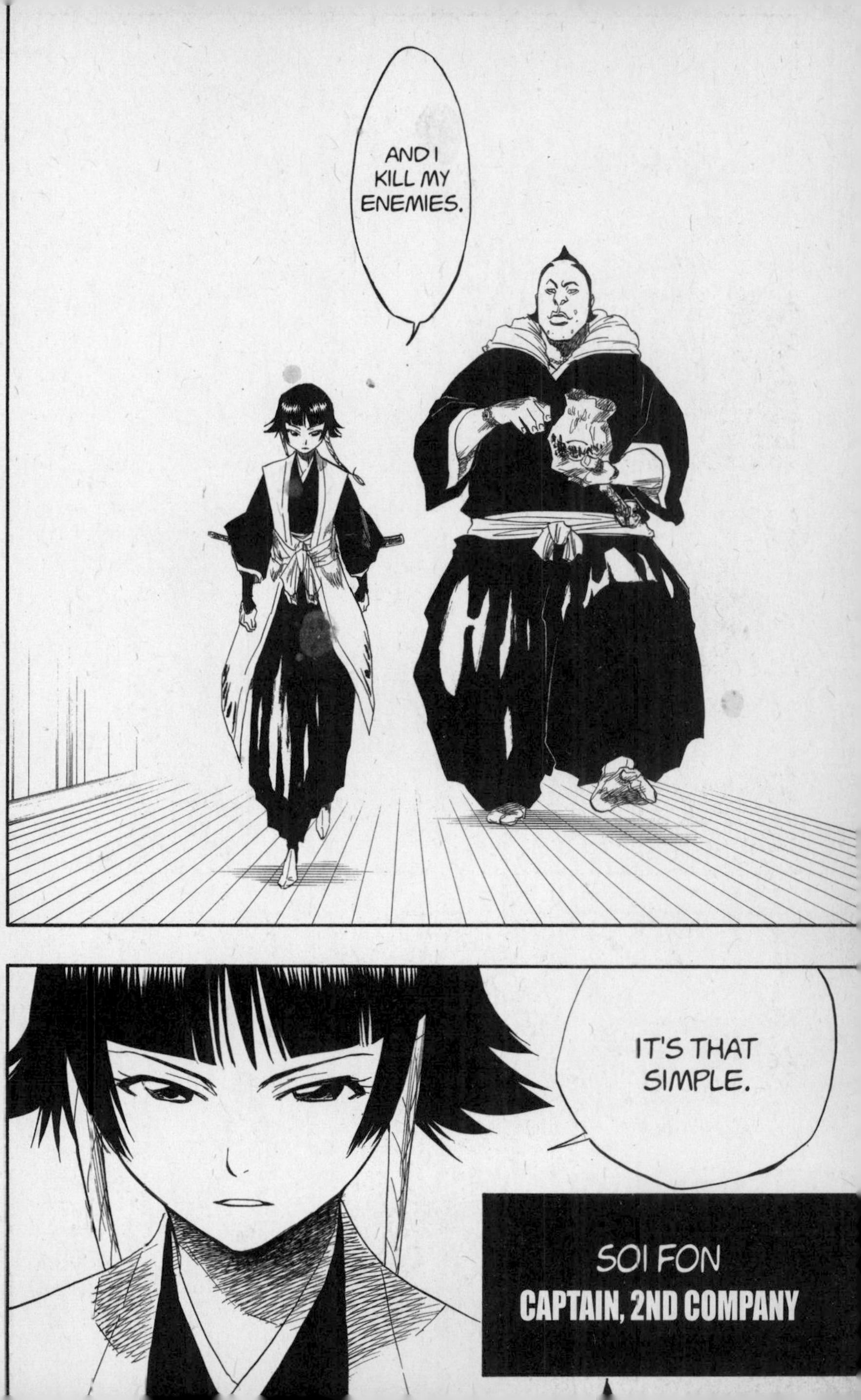
AND I KILL MY ENEMIES.
IT'S THAT SIMPLE.
SOI FON
CAPTAIN, 2ND COMPANY

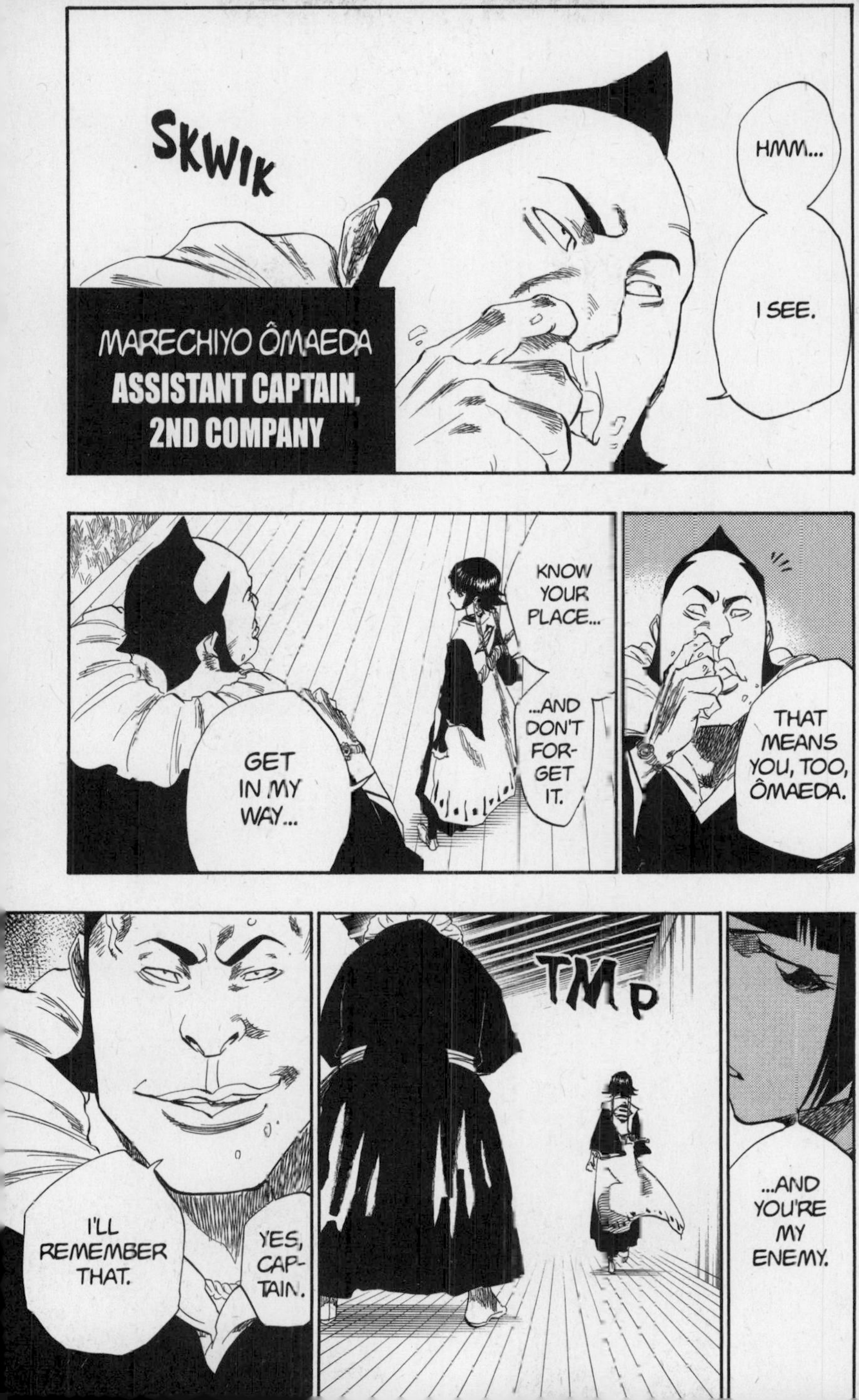
HMM...
I SEE.
SKWIK
MARECHIYO ÔMAEDA
ASSISTANT CAPTAIN, 2ND COMPANY
THAT MEANS YOU, TOO, ÔMAEDA.
KNOW YOUR PLACE...
...AND DON'T FOR-GET IT.
GET IN MY WAY...
...AND YOU'RE MY ENEMY.
TMP
YES, CAP-TAIN.
I'LL REMEMBER THAT.

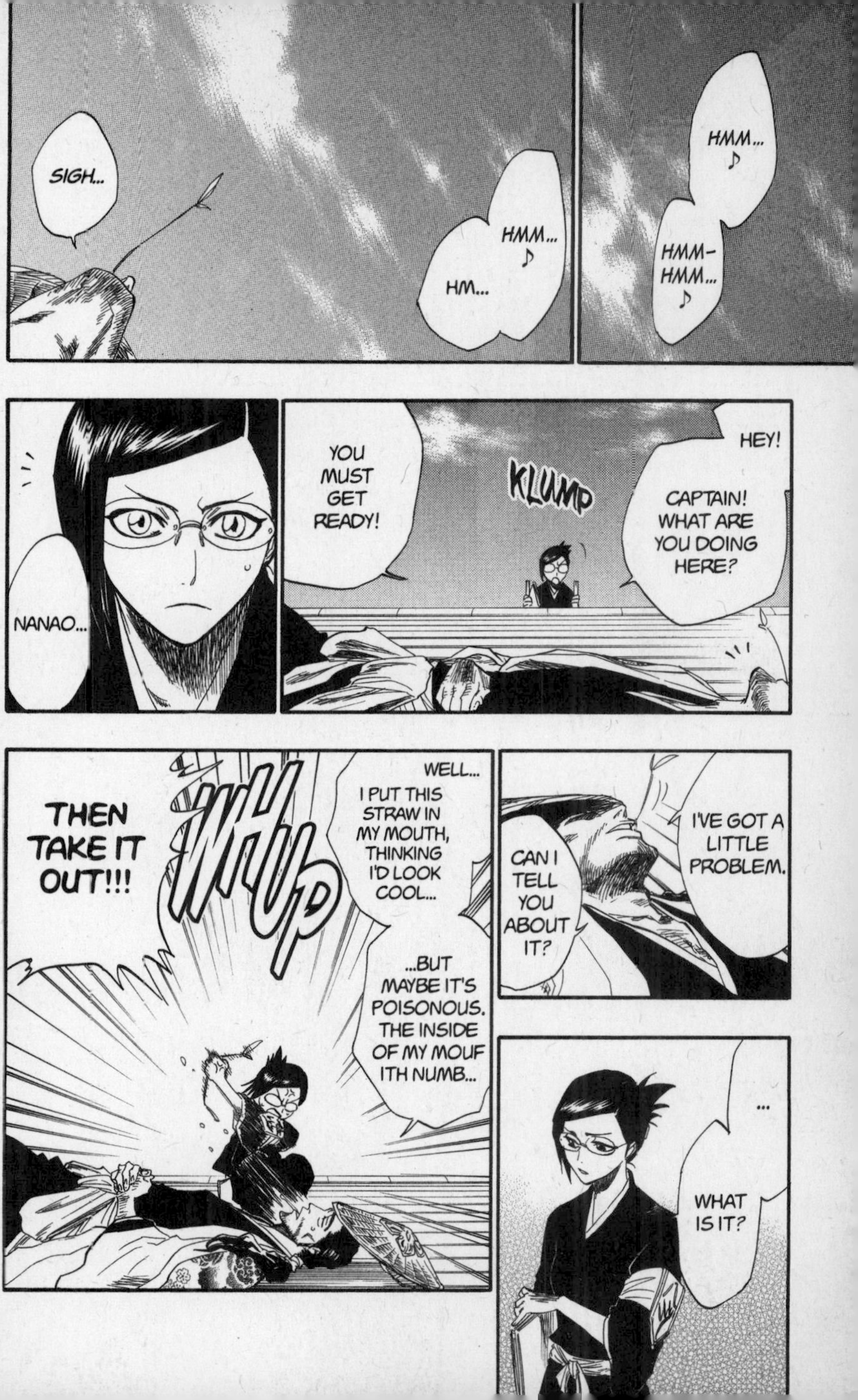
HMM... ♪
HMM-HMM... ♪
HMM... ♪
HM...
SIGH...
HEY!
CAPTAIN! WHAT ARE YOU DOING HERE?
KLUMP
YOU MUST GET READY!
NANAO...
I'VE GOT A LITTLE PROBLEM.
CAN I TELL YOU ABOUT IT?
...
WHAT IS IT?
WELL...
I PUT THIS STRAW IN MY MOUTH, THINKING I'D LOOK COOL...
...BUT MAYBE IT'S POISONOUS. THE INSIDE OF MY MOUF ITH NUMB...
WHUP
THEN TAKE IT OUT!!!

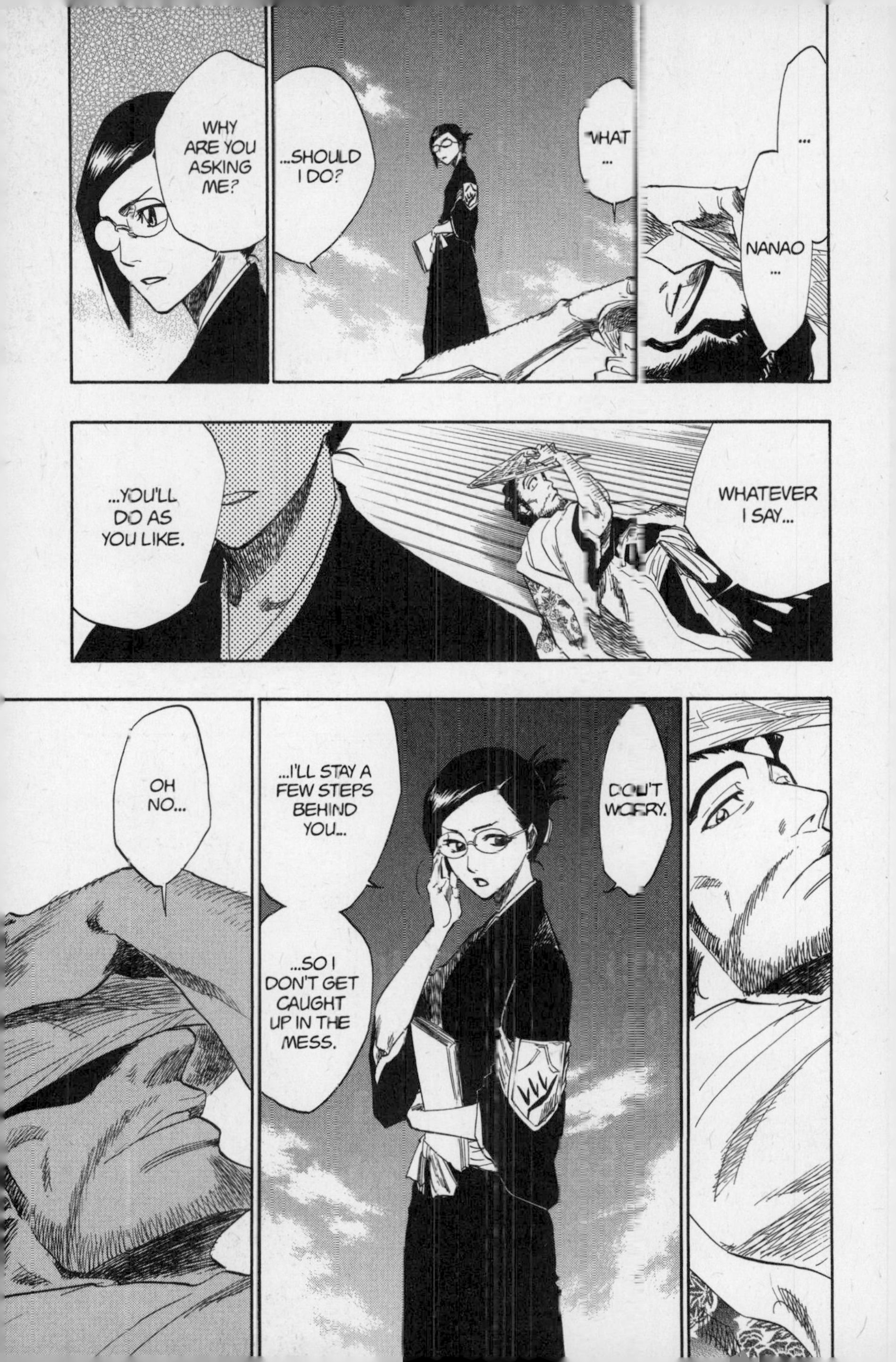
...
NANAO ...
WHAT ...
...SHOULD I DO?
WHY ARE YOU ASKING ME?
WHATEVER I SAY...
...YOU'LL DO AS YOU LIKE.
DON'T WORRY.
...I'LL STAY A FEW STEPS BEHIND YOU...
...SO I DON'T GET CAUGHT UP IN THE MESS.
OH NO...

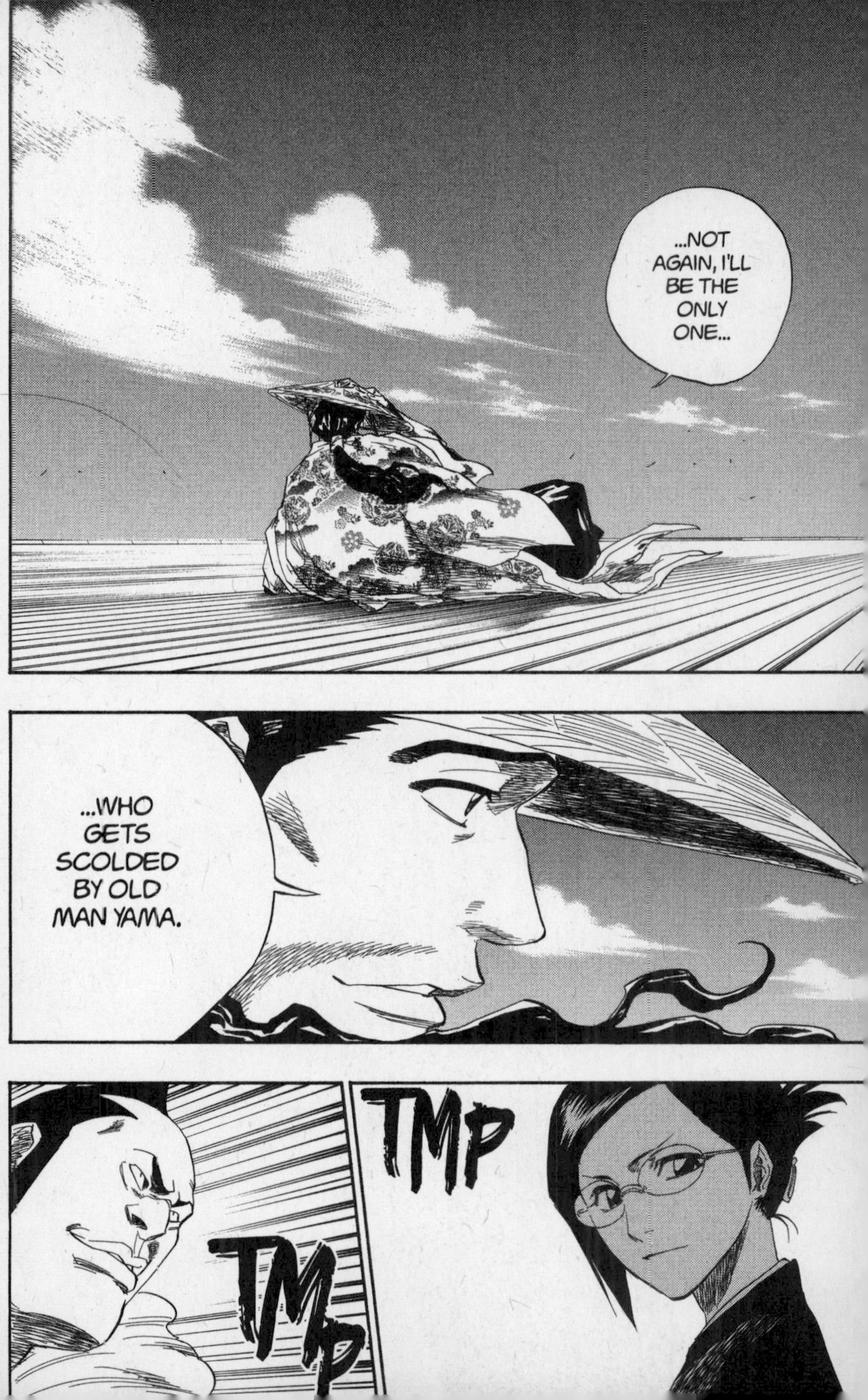
...NOT AGAIN, I'LL BE THE ONLY ONE...
...WHO GETS SCOLDED BY OLD MAN YAMA.
TMP
TMP

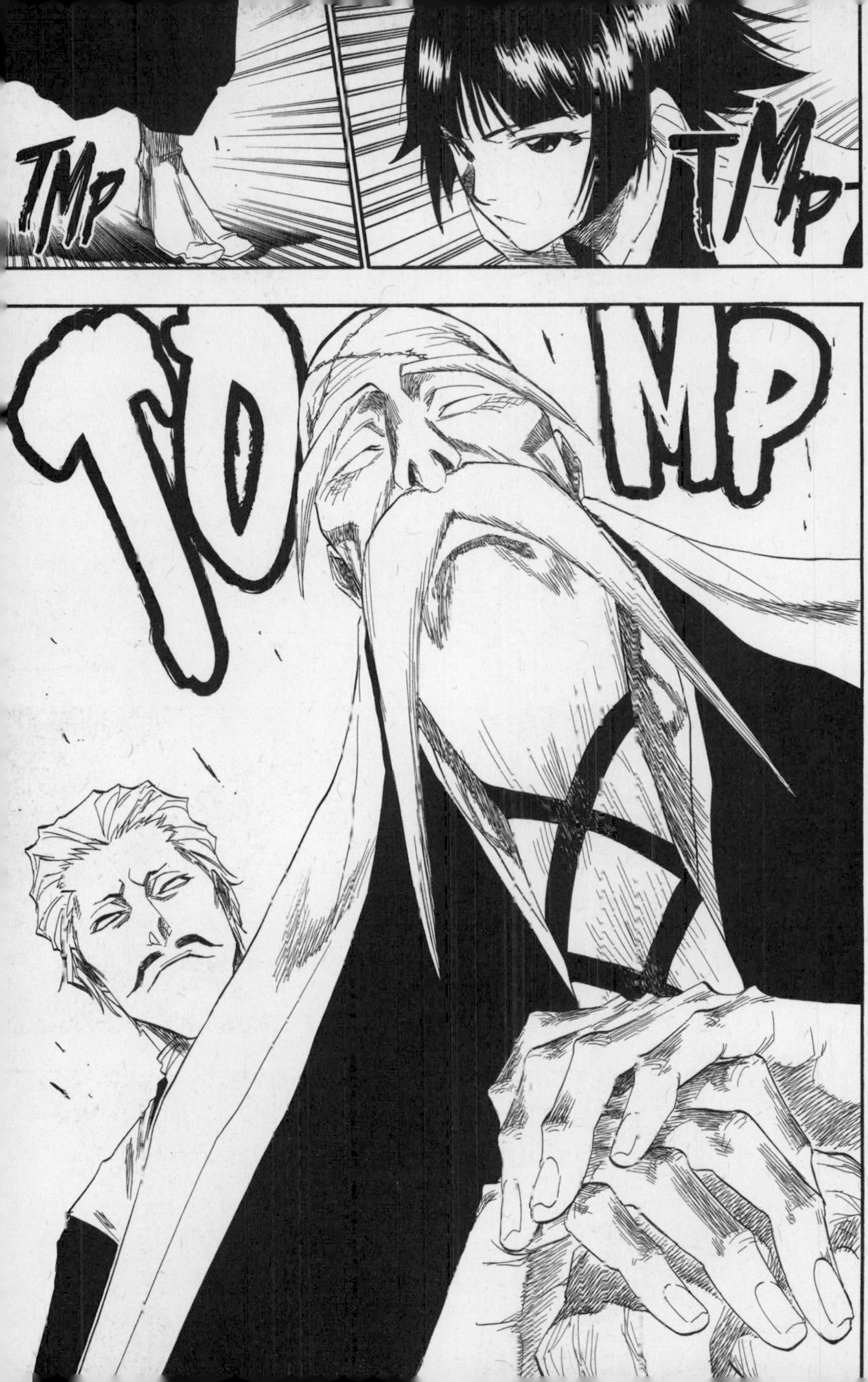
TMP-
TMP
TOMP

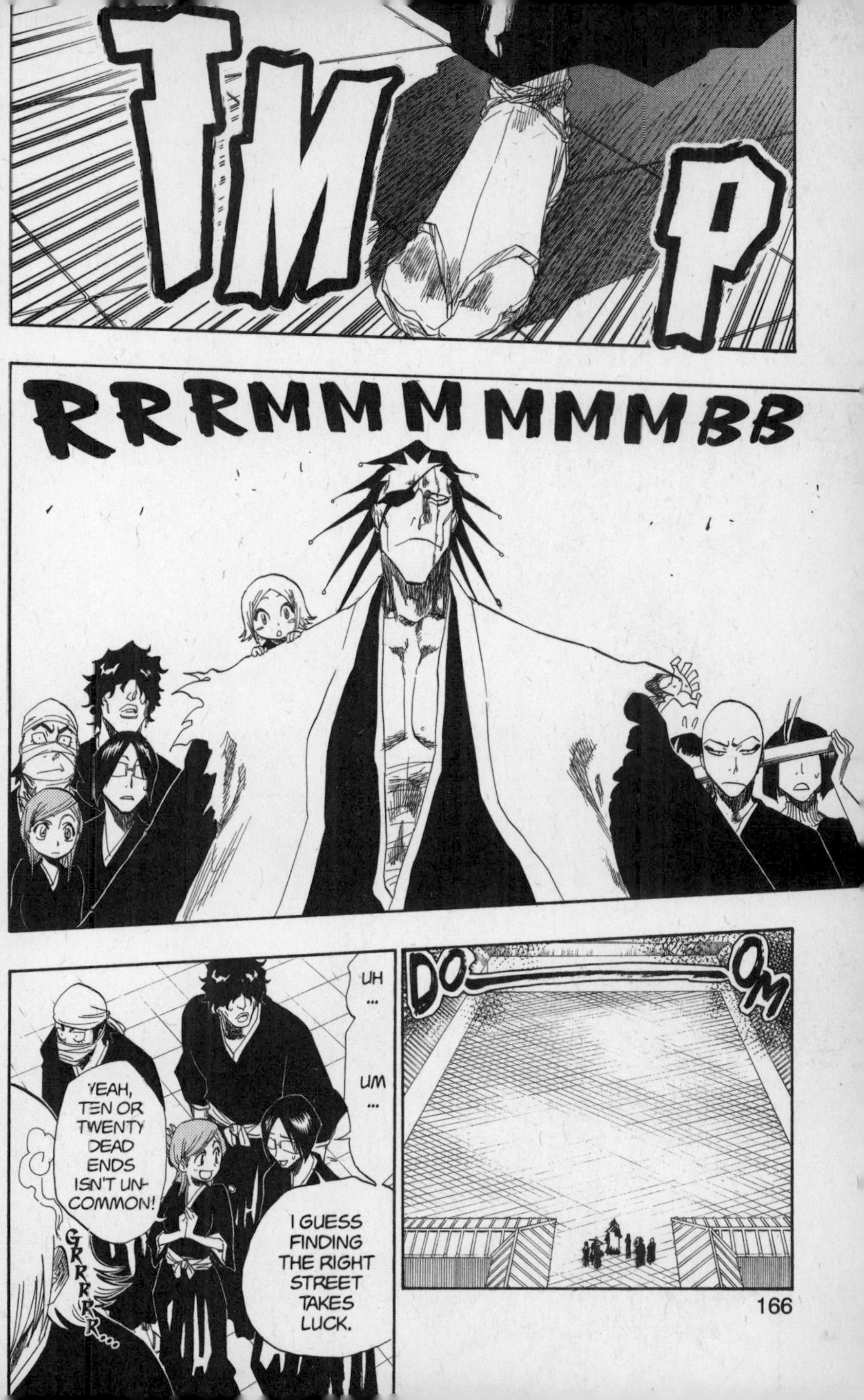

TMP
RRRMMMMMMMBB
DO-OM
UH ...
UM ...
YEAH, TEN OR TWENTY DEAD ENDS ISN'T UN-COMMON!
I GUESS FINDING THE RIGHT STREET TAKES LUCK.
GRRRRRooo

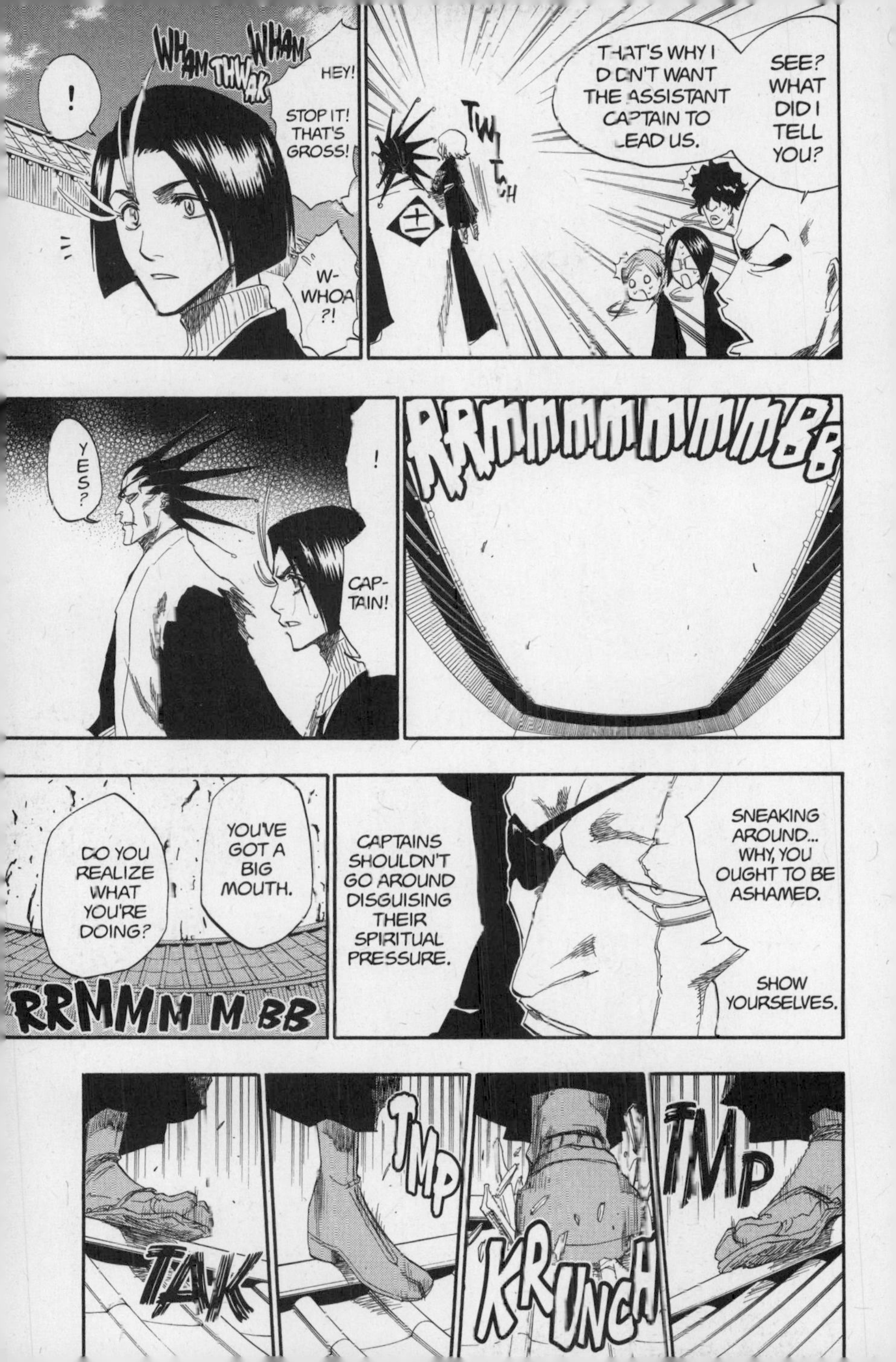
SEE? WHAT DID I TELL YOU?
THAT'S WHY I DIDN'T WANT THE ASSISTANT CAPTAIN TO LEAD US.
TWITCH
WHAM WHAM THWAK
HEY!
STOP IT! THAT'S GROSS!
!
W-WHOA?!
RRMMMMMMMMMBB
!
CAPTAIN!
YES?
SNEAKING AROUND... WHY, YOU OUGHT TO BE ASHAMED.
CAPTAINS SHOULDN'T GO AROUND DISGUISING THEIR SPIRITUAL PRESSURE.
SHOW YOURSELVES.
YOU'VE GOT A BIG MOUTH.
DO YOU REALIZE WHAT YOU'RE DOING?
RRMMMMMBB
TMP
KRUNCH
TMP
TAK

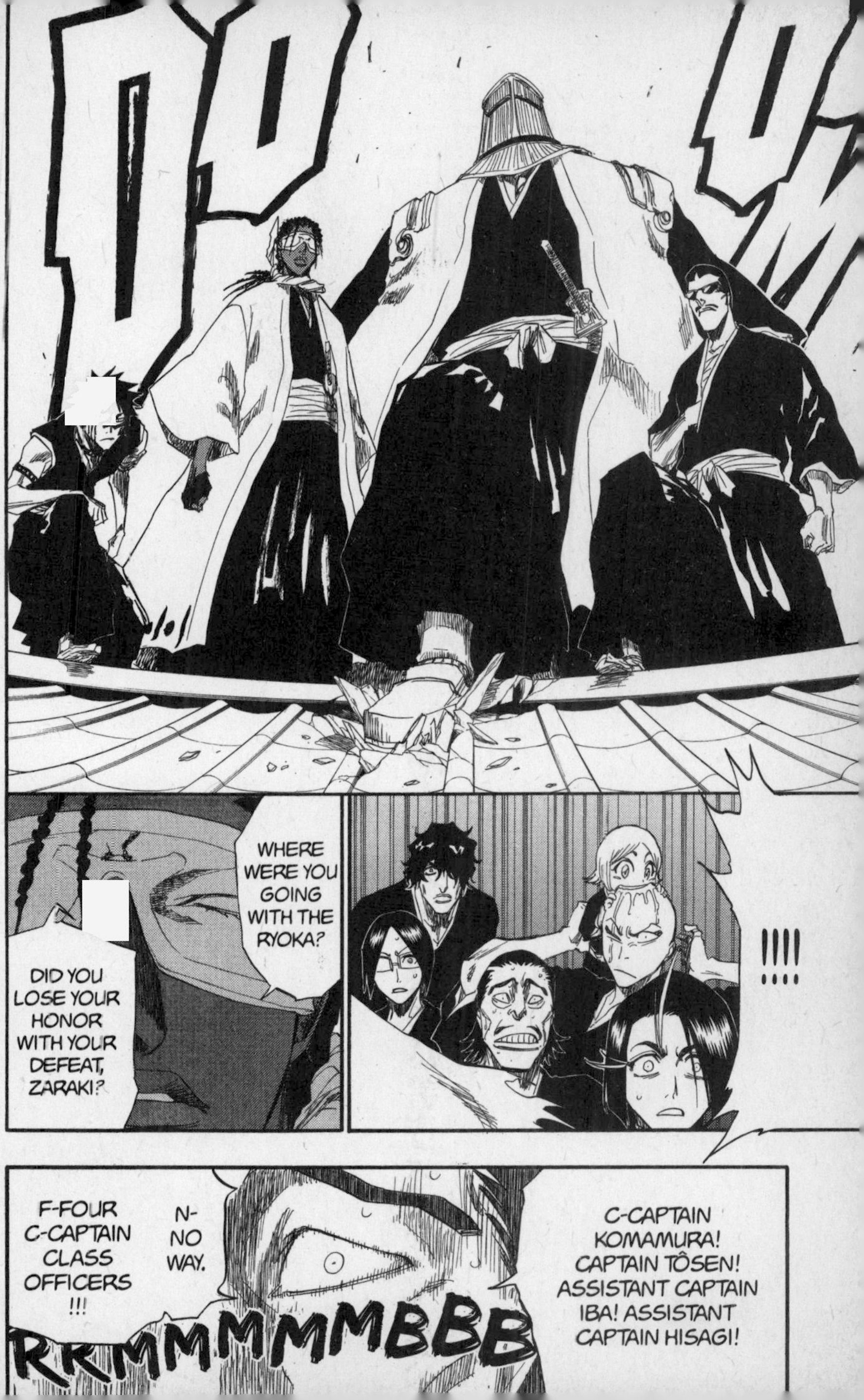
!!!!
WHERE WERE YOU GOING WITH THE RYOKA?
DID YOU LOSE YOUR HONOR WITH YOUR DEFEAT, ZARAKI?
C-CAPTAIN KOMAMURA! CAPTAIN TÔSEN! ASSISTANT CAPTAIN IBA! ASSISTANT CAPTAIN HISAGI!
N-NO WAY.
F-FOUR C-CAPTAIN CLASS OFFICERS!!!
RRMMMMMMBBB

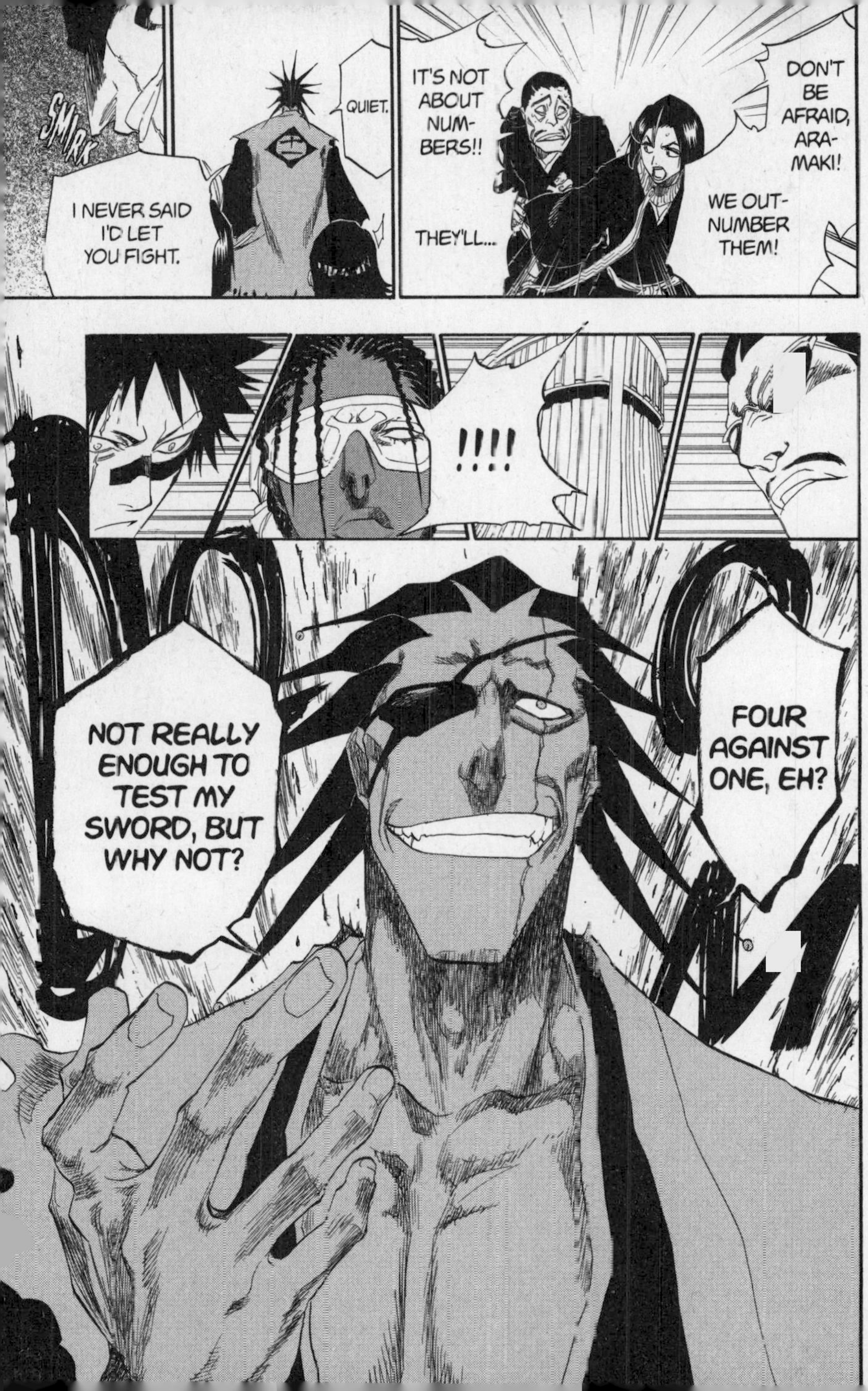
DON'T BE AFRAID, ARAMAKI!
WE OUTNUMBER THEM!
IT'S NOT ABOUT NUMBERS!!
THEY'LL...
QUIET.
SMIRK
I NEVER SAID I'D LET YOU FIGHT.
!!!!
FOUR AGAINST ONE, EH?
NOT REALLY ENOUGH TO TEST MY SWORD, BUT WHY NOT?

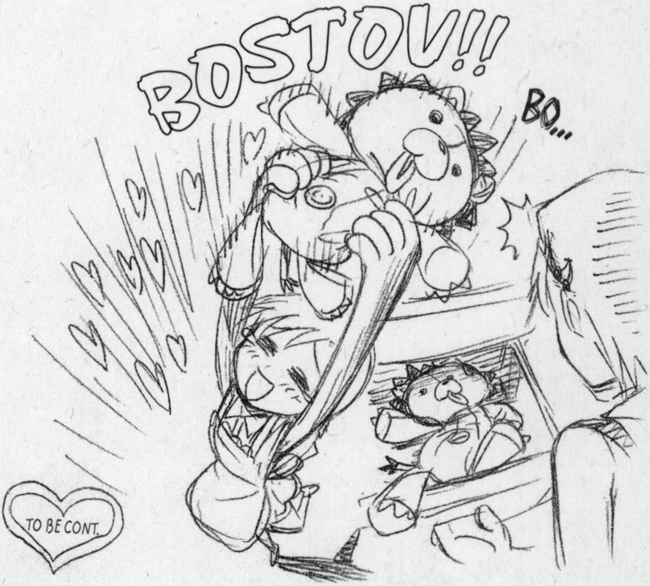
BOSTOV!!
BO...
TO BE CONT.

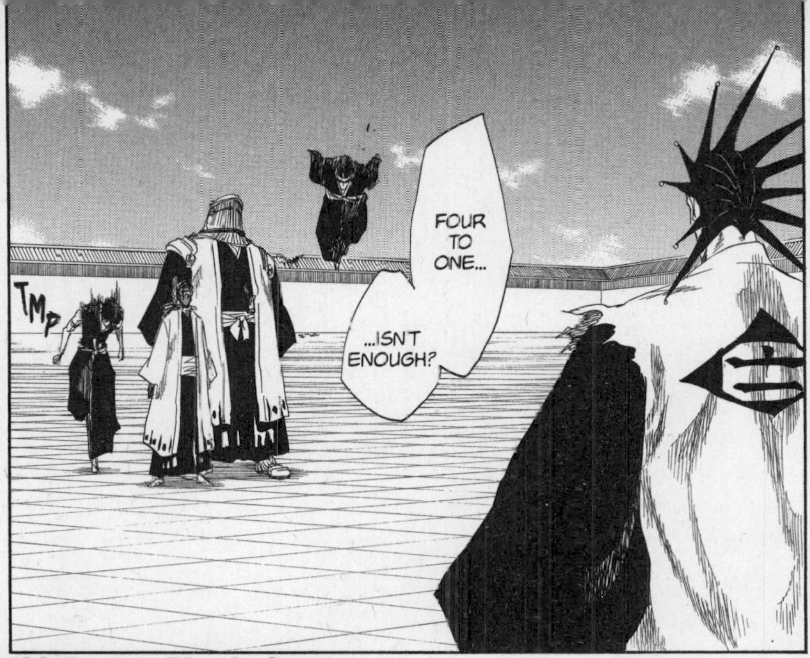
FOUR TO ONE...
...ISN'T ENOUGH?
TMP

139. Drowsy, Bloody, Crazy

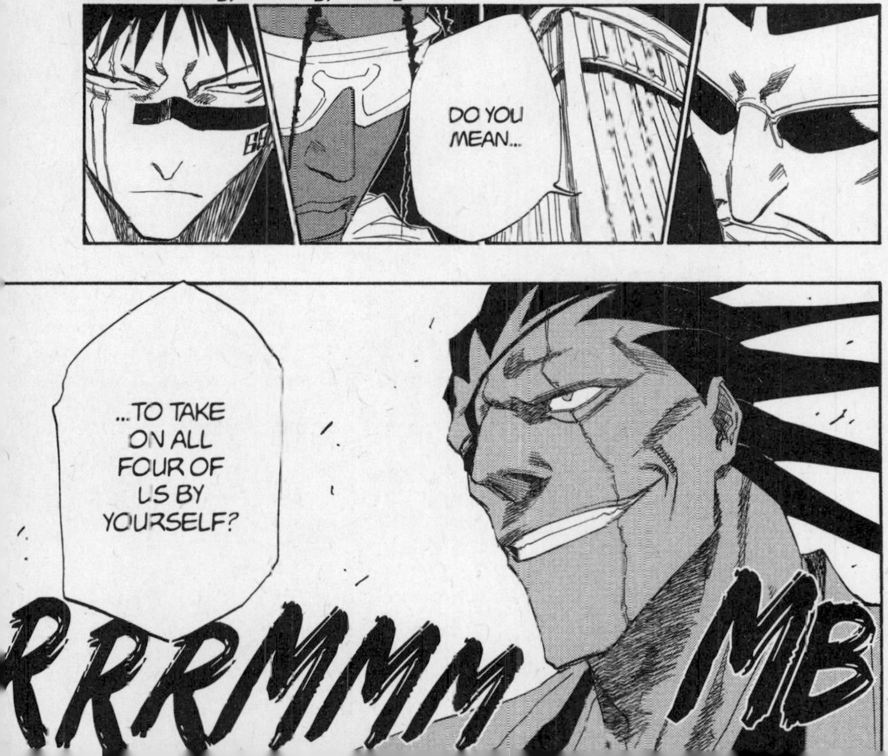
DO YOU MEAN...
...TO TAKE ON ALL FOUR OF US BY YOURSELF?
RRRMMMMMB

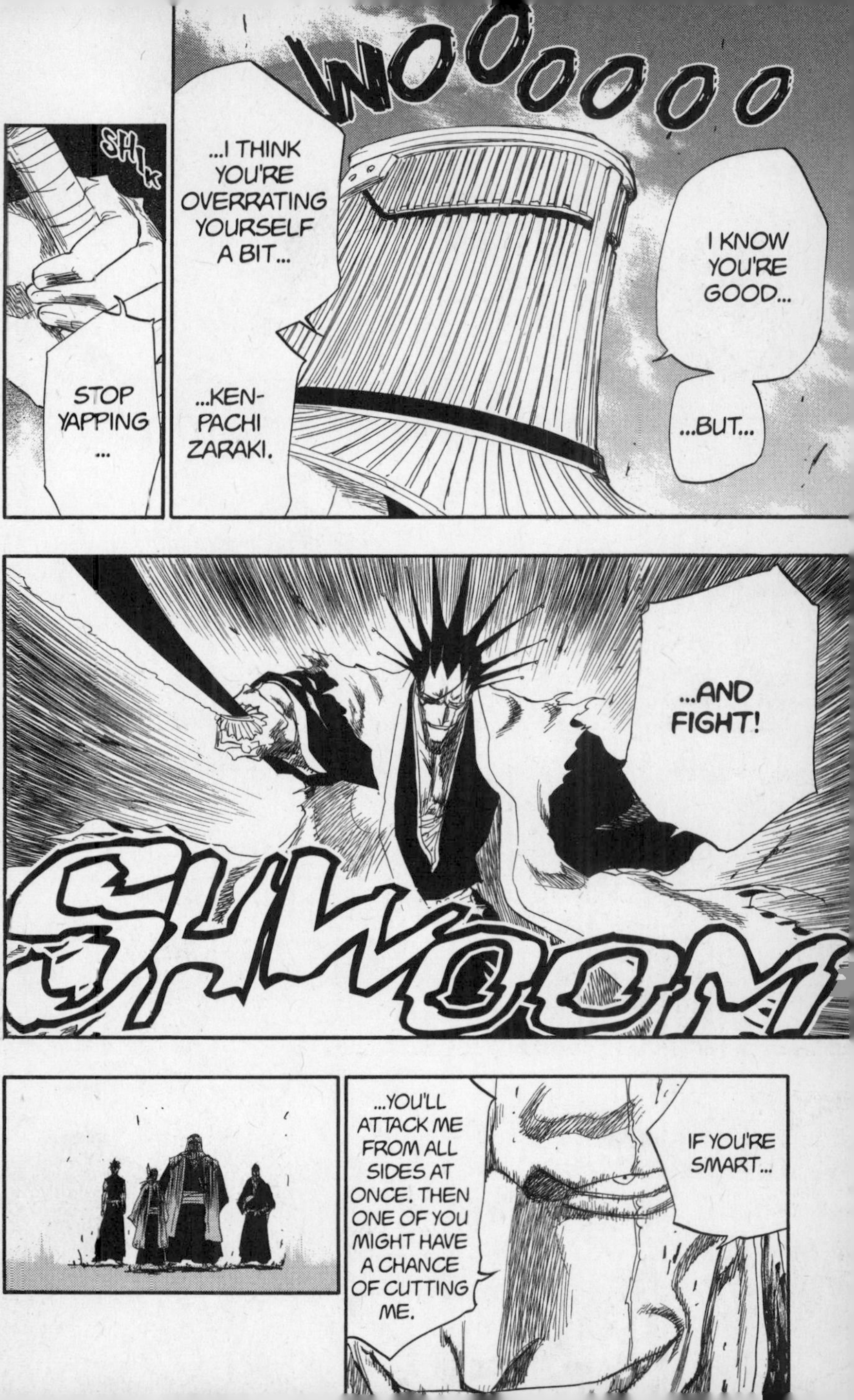
WOOOOOOO
I KNOW YOU'RE GOOD...
...BUT...
...I THINK YOU'RE OVERRATING YOURSELF A BIT...
...KEN-PACHI ZARAKI.
SHIK
STOP YAPPING ...
...AND FIGHT!
SHWOOM
IF YOU'RE SMART...
...YOU'LL ATTACK ME FROM ALL SIDES AT ONCE. THEN ONE OF YOU MIGHT HAVE A CHANCE OF CUTTING ME.

READ THIS WAY

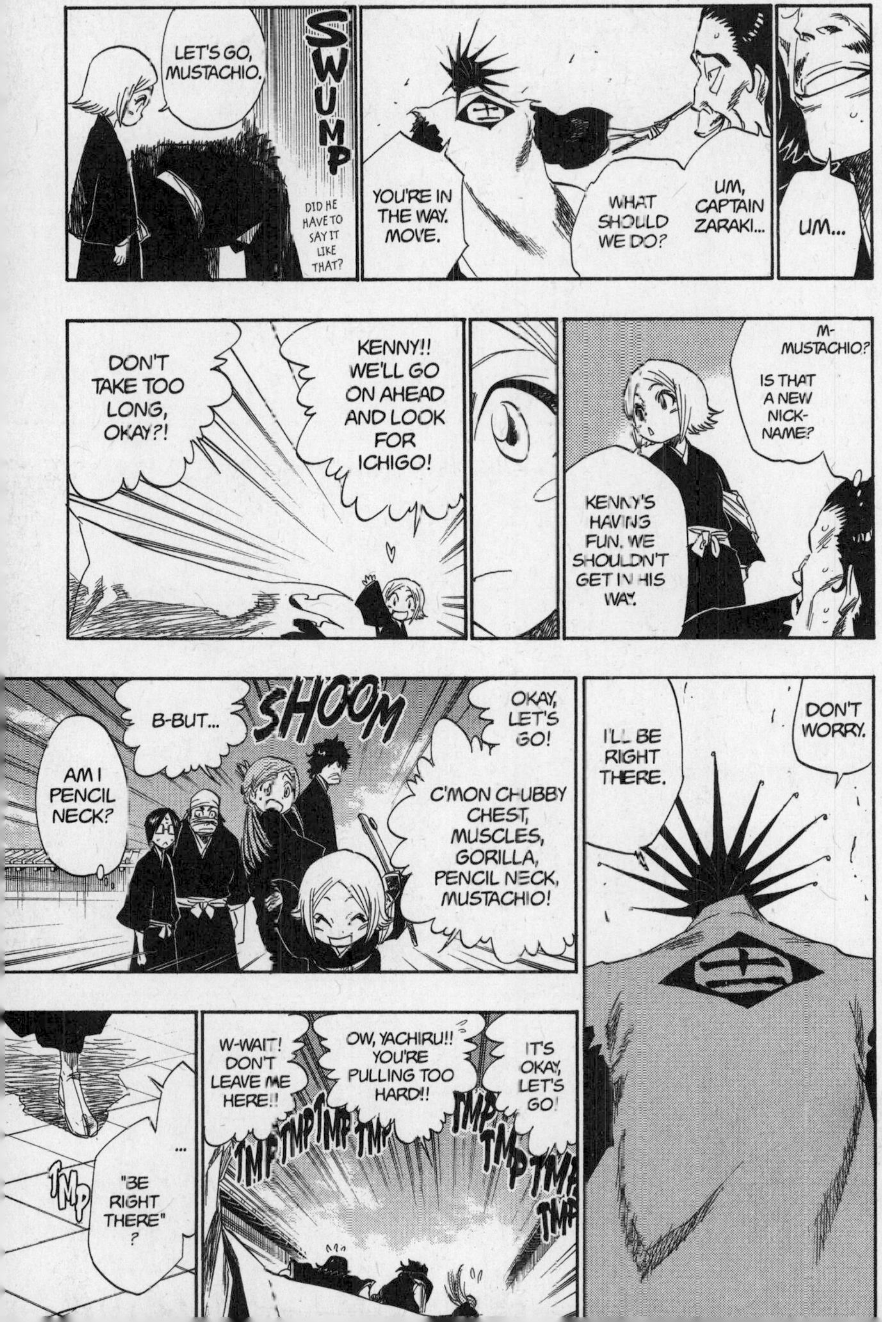
UM...
UM, CAPTAIN ZARAKI...
WHAT SHOULD WE DO?
YOU'RE IN THE WAY. MOVE.
SWUMP
LET'S GO, MUSTACHIO.
DID HE HAVE TO SAY IT LIKE THAT?
M-MUSTACHIO? IS THAT A NEW NICK-NAME?
KENNY'S HAVING FUN. WE SHOULDN'T GET IN HIS WAY.
KENNY!! WE'LL GO ON AHEAD AND LOOK FOR ICHIGO!
DON'T TAKE TOO LONG, OKAY?!
DON'T WORRY.
I'LL BE RIGHT THERE.
OKAY, LET'S GO!
C'MON CHUBBY CHEST, MUSCLES, GORILLA, PENCIL NECK, MUSTACHIO!
SHOOM
B-BUT...
AM I PENCIL NECK?
IT'S OKAY, LET'S GO!
OW, YACHIRU!! YOU'RE PULLING TOO HARD!!
W-WAIT! DON'T LEAVE ME HERE!!
TMP TMP TMP TMP TMP TMP TMP TMP
...
"BE RIGHT THERE"?
TMP

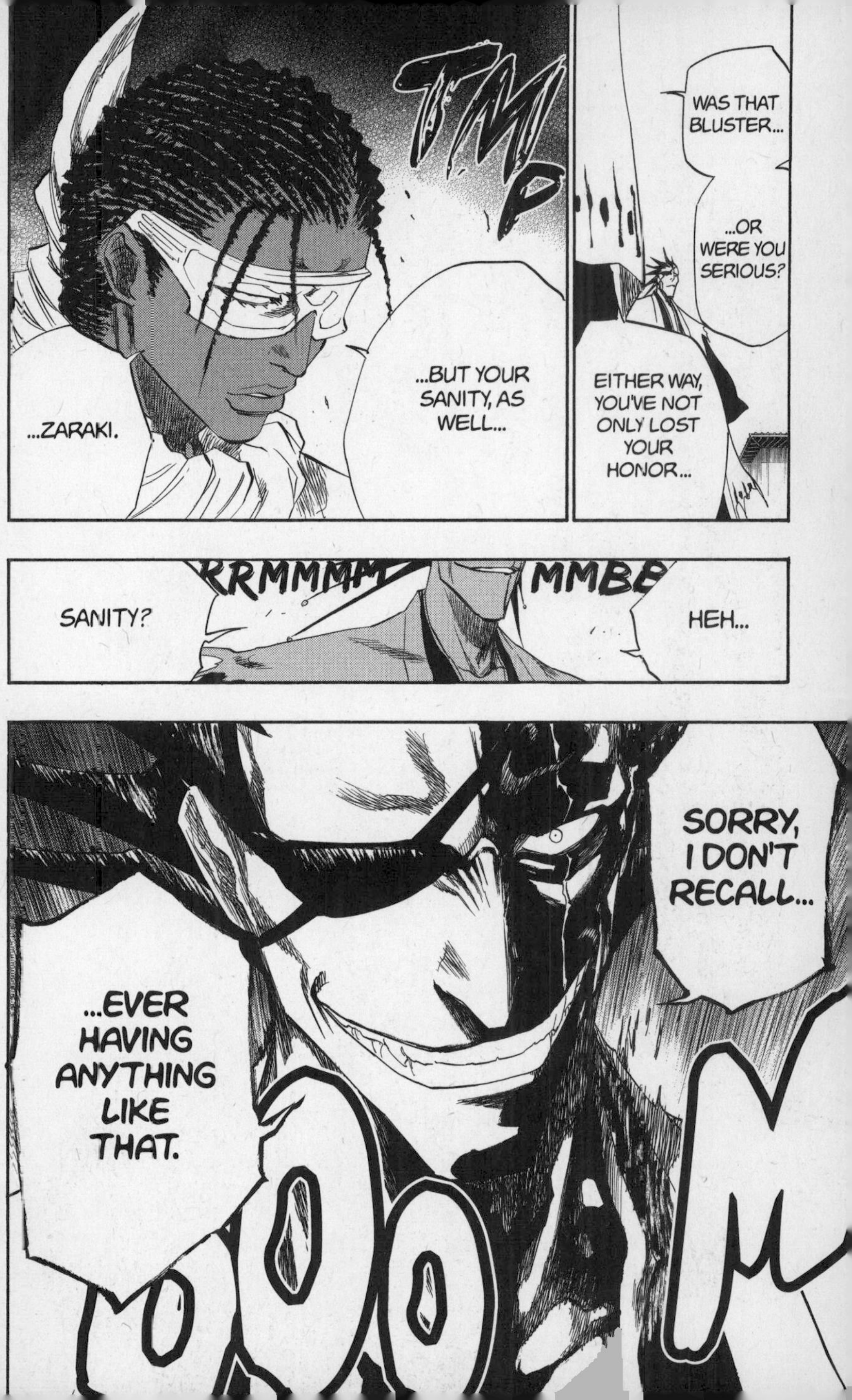
WAS THAT BLUSTER...
...OR WERE YOU SERIOUS?
EITHER WAY, YOU'VE NOT ONLY LOST YOUR HONOR...
TMP
...BUT YOUR SANITY, AS WELL...
...ZARAKI.
HEH...
SANITY?
SORRY, I DON'T RECALL...
...EVER HAVING ANYTHING LIKE THAT.

139. Drowsy, Bloody, Crazy

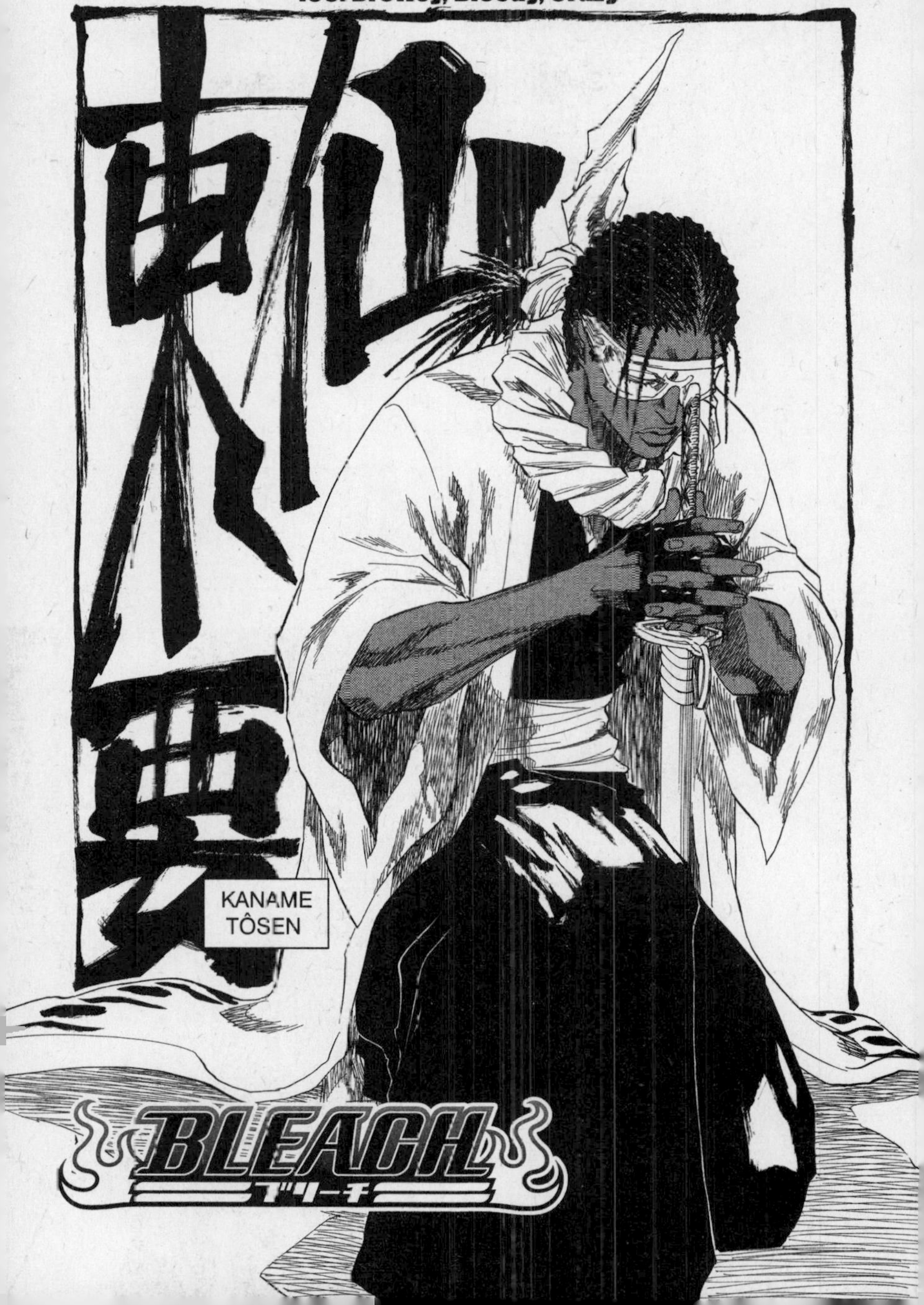
東仙要
KANAME TÔSEN
BLEACH
ブリーチ

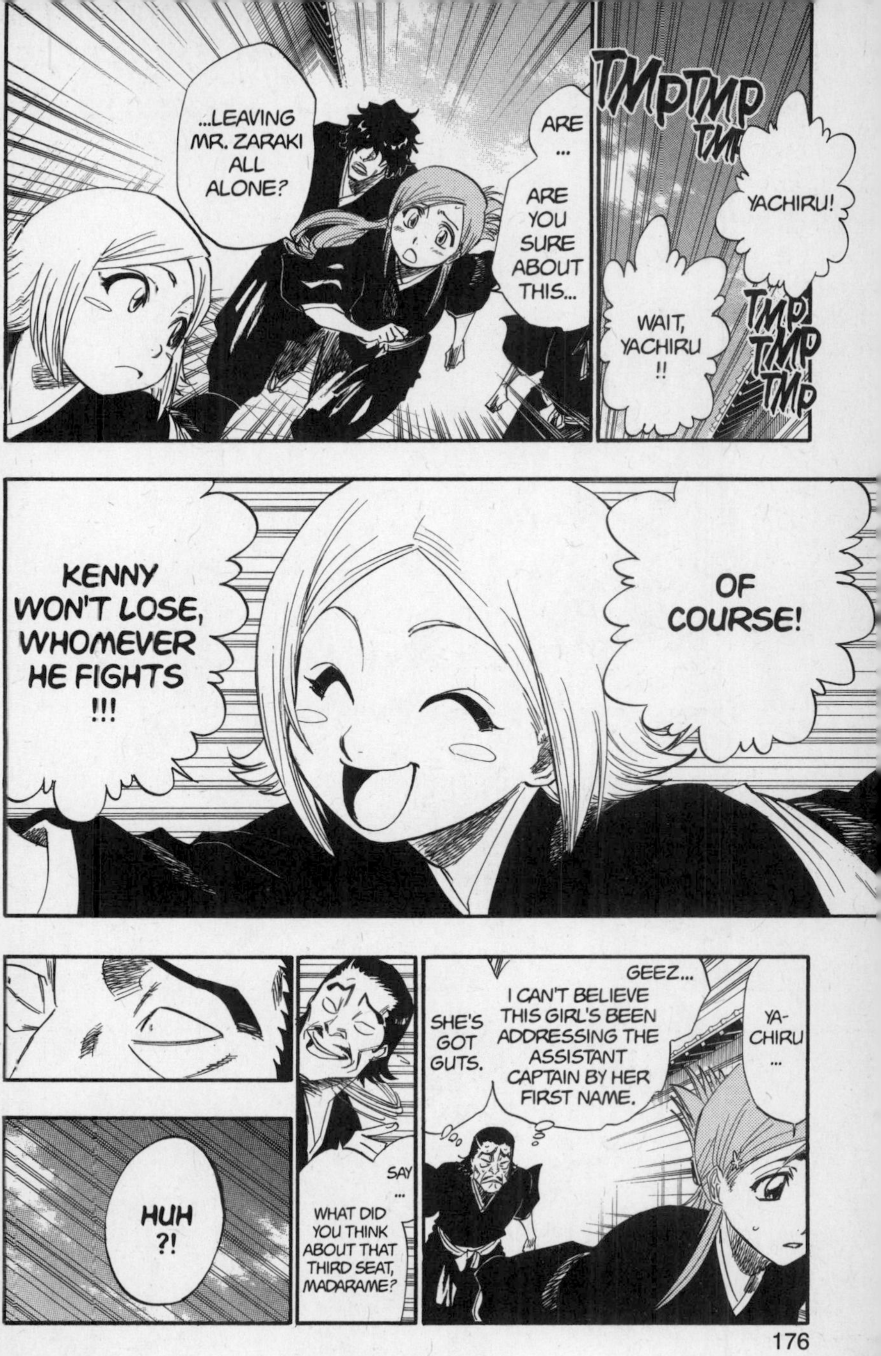
TMPTMP TMP
YACHIRU!
WAIT, YACHIRU !!
TMP TMP TMP
ARE ... ARE YOU SURE ABOUT THIS...
...LEAVING MR. ZARAKI ALL ALONE?
OF COURSE!
KENNY WON'T LOSE, WHOMEVER HE FIGHTS !!!
YA-CHIRU ...
GEEZ...
I CAN'T BELIEVE THIS GIRL'S BEEN ADDRESSING THE ASSISTANT CAPTAIN BY HER FIRST NAME.
SHE'S GOT GUTS.
SAY ...
WHAT DID YOU THINK ABOUT THAT THIRD SEAT, MADARAME?
HUH ?!

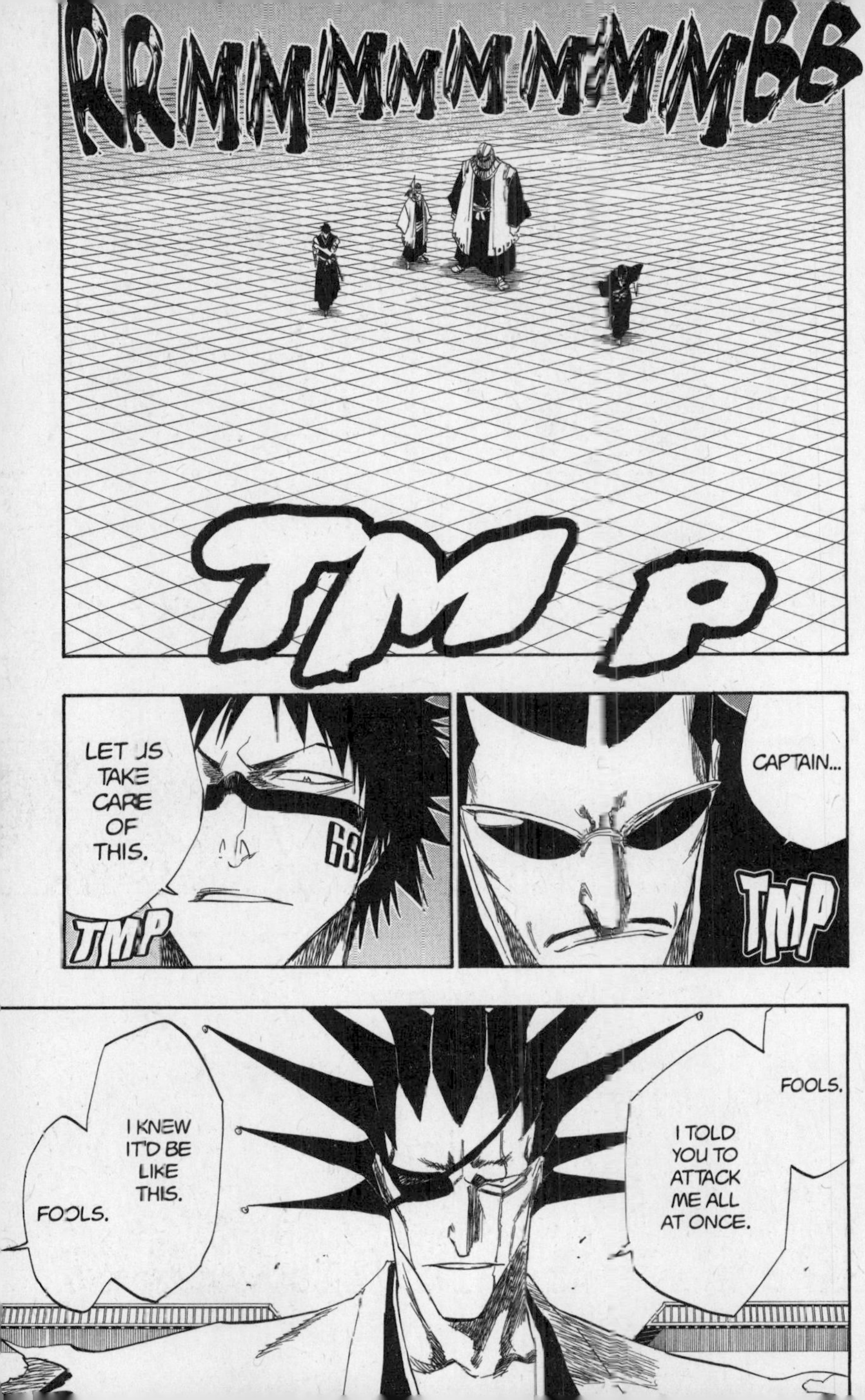
RRMMMMMMMMMBB
TMP
CAPTAIN...
TMP
LET US TAKE CARE OF THIS.
TMP
FOOLS.
I TOLD YOU TO ATTACK ME ALL AT ONCE.
I KNEW IT'D BE LIKE THIS.
FOOLS.

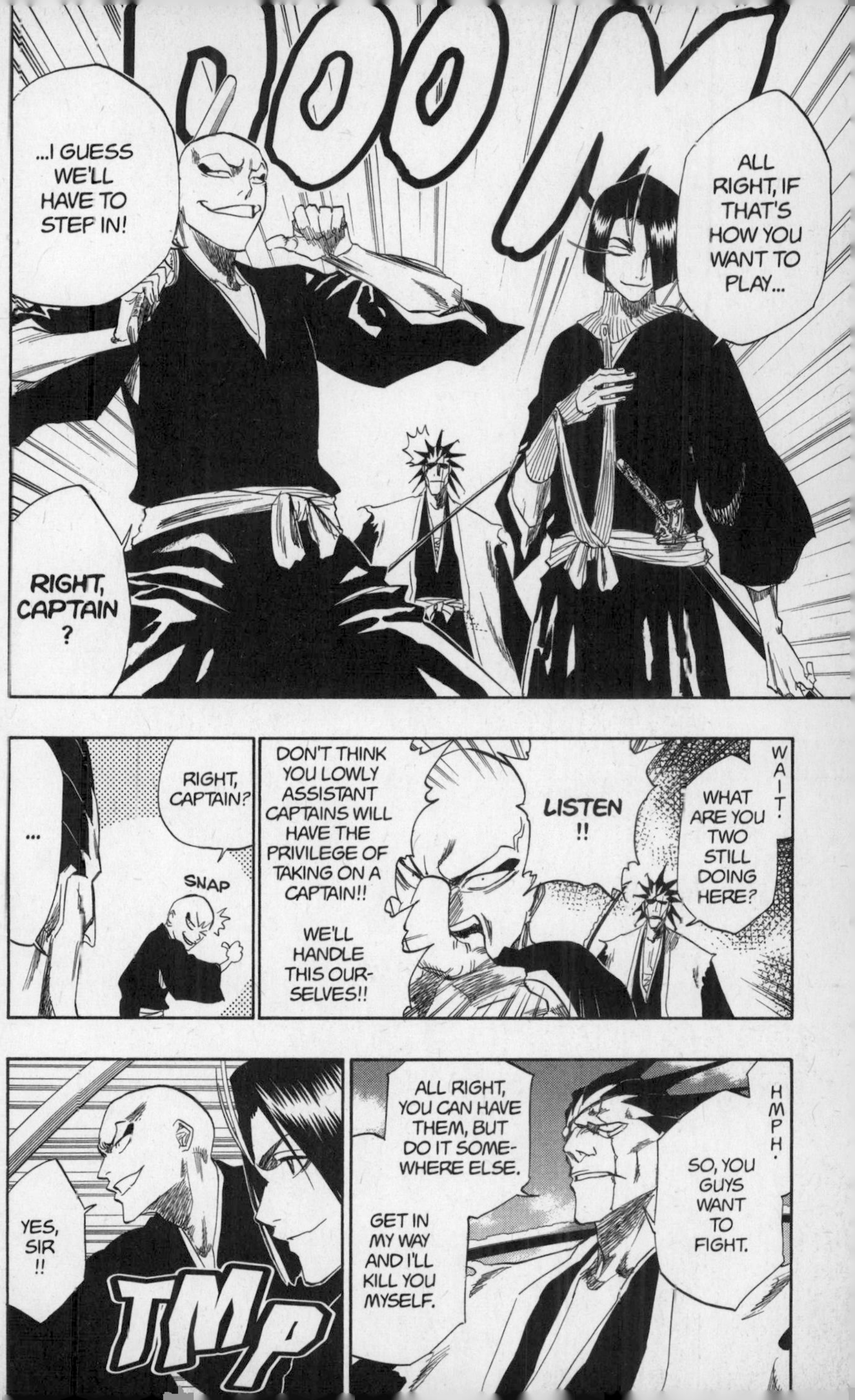
ALL RIGHT, IF THAT'S HOW YOU WANT TO PLAY...
...I GUESS WE'LL HAVE TO STEP IN!
RIGHT, CAPTAIN ?
WAIT.
WHAT ARE YOU TWO STILL DOING HERE?
LISTEN !!
DON'T THINK YOU LOWLY ASSISTANT CAPTAINS WILL HAVE THE PRIVILEGE OF TAKING ON A CAPTAIN!!
WE'LL HANDLE THIS OUR-SELVES!!
RIGHT, CAPTAIN?
SNAP
...
HMPH.
SO, YOU GUYS WANT TO FIGHT.
ALL RIGHT, YOU CAN HAVE THEM, BUT DO IT SOME-WHERE ELSE.
GET IN MY WAY AND I'LL KILL YOU MYSELF.
YES, SIR !!
TMP

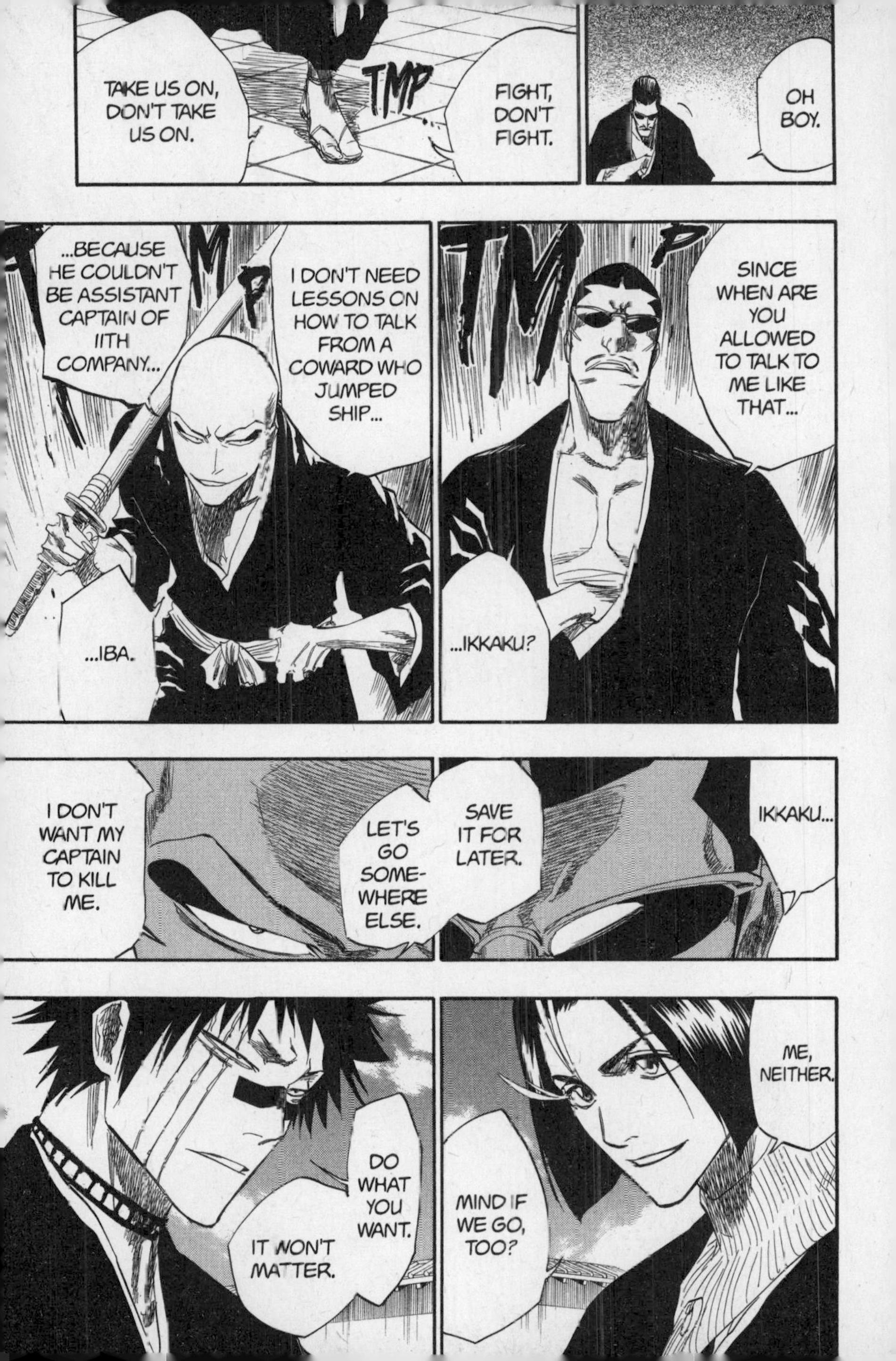
OH BOY.
FIGHT, DON'T FIGHT.
TMP
TAKE US ON, DON'T TAKE US ON.
TMP
SINCE WHEN ARE YOU ALLOWED TO TALK TO ME LIKE THAT...
...IKKAKU?
I DON'T NEED LESSONS ON HOW TO TALK FROM A COWARD WHO JUMPED SHIP...
TMP
...BECAUSE HE COULDN'T BE ASSISTANT CAPTAIN OF 11TH COMPANY...
...IBA.
IKKAKU...
SAVE IT FOR LATER.
LET'S GO SOME-WHERE ELSE.
I DON'T WANT MY CAPTAIN TO KILL ME.
ME, NEITHER.
MIND IF WE GO, TOO?
DO WHAT YOU WANT.
IT WON'T MATTER.

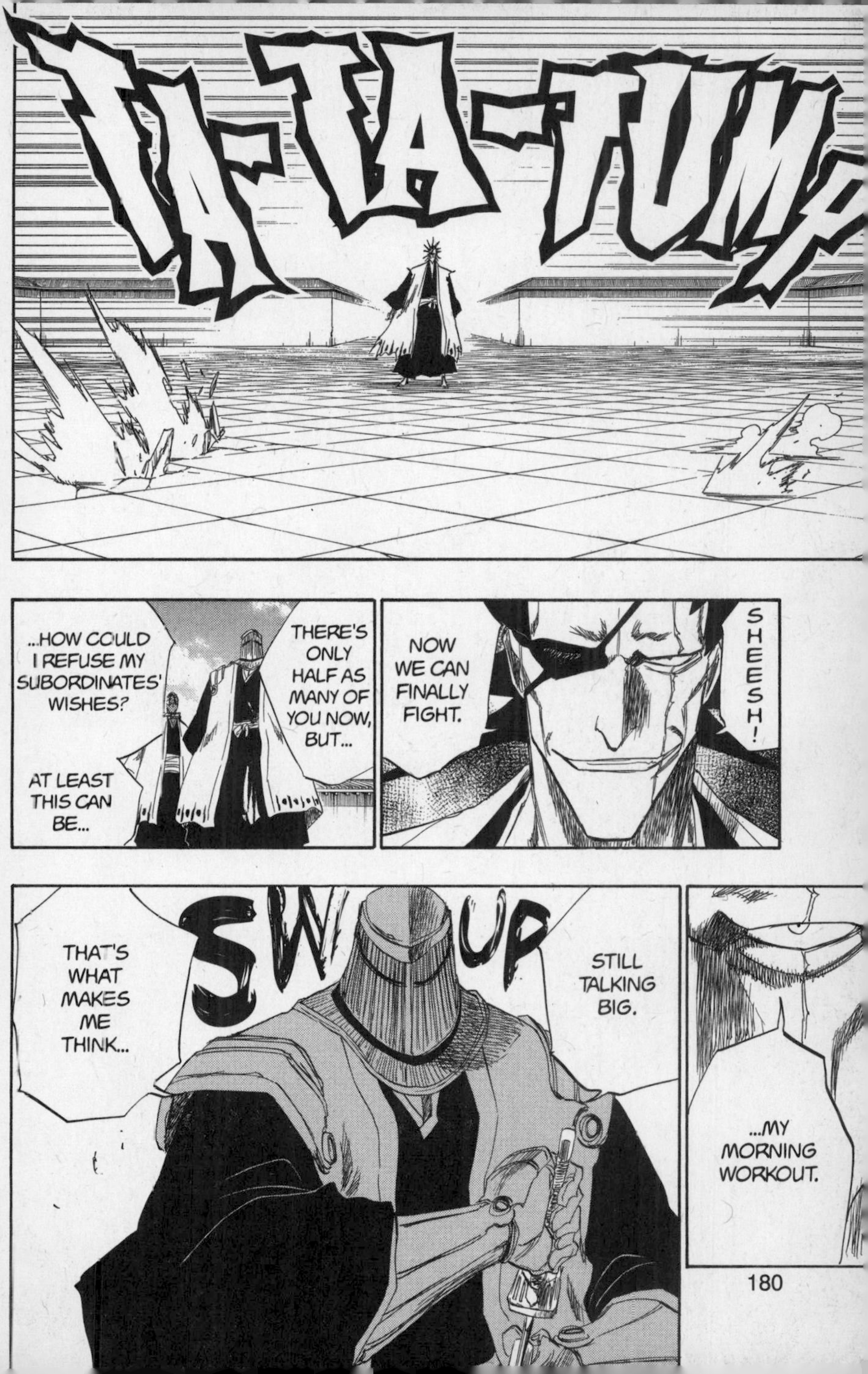
TA-TA-TUM
SHEESH!
NOW WE CAN FINALLY FIGHT.
THERE'S ONLY HALF AS MANY OF YOU NOW, BUT...
...HOW COULD I REFUSE MY SUBORDINATES' WISHES?
AT LEAST THIS CAN BE...
...MY MORNING WORKOUT.
STILL TALKING BIG.
SW UP
THAT'S WHAT MAKES ME THINK...

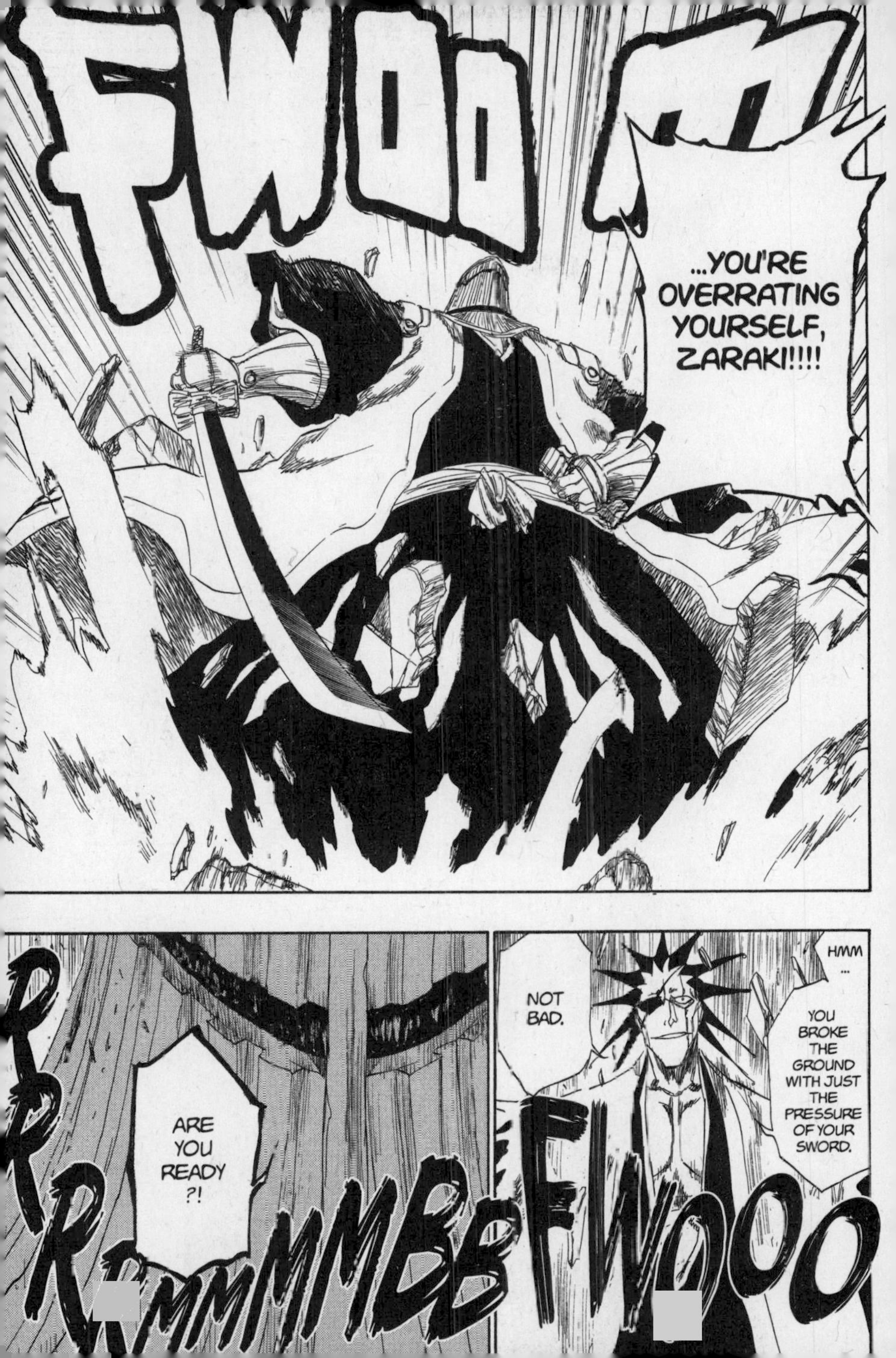
FWOOM
...YOU'RE OVERRATING YOURSELF, ZARAKI!!!!!
HMM ...
YOU BROKE THE GROUND WITH JUST THE PRESSURE OF YOUR SWORD.
NOT BAD.
ARE YOU READY ?!

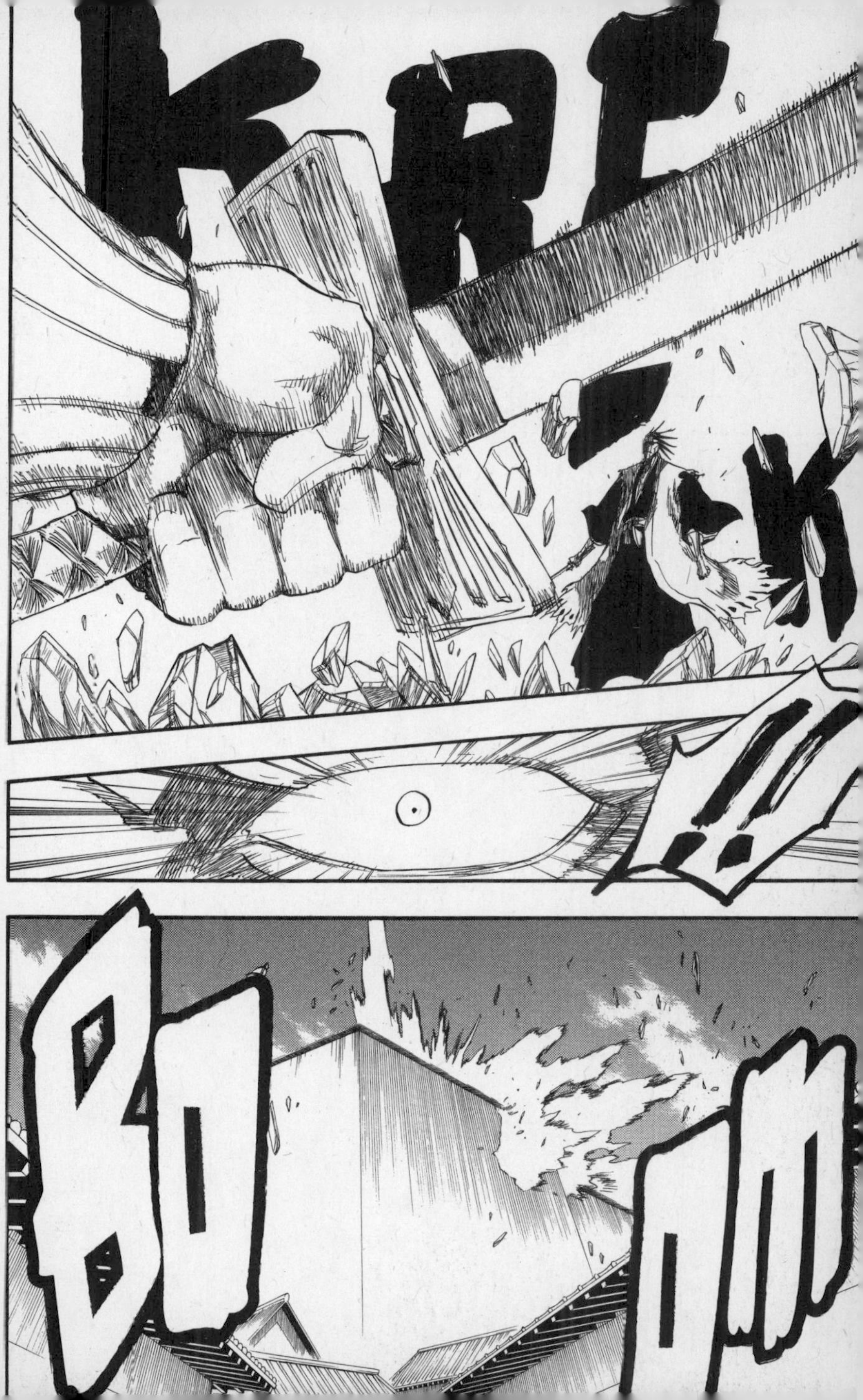
KRRK
!!
BOM

READ THIS WAY

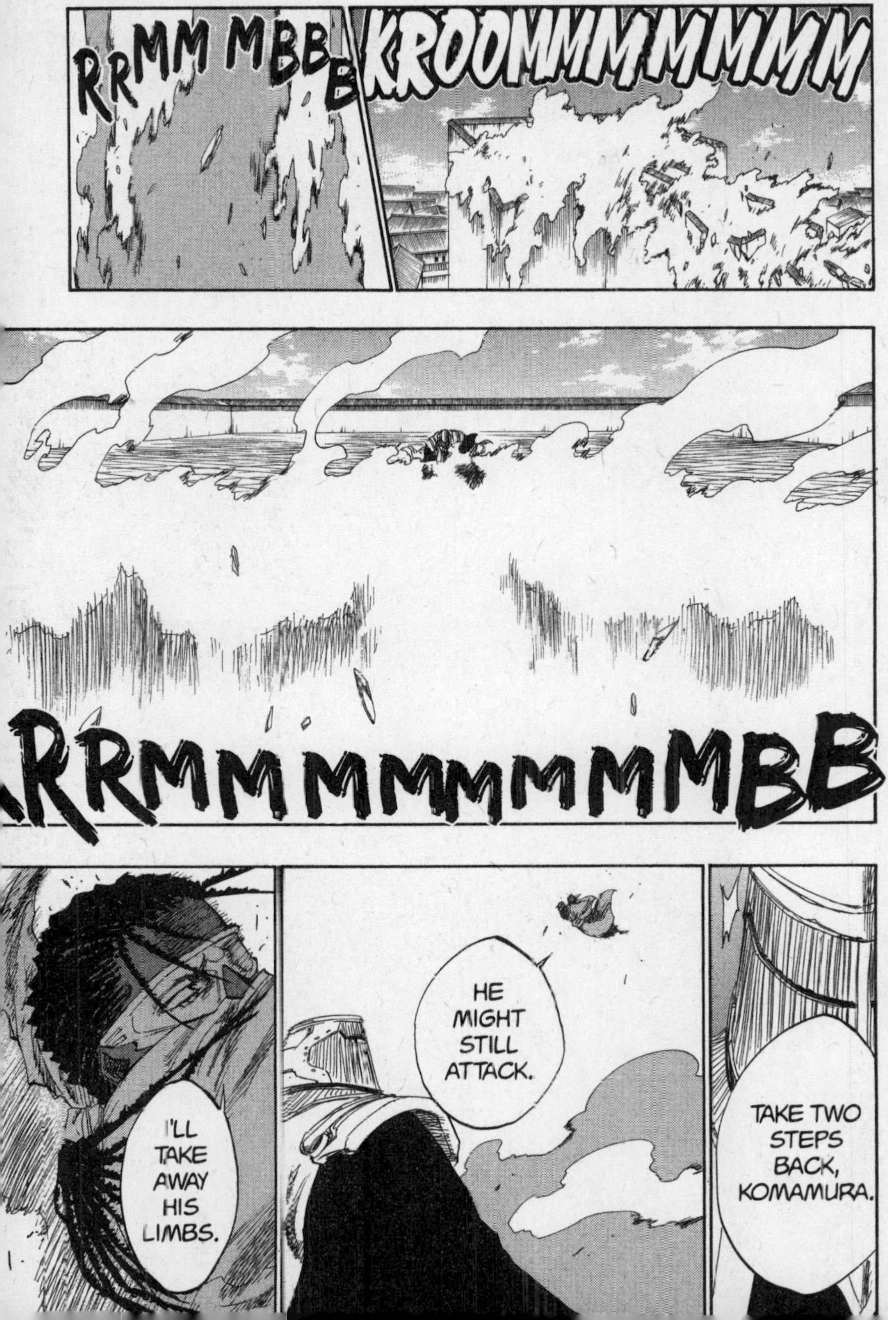
KROOMMMMMMMM
RRMM MBBB
RRMMMMMMMMBB
TAKE TWO STEPS BACK, KOMAMURA.
HE MIGHT STILL ATTACK.
I'LL TAKE AWAY HIS LIMBS.

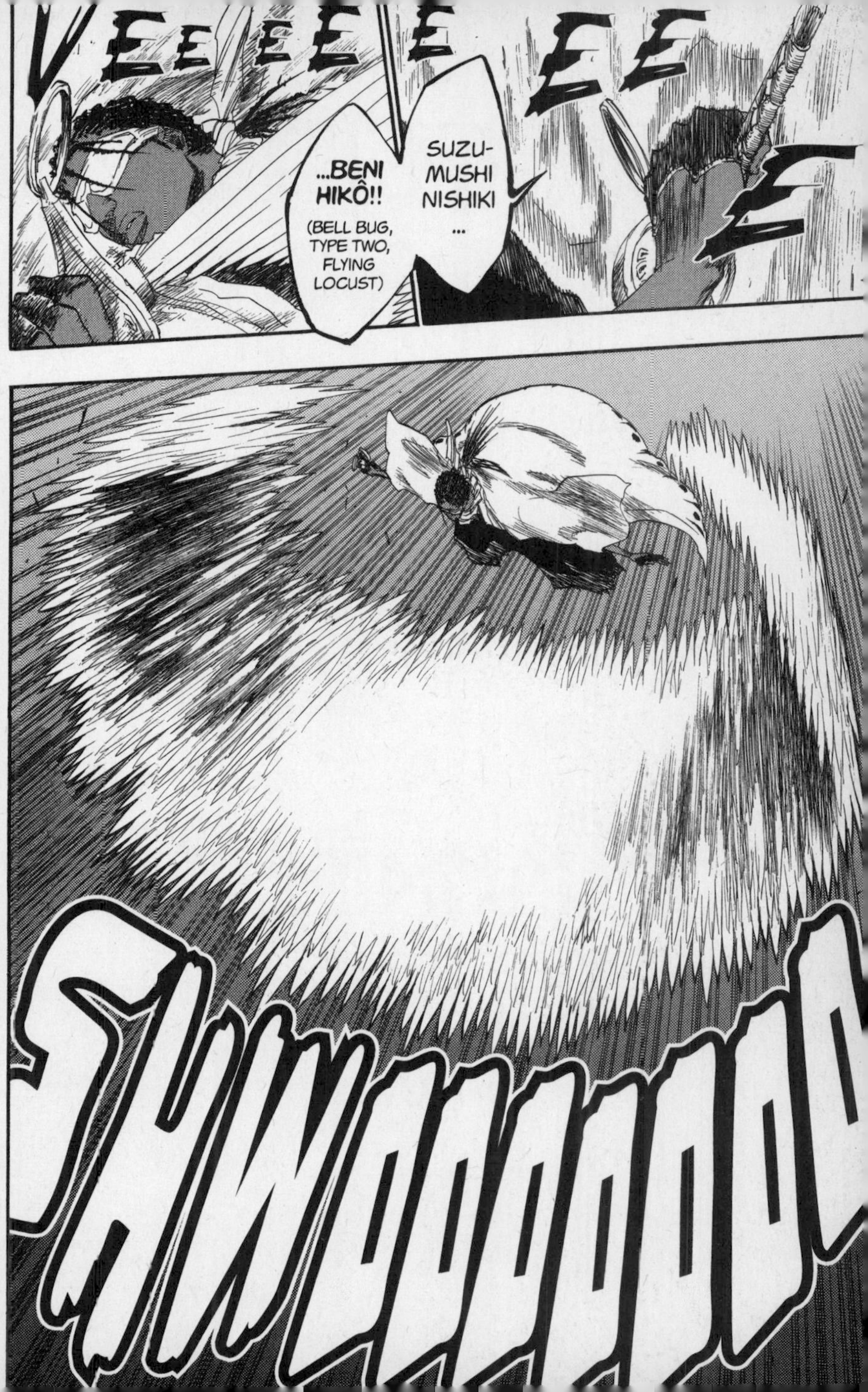
VEEEEEEEEE
SUZU-MUSHI NISHIKI ...
...BENI HIKÔ!!
(BELL BUG, TYPE TWO, FLYING LOCUST)
ZHWOOOOOO

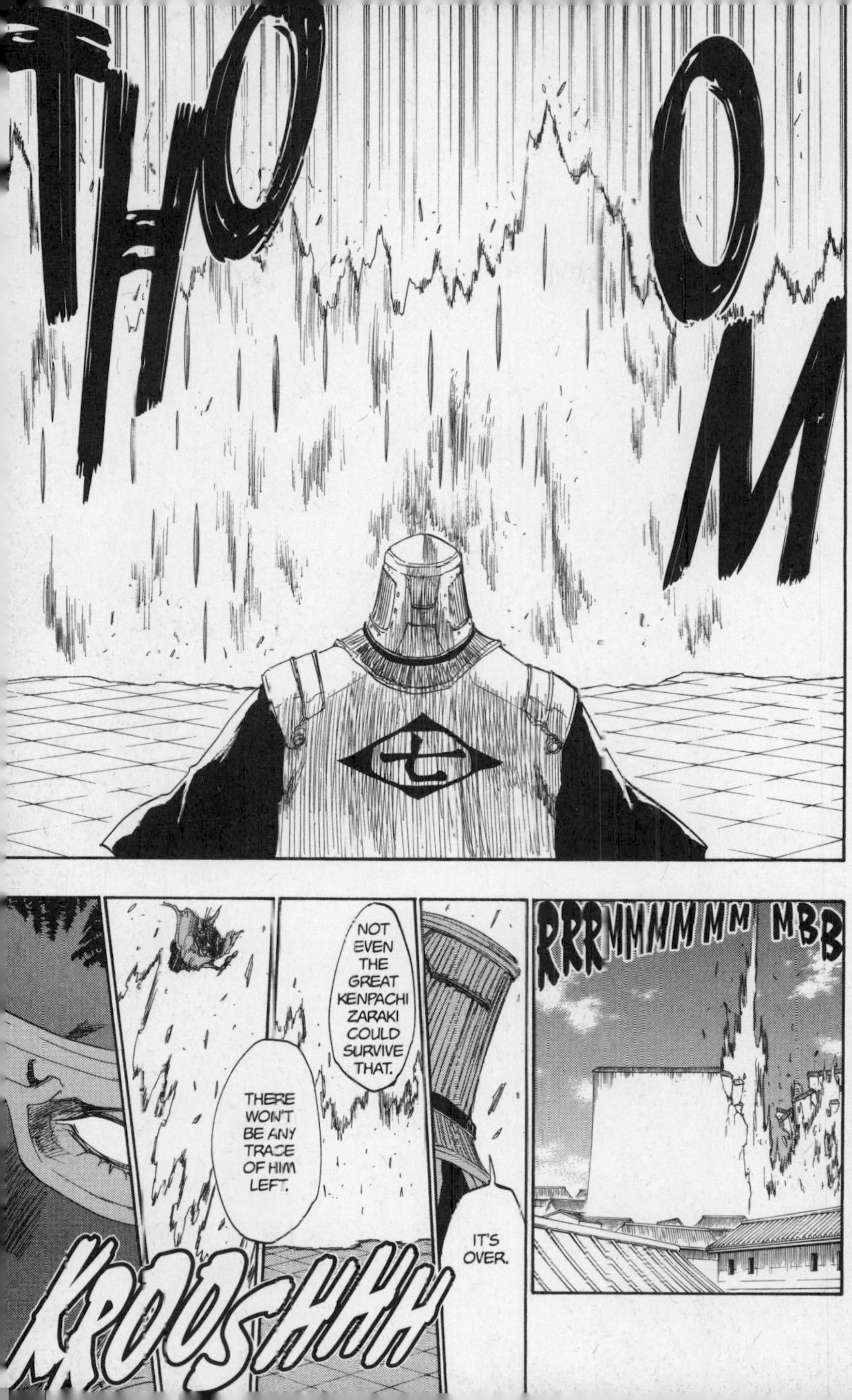
THOOOM
RRRMMMMMM MM MBB
IT'S OVER.
NOT EVEN THE GREAT KENPACHI ZARAKI COULD SURVIVE THAT.
THERE WON'T BE ANY TRACE OF HIM LEFT.
KROOSHHH

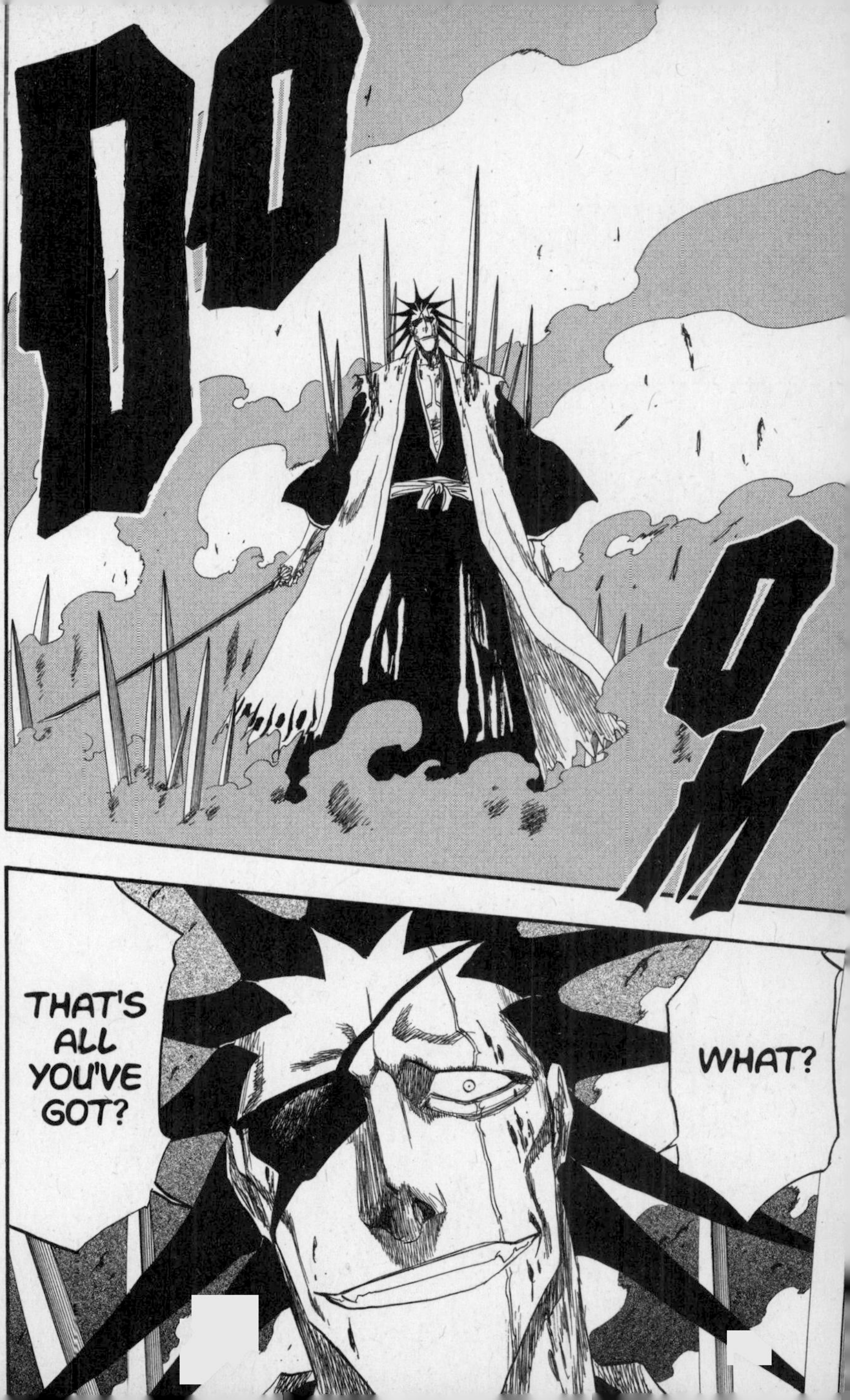
DO
OM
WHAT?
THAT'S ALL YOU'VE GOT?

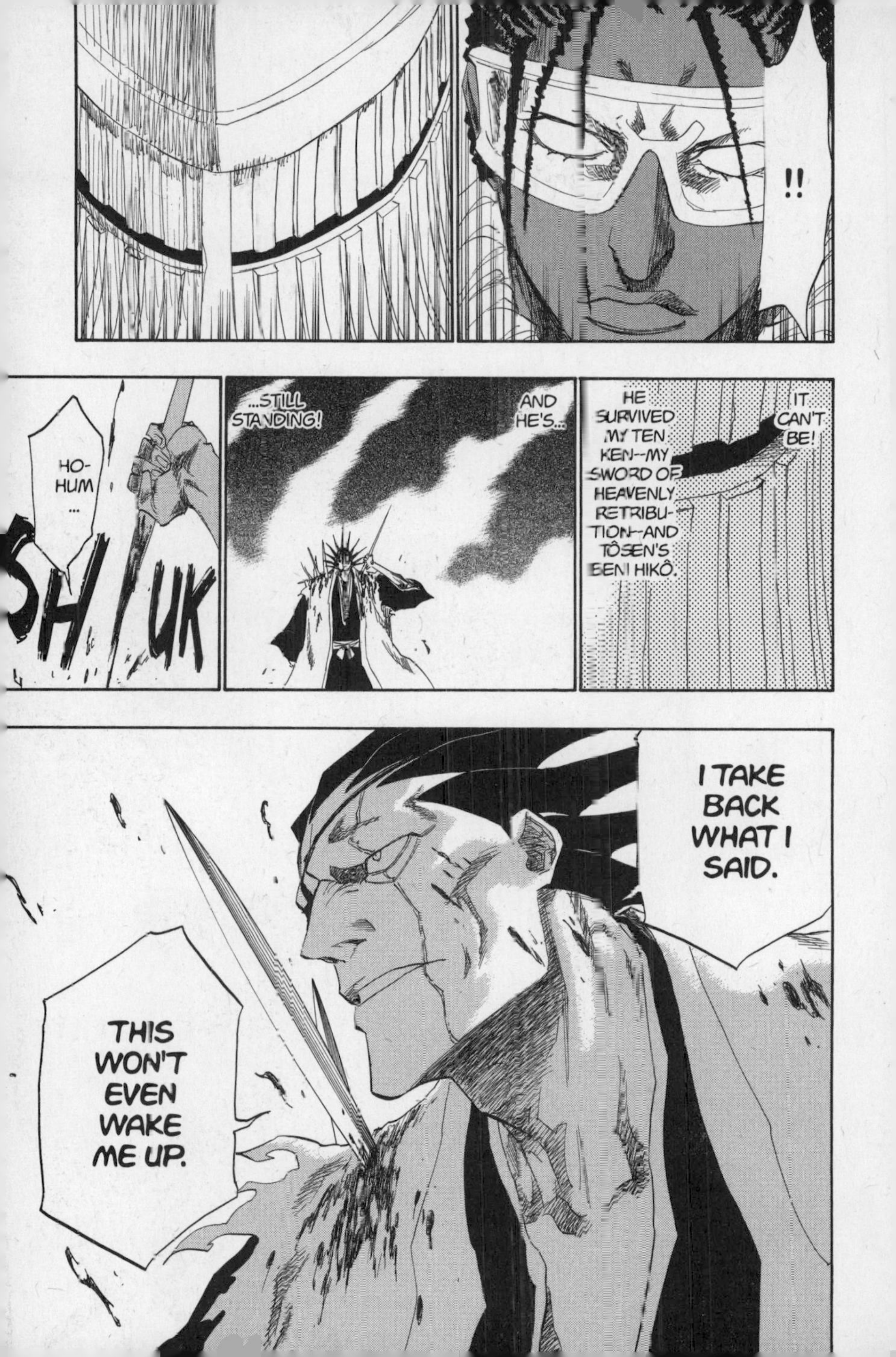
!!
IT CAN'T BE!
HE SURVIVED MY TEN KEN--MY SWORD OF HEAVENLY RETRIBUTION--AND TÔSEN'S BENI HIKÔ.
AND HE'S...
...STILL STANDING!
HO-HUM ...
SHUUK
I TAKE BACK WHAT I SAID.
THIS WON'T EVEN WAKE ME UP.

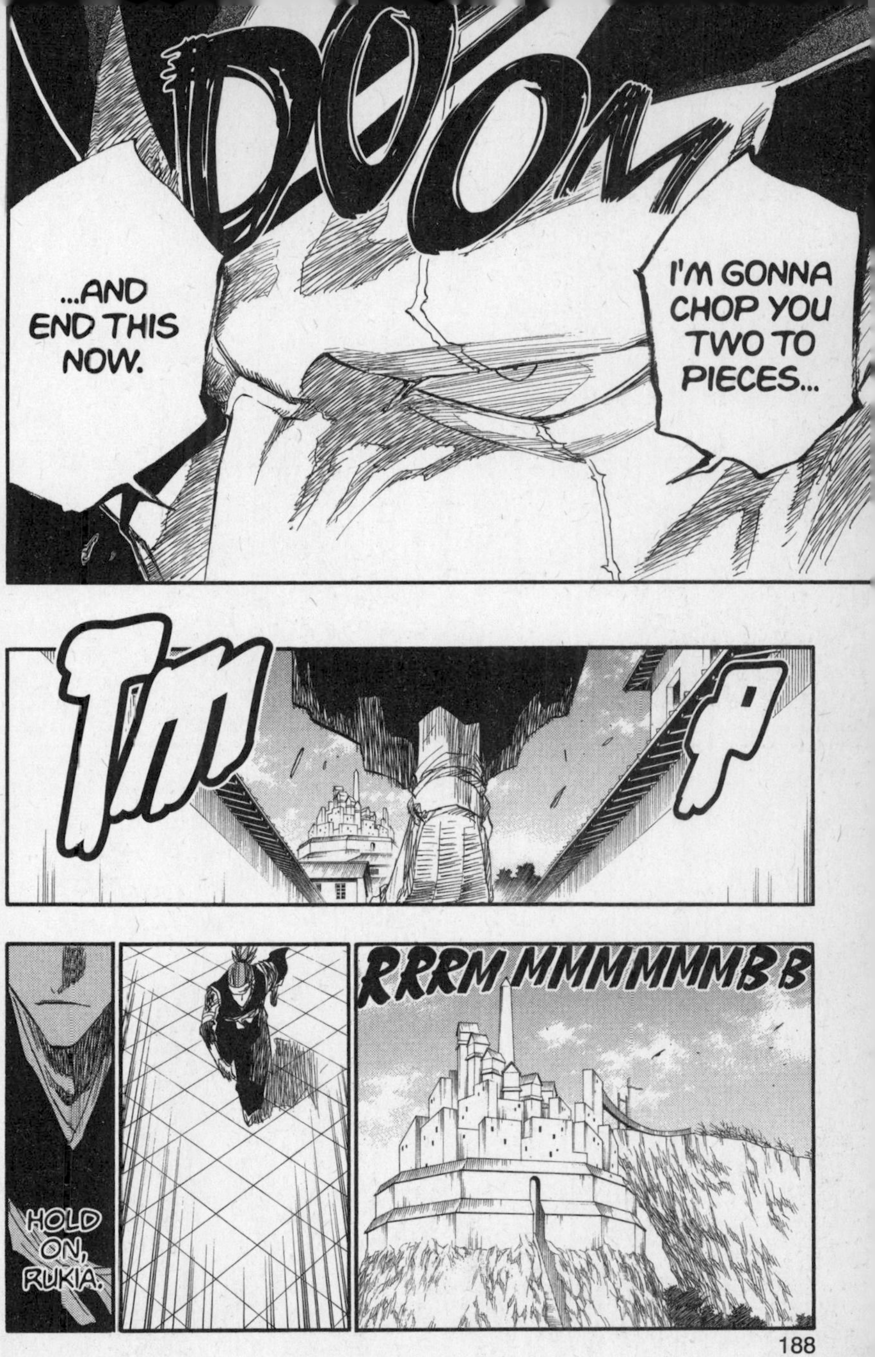
DOOM
I'M GONNA CHOP YOU TWO TO PIECES...
...AND END THIS NOW.
TM P
RRRM MMMMMMB B
HOLD ON, RUKIA.

READ THIS WAY

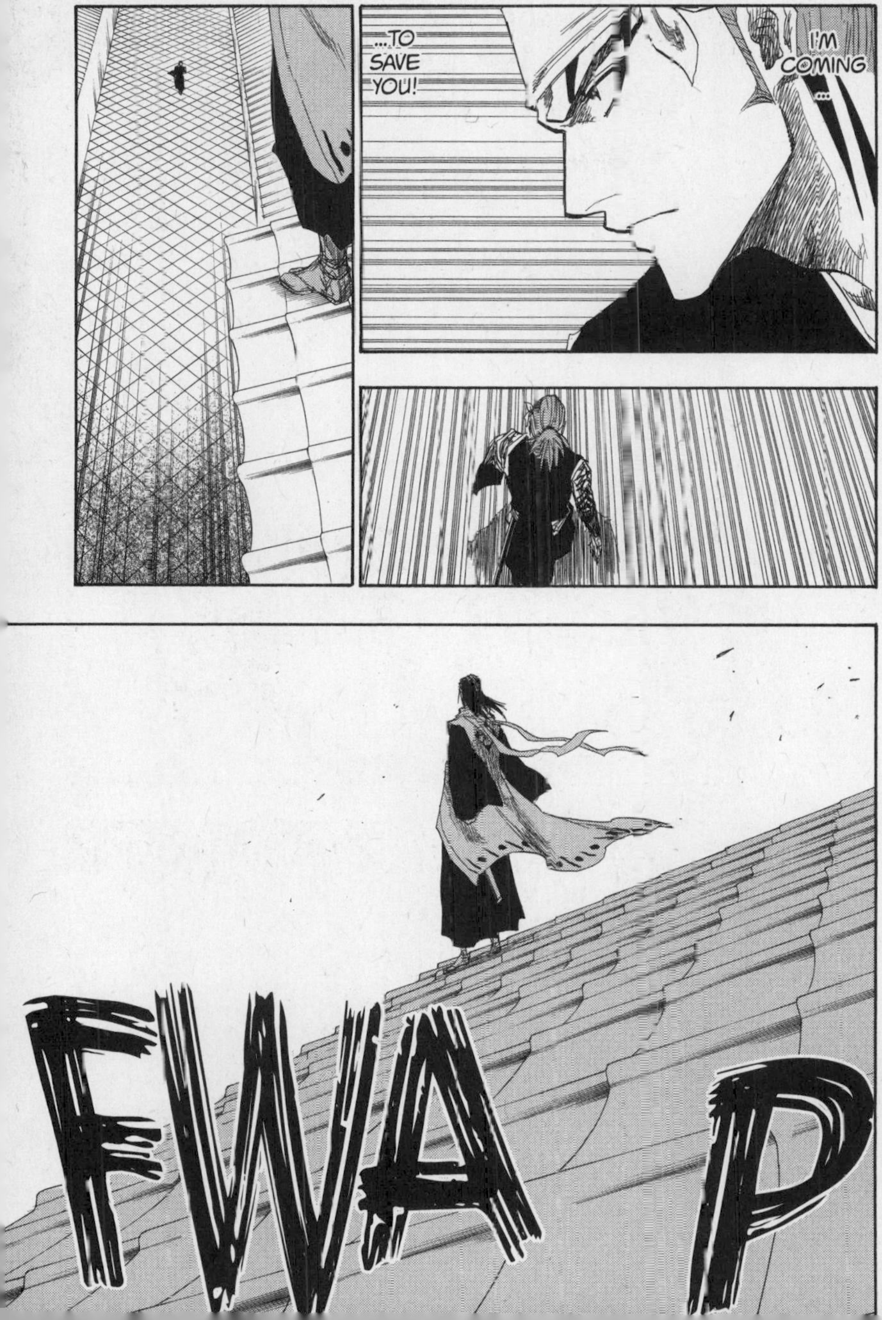

I'M COMING...
...TO SAVE YOU!
FWAP

CONTI
NUED
IN
BLEACH
17

Next Volume Preview

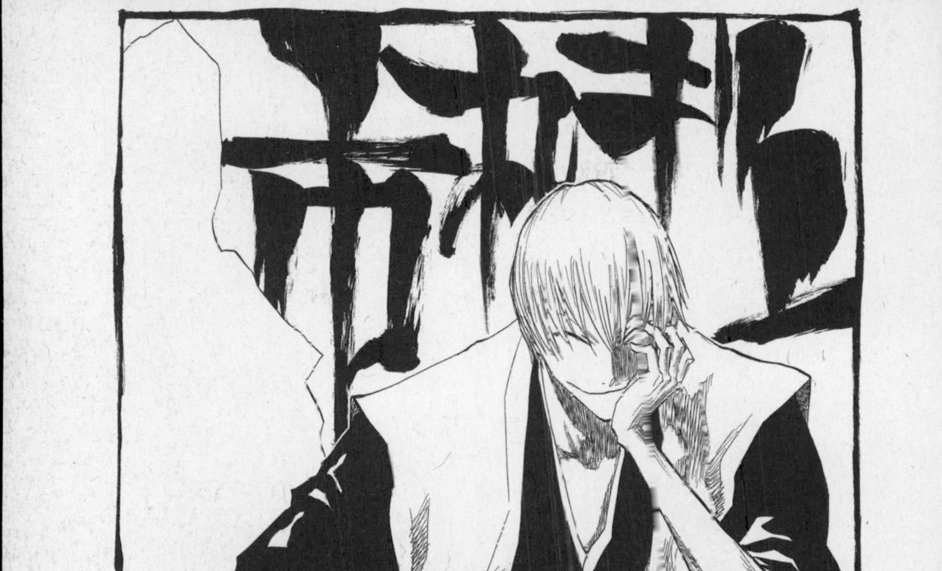

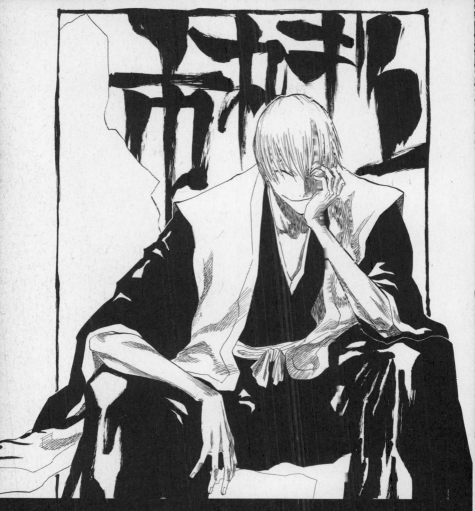

All of Renji's Soul Reaper training has been preparation for the day when he would fight Byakuya Kuchiki. And now that day has finally come. Their showdown will unleash the full force of their Bankai and show just how far Renji has come.

Available in February 2007

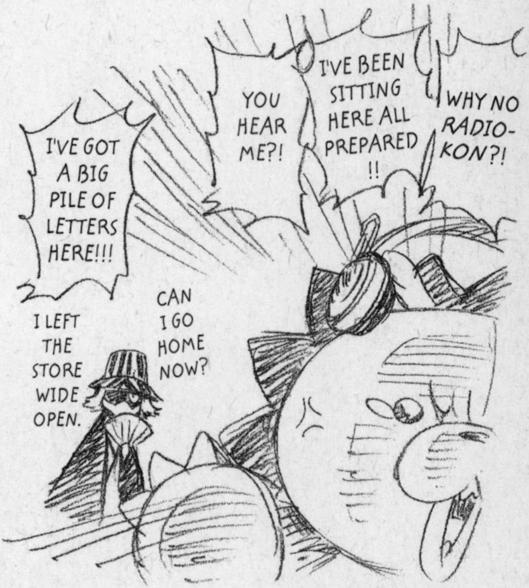
WHY NO RADIO-KON?!
I'VE BEEN SITTING HERE ALL PREPARED !!
YOU HEAR ME?!
I'VE GOT A BIG PILE OF LETTERS HERE!!!
CAN I GO HOME NOW?
I LEFT THE STORE WIDE OPEN.

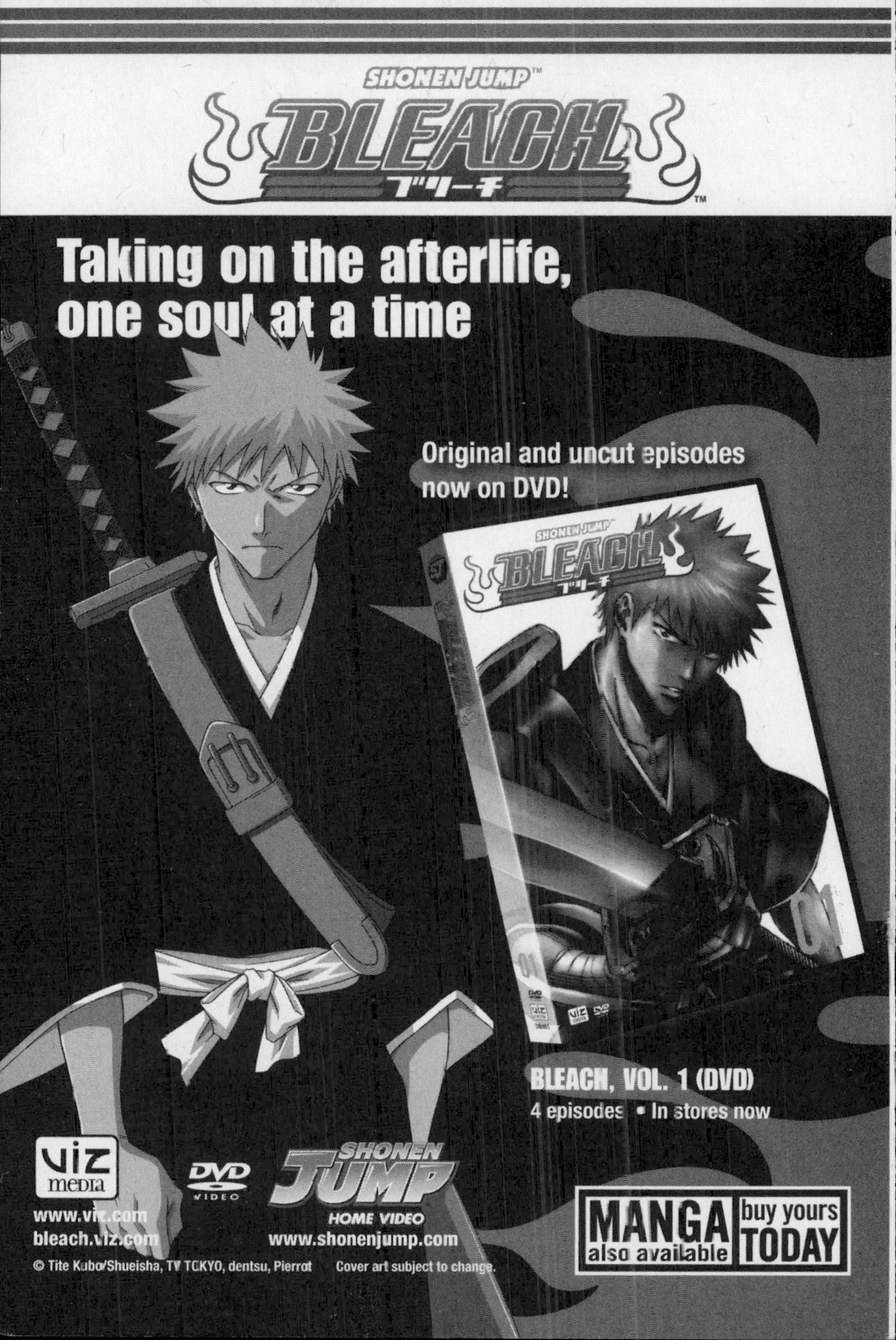

SHONEN JUMP™
BLEACH
ブリーチ
Taking on the afterlife, one soul at a time
Original and uncut episodes now on DVD!
BLEACH, VOL. 1 (DVD)
4 episodes • In stores now
viz media
www.viz.com
bleach.viz.com
DVD VIDEO
SHONEN JUMP HOME VIDEO
www.shonenjump.com
MANGA also available
buy yours TODAY
© Tite Kubo/Shueisha, TV TOKYO, dentsu, Pierrot
Cover art subject to change.

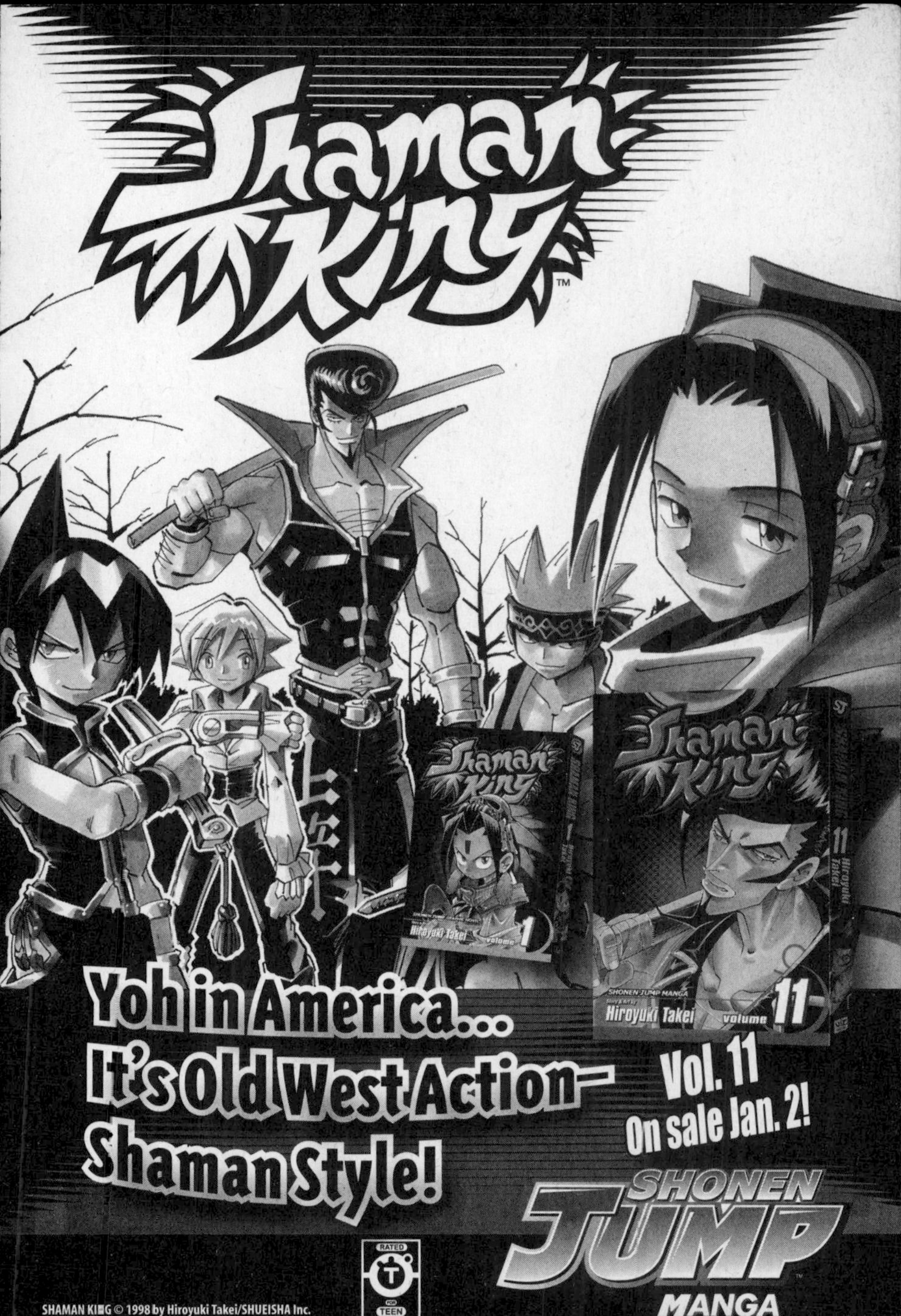

Shaman King™
Shaman King
Hiroyuki Takei volume 1
Shaman King
11 Hiroyuki Takei
SHONEN JUMP MANGA
Hiroyuki Takei volume 11
Yoh in America...
It's Old West Action—
Shaman Style!
Vol. 11
On sale Jan. 2!
SHONEN JUMP
MANGA
RATED T FOR TEEN
SHAMAN KING © 1998 by Hiroyuki Takei/SHUEISHA Inc.

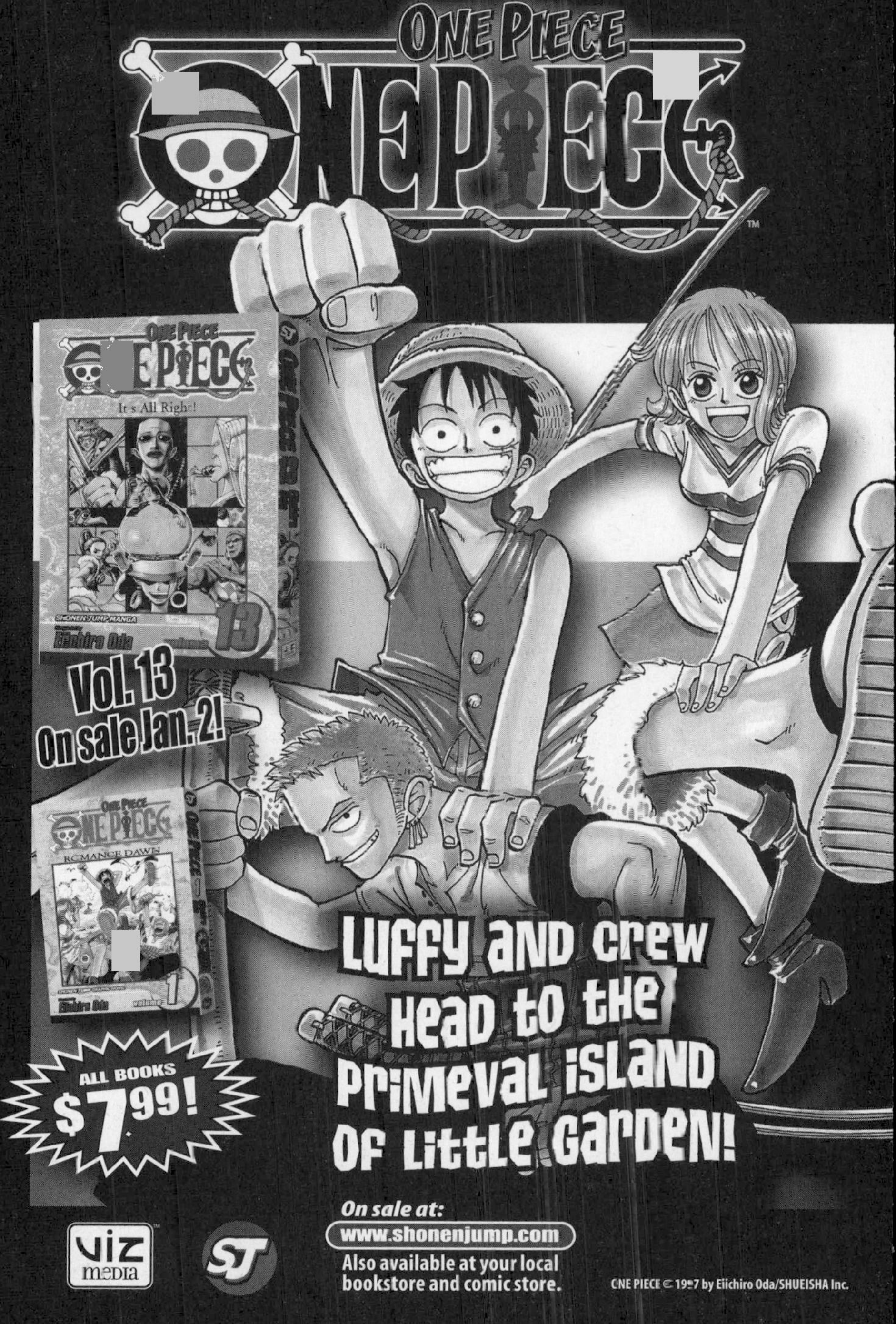

ONE PIECE
ONE PIECE
It's All Right!
SHONEN JUMP MANGA
Eiichiro Oda
volume 13
Vol. 13
On sale Jan. 2!
ONE PIECE
ROMANCE DAWN
volume 1
ALL BOOKS
$7.99!
LUFFY AND CREW
HEAD TO THE
PRIMEVAL ISLAND
OF LITTLE GARDEN!
On sale at:
www.shonenjump.com
Also available at your local
bookstore and comic store.
viz media
SJ
ONE PIECE © 1997 by Eiichiro Oda/SHUEISHA Inc.

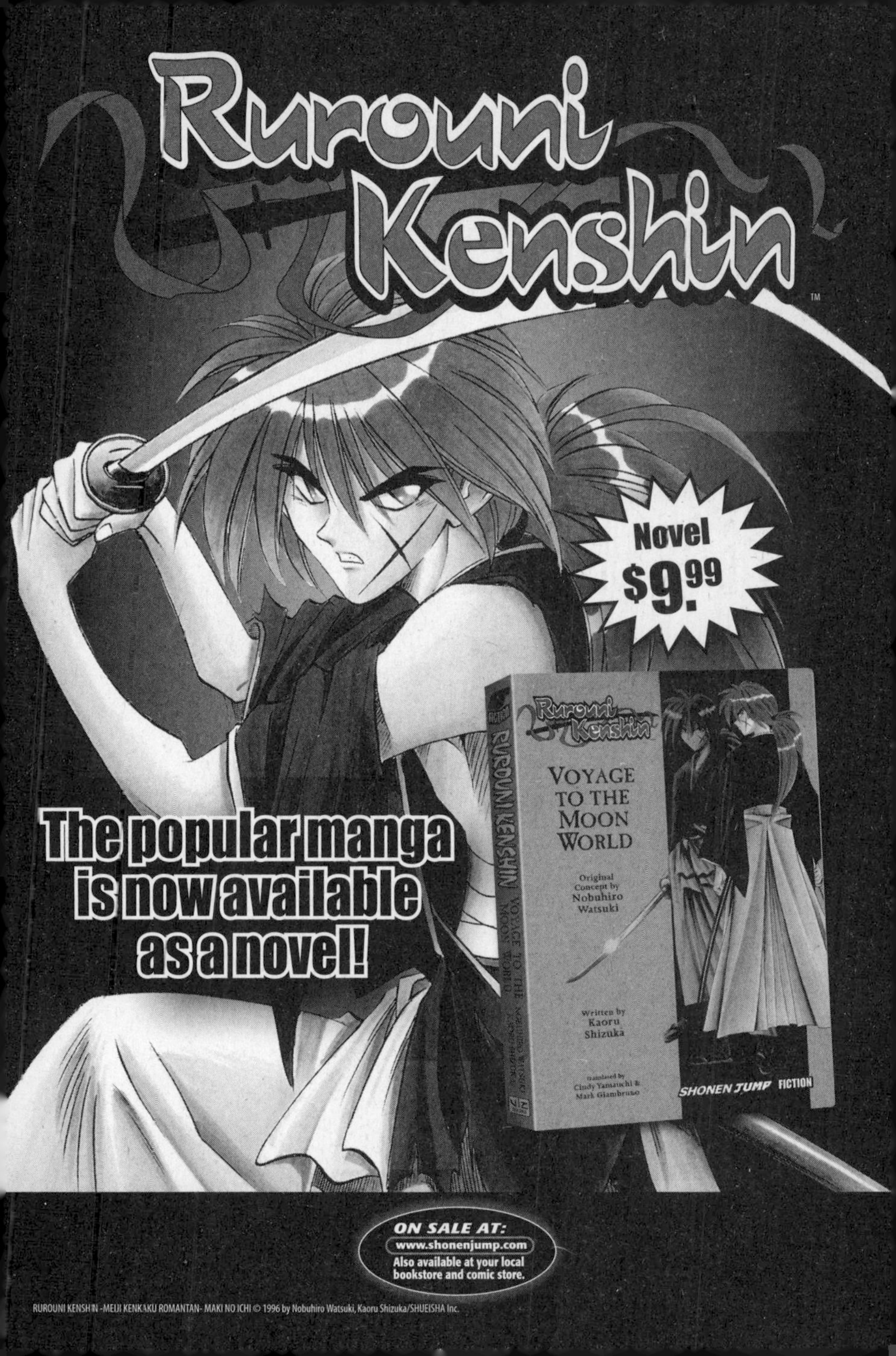
Rurouni Kenshin
™
Novel
$9.99
Rurouni Kenshin
RUROUNI KENSHIN
VOYAGE TO THE MOON WORLD
Original Concept by Nobuhiro Watsuki
Written by Kaoru Shizuka
translated by Cindy Yamauchi & Mark Giambruno
SHONEN JUMP FICTION
The popular manga is now available as a novel!
ON SALE AT:
www.shonenjump.com
Also available at your local bookstore and comic store.
RUROUNI KENSHIN -MEIJI KENKAKU ROMANTAN- MAKI NO ICHI © 1996 by Nobuhiro Watsuki, Kaoru Shizuka/SHUEISHA Inc.

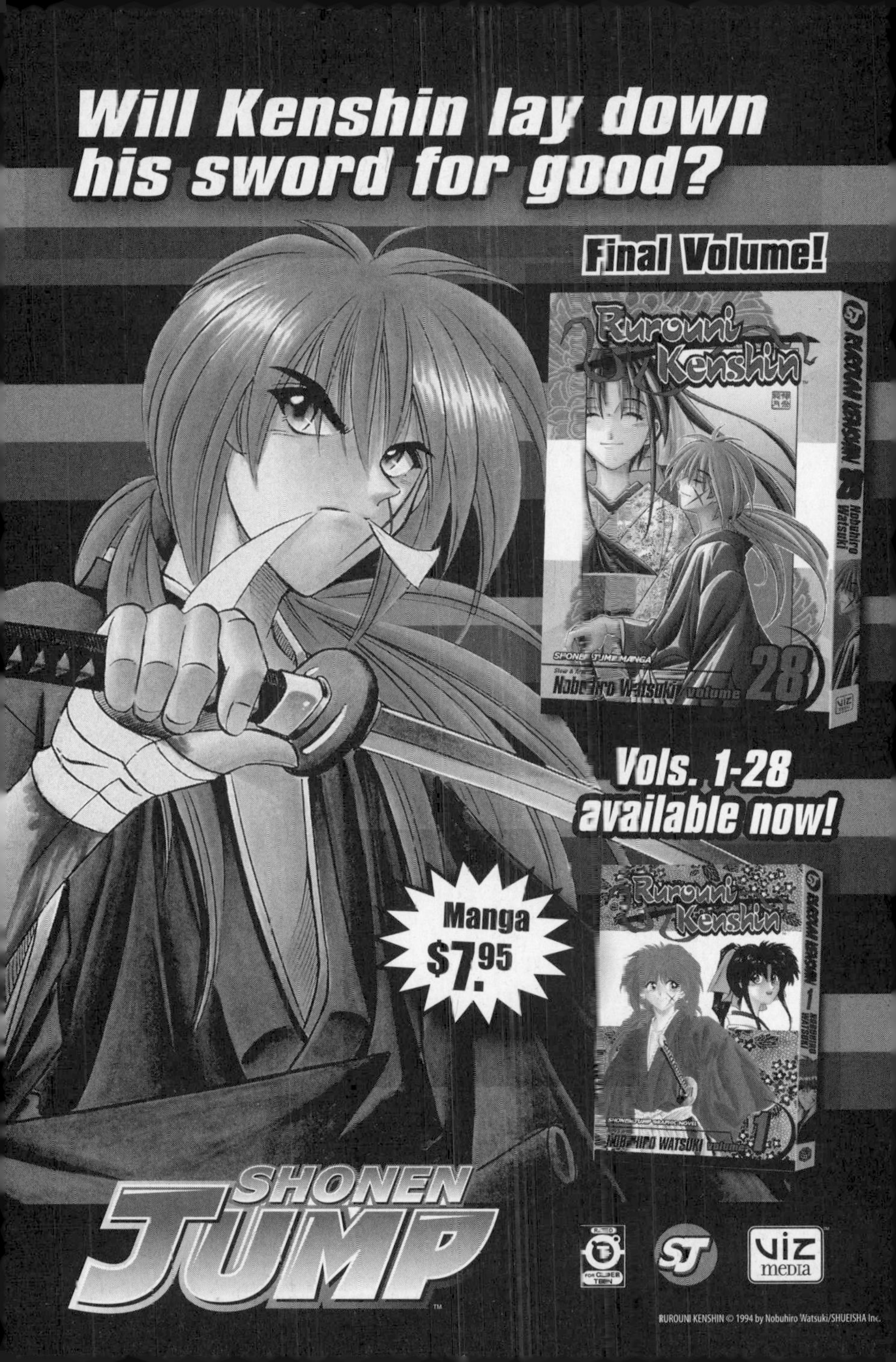

Will Kenshin lay down his sword for good?
Final Volume!
Rurouni Kenshin
SHONEN JUMP MANGA
Nobuhiro Watsuki volume 28
Vols. 1-28 available now!
Manga $7.95
Rurouni Kenshin
NOBUHIRO WATSUKI volume 1
SHONEN JUMP
RATED T FOR OLDER TEEN
SJ
VIZ media
RUROUNI KENSHIN © 1994 by Nobuhiro Watsuki/SHUEISHA Inc.

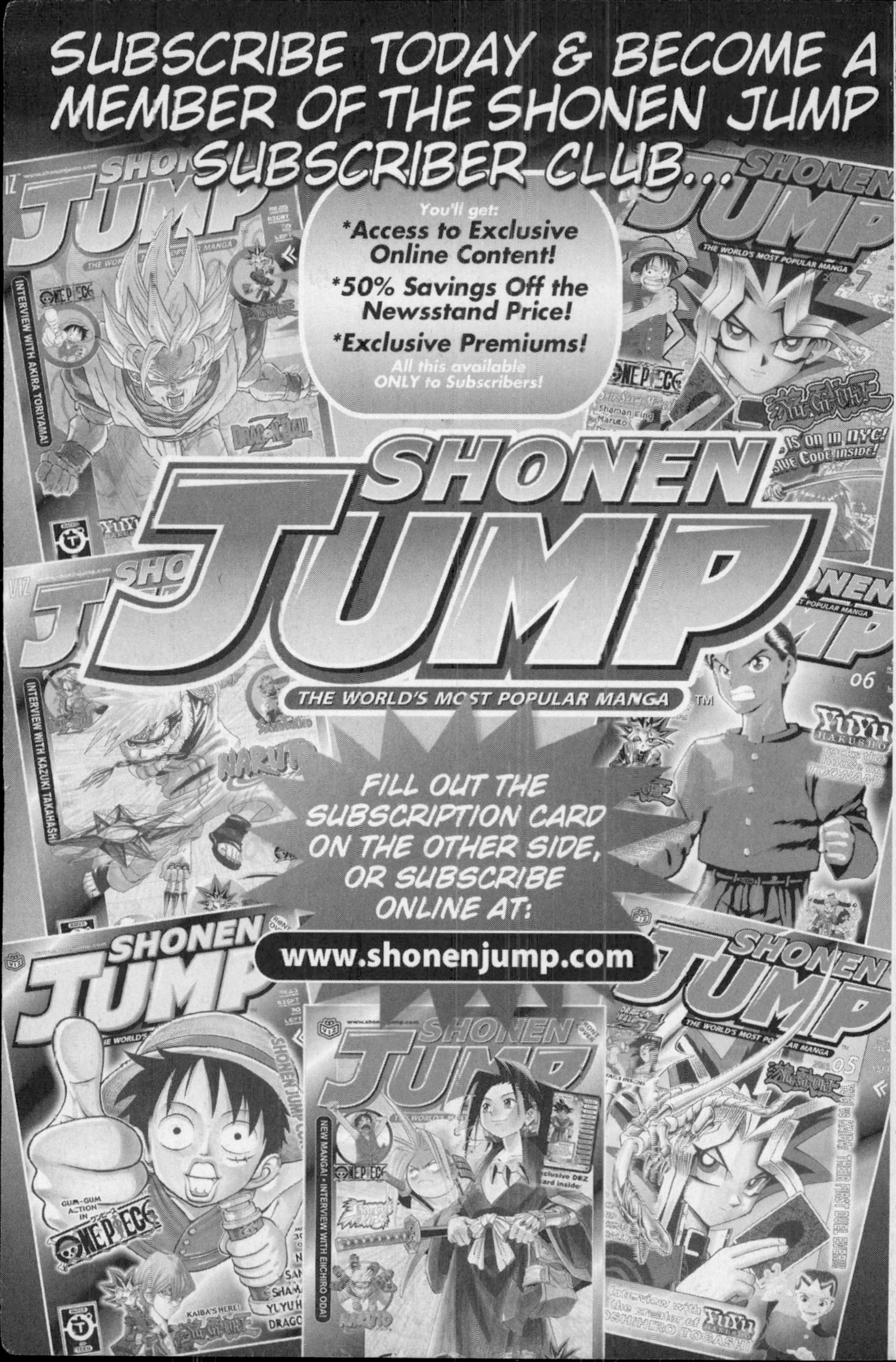
SUBSCRIBE TODAY & BECOME A MEMBER OF THE SHONEN JUMP SUBSCRIBER CLUB...
You'll get:
*Access to Exclusive Online Content!
*50% Savings Off the Newsstand Price!
*Exclusive Premiums!
All this available ONLY to Subscribers!
SHONEN JUMP
THE WORLD'S MOST POPULAR MANGA
TM
FILL OUT THE SUBSCRIPTION CARD ON THE OTHER SIDE, OR SUBSCRIBE ONLINE AT:
www.shonenjump.com

Save **50%** off the newsstand price!

**SUBSCRIBE TODAY and SAVE
50% OFF the cover price PLUS enjoy
all the benefits of the SHONEN JUMP
SUBSCRIBER CLUB. exclusive online
content**
AVAILA

☑ **YES!** P
(12 issues)
LOW SUBS
up for the

NAME

ADDRESS

CITY

E-MAIL ADD

☐ **MY CH**

CREDIT CA

ACCOUNT #

SIGNATURE

DATE DUE

Demco

95!

ept.
P.O. Box 515
Mount Morris, IL 61054-0515

Make checks payable to: **SHONEN JUMP.**
Canada add US $12. No foreign orders. Allow 6-8 weeks for delivery.

P6SJGN   YU-GI-OH! © 1996 by Kazuki Takahashi / SHUEISHA Inc.